THE ECONOMIST'S VIEW OF THE WORLD

THE ECONOMIST'S VIEW OF THE WORLD

GOVERNMENT, MARKETS, AND PUBLIC POLICY

STEVEN E. RHOADS

University of Virginia

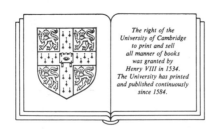

CAMBRIDGE UNIVERSITY PRESS

Cambridge

London   New York   New Rochelle

Melbourne   Sydney

Published by the Press Syndicate of the University of Cambridge
The Pitt Building, Trumpington Street, Cambridge CB2 1RP
32 East 57th Street, New York, NY 10022, USA
10 Stamford Road, Oakleigh, Melbourne 3166, Australia

First published 1985
Reprinted 1985, 1986

Printed in the United States of America

Library of Congress Cataloging in Publication Data
Rhoads, Steven E.
The economist's view of the world.
Bibliography: p.
Includes index.
1. Economics. I. Title.
HB171.R43   1985   338.9   84-14997
ISBN 0 521 30160 2 hard covers
ISBN 0 521 31764 9 paperback

To the Queen of the Forest
and our brood:

Bananaman, Poo-man-chu, and the Birdman

CONTENTS

PREFACE

This book is written, first and foremost, for intelligent, educated readers who are interested in domestic public policy and who know little or nothing about economics. Some of these readers will be found in public-policy courses taught outside economics departments. Some will be professors interested in learning more about an influential sister discipline. But many will have long since left the groves of academe. All these potential readers may associate economics with some best-selling ideological tract or with long afternoons spent in Economics 101 peering at supply and demand curves on dusty blackboards. I ask such readers to give economics another chance. The ideological tract may not have been written by an economist; even if it was, it almost certainly did not represent most economists' opinions. And there are no graphs in this book.

I hope that my book will show that economics is more substantial than the best-selling ideological tracts indicate and more interesting than most economists' explications suggest. I am a political scientist who believes that some knowledge of contemporary microeconomics is a prerequisite for intelligent citizenship. Succeeding chapters show that a large number of congressmen, consumer advocates, and business and union representatives give no evidence of having met the prerequisite. They show also that our public policy is the worse for that failure. Laurence Silberman, undersecretary of labor at the time the Occupational Safety and Health Act was passed, has said that he would have pushed hard for an alternative approach if he had had his present understanding of economics.[1] I know a number of other advanced students of public affairs who, after being reintroduced to economics, have expressed amazement that they could have so long ignored a subject so central to their concerns. Many have said that they will never again read a newspaper in quite the same way. Noneconomist readers should expect to be surprised at how often what is controversial politically is not controversial among most economists, and vice versa. I in turn will be surprised if such readers are not led to rethink a number of their current opinions on public-policy issues.

Though I am glad to have spent the last decade immersed in economics, I am also glad that, as a political scientist, I will not have to spend the next decade so thoroughly immersed. The last part of the book explains why. This is not the place to indicate the nature of my critique of economics, but the potential reader should be made aware here that the book's early praise of the discipline is followed by quite spirited criticism. I think this unusual mix of strong praise and sharp criticism is necessary to do justice to a discipline that is full of both marvelous insights and troubling blindness.

Though my principal audience is a "nonexpert" one, I hope that my attempt to assess the strengths and weaknesses of their discipline will also be of interest to economists and their students and to others in the policy-analysis community. This "expert" audience has a right to expect extensive documentation when a noneconomist attempts a comprehensive and frequently provocative assessment. The resulting notes have been placed at the end of the book so as to be as undistracting as possible to my principal audience.

STEVEN E. RHOADS
Charlottesville, Virginia
April 1984

ACKNOWLEDGMENTS

If this book has any virtues, their genesis was at the Cornell University of the 1960s. As a master's candidate in public administration, I was drawn to Cornell's economics department. There, from Alfred Kahn and Robert Kilpatrick, I learned that the fields of regulatory economics and public finance addressed issues of policy substance in a disciplined and illuminating way.

Many years later, at a chance meeting, Kahn foolishly agreed to look at a manuscript I was working on. When I later deposited 550 pages on his doorstep, he kept any groans inaudible, and, in the midst of a schedule busier than any I will ever know, he produced twenty-two single-spaced pages of detailed, exceedingly helpful comments. Those who followed Fred Kahn's career in President Carter's administration will not be surprised to learn that at Cornell he was famous for his buoyant energy, wit, and intelligence. They may know less than I do of his astonishingly generous nature.

Toward the end of my study of economics at Cornell, I had the good fortune to encounter another legendary campus figure, Allan Bloom. It was later my privilege to study with this peerless teacher when he was finishing his work on Plato's *Republic* and beginning his study of Rousseau's *Emile*. Like most other graduates of what today pass for good liberal arts colleges, I had never read these, or indeed, almost any other truly important book. From Bloom I learned of views of the world richer than those of economists. My book would be a far better one if I knew even a few of the great books of political philosophy half as well as he.

After receiving my master's degree, I worked under Charles Schultze at the U.S. Bureau of the Budget. There I was able to see the economist's view of the world as it first began to gain a real foothold in government through the studies that grew out of the old Planning, Programming, and Budgeting System.

When I returned to Cornell to obtain my Ph.D in government, I was fortunate to be able to work with Richard Fenno, Allan Sindler, and Walter

Berns. My efforts here to let economists speak in their own words whenever possible are a tribute to Fenno's more skillful use of this method to bring alive the life of the Congress. In their very different ways Sindler and Berns provided me with important models of how one can find in political science a source for thoughtful analysis of the issues of American politics. Sindler chaired my dissertation committee and has helped in many ways in succeeding years.

A manuscript that attempts to cover as much as this one does would be riddled with errors were it not for the kindness of readers more expert than I about various parts of it. The entire first draft of the manuscript, or substantial portions thereof, was read by Edward Banfield, Lawrence Brown, Donna Hawthorne Carfagno, James Ceaser, Ward Elliott, Joseph Goldberg, William Johnson, Alfred Kahn, Carnes Lord, Harvey Mansfield, Jr., Edgar Olsen, James Pontuso, Abram Shulsky, Allan Sindler, Aaron Wildavsky, Leland Yeager, and several anonymous readers. Though I think my readers' comments have made this version much improved, they are of course blameless if I have made things worse instead.

The graduate students in the public administration classes of 1983 and 1984 were involuntary, but extraordinarily helpful, readers. I extend thanks to them and to my wife, Diana, the only person who has had to read every page of every draft. She is a superb editor, but that is the least of her virtues.

Cathy Dooley, Jim Crane, and Roxanne White were the last of a long line of research assistants who performed important but unglamorous work with skill and good cheer. Barbara McCauley did her usual superb typing job. The Institute for Educational Affairs, the Earhart Foundation, and the Center for Advanced Studies at the University of Virginia provided generous fellowship support that made possible a full year for writing. The university's small grants committee and the Department of Government and Foreign Affairs provided funds to type and reproduce the manuscript. And finally, Colin Day has been a gifted and helpful editor from the very first. It has been a pleasure to work with him, my excellent copyeditor, Mary Byers, and the rest of the staff at Cambridge University Press.

1

INTRODUCTION

When the educated layman looks at the economy, he sees unemployment, inflation, and low growth. When he looks at the economics profession, he sees chaos. The cartoonist Mal captures the public perception perfectly. In one picture he depicts a frightened stranger entering a doorway labeled "Department of Economics" beside which is a sign saying "Abandon All Hope Ye Who Enter Here." In another he has his bewildered moderator standing at the podium of an economic forum say, "We will now hear from another eminent economist who will refute everything the previous eminent economist has had to say." Little has changed since the days when a wag commented, "If parliament were to ask six economists for an opinion, seven answers would come back – two, no doubt, from the volatile Mr. Keynes." One might, of course, seek to resolve this problem of conflicting advice by taking counsel from economists who consider the point of view of all schools of thought. But then the frustration felt by Harry Truman is sure to return. After an afternoon of hearing "on the one hand...on the other hand," Truman declared that he was going to get himself a "one-handed economist."

Economists feel misunderstood. People notice only their showy, disheveled, and presumptuous half, macroeconomics, while their solid, elegant, better half, microeconomics, remains unseen. Thus one can find prominent economists calling microeconomics "the Cinderella side of the discipline" or complaining that "macro gives micro a bad name."[1]

The economists have a point. The discipline as a whole is not in shambles, far from it. In academia there are more micro- than macroeconomists, and in government there are far more. Microeconomists and those associated with fields that have spun off from microeconomics, such as welfare and benefit-cost economics, public finance, and public choice, have never been more influential. In the universities economic concepts and models appear often in the work of psychologists and sociologists.[2] Economists have been so influential in political science that one of their number, Gordon Tullock, was elected to the governing council of the American Political Science Association.[3] Even contemporary philosophy has been heavily influenced by the study of economics.[4]

The pervasiveness of economic thinking in the professional schools is even more striking. Both in this country and abroad it is increasingly important to the study of public administration.[5] In the interdisciplinary public-policy programs that have grown enormously at our best universities, microeconomics is acknowledged to be the most influential specialty.[6] Almost all the best law schools now have at least one economist on their faculties, and economic principles significantly affect teaching and scholarship in traditional fields such as torts, contracts, property, antitrust, and administrative law. Economics has even reached the medical schools. A path-breaking book, *Costs, Risks and Benefits of Surgery*, edited by two doctors and a statistician, draws heavily on economic theory and cost-benefit analysis.[7]

As might be expected, this economic imperialism has met opposition wherever it travels. But even the critics of economics grant its influence, sometimes explicitly,[8] and sometimes by the very vigor and frequency of their protests. The disciplines that make up the humanities and social sciences study human beings from a wide variety of perspectives. If an award were to be given to the discipline that has had the most influence on other disciplines over the last two decades, the Cinderella side of economics would make economics an all but certain winner.

The public perception of economics as a discipline riven by schisms is largely true of macroeconomists, but that perception is wildly wide of the mark for microeconomists. Indeed, one source of microeconomists' great influence is the consensus they have reached on important questions of fact and theory. This consensus extends even to evaluative questions. Economists tend to use the same normative framework and evaluative criteria when examining domestic programs, whatever the functional area. More remarkable still, on a host of controversial policy questions, economists, whether liberal or conservative, Democratic or Republican, come to the same general conclusions. They make the same criticisms of existing government policies, and they make similar suggestions about desirable alternatives. The late Arthur Okun put it this way:

Economists of contrasting political views agree among themselves on many issues. In particular, on a number of issues, a bipartisan majority of the profession would unite on the opposite side from a bipartisan majority of the Congress.[9]

Opinions like those of Okun have been voiced by a number of other prominent economists, and the existence of the consensus he describes has been confirmed by a recent poll of the profession as well.[10]

Macroeconomics focuses on broad economic aggregates such as total output, total employment, the price level, and the rate of economic growth. Macroeconomic policy seeks to keep inflation and unemployment low and economic growth high. Microeconomics focuses not on broad aggregates, but on particular sectors of the economy and the relations among the sectors. Microeconomics seeks to determine how scarce resources are allocated among competing sectors and among competing societal ends and who gets the goods and services provided. Policy-oriented microeconomists usually want to change the mix of goods and services produced by the economy so as to more efficiently satisfy consumers' preferences. Typical policy concerns of microeconomists are government's inefficient regulation of transportation and communications, inefficient controls over rent and energy prices and over minimum wages, and the inefficient design of environmental and occupational safety policies.

Growth, unemployment, and inflation sound more important, and in the final analysis they probably are. But microeconomics is concerned with more than technical, uninteresting details. For one thing, micropolicies affect macroproblems. As discussed in Chapter 6, micropolicies that discourage savings and investment hurt economic growth, and laws requiring minimum wages increase unemployment rates among poorly educated, inexperienced workers. And though the design of environmental policies sounds pretty dry, the stakes are not small. As will be discussed in Chapter 4, economic studies show that better designs could save tens of billions of dollars at no cost to the environment. Thus, good solutions to macroquestions must take account of microparticulars. There would be no cause for congratulations if all our workers were fully employed producing low-priority goods in a wasteful manner.

This book explains and assesses the way that most micro, welfare, and benefit-cost economists look at the world of public policy. It evaluates the views of mainstream economists, those whose outlook has been shaped by the principles discussed in standard microeconomic or public finance texts. As I use the term, "mainstream economist" encompasses a clear majority of economists – liberal and conservative, Democratic and Republican. Though Chapter 9 contains a brief discussion of John Kenneth Galbraith, I make no attempt to consider systematically the spectrum of opinion among radical, socialist, or Marxist economists.[11]

Academic economists working in government are often appalled by the ignorance of economics that they encounter.[12] Yet they readily acknowledge that what they add to the policy process is primarily "a basic orientation and general framework" or "the simplest, most elementary concepts of economic theory."[13] This book explores that basic orientation, those elementary concepts, and the policy conclusions they point to.

Parts I and II consider the two types of policy guidance provided by the micro, or resource allocation, side of economics. Part I discusses opportunity cost, marginalism, and economic incentives, three illuminating concepts central to the world view of almost all economists. Opportunity cost reminds us that since resources are scarce and ends multiple, to worry about costs is to care about benefits, benefits forgone in other sectors. This seeming truism has not in fact been fully understood by a number of intelligent politicians and public administrators. Marginalism shows why neither the intrinsic importance of a public function nor a ranking of problems facing a community provides much guidance for public-expenditure choices. Marginalism suggests looking at the details – understanding that most budgeting decisions concern spending a little more or a little less, not whether we should address a problem at all. After looking at the details we may find that added expenditures will have little effect on the relatively intractable ''most important'' problem while they could dramatically alleviate the third most important. Finally, the economic-incentive insight allows us to see how we can achieve a number of our public goals more cheaply and successfully if we pay more attention to private self-interest when designing our government programs. Many of our new regulatory programs, such as those for environmental protection and worker safety, try to change the behavior of millions of individuals and business firms by way of detailed laws and regulations. Economists have convincingly shown that changing material incentives so as to make private interests more congruent with public goals is, in many cases, a dramatically superior approach.

The concepts of opportunity cost, marginalism, and economic incentives are less ambitious than the economics discussed in Part II. They do not seek to provide comprehensive frameworks or conclusive answers. They are instead ideas to be kept in mind – factors to be weighed against other relevant factors when thinking through a problem or policy. Though these concepts are less ambitious, they are not necessarily less useful. One can reject the evaluative principles behind the economics discussed in Part II and still learn from Part I's concepts.

Chapter 5, the first in Part II, explains why most economists, liberal and conservative, have great respect for market systems and great skepticism about the efficiency of governments. Markets do, however, fail in some situations, and these are outlined and explored in the fields of public finance and welfare economics. Economists working in these fields believe that reflection on market failures, particularly on the type of failure called an externality (an effect on a third party that is not transmitted through the price system), can lead to conclusions about the desirable scope of government. When externalities can justify government programs, economists then look at the geographical scope of the externalities to help decide whether federal, state, or local governments should take the lead in addressing the problems at hand. Chapter 7 outlines and explores the policy relevance of these teachings. For example, it shows how the externality concept can be used to criticize some political arguments concerning the desirability of voluntarism in environmental enforcement and of subsidies for rail transportation.

The principles of welfare economics provide guidance about the appropriate agenda for government. Benefit-cost economics, the applied branch of welfare economics and the subject of Chapter 8, goes even further and gives advice about how much money should be spent on justifiable objectives and functions. For economists the benefits of a government program are entirely dependent on the preferences of consumers, that is, on their willingness to pay for the program. Chapter 8 contains a nontechnical explanation of the way economists estimate consumers' willingness to pay for several domestic programs. It also assesses the political and intellectual controversy concerning the legitimacy of benefit-cost analysis.

Welfare and benefit-cost economics tell economists that societal welfare is maximized if individuals' preferences determine the use of scarce resources, but they say nothing about whose preferences should count the most. The standard economic framework, however, does acknowledge that achieving whatever society considers a fair distribution of income is a legitimate purpose of government. Chapter 6 explores the controversy among economists about the equity or fairness issue. It shows that there are large differences in the profession over evidence and appropriate societal values. Still, even on this controversial equity question economic analysis is more than an amalgam of conflicting ideologies. Economists have reached a remarkable consensus about the best way to achieve an equity objective, and they agree that there is a tension between the goals of economic efficiency and growth on the one hand and a more equal distribution of income on the other. The substance of the consensus on these issues will seem provocative to most noneconomists. Noneconomists may also be surprised to learn that liberal Democratic economists join conservative Republican economists in advocating a tax on unemployment insurance benefits and an end to the tax on corporate income. And that most economists, Republican as well as Democratic, believe that welfare and Medicaid should be primarily federal, not state and local, responsibilities.

Parts I and II of the book emphasize the ways that economics can improve public policy. Part III focuses on weaknesses in the public-policy perspective of most economists. Economists hope to avoid controversy by simply taking preferences as they find them. Chapter 9 shows that this procedure does not avoid controversy, however, since it can sometimes make policy choices turn on the gains to the criminal from crime or the costs to the malevolent from saving lives. Moreover, in practice economists are often not neutral about preferences. Despite the formal openness of welfare economics, in their policy work many economists overemphasize the importance of money as a human motive and source of happiness.

Welfare-economic principles do not allow one to distinguish between high and low or moral and immoral pleasures. The externality concept does, however, allow for government encouragement of activities that bring third parties pleasure and government discouragement of activities that bring third parties pain. Thus one might expect to find economists emphasizing policies that promote serious learning, ethics, good will, civility, and other human traits or activities that yield benefits throughout society. In fact, one finds that most economists adopt a cramped view of externalities that ignores many considerations important to public welfare, even as welfare economics itself defines it. In Chapter 10, I illustrate this tendency with many examples and trace it to a narrowly technical understanding of economic research and to a world view that overemphasizes money and narrow self-interest.

Welfare and benefit-cost economics make recommendations about good policy. They have no explicit teaching about desirable characteristics of the policy process or of political institutions. Still, there is an implicit teaching. It is assumed that consumers know what they want and should get what they want. In applied economic studies the desires of the public are determined by deducing preferences for public goods from private market decisions or, in the absence of such decisions, from public polls. This assumes that participation in discussion and deliberation prior to decision does nothing to improve public policy. It thus ignores one of the principal functions of and arguments for representative political bodies. Moreover, deliberation aside, welfare and benefit-cost economics leave no room for independent representatives or political leadership. By advocating that public policy be based on consumer "willingness to pay," welfare and benefit-cost economists silently assume the desirability of passive representatives. If political judgment or political leadership is needed at all, it is only to find the best tactical route for implementing the policy desires of today's consumers.

On these topics the explicit teaching of those economists who do address political-institutional questions differs little from the implicit teaching of their benefit-cost cousins. The good representative is a clerklike aggregator of consumers' preferences. In Chapter 11, I consider these economists' views in conjunction with those of democratic politicians and political theorists who have advocated a more substantial and creative role for political representatives.

Readers will find that this book contains many inelegant and imprecise phrases such as "most economists," "many economists," "some economists," and "almost all economists." In reaching the judgments that produced these phrases I have relied primarily on my own extensive reading in economics. I have, of course, been especially attracted to research where economists themselves have tried to summarize or synthesize studies, trends, attitudes, and schools. I have profited from an interesting poll of economists on policy issues and from the results of a number of interviews both formal and informal. Five economists of varying political persuasions have read the entire manuscript, and others have read parts of it. Their comments have improved my judgments immeasurably. I have tried to be cautious, using "many" rather than "most" whenever I am in doubt. Still, I am sure that a year or two from now I will wish that I had transposed some adjectives.

Opportunity cost, marginalism, economic incentives, externalities, free markets, benefit-cost analysis – I doubt that many knowledgeable people would deny that all are central to the policy outlook of most economists. I am less sure that the views I criticize in Part III are a part of the world view of most economists. After reading the first draft of Part III one economist said, "I think that the views criticized are held by at least a substantial minority and in many cases by a majority of economists." A second questioned whether I was being "entirely fair to economists in general" but thought what I said "descriptive of enough of them and of a common tendency of all economists." A third was "not sure whether such thinking is dominant in the economics profession" but thought there was "easily" enough of it to save me from attacking a mere straw man. Alas, a fourth economist reader did not recognize himself or his colleagues in any part of the critique, a charge I find hard to reconcile with the stylistic complaint that I quote "everyone under the sun."

I claim no more than the first three economists acknowledge. I would add only that there are far more economists voicing views like those I criticize than there are economists criticizing such views or voicing alternative ones on the subjects at issue.

As a political scientist, I would have no reason to write this book if I did not believe that ideas about good policy influence political outcomes. I recognize that factors such as electoral strategy, public moods, and interest-group pressures also influence public policy, and I know that it can be extremely difficult to weigh the relative importance of all such factors. But if ideas matter at all, and in recent years a number of good political scientists have stressed their political importance,[14] then an examination of economists' views seems especially important. Many economists' ideas that have recently become government policy – the Environmental Protection Agency's use of economic-incentive approaches for policy implementation, rent subsidies for low-income housing, a more relaxed antitrust policy, and reforms in the regulation of airlines, trucking, and communications – appeared years ago in economic books and journals. One knowledgeable observer recently said that the annual books on the federal budget compiled by Brookings Institution economists have "fundamentally changed the ways in which American politicians think about the budget," and, as the intellectual foundation for the passage of the 1974 Budget Reform Act, the books were also an important cause of what is "probably the most influential change in the structure of American government in the past generation."[15]

Economists these days are also having a more direct impact on public policy. Increasingly, economists hold important political offices in their own right. Under President Reagan economists have headed the State Department, the Federal Trade Commission, and the White House's domestic policy council. Under President Carter four Ph.D economists served as secretaries of cabinet departments, and two others headed the Civil Aeronautics Board and the Interstate Commerce Commission.[16] Many of these have argued that the economic training they brought to their jobs was central to their performance. For example, Alfred Kahn, who headed New York State's Public Service Commission before becoming chairman of the Civil Aeronautics Board, has said that he has "closets full of memoranda" to demonstrate that "not a week went by in which I did not find in some problem we were confronting a lesson that could fruitfully be applied from the academic literature." Often the solutions to problems were just "neat application[s] of simple economics."[17]

The economics discussed here tries to point the way toward substantively good public policy. Good politicians will want advice that assesses policy proposals on their substantive merits, but good politicians, of course, must consider political strategy and tactics as well. They will want to weigh questions of timing and sponsorship. They may support a policy they think is substantively bad in order to head off political pressure for one they think is even worse. Alternatively, they may fail to support a substantively good policy because they believe that the legislative struggle for passage will hurt the prospects of still more important parts of their programs. Good politics thus requires both finding good answers to substantive policy questions and strategic and tactical skill.[18] Though both parts of the political art are important, economists concern themselves only with policy substance. I assess their success in carrying out the function they seek to perform.

My book appears in a world in which economic analysis is exceedingly controversial both in academia and in politics. Noneconomists who know a little about microeconomic analysis often think economics is mainly theory built on unrealistic assumptions. Many also think economists are presumptuous, materialistic, mean-spirited, and incapable of understanding the important characteristics of a good society. For their part, economists think of themselves as the spokesmen for facts and rationality – the arch-opponents of unrealistic theory and ideology. They think most noneconomists would agree with them if they knew more economics, and they point to the large number of practitioners of other disciplines who became their fellow travelers once they took the time to learn some economics. But most economists pay little attention to their critics. They are content to collect their lucrative consulting checks while other social scientists howl.

I think there is truth and error in both camps, and my book's final chapter tries to weigh the strengths and weaknesses of the economists' view of the world. I would be delighted if the book caused others to share what I believe to be lonely but solid middle ground. I would, however, be more than content if it helped make the debate more fruitful and informed.

Part I

USEFUL CONCEPTS

2

OPPORTUNITY COST

Economics is still something of a dismal science though not for the original Malthusian reasons. As Nobel laureate Kenneth Arrow notes, the economist's frequent job is to say "this or that, not both. You can't do both."[1] There is much talk these days of government programs that do not achieve their objectives. The economist, however, sees a bittersweet quality in even those programs that *do* achieve their objectives. The crowd at the ground breaking for the new community recreation center finds it a happy occasion that will soon make available wholesome sports for the young and community-building opportunities for senior citizens. The economist broods: "Yes, but by spending the money here and not elsewhere we give up the mobile heart units that would save four lives a year; the remedial reading program that might raise low-income students' test scores a full grade; and the larger, modern jail that would reduce our crime rate. And what about the recreational opportunities that local families might enjoy if the tax dollars to pay for this center were left in their pockets?"

Economists are sometimes defined as those who "know the cost of everything and the value of nothing." In their defense they point out that a concern with costs is really a concern with values. Our brooding economist was worrying about recreation center costs because he cared about the victims of heart attacks and about slow-learning children. Added costs leave us with fewer resources available to further values in other policy areas. In other words, whenever the costs (and benefits) of one program increase, the expenditures on and benefits obtained from some other program (or from private expenditures) decrease. This is the opportunity-cost insight, the understanding that spending and regulatory decisions that use scarce resources or require their use incur costs in terms of forgone alternatives (that we no longer have the capacity to undertake) elsewhere.

This seems so obvious that one can wonder why it is worth discussing. Anyone who has to balance a checkbook certainly knows something of opportunity cost in the family context. But in the public-policy context it is more easily forgotten.

Some time ago a high-ranking city administrator in Virginia described his jurisdiction's recreation policy as follows: "We give primary consideration to the public welfare, but cost considerations are also important." Economists worry about this sort of formulation because it suggests that costs are something other than public welfare forgone in other public programs and in the private sector.

When visiting Mexico, columnist James J. Kilpatrick observed fifty men in Puerto Vallarta with picks and shovels digging up cobblestones, a job "one big Caterpillar" could do in a tenth of the time. He noted that though unemployment was high, underemployment was worse "partly because of a policy that puts manual labor ahead of efficiency."[2] Kilpatrick, however, neglected to consider opportunity costs. Where unemployment is high, the opportunity cost of labor is low. If investment capital is quite scarce, its opportunity cost may be too high to justify buying a Caterpillar. Once opportunity cost is in clear view, efficiency in a less developed country may look different than it does in a developed one, and "underemployment" may disappear.

Similarly, it may not be a sign that something is wrong with business management when declining industries use antiquated rather than modern equipment. The opportunity costs to society of taking from expanding industries the scarce investment capital needed to modernize the declining industries may be so high that the use of antiquated machinery by declining firms is perfectly efficient. Declining industries are always a sorry sight. The noneconomist tends to blame the plight of these industries on their antiquated equipment (and on the shortsighted management responsible for it). Economists see the equipment as the effect rather than the cause of the industry's decline.

The economically correct response [from the point of view of the firm and of society] to a steadily declining demand is not to replace old equipment but to continue to operate with existing equipment as long as it can cover its variable [operating] cost of production. To modernize at high capital costs would make the [firm's] plight worse because costs would rise in the face of declining demand and prices.[3]

Opportunity cost reminds us that we should always think about costs, but it also tells us that the costs relevant to decisions are those connected to opportunities. Money already spent and resources already used are "sunk costs." Since no conceivable alternative can avoid these sunk costs, they have no economic relevance for decisions yet to be made. But one often hears people say of a government project that too much is invested to back out. For example, in 1971 Congressman Tom Steed (D-Okla.) said of the American supersonic transport plane:

It is a strange thing why some want to stop now. I ask the question: If we stop now, who will benefit? Certainly not the people for they are going to be stuck for $1.1 billion.[4]

The economist responds as follows:

They will be stuck one way or the other. We should ask if benefits will exceed *additional, controllable* costs. If not, don't send good money after bad.

Economists are convinced that few outside their profession truly grasp the significance of opportunity costs. Thus, Wisconsin's Burton Weisbrod has said of his former role in the public-policy process, "That which we have to offer is fundamentally very simple and second nature to economists but not to others, and I think it's essentially the notion of opportunity costs."[5] And coauthors Charles Schultze (former head of Jimmy Carter's Council of Economic Advisers) and Allen Kneese sound almost schoolmarmish when asking their readers to consider the costs of overambitious antipollution goals and timetables:

These costs are not simply numbers for accountants or economists to ponder. They represent the value of the resources that must be channeled into controlling pollution and that will not be available for meeting the other wants of society. In the long run their principal source will not be the profits of industrial firms, but the higher prices and higher taxes that all of us will have to pay. Environmental goals therefore are not the simple consequence of decisions about how clean we want the air and water to be or how "tough" the government should be with particular industries. Establishing them confronts us, especially at the highest levels of control, with a set of hard choices between environmental quality and other aspects of living standards, in which the more we want of one, the less we can have of the other.[6]

But should Schultze and Kneese lecture us? Do we really need these economists always so quick to remind us over lunch that there is no such thing as a free lunch?

PROFESSIONAL STANDARDS AND ADMINISTRATIVE GOAL SETTING

Economists emphasizing opportunity costs constantly find themselves quarreling with other experts and professionals. Engineers, for example, frequently provoke an economist's ire. Engineers often ponder costs when considering alternative ways to complete a particular project. But a full concern with opportunity costs requires more than considering the relative costs of using steel or reinforced concrete when building. It also requires considering ways to solve a problem without building at all. Sanitary engineers have equated solving water pollution with the treatment of municipal and industrial waste waters while giving little thought to lower cost solutions, including changing the economic incentives to pollute.[7] The Federal Aviation Administration (FAA), an agency in which engineers have great influence, has often favored reducing congestion through costly airport construction projects rather than through less expensive regulatory or pricing changes.[8] A study of Oakland shows that the engineers who run the street and engineering department see costs as an engineering refinement to be considered after project decisions have been made on other grounds.[9]

For engineers technological promise often controls decisions without thought of opportunity cost. Though technological progress in civil aviation had been extremely rapid, government engineers pushed for government subsidies for the supersonic transport when private companies showed little interest.[10] In the FAA it is difficult to convince engineers that improved instrument landing systems that are clearly superior to existing systems may not be sufficiently better to cover the opportunity costs of replacing the old systems. It is certainly understandable that engineers should want to show the full range of their powers and pursue the most innovative technologies rather than patch up and tinker with existing systems. But opportunity costs make it clear that we should often ask engineers to do the latter.

Like engineers, professionals in every area are convinced of the importance of their work. They know less and care less about what other professionals do. As a result, opportunity costs fade from view, and professional standards of need and adequacy are equated with the public interest. These standards are almost always based on expenditure levels and other input criteria. It is rare to find any clear link between these inputs and effectiveness or benefits to the public. To get the top fire-prevention rating my community would have to double the number of fire fighters on duty and add three more engine companies. But a student of mine found that even if such measures were to eliminate completely all fire damage in the community, the costs of these measures would far exceed the benefits.[11] Still, not long ago a local fire marshall resigned in a huff saying, "My standards and priorities for providing public fire protection do not parallel those of my superiors or the current administration." The marshall complained of not being given the help needed "to adequately perform the job" at the same time that he acknowledged that he considered the level of fire prevention in the community equal or superior to that of any in the state. The fire marshall saw his role as "kind of a maverick looking out for the public's best interest, even if they don't realize it."[12]

This fire marshall is concerned about what cost consciousness is doing to fire prevention. Librarians are equally concerned about what it is doing to their institutions. The president of the American Library Association once said it would take $3.1 billion to bring the nation's libraries to a level of mere "adequacy."[13] And a college dean in the business of training welfare case workers is also concerned about reductions in public funding of his profession and its clients:

Attempts to save on costs without concern for the impact on human beings will ultimately be self-destructive. The danger is that the systems approach is deaf and blind to human values...the man who really makes the decisions will be a manager, a systems analyst, and not a social worker. He will not be a person trained to be concerned about human beings, their needs, nor will he be disturbed by society's disregard for and neglect of people.[14]

Neither fire marshall, librarian, nor social service dean, however, is more concerned about unrealized opportunities than are many doctors. The new medical director of the Virginia correctional system says that "we must make sure inmates' care is just as good as what anyone else gets."[15] At present, however, medical care for some noninmates is also of low quality. Should we not think about the possible effects on people who are not in prison before paying additional physicians to treat those in prison? And what about the possible effects on our dean's welfare clients if the medical-care portion of the budget increases? Those who resist considering opportunity costs when supporting humanitarian programs would prefer to imagine that the money spent on these programs would otherwise have gone "to pay for fancy retreats on the Carolina islands for HEW bureaucrats,"[16] but there is obviously only so much pure waste and fraud that can be eliminated. Added costs in a program usually mean lost benefits elsewhere.

Politicians and administrators regularly lose sight of opportunity costs when they support maximizing goals or achieving them with the best available technology. Before an economist became involved, administrators had been suggesting Department of Transportation objectives such as "maximizing speed and comfort and minimizing the expense of travel."[17] It is, of course, impossible to maximize speed and comfort and minimize cost simultaneously. But the economist's most telling point is that maximizing even a single policy goal is almost always a mistake: "To the economist, the phrase 'greatest possible' is almost devoid of meaning because it suggests a violation of the human condition, a devotion of all resources to the achievement of one end; it denies the economic problem of choice and conflict among competing ends."[18]

One does not have to use the word "maximize" to propose goals as extreme and indefensible as the preceding. Public-policy "crises" always seem to produce them. In the wake of President Carter's declaration that the energy crisis was the moral equivalent of war, many physical scientists, with government support, set to work developing what has been called the Btu theory of value. In its simplest form the theory holds that "all human actions should be measured in terms of how much energy they require and that, for roughly equivalent actions, that action is to be preferred which requires less energy."[19] The theory implies that all other inputs in the productive process (e.g., labor, land, and capital) are costless and that even a huge increase in the use of other resources is to be preferred to a small additional increase in the use of precious Btu's.

Before the energy crisis the environmental crisis led Congress to enact national goals such as the elimination of all discharge of pollutants into navigable waters by 1985. Accomplishing such a feat would add to air pollution and solid-waste disposal problems, since achieving zero discharge in all media simultaneously is impossible. The environmental movement also brought about a law requiring that water pollution be attacked by the "best available technology economically achievable." Though the phrase "economically achievable" made the law somewhat ambiguous, interpretations of the law ignored opportunity costs.[20] These interpretations may in fact have corresponded with Congress's intention. Former senator Edmund Muskie (D-Maine) was as influential as any congressman in shaping our antipollution legislation. Muskie saw the Clean Air Act as based on "the forced technology concept," "designed to put pressure on people to do things that may not now be technologically doable."[21] He complained about the auto companies:

All they have to offer is their difficulties. Negativism. You'd think they'd be inspired by their own history. Early in World War II, F.D.R. announced one day that we had to build sixty thousand airplanes a year. It was just a figure he pulled out of the air. We were just not equipped to do it. But we *did* it. And mostly right around their own city of Detroit. You remember Willow Run Airport near Detroit? That enormous barn of a passenger terminal was built by the automobile people to be the factory where they turned out a lot of those sixty thousand planes a year. Where is the old American spirit that enabled us to do that?[22]

The preceding quotations come from a fascinating book by Bernard Asbell, who followed Muskie around in 1975 when the Clean Air Act was being revised. Asbell's book shows Muskie to be a thoughtful and serious man, cognizant of the importance of opportunity costs in his budget committee work, but seemingly unaware of their importance for regulatory policy. Economists would argue that eliminating pollution requires government intervention, and thus, in some sense, it is good policy to force, or induce, Detroit automakers to develop technology they would not develop otherwise. Chapter 4 will discuss the way in which almost all economists recommend doing this – a way that takes opportunity costs into account. As Asbell's book indicates, however, Muskie had no idea how much it would cost to reach the pollution-reduction levels he supported on the time schedule he envisioned. Only technological feasibility, not costs, seemed to limit his enthusiasm for the strictest possible standards.

Does the pollution problem dwarf all other national problems such that we want to attack it in the single-minded way we fought World War II? Do we really want Detroit always to place the reduction of pollution above keeping costs and car prices from rising too fast?

The importance of the opportunity costs of such single-mindedness becomes clearer if we preview Chapter 4. That chapter illustrates how the concept of forced technology changes incentives in ways that end up weakening or eliminating the expected clean-air gains of "getting tough" with Detroit. The government guaranteed the purchase of those 60,000 World War II airplanes, but no one can guarantee that consumers will purchase cars that are more costly because they pollute less. It is no answer to say that consumers want clean air and will pay what is necessary to get it. The individual consumer's decision about whether to buy a car that does not pollute will have no noticeable effect on the air he breathes. One less-polluting car cannot alter much the air pollution resulting from emissions from many thousands or even millions of cars, and few, if any, owners of the other cars will change their polluting behavior because one private citizen among them buys a less-polluting automobile. If standards are set very high with tight deadlines, rising costs and prices cause consumers to keep their old cars longer than they would otherwise. The result may be more pollution than would have been produced by new cars with somewhat weaker emissions standards than those enacted.[23] This can happen because weaker standards mean lower costs and lower prices, and thus more rapid replacement of the worse-polluting old cars. In other words, the success of any Detroit effort ultimately depends on consumer willingness to purchase the final product; short deadlines, which drive up costs substantially in all development processes, may paradoxically produce lost opportunities elsewhere while yielding little or no benefits in cleaner air.

If Muskie had studied economics more closely, would he have thought differently about the Clean Air Act in 1975? Perhaps he would still have said, as all of us would have in 1941, "Keep costs as low as possible, but meet the goals *regardless* of costs." It is more likely, however, that he was simply unaware of the full opportunity-cost implications of his decisions because he did not see costs as every bit as important as benefits, indeed as another word for benefits – benefits forgone in other areas. In the Congress he was obviously not alone. Even many conservative Republicans, though more moderate in practice, seemed to adopt principles quite like Muskie's. Senator James McClure (R-Idaho), for example, summarized his position as follows:

When it's a massive expenditure like this, I say go a little slower, force them to go only as fast as we know they can go. But *do* force them to go as fast as we know they can go, and maybe set goals a little beyond our known technology. I think we've exceeded that.[24]

Charles Schultze – a liberal Democrat and Lyndon Johnson's budget director, but also an economist with a good understanding of opportunity cost – would never call for forcing technology in such an open-ended fashion as does this conservative senator less well educated in economics.

SHOULD LIFESAVING PROGRAMS BE EXCEPTIONS?

The belief that we should do whatever we can do to save human life is widespread within Congress, unions, Ralph Nader-oriented public-interest organizations, and the public at large. A United Steelworkers' representative thinks it "despicable" that the Council on Wage and Price Stability questions coke-fume standards costing at least $4.5 million per worker saved.[25] Former senator Harrison Williams (D-N.J.) finds a call for "trading off" increasing safety and economic growth "unconscionable."[26] Congressman David Obey (D-Wisc.) says, "Quite frankly, I believe that when you're dealing in questions related to human life, economic costs are irrelevant."[27] Several congressional committees have voiced similar sentiments.[28]

A large number of people feel a special concern about risks that workers face on the job. Former representative Philip Burton (D-Calif.) spoke for many when he said that American workers have an "inalienable right to earn their living free from the ravages of job-caused death, disease and injury."[29] Such sentiments led to the creation of the Occupational Safety and Health Administration (OSHA), which was directed to promulgate standards that assure, "to the extent feasible, on the basis of the best available evidence, that no employee will suffer material impairment of health or functional capacity."[30]

Like Congressman Burton, most OSHA employees have very strong pro-protection values. One study finds that when considering alternative proposed standards, OSHA officials almost invariably choose the most protective alternative with little thought of costs. This study, by Harvard political scientist Steven Kelman, also asked OSHA inspectors in the field for examples of regulations they thought too strict or too lenient. No inspector cited an example thought too strict. There are no Ph.D economists anywhere in OSHA, and most officials come from the safety engineering or industrial hygiene professions. They shun inexpensive personal protective equipment (e.g., respirators, safety shoes, or, for noise damage, earmuffs) in favor of far more expensive engineering controls. Kelman finds that the textbooks these officials read in school "impart a feeling that relying on personal protection is seen as a confession of failure, a betrayal of the can-do approach of the engineer, a renunciation of pluck and determination for laziness and defeat. 'Personal protective devices have one serious drawback,' *Fundamentals of Industrial Hygiene* states, 'they do nothing to reduce or eliminate the hazard.' "[31]

What have been the results of this single-minded devotion to worker safety coupled with a resolute refusal to consider opportunity costs? Several standards impose costs on industry of tens or hundreds of millions of dollars per life saved. For example, an OSHA contractor estimated that the benzene standard that the Supreme Court overturned (of 1 part per million averaged over an eight-hour working day) would have required $267 million in capital expenditures with operating costs of $124 million in the first year and $74 million in subsequent years. Yet Harvard physicist Richard Wilson has estimated that the new standard would have saved at most one life every three years.[32] Since the charge is often made that such horror stories come only from "business dominated cost-benefit studies,"[33] the reader should know that Wilson was considered impartial enough to have chaired the governor's panel on reactor safety subsequent to the accident at Three Mile Island. Both his father and stepmother died of cancer, and because of adverse health effects, he is on record in opposition to weakened pollution standards for fossil-fuel burning. Moreover, his study used a linear dose-response model that many researchers believe overestimates risk.

But why should industry be permitted to impose these risks on workers whatever the cost? This common retort is a misleading way to describe what is happening. After all, expensive, controversial OSHA decisions, such as those dealing with coke fume and benzene, have usually involved industries where strong unions have opportunities to discuss their priorities for wage and safety improvements with management.[34] Moreover, a number of studies present strong evidence that wage rates are higher in high-risk occupations, even after controlling statistically for education, race, experience, unionization, and so on.[35] Such data are incompatible with a view that imagines the typical worker at risk to be a poor, nonunionized coal miner in Appalachia cut off from other job opportunities and barely aware of the very large risks he faces daily. It is, however, compatible with other research that has found "a strong positive relationship between the worker's danger perceptions and both the pertinent Bureau of Labor Standards industry injury rate and his direct injury experiences." This study also found that workers who perceived their jobs to be "dangerous" or "unhealthy" received about $400 extra per year in 1969.[36]

How great a risk were benzene workers taking under the old exposure standard of 10 parts per million? Is it possible to imagine a worker, not bound by desperate circumstances, willing to subject himself to such a risk for a wage premium? The risk of death for the benzene worker was less than one-tenth the risk taken by steel or railroad workers, less than one-eighth the risk that the average member of the population has of dying in an automobile accident, and less than one-eightieth the risk that cigarette smokers voluntarily incur.[37]

Another way to think of the question is to imagine being one of the 30,000 workers exposed to benzene and affected by the OSHA-proposed standard. Without the standard one of us will die of benzene-related cancer every third year. Would each one of our band of 30,000 pay over $3,333 a year (one worker's share of the $100 million annual cost of the standard) to eliminate this risk? Certainly the wage premium studies suggest that workers are willing to undergo risks for much less than $300 million per death avoided.

The $300 million is, of course, not the workers', and government must decide if industry should have to spend it. Clearly it makes more sense to use the money for one of the many highway-improvement or cancer-screening programs that can save a life for less than $100,000.[38] Money saved will, of course, not go to these programs directly. Most of it will probably reduce product cost. But most people, including union members, want more goods and services as well as a longer life span. Reducing their real incomes through regulation-induced inflation will make them less willing to fund those programs that can save lives at reasonable cost.

One should not assume that the OSHA benzene example is the most extreme case. Wilson's research on a proposed 1980 Environmental Protection Agency (EPA) benzene-emission standard showed that the standard imposed large costs on at least one firm even though Wilson predicted that a case of leukemia would not thereby be prevented until 37,000 years had passed. The implicit cost to save a life was $33 billion.[39]

It can be demoralizing to acknowledge that high costs should sometimes rule out further efforts that we know will save lives. Some readers may be tempted to say that they would go ahead with all the OSHA and EPA programs discussed here so as to avoid any such acknowledgment. But there are an unending number of hypothetical programs that could save lives. Take highway safety, for example. We could save lives by banning all left turns; by banning any travel in rain or snow; by doubling the size of road shoulders or the number of traffic lanes; by cutting speed limits in half; by adding tanklike armor to automobiles; by having pedestrian overpasses at all intersections. Even if we did all these, we could save even more lives if we redoubled the size of road shoulders and the number of lanes and cut the speed limit in half once more. If to save lives we put up with all this environmental destruction, inconvenience, and cost, our lifesaving work would still have just begun. Doctors, police officers, fire fighters, air-quality experts, Coast Guard officers, lifeguards, and ambulance drivers, among others, would be at the door with projects that quite clearly could save lives if we were willing to fund them.

I do not mean to defend here the particular conclusions that economists have reached as to when the benefits of lifesaving programs exceed opportunity costs. I mean only to argue that the concept of opportunity costs is useful and necessary even when thinking about lifesaving programs. We must weigh in our own minds, using our own standards, the gains forgone elsewhere when money is spent on such programs. Even moral philosophers and theologians have been unwilling to say that lifesaving should always have priority over other societal goods.[40] Our life expectancy is now more than ten years greater than that of Americans living forty years ago. That is surely all to the good, but there would be nothing admirable about a society that watched the quality of its life steadily decline in hot pursuit of smaller and smaller increments of life extension. We should not let moralists with tunnel vision convince us otherwise.[41] In this task the librarians and the deans who educate social workers can be of some help.

Though opportunity cost should not be forgotten in agencies like OSHA, it is not really surprising that it so often is. We have, and should want, OSHA administrators who care deeply about occupational safety and health. Because people can care deeply about only a limited number of things, we cannot expect them to care as deeply about other ends. We have, and also should want, union leaders who are dedicated to protecting their workers' lives. It might be thought that business representatives will ensure that cost is not forgotten. But as Kelman's book shows, business spokesmen on the advisory committees and at the public hearings have put up much less resistance to strict standards than might be expected. At these gatherings union leaders speak bitterly of past exposure to carcinogenic agents that will doom "hundreds, perhaps thousands" of workers to agonizing deaths, and they speak movingly of their simple desire for a safe workplace in which to provide for their families – a workplace "like you people behind the desk [have]."[42] It is surely not all bad that businessmen do not know how to respond. They may know that most of the costs of the safer workplace will be borne by consumers paying higher prices. They may also know that remaining costs will be shared with them by stockholders with lower profits, by workers with lower wages (due to reduced demand for their services), and by potential workers with fewer job opportunities (as the result of industry contraction in response to some consumers' switching to other, less expensive products). But it is most unlikely that such calculation is the principal reason for businessmen's silence. Rather, they are understandably reluctant to discuss saving lives in economic terms, and they know that they will seem cruel and uncaring if they do so.[43]

I would agree that we should be slow to ask others to face risks we do not face even when they are paid something to face them. I would also argue that we should be sure that our unwillingness to spend $300 million to save a life does not produce a callousness and cynicism that make us indifferent to others' misfortunes. Still, we would have a better policy process in agencies like OSHA if businessmen more often played the role of cost-conscious calculators. It might help if they reminded themselves that we all face many risks with reasonable equanimity, and that, if they would not pay $3,333 every year to reduce their annual death risk by one in ninety thousand, they should not feel ashamed about opposing a policy that treats others' lives as more sacred than they would treat their own. The policy process would also be improved if businessmen, or someone else, reminded others involved that reverence for life requires spending money on programs that can save many lives before spending it on those that can save only a few. Management might also remind union leaders that it stands ready to trade union wage increases for safety improvements if workers' preferences have changed. More telling still, they might remind union leaders that since the same money spent on personal protection devices such as respirators could save far more lives than the money proposed to be spent on technology, the real issue is not money versus lives but workers' comfort versus workers' lives.[44]

Many businessmen, however, will continue to be unwilling to say publicly that worker deaths that could be prevented are nonetheless tolerable. It is too hard to make such a grave argument when the advantages of doing so, large though they may be, are so diffuse and hard to visualize. Economists care about opportunity cost, a theoretical concept that stands for the multitude of things we value, but cannot comprehend simultaneously. In a world where most of us see costs only as a constraint – as something that keeps us from living our lives or doing our work well – economists and opportunity cost can help us keep our eye on the whole.

CONCLUSION

If politicians and administrators do not fully understand opportunity cost, it should be no surprise that the general public, less involved in questions about public-resource allocation, also does not understand it. A political scientist has argued that the voters in the 1980 presidential election actually wanted more spending for social welfare programs, not less. As evidence he cited national polls of voters that questioned them about their preferences. Voters who thought we were spending "too little" on programs such as education, health, the environment, and big cities far outnumbered those who thought we were spending "too much." The more common perception that the voters wanted to spend more on defense was also found to be true.[45] Such results suggest that the voters wanted a bigger federal government. But this interpretation must be reconciled with other findings: that the public in 1980 considered inflation the nation's main problem, believed that government deficits and excessive spending should be cut, and that the government, not business or labor, caused inflation. The voters, not unlike the pre-budget-reform Congress, approve of more spending in most areas, but then look in horror at the size of what they have wrought.[46]

Some years ago a similar poll found overwhelming support for increased spending on social programs. Seventy percent of respondents wanted more spent on the elderly. Sixty percent favored increases both for the needy and for education. And 54 percent wanted more spent on hospitals and medical care. But when the same people were asked if more should be spent even if more taxes were required, those favorably disposed dropped to 34, 26, 41, and 25 percent, respectively.[47] Making clear who will pay the taxes can also have a dramatic effect. One poll that found 50 percent support for the use of tax monies to supplement the cost of operating bus services found only 27 percent support a few months later when the words "personal income tax monies" were used instead of "tax monies."[48] We, the public, seem quite willing, if given half a chance, to believe that there *is* such a thing as a free lunch.

What is one to make of 1978 poll results that found 53 percent of the public believing that "protecting the environment is so important that requirements and standards cannot be too high, and continuing improvements must be made regardless of cost."[49] The results need not be thought conclusive. As the next chapter will show, one needs a good bit of information to be able to voice intelligent opinions on resource allocation questions. Would the public have given the same answer if it knew that reducing 99 percent of water pollutants would cost $119 billion, but reducing 100 percent would cost $319 billion?[50]

Despite administrators' and legislators' greater knowledge of public affairs, their neglect of opportunity costs is not too surprising. As suggested earlier, it is not only natural, but in most ways advantageous, to have administrators who care more about their programs than the average citizen does. Doctors should worry more about diseases, and firefighters should worry more about fires. And surely librarians should have an atypical love of books. People with devotion and energy will accomplish more with the resources given them than those whose concerns are less partial. Likewise, legislators are likely to become unusually strong supporters of certain programs. Programs important to their district will, of course, get special emphasis. But beyond this, politicians will want the electoral support and psychological pleasures that come from standing for something – from being introduced to applause as "Mr. Solar Energy," "someone veterans can always count on," or "a dependable friend of occupational safety." The legislator who keeps opportunity cost in mind may have to forsake much of that.

Opportunity costs do not go away just because people stop thinking of them. It is more difficult to give them due weight when they do not appear in the sitting legislature's budget. State and local governments embark on projects using federal matching funds that would never see the light of day if the projects required their own monies. And the federal government is constantly imposing unfunded mandates on the states as the states in turn do on the localities. Our public policy would be improved if such unfunded mandates were less pervasive. New York City mayor Edward Koch explains why when discussing his current opposition to federal legislation for equal access for the handicapped, legislation that he had earlier supported as a congressman:

"Sounds terrific, doesn't it? But do you know what that MEANS? It means that in New York City we would have to spend over a BILL-Y-ON DOLLARS – the federal government doesn't provide dollar one – for elevators and other things so that people in wheel chairs could use the subways. For the number who'd use them, that comes to $50 a ride. We say we'll take them wherever they want to go by limousine. It would be cheaper."

The government also insists that the city provide special classes for emotionally and physically handicapped children. For this, the feds provide $8.5 million.

"So go do it. But the added cost is $300 million. Where is the money coming from? From the police, the firemen, sanitation, corrections? WHERE?"

This is an understandable reaction from a man charged with reducing next year's budget by $300 million when forty-seven federal and state mandates will require expenditures of $938 million. Koch concludes with a definition of opportunity cost New York City style: "Being told to do good things, when you can't afford them, is not doing good things."[51]

Making the costs of government-imposed regulations on business seem real is more difficult still because such costs are so diffuse and show up in *no* government's budget. Perhaps the idea of a regulatory budget – a fixed amount of costs that a given agency could impose on firms in any given year – deserves a try. But for some of the more subtle but significant forms of opportunity costs, nothing but a better legislative understanding of economics will suffice. In 1981 federally guaranteed loans exceeded $250 billion, and, together with other forms of federal spending support, they accounted for 21.2 percent of all funds advanced in U.S. credit markets.[52] Student loans have had an 18 percent default rate. But for most government-assisted loans the default rate has been much lower. In these cases Congress is too easily persuaded that the loans are essentially costless. Why not give Chrysler or Lockheed a chance with a guaranteed loan? The federal government will be paid first if they should go bankrupt, and American jobs may be saved as a result. So goes the argument. But guaranteed loans are not costless even when they are paid back. The amount of investment capital available at reasonable interest rates is not unlimited, and guaranteed loans make bad credit risks into splendid ones. When some move to the front of the credit line, others, often small businesses that may be more important to the economy in the long run, move to the rear. And many of these small businesses go bankrupt.

The Chrysler and Lockheed loans are widely considered success stories since neither company went bankrupt. Economists are less sure. Again, we cannot know that the companies that otherwise would have received the investment funds might not have done still better. Besides, though the federal bailout helped Chrysler workers, it hurt Ford and General Motors workers, whose companies would have gained sales if Chrysler had gone bankrupt. Moreover, even after the successful rescue effort, Chrysler's employment today is only about one-half of what it was in 1978. Similarly, if Lockheed had gone bankrupt, other companies would have received more defense contracts. The $250 million loan guarantee granted Lockheed in 1971 was aimed at saving the company's Tristar commercial jumbo jet. But in 1981 Lockheed decided the plane would never be profitable, and it was phased out. For some time, however, McDonnell Douglas had to split the DC-10 market with Tristar. As a result it could not "develop the cash flow to launch a smaller, two-engine version of the DC-10. Into that gap marched the European Airbus, now a formidable U.S. rival."[53]

As the quotation from Mayor Koch suggests, opportunity costs that affect political executives' own budgets are least likely to be forgotten. Though political executives may want to share the rewards and pleasures that come from advancing a particular cause, they cannot avoid the conflicting pressures as easily. They must propose a budget for which they assume responsibility, and they are more likely than individual legislators to be held personally responsible for deficits. Thus it is not surprising that economists have been closer to the center of power with the country's executives than with its legislators.

3

MARGINALISM

Adam Smith struggled with what came to be called the paradox of value in use versus value in exchange. Water is necessary to existence and of enormous value in use. Diamonds are frivolous and clearly not essential. The price, however, of diamonds, their value in exchange, is far higher than that of water. What troubled Smith is now rationally explained in the first chapters of every college freshman's introductory economics text. Smith had failed to distinguish between total and marginal utility. The elaboration of this insight transformed economics in the late nineteenth century, and the fruits of the marginalist revolution continue to set the basic framework for contemporary microeconomics.

The total utility or satisfaction of water exceeds that of diamonds. We would all rather do without diamonds than without water. But almost all of us would prefer to win a prize of a diamond than one of an additional bucket of water. To make this last choice, we ask ourselves not whether diamonds or water gives more satisfaction in total, but whether more of one gives greater additional satisfaction than more of the other. For this marginal utility question our answer will depend on how much of each we already have. Though the first units of water we consume every month are of enormous value to us, the last units are not. The utility of additional marginal units continues to decrease as we consume more and more.

Even if we equate diamonds with foolishness and vanity and would never wear one ourselves, we would prefer to win a diamond than a bucket of water because we could sell the diamond for money or for things worth more to us than a bucket of water. The price of diamonds is higher because people value them, and they are much scarcer. This relative scarcity reflects the difficulty we have in increasing their supply. Because both the marginal utility of diamonds and the marginal costs of production are high, the price of diamonds is higher than that of water. The high price means that many people do not buy diamonds at all, and others stop buying them though they would very much enjoy having another. Such people may assign little or no value to extra water. Actual choices then reflect not just core values or preferences (water is more important than diamonds), but also relative scarcities. They reflect a weighing of marginal utility and marginal cost of the alternative opportunities before us.

The economic term "marginal" is usually paired with another word or phrase. As in the water–diamond example, marginal benefit or marginal utility is the added satisfaction from consuming a little more of a good or service; and marginal cost is the cost to produce another unit or increment of a good or service. Similarly, the marginal tax rate is the amount a person would pay on an additional dollar of income. And the marginal savings rate is the amount he would save from an additional dollar of income.

The water–diamond example showed that choices result from weighing the marginal utility and the marginal costs of alternative opportunities. Inevitably, an explanation of marginalism brings the words "opportunity" and "cost" back to center stage. The concepts of marginalism and opportunity cost flow from the same insights. Marginal cost is defined as opportunity cost, and opportunity cost means alternative benefits – alternative marginal benefits – forgone. Though the concepts are related, they are not identical. Marginalism helps define opportunity cost, but it has wider relevance. For example, when considering the effect of tax rates on the incentive to work, it reminds us that in most cases we are less interested in the average tax rate paid on a family's entire income than on the proportion of *added* gross income that the husband or wife will keep if either works a little more. Similarly, when considering the effect of a tax cut on savings, it reminds us that we should not look at the percentage of a family's total income that is saved but rather the percentage of any *additional* income received (in this case from the tax cut).

Both marginalism and opportunity cost point to benefit-cost analysis – an attempt to quantify and compare in dollar terms the marginal benefits and the marginal costs of a policy or program. But as Chapter 8 will explain, economic benefit-cost analysis looks only to consumers' preferences, their willingness to pay, when determining the benefits or worth of a public program. Some readers will think this benefit-cost standard for good policy inadequate. Such readers may still find the concepts of opportunity cost and marginalism helpful as they weigh, according to their own criteria, the advantages and disadvantages of the policy alternatives before them.

Though the two concepts are closely related, marginalism is better suited to illustrating certain mistakes in theorizing about human nature and in framing some large public–policy questions. Economists think that most people's private decisions are based on a comparison of marginal utilities and marginal costs even if the comparisons may be only subconscious ones. They also think that looking to the margin in this way is sensible. But when theorizing about human nature, noneconomists often miss the common sense of marginalism. And in discussions of public-policy issues where most of the benefits and costs do not accrue to the individual making the policy decision (e.g., subsidies for health care), the appeal of total utility and intrinsic worth as a basis for decision can mask the insights of marginalism.

HUMAN NEEDS AND MARGINALISM

A. H. Maslow was a psychologist whose work on human motivation has been influential in fields such as organization development and industrial psychology. Maslow argued that basic human needs can be catalogued and ranked according to their importance in providing motivation and influencing behavior. He saw physiological needs such as water, food, sex, and sleep as the most fundamental, demanding, and powerful. However, if the physiological needs "are relatively well gratified, there then emerges a new set of needs" pertaining to safety. Once the safety needs of security, order, and protection are "fairly well gratified," there then "emerge" love, affection, and belongingness needs. When these have been satisfied, needs for esteem (achievement, reputation, prestige) take over, and these, when satisfied, are replaced by the need for self-actualization, "the desire to become more and more what one is, to become everything that one is capable of becoming."

Maslow did not hold rigidly to this ordering of needs. He said there will be exceptions and that a need does not have to be satisfied 100 percent before the next need emerges. "A more realistic description of the hierarchy would be in terms of decreasing percentages of satisfaction as we go up the hierarchy of prepotency." Nevertheless, the view that at any point in time a person is dominated by the most powerful of the unsatisfied needs is clearly set forth. Here is how Maslow summarized his argument:

We have seen that the chief principle of organization in human motivational life is the arrangement of needs in a hierarchy of less or greater priority or potency. The chief dynamic principle animating this organization is the emergence of less potent needs upon gratification of the more potent ones. The physiological needs, when unsatisfied, dominate the organism, pressing all capacities into their service and organizing these capacities so that they may be most efficient in this service. Relative gratification submerges them and allows the next higher set of needs in the hierarchy to emerge, dominate and organize the personality, so that instead of being, e.g., hunger obsessed, it now becomes safety obsessed. The principle is the same for the other sets of needs in the hierarchy, i.e., love, esteem, and self-actualization.[1]

Economists Richard McKenzie and Gordon Tullock have used the insights of marginalism to criticize Maslow's theory.[2] They agree with Maslow that the individual can rank his needs and wants and that he will pursue those avenues that give him the greatest satisfaction. They also note that Maslow seemed to accept the principle of diminishing marginal utility. As the hunger and then the safety needs are better and better met, they cease to motivate, and other needs emerge. But Maslow mistakenly thought that one can predict human behavior by looking at the relative strengths of the needs without considering the relative costs of satisfying them. Even if one assumes that in some total or absolute sense, the demand for satisfying a basic physiological need is greater than that for satisfying a belongingness need, there is no reason to believe that a higher proportion of the physiological need will actually be satisfied. In underdeveloped countries there are many people who satisfy a higher percentage of their total love and belongingness needs than of their physiological or safety needs.[3] The same could probably be said of some low-income families in the United States. And many who strive for esteem nevertheless feel vulnerable and unsafe, worried about their health, nuclear destruction, or violent crime. These worries, even if fairly strong, may not dominate such people's behavior because they do not think much can be done about these concerns at reasonable cost.

The demand for satisfying needs is not completely insensitive to price.[4] How much we try to satisfy our total need for anything will, in every instance, depend on the costs of doing so, as well as on our fundamental needs and beliefs. Moreover, our needs are not considered separately but in conjunction with each other. In some cases a comparison of the marginal utility and marginal cost of different alternatives may lead us to give priority to a relatively small "total utility" need rather than a relatively large and powerful one even though the latter is not close to being fully satisfied. And if the costs of meeting needs change sufficiently, choices and behavior can change substantially while basic needs and preferences remain the same.

HEALTH NEEDS AND THE DEMAND FOR MEDICAL CARE

The marginalist insight can illuminate some weaknesses in the health-policy outlook of those whose position is determined by the idea of medical needs. One view of medical needs holds, in the spirit of Maslow, that they dominate behavior. Doctors are not like books and movies; they give no positive pleasure. No one wants to see a doctor. But if a person is sick and needs to see a doctor, nothing will keep him from seeing one. When an individual's health is bad, he becomes obsessed with health, and all his capacities are directed to obtaining the necessary medical care. According to this theory economics and changes in price will have little or no effect on the demand for medical care. That demand is almost completely insensitive to price; it is either there, or it is not. Changes in insurance deductible provisions or the coinsurance percentage rate paid by consumers will not effectively limit demand.

The available evidence gives little support to this position. From the point of view of the consumer at least, a significant portion of demand for medical care gives very small benefits. These benefits are poorly indicated by thinking about total utility, that is, how important health is. For a number of small populations, scholars have observed the effects of insurance policy changes on the demand for health care. A few actual experiments have also been conducted. One asked a group of California Medicaid beneficiaries to pay one dollar for their first two office visits each month, while a similar group continued to receive completely free service. This modest charge reduced office visits by 8 percent.[5] Other studies have found that even small changes in time cost can have an effect. For example, when the health facility at one college was moved so that it took twenty minutes rather than five to ten to walk there, student visits fell by nearly 40 percent. Similarly, a 10 percent increase in the travel time to outpatient clinics among a low-income urban group caused an estimated 10 percent decrease in demand for visits to physicians.[6] Whether the health services forgone in these cases were necessary remains an open question, but surely the behavior of the potential patients was not dominated by their health needs. One study estimates that full, free insurance for ambulatory physician services would increase demand in this country by 75 percent. Differences in drug and dental usage among groups with full coverage and those with more typical coverage suggest that full coverage for these services might increase demand by 100 percent.[7]

A more sophisticated version of the medical-needs position holds that certain fundamental goods such as "health, education, food, housing, and clothing" are "essential needs" to which there should be "a social, institutional right."[8] Charles Fried has made this argument well. Fried believes that the economist's tendency to talk about ethics only in terms of the individual's right to a societally determined fair share of general resources is inadequate.[9] He maintains that

distributional schemes would not (if equality were our canon of just distribution) be satisfied by an equal distribution of money with which the chronically ill could purchase medicines while others purchased holidays, opera tickets, or other luxury goods. Good health is a need precisely in the sense that we have or we seek objective measures of good health. We try to assure this objective good, the satisfaction of this objective need apart from, or without prejudice to, the balance of an individual's distributive share.[10]

In other parts of his article Fried seems reluctant to say that health and other fundamental needs deserve absolute priority over other goods. He also acknowledges that there will be great complexities in working out the details of his idea. Still, he treats the health need as far easier to define than seems warranted. Fried seems to think of serious, medically treatable illness when he pictures health demand and medical expenditures. But again, those who have looked closely at the question find that the marginal utility of much spending for medical services does not belong in a fundamental-need category and deserves no absolute priority over other expenditures. The problem, moreover, is not just patients' unnecessary use of a heavily subsidized system, but doctors' disagreement concerning the presence of a health need.

Michael Cooper notes that hospital surgeons in the United States find twice as many patients in need of surgery as do their British counterparts. In England, decisions about referring patients to a specialist or for hospitalization show inexplicable variation among regions, doctors, and hospitals. In some areas children have twice as many tonsillectomies as in others. In Edinburgh some general practitioners refer less than 1 percent of their patients to hospitals, whereas others refer nearly 26 percent. Even after controlling for age and sex and rejecting certain extreme values that fluctuate from year to year, the average lengths of stay in different British hospitals are found to vary fivefold for treatment of hernia, sixfold for appendicitis treatment, and ninefold for treatment of bronchitis and pneumonia. The recent average hernia treatment in England is eleven days (and treatment in some hospitals averages twenty-one days), though a study has found that discharge after one day produces no observable effect on the patient compared with discharge after one week.

Cooper presents this information as part of his assessment of the 1946 British Health Service Act, which established access to health care resources as a "human right" of all those shown to be in need as assessed by the medical profession. He concludes that

the Health Service was founded upon a basic misconception of the nature of the need for health care resources. The conception of sickness as an unambiguous and absolute state led to the false hope that unmet need could be abolished. In practice, sickness has been found to be a relative state capable of almost infinite interpretation by both potential patients and the medical profession. There has proved to be no allocation of national resources which would eliminate the necessity for the Health Service to ration its services among excess competing claims upon them.[11]

From the patient's point of view the potential for entry into the category of needy is enormous. Large numbers of people do not feel entirely well. An English study found that 95 percent of the people in one community considered themselves unwell during the fourteen days prior to questioning. A survey in Rochester, New York, found that adults suffered from at least one disorder on 20 percent of the twenty-eight days covered. Further, 46 percent of American draftees were rejected on "genuine" medical grounds.[12] In the absence of money costs, queues, or other allocative devices, many of those who are not now seeing doctors would do so. They could easily swamp even greatly expanded medical facilities.

Doctors know that their science is uncertain, and if there is no cost to them or their patient, many will do something. After all, further tests *might* find something, and extra days of hospitalization *might* prevent complications. Physicians are supposed to do everything they can for patients, and if given the freedom to do so, they could become concerned with risks as remote as those that trouble the dedicated occupational safety professionals who populate the Occupational Safety and Health Administration.

Cooper notes that both demand and need tend to grow in line with provision.

Doctors react to any expansion in supply by realigning their conception of need. Thus one study of acute-care hospitals found that both admissions and length of stay increased with bed availability. It could not discover a level of bed provision that would have fully satiated doctors' demands.[13]

Nothing said heretofore is meant to argue that the concept of medical need is meaningless. Good health is not simply subjective, and it, as well as water, is more important than diamonds. As Fried argues, when physicians can significantly help the seriously ill, the needs of such patients should have a special claim on resources. But most of the time they already do. In any case, when considering whether all those with medical complaints should have free and immediate access to physicians, one should not think mainly about a catastrophically ill patient with low income. Those patients' problems are very real, but they could be resolved with policies far less costly than providing free and immediate access to doctors for everyone with a medical complaint. The more typical patient whose demand would be restricted by coinsurance or deductibles is one whose disorder is fairly minor, its cause uncertain, or the chance that doctors can help, slim. Many doctors will want to use scarce resources to the point where the marginal utility of further expenditures equals zero ("everything possible for my patients"), not to the point where it equals opportunity cost. One should encourage them to do so only if good health is the only important component of a good life and if greater access to physician services is the only route to better health.

The concept of need brings to mind things solemn and important. Where it is used to call our attention to genuine suffering, it is good that it does. But overemphasizing need can make us even needier. If we equate the demand for health care or even doctors' views of the need for health care with the true need for it, we will encourage the view that keeping us healthy is principally someone else's job. Eating, drinking, and smoking less, however, could improve our health far more than seeing doctors more frequently.

SETTING PRIORITIES AND MARGINALISM

Government leaders and agency heads often talk of the need to set priorities so as to give direction to their activities. Though this setting of priorities is often seen as little more than common sense, it is difficult to do without ignoring the insights of marginalism. The resulting effects on government policy can be almost as unfortunate as those produced by overemphasizing needs.

Economists believe that even good answers to certain grand questions give little guidance for rational public-policy choices. What is more important – health or recreation? Clean air or economic growth? Natural-setting recreational opportunities for some or developed recreational opportunities for far more? Marginalism suggests that our real concern should be with proportion, not rank. If forced to choose, everyone would find health more important than recreation, but this finding does not imply that all swimming pool diving boards should be removed just because a few people die in diving accidents. Similarly, we clearly want cleaner air and economic growth, natural-setting recreational opportunities and developed ones. Reasonable policy choices require knowledge of how well we are now doing in all of these areas and of the alternative opportunities available.

In addition, costs must be determined. Even the biggest *remaining* problem may not deserve most of the extra money. One writer, for example, argues that early deaths of the young are our greatest lifesaving problem, and therefore the health budget should emphasize preventing the largest killers of the young, such as accidents and suicides.[14] But even if one accepts this writer's values, his policy conclusions do not follow. We may not know how to prevent suicides at reasonable cost, but perhaps a medical breakthrough has made it possible to cure at low cost a disease that is the sixth leading cause of death among the young. We would then save more lives among the young if we devoted more of our resources to their sixth largest health problem rather than their first or second. Marginalism thus requires looking at the details – looking at the costs and benefits of particular opportunities.

Social scientists who are not economists sometimes want a community's budget policy to be heavily influenced by poll results about the major problems facing the community or the functional areas that the public thinks should be cut in times of fiscal stringency. Economists are skeptical. When consumers are asked such questions, they are almost never provided with any detailed information on probable effects and costs. Thus respondents usually look to total utility when giving their answers, and cuts in lifesaving departments such as police and fire receive almost no support. After enactment of Proposition 13, for example, only 8 percent of Californians thought that any cuts should be made in police budgets, and only 6 percent wanted any cuts in fire departments.[15] But perhaps cuts in the police budget could be accomplished by replacing police officers doing desk work with less expensive clerks, and fire department cuts may involve replacing some full-time firefighters with supplementary reservists, fully trained and paid a monthly retainer and an hourly wage while fighting fires.[16] The public cannot be expected to be aware of these possibilities, and thus the most common types of polls will tell little about their true preferences.

In 1974 the Federal Aviation Administration had new leadership eager to take charge of the agency by reshaping priorities, setting and achieving quantitative objectives, and systematically using benefit-cost analysis when deciding on levels of program funding. The FAA implemented these changes in a way that placed the priority- and objective-setting processes in conflict with benefit-cost analysis, a fact that went unrecognized because of the neglect of the insights of marginalism.

The FAA established priorities by first developing end-product objectives it thought could be achieved over the next two years, objectives such as reducing air-carrier accidents by 6 percent, general aviation accidents by 10 percent, delays by 25 percent and noise by 10 percent. But in order to be consistent with marginalism the establishment of even one such objective or priority would have to be preceded by some weighing of the marginal gains and marginal costs of expanding each of the programs dealing with the objective in question as compared to the marginal gains and costs of expanding programs advancing other agency objectives. We can know how high to set any one objective only if we know what we give up in progress toward other objectives. Moreover, it makes little sense to say that achieving one of these objectives has a higher priority than achieving another. Chances are that some of the programs aimed at all three of the principal problems – safety, congestion, and noise – will provide high marginal benefits compared to marginal costs. Thus a list of priorities guided by the marginalist insight would have to be incredibly detailed. The highest net benefit program or the one with the highest ratio of benefits to costs might aim at congestion, the second highest at safety, the third at congestion, the fourth at noise. The resulting list of agency priorities would thus be terribly complicated: "Our top priority is reducing congestion by about .4 percent" (by implementing the highest net benefit program); "our second-highest priority is reducing general aviation accidents by .8 percent" (by implementing the second-highest net benefit program); "the third-highest priority is reducing congestion by another .9 percent" (by implementing the third-highest net benefit program, which is also the second-best congestion program. Though this second-best congestion program reduces more than twice as much congestion as the best, it is ranked second because it costs four times as much as the best), and so on.

Once objectives were set, they would have to be updated continually. If the traffic at an airport that was to get an instrument landing system should go below minimum facility-establishment standards, safety and delay-reduction goals would have to be reduced, and priorities might have to change to take account of the abandonment of this project. If an increase (decrease) in development costs should make a planned piece of equipment inadvisable (advisable), again, goals and priorities would have to change.

Any agency leadership should, of course, keep in mind the fundamental goals of the agency. In the case of the FAA this means thinking a lot about safety, congestion, and noise and about developing and analyzing alternative ways to address these problems. But if the insights of marginalism are not to be ignored, the establishment of quantitative agency objectives and priorities must be the last step in a planning process, not the first. Because sensible quantitative objectives depend on deep thought about marginal costs and marginal benefits, they must be a by-product of an independent assessment of all agency programs. If this assessment supports institution of air-carrier safety programs x, y, and z, little is gained analytically by adding up the expected safety gains from these programs and then noting that our safety objective for the year thereby becomes a certain percentage reduction in accidents. Quantitative objectives determined without a careful look at particular programs should not give direction to the agency. For example, suppose money becomes available and there are additional safety programs whose benefits exceed costs but no such noise programs. Should the noise programs be given priority just because an arbitrary safety objective set months ago has been achieved, but the arbitrary noise objective has not?

Some members of the FAA saw their quantitative objectives as being similar to rate-of-return objectives in business. But a rate-of-return objective takes account of both revenues and costs, whereas the FAA's focused on either benefits or costs but not both. One can know how high to aim at achieving a safety objective or how low in reducing costs only by considering the implications for the other side of the equation. This can be done only after assessing specific programs. Given the way in which FAA objectives were established, they could become a club with which program enthusiasts with tunnel vision attack those who would balance a monetary commitment to programs with the insights of opportunity cost and marginalism – a club to attack the "false economizers" who are preventing the agency from meeting its proclaimed objectives.[17]

THE COSTS OF MARGINALISM

There are costs to the kind of calculation inherent in marginalism, costs apparent to the most thoughtful of economists. Kenneth Boulding observes that it is profoundly unromantic: "No one would want his daughter to marry an economic man, one who counted every cost and asked for every reward, [and] was never afflicted with mad generosity or uncalculating love."[18] Marginalism is also unheroic. The military's motto, "Theirs not to reason why, theirs but to do and die," is very far from the economist's view of the world. So too is the prayer of Saint Francis: "To give and not to count the cost, to labor and ask for no reward." Boulding reminds us of the powerful critique of marginalism in Wordsworth's sonnet, "Inside of King's College Chapel, Cambridge":

> Tax not the royal Saint with vain expense,
> With ill-matched aims the Architect who planned –
> Albeit labouring for a scanty band
> Of white-robed Scholars only – this immense
> And glorious work of fine intelligence!
> Give all thou canst; high Heaven rejects the lore
> Of nicely-calculated less or more;
> So deemed the man who fashioned for the sense
> These lofty pillars, spread that branching roof

Self-poised, and scooped into ten thousand cells,
Where light and shade repose, where music dwells
Lingering – and wandering on as loth to die;
Like thoughts whose very sweetness yieldeth proof
That they were born for immortality.

In principle, economic-welfare theory offers no objection to uncalculating dedication to a single end. As we shall see in later chapters, it has nothing to say about the best end or ends for individuals to pursue. But marginalism and opportunity cost show their full power only when the ends are plural, and for most people they are. Because economic calculation is so useful most of the time, it can become a habit. And despite its many uses, that habit of looking at the world through the eyes of marginalism and opportunity cost could lead us to forget that single-mindedness, though uncommon, can produce great results. A society without some single-minded people loses sight of an important aspect of human nobility.

As Alexis de Tocqueville notes, democratic, egalitarian societies are quick to tax with vain expense those who give all they can. There are not, as in aristocracies, tight groups of artisans who honor the most skillful of their number nor persons "who derive from their superior and hereditary position a taste for what is extremely well made and lasting." Instead there is "a multitude of persons whose wants are above their means and who are very willing to take up with imperfect satisfaction rather than abandon the object of their desires." Artisans and artists soon learn to be "sparing of their powers," to "remain in a state of accomplished mediocrity" far from the limits of their art.[19]

A person totally dedicated to philosophy, to art, or to the worship of God has no need of marginalism. Although he must manage his time and resources, food, for example, is not an end but a constraint that must be satisfied so that he may continue his only valued activity. Tocqueville reflects on Pascal's ability

to rally all the powers of his mind ... for the better discovery of the most hidden things of the Creator. When I see him, as it were, tear his soul from all the cares of life to devote it wholly to these researches and, prematurely snapping the links that bind the body to life, die of old age before forty, I stand amazed and perceive that no ordinary cause is at work to produce efforts so extraordinary.[20]

Tocqueville doubts that such passions, "at once so rare and so productive," will grow as easily in democratic communities. It is hard to disagree with him. Indeed, by emphasizing the principal of inclusiveness (of different aims) as a component of what little there is to say about the rational way to choose a good life plan, our best-known contemporary philosopher, John Rawls, encourages us to forget even the possibility of Pascal-like single-mindedness.[21] Marginalism, like Rawls, could lead us to forget even the past existence of such rare and productive passions.

CONCLUSION

The costs of marginalism suggest that a good education should include much more than a knowledge of Rawls and economics. Reflecting on these costs may have other implications for public policy as well. On occasion, statesmen may want to carve out some projects where they abandon nicely calculated less-or-more and do all they can. Give the artist or professional his head, and show what mankind can accomplish. Nevertheless, whatever its usefulness for philosophers, artists, and members of religious orders, marginalism must be one important part of a policy analyst's or statesman's perspective. The statesman's art is prudence or the use of reason and forethought to skillfully select and use the best means to achieve good ends. And for the statesman in peacetime the ends must be plural. Politics remains the architectonic art. The librarian, prison doctor, welfare dean, and occupational-safety expert still come to the politician with their competing claims for resources. The politician who distinguishes marginal and total utility will do a better job of judging these claims.

The temptation not to distinguish the two will, however, be very great. Polls cited in this and the preceding chapter show that when thinking about government programs the public is likely to ignore opportunity costs and see the policy world through the eyes of total utility. The people will oppose cuts in the police department budget, will believe that environmental standards cannot be too high, and will support further environmental improvements regardless of cost. Asbell describes the awkward moment in 1975 when the Senate Public Works Committee concluded that it had carried even its single-minded pursuit of clean air too far:

With the exception of Hart and possibly Culver, every committee member now seems convinced that if the Clean Air Act is to be enforceable the requirement of .4 Nox must be expunged. But whoever proposes this change will be accused of leading a retreat from clean air and virtue. Who will be first? And what euphemism will he employ to make it easier for others to join him?[22]

The politician must rely in part on euphemism to sell the economist's platform of slightly dirty air.[23] Although increased attempts by congressmen to educate the public would be helpful, such attempts cannot eliminate the need for euphemism. It is unlikely that the voters will ever be deeply knowledgeable about public affairs. The politician who sets his priorities, who focuses on and accomplishes a few things, will not only get reelected, but will boost public morale and give people more confidence in their ability to control events. The complexity of the marginalist perspective and the necessity to qualify, to back and fill as circumstances and technology change, would, if presented unadorned, leave the people with a demoralizing sense of governmental drift and indecision. The tension between marginalism and politics requires that the statesman's art include rhetoric.

The statesman, however, must not ignore marginalism. Even accomplishing a few publicly supported objectives will not yield reelection if it is accompanied by significant deterioration of other public services or by a substantial increase in taxes or prices. That 1975 Senate Public Works Committee meeting would not have been so awkward politically if politicians had given more thought to opportunity cost and marginalism when the previous air-quality standards were enacted.

The principal problem to date has not been the lack of rhetorical skills through which knowledgeable politicians could make their marginalist insights compatible with public misunderstanding. The principal problem has been the politicians' own ignorance of marginalism. Unfortunately, institutions that are potentially capable of overcoming this ignorance are poorly equipped to do so. Kneese and Schultze have noted that most congressional staffs are chosen for their negotiating skills, and few have much knowledge of economics.[24] And Washington political reporters' ignorance of the subject is scandalous. Even the *Washington Post*'s economics editor forgets marginalism in arguing that reduced taxes will probably produce little new savings and investment given the historical average national savings rate of only 7 percent of the gross national product.[25] The relevant question is what percentage of additional, *marginal* income will be saved. Even at the lowest income levels the long-run marginal savings rate is more than double the 7 percent national *average* savings rate. In the highest income brackets the long-run marginal rate has been estimated at 55 percent.[26]

The remaining chapters in Parts I and II of the book will provide additional cases in which marginalism helps illuminate public-policy issues. Before leaving the subject here, however, it is worth noting how the concept can help the politician evaluate some popular political maxims and conceptions of fairness. For example, marginalism calls into question the maxim that one cannot legislate morality. The law surely affects, to some degree, conceptions of morality. The 1964 act guaranteeing equal access to public accommodations has helped lead to different beliefs among white southerners about whether it is wrong for blacks to eat in the same restaurants with whites. But even if law could not change moral beliefs, marginalism shows that changing costs can change behavior even without affecting underlying moral opinions.

It is said to be only fair to ask all polluters to clean up to a similar degree. But some water has important uses, and other runs into the ocean. Some is clean enough to cleanse itself through its natural exposure to oxygen. Some plants can meet a cleanliness standard with little added expense, but others meeting the same standard will have to junk equipment with many years of useful life remaining. Since the benefits and costs that flow from a common standard vary so dramatically, alternative policies (discussed in chap. 4) that account for these variations can save tens of billions of dollars while achieving an equivalent level of cleanliness and meeting defensible standards of equity.[27]

Both opportunity cost and marginalism lead one to question the old maxim that anything worth doing at all is worth doing well. James Buchanan has suggested that an economist can be distinguished from a noneconomist by his reaction to this statement.[28] Another economist actually polled a group of economists to judge their agreement or disagreement with this and four other maxims. "Anything worth doing ... " was by far the least popular, with 74 percent of respondents disagreeing.[29] McKenzie and Tullock have gone so far as to entitle a chapter of their book, "Anything Worth Doing is Not Necessarily Worth Doing Well."[30] A careful weighing of marginal cost implies that we should use well the money we devote to a task, but we should rarely do as much as interested professionals think necessary.

4

ECONOMIC INCENTIVES

Since the time of Adam Smith, economists have been at work figuring out ways to use monetary incentives to accomplish public purposes. A recent landmark showing this orientation was Charles Schultze's Godkin Lecture series delivered at Harvard University in 1976. The lectures attracted the attention of the newly elected president, Jimmy Carter, and helped to convince Carter to make Schultze the chairman of his Council of Economic Advisers. They later became *The Public Use of Private Interest*, an influential book that nicely synthesized an important theme in contemporary economists' criticisms of a host of current government policies.

Schultze argues that the growing industrialization, urbanization, and interdependence of society have generated problems that require a more active government than we have known throughout most of our history. In the newer forms of social intervention, however, successful policy "depends on affecting the skills, attitudes, consumption habits, or production patterns of hundreds of millions of individuals, millions of business firms, and thousands of local units of government." To perform these difficult tasks we have passed detailed laws and adopted detailed bureaucratic regulations. Such "command and control" methods worked well when the typical governmental task was to build a dam or mail out a check, but they are a costly and ineffective way to change the private behavior of a large portion of society. Schultze notes that we have largely ignored an alternative method of collective intervention – marketlike incentives such as taxes and subsidies that make private interests more congruent with public goals. We acknowledge the power of markets and economic incentives to foster steadily improving private-sector efficiency and a higher standard of living. And "we would laugh if someone suggested that the best way to reduce labor input per unit of production was to set up a government agency to specify labor input in detail for each industry. But that is precisely how we go about trying to reduce environmental damage and industrial accidents."[1]

ECONOMIC INCENTIVES AND ENVIRONMENTAL POLLUTION

Though economists have talked at length about the public use of private interest in many policy areas, environmental pollution has been their favorite example. Many in their profession have found the benefits of certain environmental laws and regulations less than the costs. Economists, however, argue that the economic-incentives approach is a question of means. It is thus relevant regardless of one's views of these end-oriented, benefit-cost studies. Though one can make pollutants more manageable and change their form by, for example, converting waterborne wastes into solids or gases, it is impossible to eliminate all pollutants in every form. Since zero discharge simultaneously in all media violates the laws of physics, since the air and water will, in any case, cleanse themselves of a certain amount of some pollutants, and since opportunity costs, however calculated, are important, we must accept many pollutants in some degree at some places at some time. Regardless of how we determine these questions of level, time, and place, there will be cost savings and/or effectiveness gains from abandoning current modes of pollution control in favor of means that alter private incentives.[2]

Weaknesses in the current regulatory system

The public strongly supports a clean environment. The prevalent view among the people and throughout much of Washington is that the air and water legislation enacted in the 1970s led to important gains that must be preserved and strengthened by resisting the efforts of industry to "weaken" the fundamental law. The prevalent view among economists and others with expertise in the area is far different. In a recent Brookings Institution monograph, Lester Lave and Gilbert Omenn say that our current system for abating air pollution "desperately" needs attention.[3] Independent research has led Robert Crandall to view the Environmental Protection Agency's rules on clean air as "among the most expensive and inefficient" regulatory programs.[4]

What is the regulatory system we have used in the last decade? In 1970 the Environmental Protection Agency (EPA) was established to implement the Clean Air Act of 1970. That statute and subsequent amendments attempted regulation on an unprecedented scale and in great detail. The EPA administrator was to establish national primary "ambient" (outdoor) air-quality standards to protect the public health and secondary standards to protect the public welfare (soils, crops, etc.). He was to review state implementation plans to meet the standards in nonattainment areas. He was also to set federal standards limiting the amount of emissions from new or modified stationary pollution sources, such as factories, in all areas that had met the federal standards. In addition, together with the Congress, the EPA administrator was to set and enforce national emission standards for new motor vehicles.

The 1970 legislation set strict standards and rigid deadlines. Since then, however, the Congress, the courts, and the EPA have continually ignored or postponed deadlines and revised timetables for motor vehicles, stationary sources, and overall air quality. Lave and Omenn note that this "charade reached its culmination in the conclusion of the National Commission on Air Quality that stringent standards should continue to be set without regard to costs or feasibility but that federal deadlines should be removed altogether!"[5]

To be sure, there have been some gains in air quality in recent years. According to the EPA's pollutant-standard index, between 1974 and 1978 there was a 35 percent reduction in the number of "very unhealthful" days in our twenty-three major metropolitan areas. Moreover, between 1973 and 1978 two of the pollutants of nationwide distribution that appear to be the most harmful to human health, sulfur dioxide and particulate matter suspended in the air, declined by 20 and 7 percent, respectively. However, volatile organic matter was reduced very little, and nitrogen oxides actually increased 17 percent. Even the gains that have occurred may not be attributable principally to the federal clean air legislation. Increases in fossil-fuel prices have reduced consumption and encouraged the use of more efficient equipment. Many localities have severely restricted open-air burning of leaves and garbage. And many firms have substituted oil and natural gas for the much dirtier coal. Perhaps most telling of all, EPA and Council of Environmental Quality data show that air quality for sulfur dioxide and particulate matter was improving as fast or faster before 1972 as after.

It would be incorrect to suggest that all the federal air pollution laws and regulations have accomplished nothing. Lawrence White finds, for example, that the motor vehicle standards have led to substantial reductions in emissions. White also finds, however, that alternative approaches could have done as well at much less cost.[6] And all in all the clean air gains over the last decade are less than one might expect could be achieved from policies costing over $25 billion a year.[7]

Economists are not surprised by this unimpressive performance. Crandall notes that "no organization could possibly cope with the continuing flow of legislation and the detailed regulatory responses required of EPA."[8] For example, there are more than 200,000 existing stationary sources subject to air-emission limitations. Approximately 23,000 of these are major sources, each capable of emitting more than 100 tons of pollutant per year. Though 94 percent of these major sources are in "compliance" this does not necessarily mean that they have done anything. Typically it means that they are continuing to use the required "best engineering practices." In most cases the firms are certified on the basis of their own reports that they are complying with the state plan and all relevant standards. The General Accounting Office has found many errors in reports of compliance. As one would expect, the over 1,400 major sources not even "certified" as being in compliance are the most serious sources of pollution.

These uncertified major sources use the courts to fight the EPA regulations with great vigor. As one authority notes, each source argues that "(1) he is in compliance with the regulations; (2) if not, it is because the regulation is unreasonable as a general rule; (3) if not, then the regulation is unreasonable in this specific case; (4) if not, then it is up to the regulatory agency to tell him how to comply; (5) if forced to take the steps recommended by the agency, he cannot be held responsible for the results; and (6) he needs more time."[9] The EPA, unable to fight every battle, negotiates as best it can, and, for the worst violators, it often welcomes agreements promising future action. If not carried out, these agreements are then subject to renegotiation.

The problem is not just indulgent regulators. Asbell's book on his year with Muskie shows how the process works. In the negotiations over one of the relaxations of the congressionally mandated standards for new automobiles, evidence that the auto companies' technical staffs withheld information at the behest of their policy staffs was clear. But given the system, the policy staffs' concerns were certainly understandable. At one meeting a Chrysler vice-president was surprisingly candid: "They're all − all the companies including us are trying to tell you we're making progress. But we're afraid to say it. We're all worried that if we sound hopeful, what will the damned standards be tomorrow?" Though Muskie was a "get tough" type and had reports from the National Academy of Sciences and other sources at his disposal, it was clear that he did not feel he knew what the auto companies knew. At one meeting he told their representatives, "You fellows in the industry have got to look into your own hearts and ask yourselves what you can really do and how we can devise something that will really give assurance that you'll do it."[10] On most of the thousands of smaller decisions that they must make, the EPA's knowledge disadvantage is far greater than it is on the auto pollution question.

The law requires that the agency pay special attention to new sources of pollution even in areas that meet EPA air-quality standards. Thus, before any new plant or new addition can be built in clean areas, a firm must convince the EPA that it is installing the "best available control technology." It must also demonstrate, using air-quality models, that construction of the plant will not violate any allowable increment, either around the plant or in any other region. If there has been insufficient air-quality monitoring previously to demonstrate that the plant's addition will not violate any standards, the company will have to take the time (it can take up to two years) to establish a baseline. Then there is the required public hearing. The potential for wrangling there and in court about the best available control technology or competing air-quality models is obvious. And if the owners want the plant built in an area where some pollutants meet the EPA ambient standards and some do not, they may find themselves also involved with an entirely different state-run process dealing with the "nonattainment" problem.[11]

This gives only a glimpse of the air pollution control process for individual stationary sources. The agency must also enforce congressionally set emissions standards for new cars. And beyond air pollution there are the programs for pesticides standards, new chemical-testing procedures, water pollution standards, drinking water standards, hazardous waste standards, as well as noise and radiation standards.

A brief look at the 1972 water pollution legislation and its implementation can show that the difficulties with the command and control approach to regulation are not limited to air pollution. This legislation mixed tens of billions of dollars of grants for the construction of municipal waste-treatment plants with the same sort of detailed effluent emission standards for individual sources that we saw in the clean-air program. It was originally hoped that the EPA could avoid setting standards for individual plant processes by setting national standards differentiated by industry. However, the National Commission on Water Quality has noted that there is too much complexity, variation, and change within modern production processes for this to have been possible. The result has been "a staggering array of technical distinction and subcategorization which has still been inadequate to make the guidelines the kind of equitable, unchallengeable regulations the framers of the law anticipated."[12] For example, the promulgated guidelines for the Canned and Preserved Seafood Processing Point Source Category contain thirty-three subcategories for items such as conventional blue crab, mechanized blue crab, and nonremote Alaskan crab meat. There are thirty-five subcategories for iron and steel manufacturing and sixty-six for canned and preserved fruits and vegetables. Despite the elaborate subcategories the EPA has still had to tell its regulators that "these limitations should be adjusted for certain plants in the industry."[13]

Hundreds of major industrial polluters, including many of the most significant ones, are challenging their EPA-issued permits. No enforcement action can be taken until a permit has been adjudicated. Though the EPA's figures, based largely on industry self-reporting, show that 85 percent of all firms are in full compliance with their permits, a GAO review of 165 found 55 percent violating at least one discharge limitation, some in an extreme way.[14]

In negotiations with industry and in court EPA regulators are at a substantial disadvantage because, as with air pollution, they do not have as much relevant information as the firms do. The water law requires the EPA to determine effluent limits based on factors such as the age of existing equipment, process changes, technological opportunities, what is "economically achievable," and "such other factors as the Administrator deems appropriate."[15] Even decisions on the kind of product to be allowed may have to be made. Unbleached paper, for example, pollutes much less than bleached paper, and thus, if it is reasonable to ask consumers to do without some bleached paper, it is reasonable to set lower effluent limits. Firms will deny that there will be a market for unbleached paper and predict disastrous consequences from this or any other proposed EPA decision. Many times they will be lying, but sometimes they will not. Without adequate information on the hundreds of thousands of questions at issue, the EPA and the courts will not be able to distinguish the two situations. And, of course, requirements do not have to bring disaster to be unjustified.

The municipal waste-treatment program has also been plagued with problems. Congressional politics has led to the construction of many unnecessarily large plants all over the countryside. Eighty percent of all grants have gone to towns with populations under 25,000. Moreover, municipalities fail to maintain and operate new plants properly. The GAO has found that more than 60 percent of the plants they checked were not performing up to antipollution requirements more than half of the time.[16]

The results of the effort to control water pollution have been about like those to control air pollution. For most pollutants there has been improvement, but the improvement seems to have been as rapid in the 1960s and early 1970s as it has been since the massive subsidies and cumbersome processes of the 1972 act were introduced.[17]

The economists' alternative

How do economists think they can improve on this administrative quagmire that has produced regulations costing the economy hundreds of billions of dollars with but modest benefits to show for it? They suggest two approaches, either of which would be preferable to the existing system. One is to tax pollution. A tax per pound of sulfur (or other pollutant) emitted could be imposed on power plants and other industrial firms. A tax could also be imposed on automobile emissions based on each car's expected lifetime emissions or based on actual emission levels (as judged by periodic inspections) multiplied by the number of miles driven. Many economists would argue that the tax should be set at a level that approximates the harm a marginal unit of effluent does to the public. But the tax could be set higher, and the efficiency advantages of achieving more pollution reduction for a given cost (or, if one prefers, the same reduction for less cost) would remain.

The alternative method economists recommend is tradable discharge licenses. The regulatory authorities could determine the total amount of emissions to be allowed in an airshed or river basin and then issue permits or licenses for these emissions. The permits would be bought and sold like industrial property. Those planning to build a new plant would negotiate to purchase discharge licenses from existing firms the same way they now negotiate to buy the property for the plant.

Both of these mechanisms have an overwhelming advantage over our existing system in their ability to rechannel self-interest so that it becomes congruent with the public interest. Emissions become costly to a firm. They result either in higher taxes (under the first scheme) or in tying up money in costly emissions permits (under the second). When economic incentives have changed, many firms will find it profitable to clean up rather than to delay cleaning up by fighting the EPA on questions on which the firms are more knowledgeable.

The United States encourages so much litigation about regulatory matters that it would be folly to assume that all the litigation costs in the current administrative snarl would be eliminated with effluent taxes or marketable licenses. But at least things should improve. As it stands now if delay saves a company more than it loses in court costs, the company has an incentive to appeal at every stage even if it thinks it will finally lose. Under the tax scheme it would owe back taxes if it lost. There would also be less to litigate. Since the EPA would not be requiring each firm to meet a certain standard for emission or to install a particular technology by a particular date, the courts would not have to determine whether the EPA's rules for each firm were reasonable. The court need simply find that the tax reflects the agency's or Congress's best judgment about the harm done to society by the firm's pollution, and it is up to the firm to decide whether it wishes to eliminate some or all of the effluent or pay the tax. Or, alternatively, the court would find that the Congress has determined that it wants air or water of a given cleanliness. To get it requires limiting emissions to the level indicated by the emissions licenses. If a firm believes it must go to unreasonable and disproportionately great expense to clean up, the court can point out that the firm has the alternative of buying a marketable license from one of the firms with proportionately lower costs.

The court's hypothetical argument suggests why the incentive schemes lead to a more efficient distribution of the costs of cleaning up. Each firm would be faced with different removal costs depending on the nature of its production processes and economic situation. And, as Kneese and Schultze argue, for any given level of tax or effluent licenses,

firms with low costs of control would remove a larger percentage than would firms with higher costs – precisely the situation needed to achieve a least-cost approach to reducing pollution for the economy as a whole. Firms would tend to choose the least expensive methods of control, whether treatment of wastes, modification in production processes, or substitution of raw materials that had less serious polluting consequences. Further, the kinds of products whose manufacture entailed a lot of pollution would become more expensive and would carry higher prices than those that generated less, so consumers would be induced to buy more of the latter.[18]

Simple, general rules that try to anticipate this kind of efficient distribution of the costs of cleaning up cannot do so. In part, the Congress had such a rule in mind when it required new plants, new additions, and new cars to meet much stricter standards than the old equivalents. It should usually be cheaper to achieve any given level of pollution reduction if it can be planned for ahead of time. But marginalism shows the limits of this insight. Maybe new plants can be made 80 percent cleaner than old plants, and still it would cost these new plants less to go even further and become 81 percent cleaner than it would cost the old plants to clean up just 1 percent. But the new plants will plan to use the cheapest clean-up methods first so their marginal costs per unit of pollutant reduced will continue to rise. At some point it is likely that it will be less costly for the old firms to clean up a little bit than for the new firms to do still more. All depends on the host of factors indicated earlier and others besides. Moreover, in the case of automobiles, focusing on new vehicles at the time of purchase has ignored the problem of the gradual degradation of new vehicles' emissions systems. Perhaps no further improvements will be able to overcome this problem as long as drivers save money by using leaded gasoline or by tampering with their antipollution equipment in an effort to improve their cars' gas mileage or performance. Recent EPA surveys show that 18 percent of vehicles have certainly been tampered with and another 46 percent may well have been tampered with. An effluent fee based on measured emissions or other types of inspections would address this problem.[19]

All effluent standards tell a firm that it is all right, at least for now, to pollute to the legal limit, but under no circumstances may it go beyond. Effluent standards make sense only in a world in which pollution damages are trivial to the limit but devastating beyond. The Congress implicitly assumed that we lived in such a world with respect to health when it determined that primary ambient air standards should be set at a level low enough that the health of even sensitive individuals would not be adversely affected. Scientists have found that there is no such level achievable in an industrial society.[20] In the real world there are rarely sharp points that separate harmless amounts of an activity from harmful amounts. Instead, marginalism prevails. Rigid standards, like rigid goals and priorities, ignore that concept's teaching.

The rigidities in the harmless/harmful-threshold approach were illustrated in the case of Procter and Gamble's Port Ivory plant. In 1980 the company wanted to save nine million gallons of oil a year by replacing its existing boilers with ones that would burn wood waste. Because of difficulties in proving that the area's carbon monoxide level met the national air-quality standards, the EPA did not give final approval for the project until February of 1982. Though the EPA and the state environmental agency thought that the area was "most likely" in compliance, they had no data to prove it. When Procter and Gamble determined that monitoring of actual air quality was impractical (motor vehicles, not other plants, are the only other sources), the company conducted a hypothetical ''worst case'' computer analysis that demonstrated compliance. The EPA at first rejected the analysis because of the absence of ''site-specific'' traffic data but later reversed itself. Once the *area* passed muster, Procter and Gamble's particular *project* had to make its way through an additional process.

Not in dispute was the fact that though the new plant would emit more carbon monoxide it would emit less sulfur oxides and nitrogen oxides. But the either/or EPA thresholds do not give the flexibility to take this into account, nor do they allow for consideration of energy conservation gains or Procter and Gamble's losses from the delay in their cost savings change (over $1 million).[21] The two incentive schemes would give this flexibility without the need for a special EPA determination in this or other particular cases.

In the long run the pollution problem will become overwhelming without improved technology. Even if our living standards should improve at only one-half the rate of the past century, pollution per unit of output must be cut by two-thirds 100 years from now if we are to maintain even current environmental performance.[22] On the crucial issue of encouragement of new technology, the existing standards approach is radically inferior to either of the incentive schemes. This is ironic because the Congress, obsessed with technology, often mandates the best available. But though such laws give an incentive for firms that develop pollution abatement equipment to continue to innovate, such firms typically supply only the end of the pipe equipment that prevents some of the pollution produced by a dirty manufacturing process from reaching the air or water. The polluting plants' owners, however, have no incentive at all to develop a fundamentally cleaner manufacturing process since they would thereby hand regulatory authorities the means to impose higher costs on them. Indeed, because of the disparity between new source and old source standards, plant owners will often delay the implementation of even improved *known* technology as long as possible by fixing up their old plants.

Even if it were possible for the EPA to set standards for every firm at precisely the right level, given today's technology, the incentive methods would be preferable because they would spur needed innovation. Under the current system once a firm is in compliance it has no incentive to do still better. With the incentive schemes the possibility of increasing profits by reducing pollutants remains as long as any taxes are paid or capital is tied up in marketable effluent licenses, that is, as long as any pollutant remains. Moreover, the standards approach also discourages innovations because it provides no incentive to develop something that might bring cost savings and dramatic reductions in two effluents if it also entailed an increase in the amount of a third. The incentive systems are flexible enough to encourage a firm to proceed with these innovations.

There is some disagreement among economists about whether it would be better to tax or to sell permits to polluters. All agree that either would be a large improvement. Most also agree that the tax scheme would be preferable for automobiles and in areas where there are too few firms to form a market. If the tax were set at a level that reflects the effluent's harm to society,[23] the tax approach would yield an optimal level of pollution, taking into account opportunity costs. If air or water quality is not to deteriorate, however, taxes would have to be adjusted with economic growth. Depending on the technology for monitoring, the EPA's administrative burden might also be greater with taxes since the total quantity of emissions would have to be assessed, not just whether emissions exceeded the licensed amount.

Emission permits seem more attractive politically. Congress does not have to decide if the EPA usurps its taxing power if it sets differing effluent fee levels in the various river basins and air sheds. Environmentalists will be happier with a system that assures that emissions will not go above a certain level. A tax scheme cannot do this. If the marketable effluent licenses are auctioned off, government coffers will receive a substantial windfall. If they are instead given to existing firms in accordance with their legal effluent levels, business is likely to be favorably disposed. Indeed, under any of the emission permit systems existing firms would have an incentive to preserve the value of their licenses by reporting other polluters who exceed their allowable emissions.[24]

The incentive schemes would not be simple. Political pressures could lead to an unjustified level of tax or number of licenses. Monitoring of important sources of pollution would have to improve. Some variation in taxes or licensed levels depending on location and time of year would probably be advisable.[25] But parallel political and monitoring problems have also plagued the standards approach. And, if opportunity costs are to count at all, the standards too should more closely reflect location and seasonal differences than they have in the past. It is absurd, for example, for the Clean Water Act to require the EPA to mandate the same technology regardless of the nature of the water that the discharge enters. This provision led the EPA to deny a recommendation from the California Water Resources Control Board for variances for two companies that discharged their wastes far offshore. The denial was required though there was no dispute over the control board's finding that the companies' proposal would have little or no effect on water quality.[26]

The cost savings from switching to an incentive system would be great. For air, most studies show that current control costs could be cut by more than one-half if the burden could be shifted slightly from those finding pollution control expensive to those finding it relatively inexpensive. Some recent studies have found that incentive schemes could achieve equivalent air quality for as little as 10 percent of the costs of existing methods. These studies' findings seem perfectly plausible once one has seen data on the wide variation in abatement costs among different sources of the same pollutant. For example, one study in St. Louis found that particulate emissions could be removed from one boiler in a paper products factory for $4 a ton whereas to remove a ton of emissions from one brewery's boiler would cost $600 per ton. Similarly, one St. Louis power plant could remove emissions for $5 a ton, but for another the cost was $909 per ton.[27]

The savings for water from the use of incentive systems are only slightly less than for air and are largely achievable even with a relatively simple system.[28] Moreover, the savings in all these studies consider only direct expenditures for control. The less easily quantifiable savings from removing the economic growth-inhibiting hurdles now placed in the way of new plants and new technology would also be substantial.

Other industrialized democracies are far ahead of us in the use of incentives to achieve pollution reduction,[29] but economists' carping has had beneficial effects on the EPA in recent years. In the late 1970s, incentive-attuned "offsets," "banking," and "bubbles" were all begun. Under the offset policy new plants may enter nonattainment areas if they secure emission reductions from other polluters in the area in excess of their own emissions. Firms that reduce emissions below their permit level may bank these savings for use in their future expansion or may sell them to expanding firms looking for offsets. And as of 1979, a manufacturer can apply for permission to draw an imaginary bubble around his plant, or even all his plants in the region, and treat it (or them) as a single source, with all the pollution coming from a hole at the top of the bubble. Freed of detailed technology-based standards on particular emission points, the firm can decide for itself the most cost-effective way to meet air-quality standards. At first, restrictions placed on the use of these devices negated much of their good intent, but the rules have recently become somewhat more flexible. In some cities there are currently active markets complete with specialized brokers under the offset program.[30]

The potential savings from the adoption of these administrative reforms are large. The first bubble application approved in late 1980 was that of an electric utility that will substitute high- for low-sulfur coal at one plant while burning natural gas instead of low-sulfur coal at another. Total sulfur dioxide emissions should fall and savings will total $27 million per year.[31] The steel companies will find it less costly and more effective to clean up by spraying acres of coal and iron ore piles to reduce windblown particles than to install in-plant technology.[32] And a detailed study done by two economists for DuPont found that a regional DuPont bubble could achieve an overall 85 percent reduction of pollution for $14.6 million. Reaching the same overall level by requiring *each* DuPont emission source to reduce its output by 85 percent would cost $105.7 million. The regional bubble approach could actually get an overall 99 percent pollution reduction for less ($92.4 million) than this.[33]

There are still many restrictions on the use of the new devices. For example, offsets are not allowed in areas that now meet the ambient air standards. In nonattainment areas new plants must first use prescribed technology, and only then may they use an offset to balance against the pollutants that remain.[34] We are still a long way from the adoption of the economists' marketable license approach, but the progress in recent years is undeniable.

REASONS FOR THE SLOW ADOPTION OF INCENTIVE
APPROACHES

Though final conclusions on such matters are never possible, some reasons for the slow adoption of incentive approaches to pollution reduction are clear. First, the air and water legislation of the early 1970s was passed at a time of great political emotion about environmental matters. Many of those who voted overwhelmingly for these bills are still in Congress, and to accept the economists' critique of their handiwork they would have to admit to having made a significant error. People are slow to make such admissions. Second, the approach adopted in the legislation is one lawyers find congenial. Although there are fewer lawyers in the Congress than there were a decade ago, they remain by far the largest occupational group. Economists have been quick to point out that lawyers learn to affect people's behavior by changing rights and duties. Law schools tend to neglect the economists' alternative and often more efficacious method of affecting behavior: changing the channels of economic self-interest.[35]

Lawyers' emphasis on rights and duties leads them to expect knowledge of precise effects of a law – for example, exactly what level of air quality an area or firm will be required to meet. Until quite recently the tax scheme has been the only well-known economic alternative. Here everything depends on decentralized reactions to new price signals. No exact short- or long-term effect on the firms or air in a congressman's district can be determined. Of course, as argued earlier, the results from the existing-standards approach also are less certain than those passing the law expect. And the more certain one wants to be about results, the less certain one can be about the costs imposed on the economy. Nevertheless, a congressman interested in a reputation for strong leadership would find it easier to say "Do this, do that" than "Let's put this tax on and see what happens. If we don't get enough results, we can always raise the tax a couple of years down the road."

Congress does not operate in a vacuum. Though the internal explanations offered here are significant, they are probably less important than the fact that none of the principal interest groups concerned with environmental matters has consistently supported the economists.

The two principal groups have been business and environmentalists. Businessmen have supported policies that save them money, namely, the bubble and the offset, and have opposed schemes that increase costs to them, for example, emissions taxes.[36] Environmentalists, however, have not been very receptive to either of the incentive approaches. Many were strongly opposed to the EPA bubble and offset innovations, one going so far as to call such ideas "something that's got to be so thoroughly smashed that there's no residue."[37] The flavor of the opposition of most environmental lobbyists to the tax approach is best seen in the way they scornfully say, "I want to get rid of pollution, not license it."[38] Senator Muskie spoke for them on the floor of the Senate in 1971 when he said, "We cannot give anyone the option of polluting for a fee."[39]

Economists, exasperated, explain that there is evidence that pollution taxes will not just be paid and passed on to consumers, while all the firms pollute as before. Such taxes will reduce pollution.[40] Economists wonder how they could help but do so. Businessmen will sell more of their product and make more money if they can keep costs and prices down. If a businessman can avoid $1 million in annual taxes by making a technological change that costs $2 million, he will do so because the investment will very soon have paid for itself. Just as a businessman looks for ways to minimize what he must pay for electricity or raw materials so he will look for ways to minimize his expenses from dealing with the pollution problem. If he blithely pays the tax and passes the expense on to consumers even though it would be cheaper to clean up, he risks losing business to competitors whose prices can be lower because they behave more efficiently.

At this place in the argument, my students often say: "But you have chosen convenient numbers. Suppose the cost of technological changes is $200 million, not $2 million. Then the taxes will not induce the firm to clean up; it will just pass the tax on to consumers." So it will. But the absolutely crucial element the St. Louis firms' cost figures boldly demonstrate is that no two firms are the same. For some firms, my example will be more appropriate; for some my students' will. But taxes will lead some firms to clean up. Those firms will be the ones whose costs to clean up are low. If not enough firms clean up, we can raise the taxes. Under the tax scheme, the high-cost firms will, it is true, just continue to pollute as before. They will have purchased a "license to pollute." But after all, even under the current standards approach, firms have the right to emit pollutants up to the standard; they in effect are already given a license to pollute. Economists ask why environmentalists should object to having businesses pay for the polluting they still do rather than letting them do it for free.

In his interesting book, *What Price Incentives?* Steven Kelman argues that the environmentalists' "license-to-pollute" retort reflects incompletely developed intuitive concerns that the economists' responses cannot so quickly dispose of. Kelman notes that environmentalists are quite concerned with developing an environmental ethic. They want to heighten the public's environmental consciousness. For these reasons they want to stigmatize polluting behavior and avoid doing anything that might lower the value the public places on clean air and water. But a price for pollution may end the stigma by saying in effect, ''It's okay to pollute as long as you pay a fee.'' And the price itself may make it impossible for us to see unspoiled nature as priceless.[41]

Kelman convincingly shows that an extremely strong environmentalist has reasons to have reservations about pollution taxes. Kelman may be wrong, however, to suggest that a pollution tax would remove the stigma from pollution. Although we tax and license many things about which we have positive or neutral feelings (driving, marriage), we do the same for others of which we do not wholly approve (gambling, liquor, cigarettes). It is not likely that people will stop having negative attitudes toward pollution merely because it is taxed. Environmentalists, however, argue that we do not just tax murder or ''rape, pillage and burning,'' and some say that they feel the same way about polluting behavior (''crimes against nature'') as they do about these (''one day a courageous district attorney will prosecute these people for murder'').[42]

Opportunity cost becomes relevant here. If it is impermissible to sanction any polluting activity that places others at some risk, then industrial society must end because even the best technology leads to some deaths among those with serious respiratory problems.[43] And if all pollution is a crime against nature, the crime problem is truly pervasive. All humans inhale air with 21 percent oxygen and exhale it with 17 percent and drink water with about 200 parts per million dissolved solids and release it with perhaps 20,000 parts per million.[44]

If opportunity costs are relevant and some balancing of multiple goals is necessary, one is forced to think again about the nature of the stigma that should be attached to polluting behavior. It is not like murder. If all murderers were suddenly willing to do what we asked them to do, we would ask them to stop killing people immediately. If all industrial polluters were equally malleable, few, with knowledge of the consequences, would ask them to stop all pollution immediately. The quality of our lives would suffer too much. So would their length as the hospital equipment fueled by all those power plants shut down. And if balancing with other goals is necessary, then some reduction in value, to a level below priceless at least, is inevitable whether it occurs with taxes, effluent licenses, or nonzero standards.

Admitting the existence of competing goals may not even reduce the quality of the environment if economic incentives are adopted. As was mentioned earlier, the incentives lead to the faster development of new technologies. Furthermore, conditions are not always as they seem. In their own way incentives expose the real environmental criminals far better than can the most vigilant environmentalist. Businesses that have been hiding effective low-cost pollution-reduction opportunities will suddenly become quick to show them with the incentive schemes.

The environmentalist with his strong law and stiff penalties does not frighten polluters as much as does the seemingly more easy-going economist. The Clean Air Act's criminal penalties of up to $25,000 per day of violation have almost never been imposed. Judges have proved quite reluctant to make criminals out of air polluters.[45] The enormous $10,000 fine per vehicle not meeting congressional standards frightened Detroit not at all. In 1976 the president of General Motors said, "They [the federal government] can close the plants, put someone in jail – maybe me – but we're going to make [1978] cars to 1977 standards."[46] Since auto companies do not make $10,000 per car, the G.M. president would have shut down all operations if the law were implemented. And he knew that Congress was not going to allow a law that would shut down Detroit to go into effect. He was right. Just as the 1978 models were being shipped to their dealers, Congress postponed the deadline. Paradoxically, the weaker penalty is often the strongest. A fine that took 20 percent of the profit per car would be a far more effective spur to reduce pollution.

The business world knows that some environmentalists prefer a pure law to pure air. And they know what to say to them and to their supporters. Thus with big, wide eyes Dan Cannon of the National Association of Manufacturers told a 1976 congressional seminar that "industry needs clear, precise standards that tell us we must maintain a certain quality of environment to maintain health. Surely you wouldn't let a guy violate public health standards by paying a tax?"[47]

Not all environmentalists are deceived. Kelman finds that a substantial minority are impressed with the power of self-interest to achieve a cleaner environment at the same time that they see something a little unethical about using this impure motive. Some of these reluctantly support tax schemes or are willing to see them tried. ("Unfortunately, you can't turn everyone into an environmentalist on principle"; "But I know that's an idealistic approach to things, and I've been around.")[48]

Kelman treats sympathetically the concern for motives behind this ambiguity about a powerful method to achieve environmental goals. He argues that we care about motives, not simply results. Good motives tend to produce better results over a series of cases. Moreover, good motives produce valued feelings in themselves. When a stranger returns a wallet with fifty dollars in it, the owner values the act above and beyond the fifty dollars. Altruism is reinforced through practicing it and through observation of others practicing it. Preserving occasions for it is thus important. Children should not grow up in a society where everything is bought and sold.[49]

In part, Kelman's discussion of motives is a reaction to a remarkable passage in which Schultze praises economic incentives because they "reduce the need for compassion, patriotism, brotherly love, and cultural solidarity as motivating forces behind social improvement." Schultze goes on to say, "Harnessing the 'base' motive of material self-interest to promote the common good is perhaps *the* most important social invention mankind has yet achieved.''[50] He suggests what Kenneth Arrow has argued, namely, that altruism is a scarce resource that society should avoid depleting recklessly.[51]

Although Kelman's support of altruism is persuasively argued, he strains to make motives relevant to pollution-reduction alternatives. As he himself seems to half acknowledge, neither legal standards nor incentive systems encourage polluters to clean up for altruistic reasons. Even if altruism were a strong enough motive to produce clean air and water, how could an altruistic businessman know what he should do? Because the water cleanses itself to some degree and because opportunity costs are relevant, all effluents should not be eliminated. A businessman could not know what his fair share of reduction would be. Though incentive schemes abandon altruism, they actually help signal and achieve fair-share results by, in effect, telling people when they are the ones who can clean up at relatively low expense.

At one point Kelman says that ''the expression 'businesslike' may be fine to describe the relationship among businessmen, but hardly between parents and children or between friends.''[52] Agreed. But pollution is a part of business. It is largely a side effect of ongoing industrial activity. We can all hope that businessmen are altruistic in other areas of their life, and Chapter 10 argues that we may want to think about ways to encourage such motives. But at work a businessman's principal function should be running his business well. We should be pleased if he reacts in a ''businesslike'' way to economic incentives designed with our wishes to reduce pollution in mind.

Given the desirability of a world where there is more compassion, patriotism, and brotherly love, it is not clear why Schultze thinks readers should be delighted with a mechanism requiring less of them. But he is surely on firmer ground when he says that such qualities are in ''too short supply'' to be relied on to achieve a high standard of living. In my small community, designated an ''All-America'' city a few years ago, calls for voluntary water conservation during a serious drought brought no noticeable decrease in consumption. At the national level warnings about the energy crisis and ''don't be fuelish'' slogans accomplished little. But higher prices made a difference. Such results may be a commentary on human nature, and there is no reason for them to make us gleeful. But if China and Cuba can now rely on material self-interest despite strong ideological reasons for resisting, the United States also should be able to do so. From our Lockean origins to the present we have shown what enlightened self-interest can accomplish. Without making self-interest our god, we can respect it and give it some room to help us accomplish important public goals as well as the more traditional private ones.

Kelman is right to notice that much of the opposition to incentive systems is traceable to a distaste for market mechanisms and self-interested motives. But he also shows what abundant evidence from elsewhere reveals – that his

respondents possessed a rather remarkable ignorance about the simple economics of incentives-based methods. This in itself is an important independent
cause of the weak support such methods have garnered. The misunderstandings are of consequence. In a book widely read in environmental circles,
William Ophuls claims that pollution taxes will lead to serious inflation.[53]
This confuses rises in particular prices with a general price rise. Inflationary
pressures will be greater when the real costs of doing business rise faster.
We have seen that rigid standards raise costs more than taxes because they
are a less efficient way of achieving the same environmental result. The added
pollution tax revenues may have an additional deflationary effect if they are
not offset by corresponding additional spending.

Environmentalists have also been concerned that the poorer businesses
would have to clean up with the tax schemes while the richer ones would not
and would just pass the charge through to their customers. However, since
polluting behavior per se gives no satisfaction, rich as well as poor businesses
will reduce pollution as long as it is cheaper to do so than to pay the charge.[54]
As argued earlier, to do otherwise raises costs and prices and leads to fewer
sales and lower profits.

Senator Muskie's principal staff aide on pollution policy claimed that to
be effective a pollution tax would have to be of confiscatory dimensions, and
"if it's not fairly close to being confiscatory, it isn't going to work."[55]
Similarly, on the floor of the Senate, Senator Muskie argued that the fee
would lead to investment only "if the fee were sufficient to cause plant closure
if control were not implemented." He wondered how we could avoid "setting
the fee below the level of cleanup cost."[56] Again, Muskie and his staff aide
seem to think there is a single cost of cleanup. The marginalist insight has
not been grasped. Some firms will find the cost of cleanup less than the tax,
some more; some will clean up nothing, some a little, some a lot, some
entirely. And remember those who clean up nothing do not gain an inequitable
advantage over those who clean up a lot because the former pay a substantial
pollution tax that reflects the costs of their behavior to society.

It is surely noteworthy that when Kelman interviewed sixty-three members
of congressional and Washington interest group staffs concerned with environmental matters, he found not a single economist among his sample. He
found that only 16 percent of those sampled could explain why some think
a pollution tax could obtain any given degree of environmental quality for a
lower cost than standards could. Most of the rest said that they had heard
such an argument made, but when asked if they could explain the basis for
the argument, not a single one could. Moreover, a significant number said
that evidence could make a difference to them on this point. Environmentalists
who had opposed pollution taxes and could not explain the efficiency argument
for them were asked if convincing evidence that taxes could achieve any given
degree of environmental quality for 20 percent lower cost to society would

make pollution taxes acceptable to them. Five of eight said such evidence would make them favor pollution taxes.[57] As discussed earlier, there is reason to think that the efficiency gains would be much greater than 20 percent.

Much of the explanation for the slow adoption of incentive approaches is ignorance of elementary microeconomics, not the broader concerns Kelman articulates so well. Exhibit A in this regard is Kelman's own conclusion. Though the broader concerns are "frequently weighty enough" so that we should avoid using incentive approaches, "in the specific case of environmental policy, the efficiency advantages of the approach may well be great enough to make it, on balance, merited."[58] An environmentalist could not ask for one who values these broader concerns more deeply than Kelman. But Kelman also understands economists' arguments. The tens of billions of dollars at stake is a substantial amount.

OTHER APPLICATIONS

In the case of pollution economists make a convincing argument for controlling the problem by economic incentives, not by engineering-based standards. They are at least as convincing when discussing these two alternative approaches to dealing with worker safety problems. Here it is clear that the solution depends not just on safe equipment in a safe plant, but also on workers' attitudes and behavior. As two economists have noted, "Firms with unusually good safety records, such as DuPont (whose injury rate is only a small fraction of the chemical industry's average), are generally suffused with tremendous safety consciousness at all levels."[59] OSHA's current policies can change equipment, but they cannot change attitudes. An injury tax could, by ensuring that poor safety practices cost a firm money.[60]

The fruits of thinking about "the public use of private interest" are by no means limited to applications involving profit-seeking firms. Both theory and evidence have convinced economists that if the price of something valued goes up, some people will consume less of it, and if the price goes down, some will consume more. Economists thus spend considerable time thinking about the public-sector applications of simple supply and demand curves. Because air travelers, tennis players, and electricity users respond to price signals, higher prices at periods of peak use can spread out demand and thus avoid expensive capital investment. Prices can also help when the problem is not temporary peaks in demand but, as with water, temporary valleys in supply. Because many uses of water do not have high value to consumers, an increase in price at such times could make a large difference in demand. Yet one study of the water-use forecasts prepared for nine large American cities found that none of them considered the possible effects of changes in water price on expected demand.[61]

Failing to consider fully the effects of changes in law on private incentives has led to many disappointing policy results. The National Highway and Traffic Safety Administration is quite proud of the steady reduction of the fatality rate per 100 million miles driven since its creation in 1966. It never mentions that the rate fell in a similar fashion from 1946 to 1961. The temporary reversal of this trend in the early 1960s may be largely explained by the increase in young, inexperienced drivers as children of the postwar "baby boom" came of age.

Because of drivers' reactions to changed incentives, the dramatic gains predicted to follow the auto safety improvements have not appeared. By reducing the severity or likelihood of accidents, safety equipment (seat belts, dual brake systems, energy-absorbing steering columns, stronger windshields, padded instrument panels, air bags, and such) makes the worst results of hurrying less likely and thus leads to somewhat more dangerous driving. Though even the most elementary economic texts mention this effect, non-economists are usually skeptical. There is, however, evidence that the effect is present to some degree. Since 1969 new cars subject to stricter safety regulations have accounted for a larger share of all accidents than the same age class of automobiles did before stricter safety regulations.[62] The National Safety Council finds that women drive less carefully when their children are not in the car and the costs of potential accidents are lower.[63] A Swedish study finds that drivers of cars equipped with studded snow tires drive faster and follow more closely than drivers with regular tires when road conditions are icy but not when they are dry. In other words, in Sweden drivers who are safety conscious and voluntarily purchase safer tires offset some of the safety gain by increasing their driving intensity.[64] With mandated safety equipment the offsetting behavior will be at least as great.[65]

Neglect of incentives has produced other disappointing results. Because flood-protection projects and disaster-relief programs reduce the costs of building on flood plains, the more than $7 billion spent on flood-protection projects since 1936 has not produced the expected level of reduction in total flood damages. And because doctors can still bill insurance companies and because they want to provide the best care for their patients, federal and state regulations limiting the number of expensive computer-assisted X-ray machines in hospitals within any community, have led to an increase in the number purchased by unregulated physicians in private practice.[66] Chapter 6 will discuss cases where private interests reacting to changed incentives have hindered the achievement of legislatively determined fair distributions of benefits and burdens.

To avoid these failures policy makers must consider economic incentives, but before they rechannel them, careful analysis is essential. Consider crime control, for example. As with highway safety, the costs at issue here are not primarily dollars, but the incentive concept is useful nonetheless. Does mandatory capital punishment for murder increase the costs of murder and thus reduce its rate? Perhaps. But perhaps not if some people on juries think execution too harsh a penalty and thus refuse to vote for convictions. Does a ban on handguns actually protect burglarized homeowners as some have argued?[67] Perhaps, if burglars with illegal guns feel less threatened by victims without guns and thus have a reduced incentive to fire quickly when surprised. But perhaps not, if the lower rate of deaths per burglary is more than compensated for by an increase in the number of burglaries. Members of an antigun group in New England decided to show their colors by putting signs in their windows saying "There are no guns in this house." The signs came down when the burglary rate at those houses went way up.

One should not just think about the first incentive to come to mind. To do so means to risk the fate of the poor little town of Abruzzi, Italy. The city was plagued by vipers, and the city fathers determined to solve the problem by offering a reward for any viper killed. Alas, the supply of vipers increased. Townspeople had started breeding them in their basements.[68]

Before laughing at such rustic ignorance, note the way in which the urbane Senator Abraham Ribicoff and the grandiloquent James J. Kilpatrick reacted to proposals for taxes on oil products coupled with a general tax rebate to maintain purchasing power. Such a scheme would conserve oil by raising its relative price and inducing (some) consumers and businesses to spend less on oil products and more on other goods or factors of production. This is not just elementary economics but pretty close to Chapter One elementary economics. Yet Kilpatrick and Ribicoff ridiculed the notion that you could conserve anything by raising taxes on oil and then giving the money back to the same people. Kilpatrick took presidential candidate John Anderson to task for such a silly idea.[69] And Ribicoff, when it was first presented, complained that some economist must have "dreamed this up." Alice Rivlin reports that many other congressmen were also mystified by the proposal.[70]

Part II

GOVERNMENT AND MARKETS,
EFFICIENCY AND EQUITY

5

GOVERNMENT AND THE ECONOMY

Contemporary public finance texts usually begin by discussing three separate functions of government in the economy: allocation, distribution, and stabilization. Allocation questions ask whether particular government tax, expenditure, or regulatory programs improve the mix of goods and services produced by the economy. Distribution questions ask who benefits and who is harmed by such policies. Stabilization questions ask what effect all taxes and expenditures, together with monetary policy, have on aggregate employment, output, and prices.

Policies centrally concerned with one of the three functions will affect the other two. For example, U.S. environmental policy seeks to shift resources from making products to making cleaner air. But this allocation effect is accompanied by a distribution one as some firms' owners and employees gain and others lose. Similarly, a decision to build a highway will change the allocation of resources but will also provide more income for manual workers, and it may reduce unemployment or increase inflation.

Though the three separate functions of government are never isolated from one another, economists argue that one should not let particular allocation decisions be unduly influenced by any spillover effects on the other two functions. If, for example, a highway is a better use of resources than alternative public or private opportunities, then the highway should be built even if inflation is a serious problem. To cope with inflation one can tighten monetary policy, cut other expenditures, or raise taxes. On the other hand, if the highway is not a justifiable project, it should not be built anyway, regardless of its favorable effects on unemployment. Expanding more needed government programs or cutting taxes can help meet employment goals without wasting resources on a low-priority highway.

Stabilization policy is at the heart of macroeconomics and will not be further discussed here. Chapter 6 will cover distribution. This chapter, together with Chapters 7 and 8, will be centrally concerned with the heart of microeconomics, allocation, as well as with the allocative standard economists most frequently use – economic efficiency.

CONSUMER SOVEREIGNTY, WELFARE ECONOMICS, AND UTILITARIANISM

Most economists look to welfare economics for principles to guide government when it concerns itself with questions of resource allocation. The word "welfare" here signals no special concern with public-welfare programs aimed at the poor but rather welfare more generally, societal welfare. Welfare economics is an outgrowth of old-fashioned utilitarianism. Like Bentham's utilitarianism, it has no essential connection with democracy. Its concern is with the consequences of policies, not the policy process or political institutions.

Welfare economics rests on two fundamental normative assumptions, both of which Bentham would find congenial: that societal welfare depends only on individuals' subjective senses of satisfaction and that satisfaction is best achieved by letting individuals' preferences determine the use of societal resources. Welfare economics has no room for any policy standards that limit or guide human wants. The basic starting point is individuals with their bewildering variety of idiosyncratic preferences. Welfare consists of having what one prefers. The modern economist is as concerned about "bluenoses" imposing their standards on others as Bentham was about those who insist that poetry is better than pushpin.[1] Galbraith is thus correct when he says that the standard model in economics instructs the economist as follows: "The consumer wants more. Theirs not to reason why, theirs but to satisfy."[2]

What is most distinctive about modern evaluative microeconomics is this radical individualism, not simply a concern with narrowly economic ends or the materialistic side of mankind. Adam Smith explored *The Nature and Causes of the Wealth of Nations*, and modern macroeconomists continue to do so. But as the name suggests, the welfare economist's concern is welfare, not just wealth. His concern is not so much with quantities of goods and services as with the subjective sense of satisfaction they and other things bring. Economists, of course, notice that many people seem to have a strong preference for more wealth. Chapter 9 will argue that in practice many economists do overemphasize money as a human motive and source of human happiness. But, in principle, a welfare economist is concerned with anything that any individual values enough to be willing to give up something for. Fulfilling people's environmental, aesthetic, educational, or charitable desires is an economic benefit just as much as is a new car.

Bentham, too, was concerned with more than the pleasures of wealth, but he thought that all people were moved by some sort of pleasure, and he wanted societal policy to aim at maximizing the summation of all individual pleasures. It is here that modern welfare economics differs. It does not know or care whether the desire for pleasure determines our preferences. And it makes no claim to be able to make interpersonal comparisons of intensity of satisfaction or of levels of welfare. Thus it abandons any attempt to develop a hedonistic calculus that could yield an unambiguous societal optimum. In welfare economics, individuals' preferences are all that counts, but, as argued in the following chapter, welfare-economic principles cannot tell economists whose preferences should count the most.

ECONOMIC EFFICIENCY

If a society accepts subjective sense of satisfaction and consumer sovereignty as its standards, economists can show that it should be interested in achieving economic efficiency. The word "efficiency" brings to mind manufacturing, engineers, getting the same output with less input, keeping costs low. Like the word "economic" it sounds narrower than it is and is thus a source of much confusion.[3] In fact, like "economic," it in principle includes everything that anyone cares about. When nutritionist Jean Mayer suggests that it would be more efficient to produce calories through cereal grains than through meat, the economist objects because the subjective standard of economic efficiency is ignored: Most consumers value a calorie of meat more highly than a calorie of grain.[4]

An understanding of economic efficiency begins with Pareto optimality. A Pareto optimal allocation is one in which we cannot reallocate resources to improve one person's welfare without impairing at least one other person's welfare. Pareto improvements are those where a change in resource allocation is preferred by one or more members of society and opposed by no one. Such a change avoids the problems that Bentham encountered with interpersonal comparisons. But obviously such changes are very hard to find. If a single person objects to changing the status quo, then the Pareto improvement criterion gives no unambiguous public-policy guidance. The existing situation may be Pareto optimal. But there are a nearly infinite number of other non-comparable Pareto optimums, and the concept is of little policy use.

Economically efficient allocations are always Pareto optimal allocations. But if the initial allocation is inefficient, the achievement of economic efficiency does not require that no one be made worse off before a change can be recommended. Economic efficiency requires only that recommended changes use resources in such a way that it would be theoretically possible – assuming costless transfers of income among gainers and losers – to make some better off and no one worse off. Suppose that most people would gain from some change, but some would lose. If the gainers gain enough so that they *could* fully compensate the losers with money or goods and still have an improved situation themselves, the change meets what some economists call the "potential Pareto" criterion and would improve economic efficiency. The change is economically efficient even if the transfer to the losers does not actually take place.[5]

Thus, as we will see in Chapter 6, changes that improve economic efficiency may fail an equity standard. But the concept is not useless. Politicians understand that changes never benefit everyone. Some of them may find it helpful to know when the gainers from a change gain enough that they could fully compensate losers and still be better off. If politicians can find a way to make the potential compensation actual, they can create a better situation from the points of view of all parties concerned.

FREE MARKETS AND FLEXIBLE PRICES

Economists believe that in most situations free markets come closer to achieving economically efficient outcomes than do alternative institutional arrangements. As Arrow and Hahn note, to one unschooled in economics an economy motivated by individual greed and controlled by a very large number of different agents brings to mind chaos.[6] But in fact, free markets with flexible prices coordinate the activities of millions of people in different countries in a remarkable way. Consider a simple wooden pencil. To produce it people must cut down trees, and this alone requires saws and trucks and rope, which in turn require "the mining of ore, the making of steel and its refinement into saws, axes, motors; the growing of hemp and bringing it through all the stages to heavy and strong rope; the logging camps with their beds and mess halls," not to mention the thousands who have a hand in every cup of coffee the loggers drink.[7] And still to come is the millwork to convert the logs to slats, the graphite from Sri Lanka that much later becomes pencil lead, the brass made from zinc and copper that holds the rubberlike eraser, which is made by reacting Indonesian rapeseed oil with sulfur chloride.

A single person acting alone could not have the time and knowledge to make a pencil of today's quality in a year, perhaps not in a lifetime. Yet one can buy a pencil for a few cents. Economists explain why. Markets permit a productive division of labor by efficiently transmitting information. When consumers decide that they want more pencils, no central authority has to tell everyone involved what to do. Retailers order more from wholesalers, and wholesalers in turn order from manufacturers. The manufacturer orders more wood, brass, and graphite. As Milton and Rose Friedman say, "A major problem in transmitting information efficiently is to make sure that everyone who can use the information gets it without clogging the 'in' baskets of those who have no use for it. The price system [free markets] automatically solves this problem."[8] The pencil manufacturer, for example, does not have to worry about whether he should hire more loggers or instead use more powerful, expensive saws to fell and process the additional trees needed. Similarly, the producer of wood does not have to decide whether, in light of the temporary shortage of rapeseed oil, eraser size should stay the same while price goes up or price should stay the same while eraser size goes down. Indeed, the producer of wood may not know or care that the increased demand for his wood has anything at all to do with pencils.

Free markets with their flexible prices provide more than the right information. They also give people an incentive to act on it. Economists find that the desire for wealth is a sufficiently common goal to ensure that resources will shift when financial incentives do. When consumers start to demand more pencils, the price of pencils goes up to ration the limited supply. The higher price induces the least eager (or the poorer) buyers to drop out of the market. The higher price also makes retailers quick to want to increase their supply of pencils so they can take advantage of the new demand and high price. They put pressure on their wholesalers, the wholesalers on their manufacturers, their manufacturers on the producers of wood. Each offers to pay more if necessary – they can do so and still increase profits given the higher price for pencils. The wood companies may in turn pay overtime to their employees to get an increase in production or cut back sales to other manufacturers whose consumers are less eager to buy and who thus cannot afford to pay as much. When consumers are especially eager and drive up the price further and faster, businesses are more eager to meet their demand and they respond more quickly.

Firms that thrive do not often respond clumsily to consumers' demands. Those that waste scarce resources when making their product have difficulty matching the price and quality of firms that do not. Firms with an inefficient scale of operation come under pressure from those of more optimal size. And firms that guess wrong about whether consumers would prefer a higher pencil price or a smaller eraser lose business to competitors.

Consumers bid in all markets for various goods and services, and businesses bid on their behalf for the resources needed to provide the goods and services. Given scarcity, all consumers cannot get all they want at a low price. But in the market, resources flow toward those goods and services where the consumer dollar votes are greatest. If consumers prefer more pencils and fewer toothpicks, they can get what they want by bidding up the price of pencils. This enables pencil manufacturers to make a normal profit or, temporarily, even better than normal while still paying a higher price for wood if necessary. Pencil manufacturers expand, and the added supply then eradicates most, if not all, of the price increase. The toothpick manufacturers contract since they can no longer make the profit needed to maintain past production while paying the new and higher opportunity cost of using the scarcer wood. The costs of providing a commodity thus reflect the competing offers of other producers for the services of the factors to produce it. Consumers through their demand determine what those competing producers will offer, and thus, given the distribution of income, the market satisfies consumers' desires as well as scarcity will allow.

MARKET FAILURE

If you like consumer sovereignty, you should be interested in achieving economic efficiency. If you care about economic efficiency, you should like free markets. Almost all economists would find these propositions fundamentally persuasive. But they would also believe the second one should be qualified. In addition to its stabilization and distribution functions, government will be needed to correct for market imperfections that prevent the allocation of resources in accord with consumer valuations. These imperfections may include concentrations of market power (monopolies and powerful labor unions), externalities, and public goods.

The case for government intervention is strongest for public goods. A public good is not everything that government now provides or even everything that government should provide, and the term is thus somewhat misleading. "Collective consumption good" more accurately captures the phenomena that economists wish to distinguish.

Public or collective consumption goods are goods where consumption is nonrival (i.e., a number of people may simultaneously consume the same good) and where it is either prohibitively expensive or impossible to confine the benefits of the good to selected individuals. Only the person who consumes a steak enjoys it; his neighbors do not benefit from it. But an individual spraying for mosquitoes by plane or building a levee to protect against floods benefits no more than do his neighbors. Any individual may thus wait for one of the neighbors to spray or build or pretend to lack of interest in the projects if the neighbors decide to take up a collection to perform the tasks. (Economists call such individuals "free riders.") Almost everyone might benefit from the projects by more than the proportionate cost he incurs, but each may benefit still more if others pay all the cost. As a result, the projects may not be undertaken unless government steps in and ensures that all pay their fair share through compulsory taxes. The chances for voluntary agreement without government involvement become close to zero for national defense and pollution abatement where the benefits flow far beyond a single neighborhood.[9] In other cases, as with intracity streets, it is technically possible to exclude free riders (nonpayers) from the benefits; but the costs of controlling access and collecting tolls would be so large compared to the costs of building and maintaining the streets that it makes sense to have government provide the service and have all pay for it through taxes.

If economic efficiency is to be obtained, public goods should be provided only if consumers are collectively willing to pay more than the opportunity cost of provision (i.e., the consumers' gains from forgone alternatives else-where). Economists' efforts to determine willingness to pay for public goods is at the heart of benefit-cost analysis and will be discussed in Chapter 8.

Externalities or spillovers are more common examples of market failure that may justify government intervention. Externalities are effects on third parties that are not transmitted through the price system and that arise as an incidental by-product of another person's or firm's activity. They may be positive effects on others, such as education, or negative, such as pollution. Sending a child to school benefits the child and his parents, but others also benefit somewhat if the child becomes a more informed voter and a more reliable taxpayer. The private market can capture only the dollars the parent or child is willing to pay for the child's education. The numerous external beneficiaries cannot be charged. As a result, without government subsidies the market is likely to provide less education than the community as a whole wants and is willing to pay for. Negative externalities represent the cost side of others' actions. Pollution, for example, hurts the community at large, but if the costs do not appear on the firm's profit and loss statement, they are usually ignored. The community then gets more pollution-causing production than it desires. As argued earlier, a tax on effluents can internalize the external cost and help us produce a lower, more satisfactory level of pollution.

Externalities are everywhere. Polio shots, newly painted houses, and newly planted flowers benefit many people besides those directly involved. Crabgrass, loud radios, and Cadillacs bought by those with emulating, or merely envious, neighbors all impose incidental costs on others. And honking horns, flashy ties, and miniskirts produce external benefits for some and costs for others. The externality concept is both terribly useful and terribly troublesome and will be explored at length in Chapters 7 and 10. What should be noted here is that it could be used to justify an extremely pervasive government role in the economy. Most economists do not think externalities should justify such a role. The concept of government failure helps to indicate why.

GOVERNMENT FAILURE

Twenty years ago economists wrote about market failure but rarely about government failure. Today they consider both. Imagine a perfectly democratic New England town meeting in which all citizens participate. Economists show that whatever its other virtues, such a meeting possesses no inherent tendency to allocate resources efficiently. When the citizens vote two to one against an addition to the local public school, that does not necessarily mean that the losers from the addition would lose more (in taxes) than the gainers would gain (in net benefits) or that there is not collectively enough willingness to pay to cover the costs of the addition. The question put at the town meeting was, "Should all taxes be raised 5 percent to pay for the addition?" But perhaps the minority would have been willing to pay 15 percent more. Or, more realistically, some of them might have paid 30 percent more, some 10 and even some of the nay sayers 2, to obtain the addition. In either case there may be enough people willing to forsake other goods to pay for the addition. Yet the local newspaper says the people have spoken and have decisively rejected the project.

The problem here is that voting is not a very finely tuned device for gauging public preferences. In particular it ignores the intensity of preferences. This can lead to too much, as well as too little, spending. The vote might have been two to one for a project that enjoys mild support among the majority but is considered useless, perhaps even perverse (for instance, a teenage social center), by the minority.

The town meeting is likely to encounter a second problem as well: the tendency of voters to be "rationally" ignorant of the consequences of their choices. Many economists believe that voters have good reason to be less informed about political decisions than about comparable market decisions. Because it takes time to acquire information, few consumers take the trouble to obtain all possible information on even their major private purchases. But if one is deciding whether to buy a new car or repair the old one, there is a strong incentive to learn a good bit about the alternatives because the potential gains or losses of the decision for the individual are great. They are less great if the decision is the public one of whether to replace all the old school buses. Here costs of a bad decision and gains from a good one are spread among all citizens. Since the personal stakes are less, citizens who do not find politics intrinsically interesting, and are not unusually public spirited, will not be as well informed. This tendency will be magnified because the individual gains from the correct decision on the buses are not assured once one takes the time to get good information. Once an individual decides that he should buy a new car, he can do so. But taking time to decide if the town should buy new buses does not ensure that buses will be purchased or not purchased. A majority may disagree.

Whatever the economic efficiency problems in a town-meeting setting, those flowing from decisions made by representative political institutions and by governmental bureaucracies are potentially much greater. A school of economics called "public choice" explores them. Assuming that people in political organizations are moved by narrowly selfish motives just as they are in markets, public-choice scholars predict that the government bureaucracy will have little interest in efficiency or in satisfying citizen preferences. A federal administrator who spends more money on his program will find this has almost no effect on his tax bill. But it may help him in other ways. His salary, his power, his patronage, his public reputation, and his perquisites of office (free parking, cheap lunches, etc.) are all likely to be greater if his budget is large and he has a lot of people working for him. What incentive is there then to run a lean and efficient bureau?

If one responds that we elect representatives to make certain that bureaucrats do not behave in this way, the public-choice economist points out that many government bureaus have a monopoly on performing their function, and thus the representatives will have little real knowledge about whether the bureaus for which they appropriate money could do things more cheaply. More important, they will have little incentive to get good information. Politicians know that they get votes by talking about efficiency in government, but they also know that few voters will know if they do anything besides talk. More votes, campaign contributions, and speakers' fees can be obtained by keeping in touch with groups in the district than by spending time in Washington carefully studying agency budgets. Politicians will tend to vote for programs with visible, immediate, and concentrated benefits and hidden costs. They will shy away from programs with long-term, diffuse benefits and concentrated, visible costs.

Politicians can find economically inefficient programs the best path to reelection because of a "rational voter ignorance" problem many times greater than that explored in the town-meeting setting. A typical voter will have little interest in deeply studying how he would be affected by a policy proposal. More information on that issue will probably not lead him to change his mind about whom to vote for in an election in which the candidates differ on many other issues as well. Moreover, his vote and campaigning almost certainly will not decide the election; nor will his representative's vote often be decisive in the legislature.[10]

Public choice is just one school of economics, and it has by no means swept the discipline. As argued in Chapters 9 and 11, its narrowly self-interested motivational assumptions are too simplistic to explain much government behavior. By themselves they have a hard time explaining why people vote at all or why some programs at some times grow much more rapidly than others. But the work of public-choice economists has produced some useful insights, and it has had some influence on the profession as a whole.[11] Moreover, a belief central to public choice – that governmental processes do not have mechanisms for promoting efficiency that are as powerful as the market's – is widely shared by most mainstream economists. This belief has been strengthened by empirical findings from a number of studies.

Among the most interesting of these studies are those that compare the relative efficiency of government agencies and their private-sector counterparts. Public-choice theory would predict greater private-sector efficiency because of competitive pressures and the greater ability of private firms' managers to reap the rewards of efficient behavior. One of the most systematic of the comparative studies looked at residential refuse collection. The study found that on average U.S. cities with over 50,000 residents get roughly 30 percent cheaper service when they hire firms to pick up refuse than when a city agency performs the work. This was so even though the private firms also paid taxes of various kinds and thus produced fifteen dollars of revenues for the general public for every hundred dollars they received for collecting trash. Reasons suggested for the differences included higher municipal employee absentee rates (12 percent vs. 6.5 percent); larger municipal crews (3.26 workers vs. 2.15); and the longer time it took the municipal crews to service each household (4.35 work hours per year vs. 2.37).[12]

A study contrasting federal agency efficiency with private firms was done by the General Accounting Office in 1975. It found that it costs the government nearly twice as much as it costs private insurance carriers to process each medical claim. The government was also found to be slower in paying claims. The cost results were explained by higher government salaries and lower government productivity. For example, federal accountants and auditors averaged $21,600 in wages and fringe benefits compared to $18,000 for Blue Cross of Chicago, $17,300 for Blue Cross of Maryland, $13,800 for Travelers, and $13,700 for Mutual of Omaha. Similar salary differences existed for claims examiners and nurses. Despite higher wages, federal employees processed an average of just 2,500 claims a year compared to 3,900 for Travelers, 4,200 for Mutual, 5,700 for Blue Cross of Maryland, and 6,600 for Blue Cross of Chicago.[13]

Other federal government surveys have shown an average savings of 30 percent when various services (for restaurant workers, mechanics, security guards, etc.) are contracted out to private firms.[14] At the local level, in addition to trash collection, cost savings have been found by contracting out for other services such as fire fighting, utility billing, tax assessment, and municipal transit.[15]

There is other, less systematic, evidence about the efficiency of governmental allocation of resources. In communist countries and others like Argentina with vast state industrial sectors and centrally fixed prices, many problems result. The discussion in Chapter 3 of priority setting without good information on marginal values is relevant here. The literature on Maoist China is replete with self-confessions about failures to balance properly capital construction projects with building supply materials or coal and iron goods with transportation requirements. Mao himself said at one point, "Coal and iron will not walk by themselves...I did not anticipate this point."[16] The example of the pencil suggests the kind of information that would be needed to coordinate resources for a whole economy, all the while keeping opportunity costs in all sectors in mind. Most of the major communist regimes are now talking of incorporating more market forces in their systems though the accompanying ideological and political risks to them are so great that it is unclear if much will come of this.[17]

Still, this whole movement by ideological opponents of capitalism provides striking evidence on the question of government allocative efficiency. China has given its official blessing to profit-seeking businessmen who operate virtually free of government control and who may hire up to seven employees.[18] Cuban advisers to Nicaragua are said to be warning against "creation of a stifling omnipresence of the state in daily life." They believe the planning sector should be kept much smaller than theirs, and reliance should be placed on a market system rather than a "more costly and less efficient" state distribution system.[19]

Closer to home, there is much unsystematic evidence of the inefficiency of government bureaucracies. Business owners and managers have a strong personal incentive to make certain that money owed their companies is paid on time. No one has a similar incentive for money owed the government. In 1980 the federal government was owed at least $139 billion in unpaid bills, a figure that Representative Jim Jones (D-Okla.) says materially understates the problem because many agencies keep inadequate records of accounts receivable.[20] Many of us who have been in the armed services know how wastefully the government can spend money near the end of a fiscal year. In 1975 the Maritime Administration awarded 42 percent of its research and development contracts in the last two days of the fiscal year. At the end of fiscal 1978, the Department of Housing and Urban Development ordered $65,000 worth of furniture and then spent $800 per month to store it because it was surplus.[21] A year later the *Washington Post* had a story about surplus furniture dealers who obtain many of their wares by sifting through items federal agencies throw away at the local landfill.[22] There are no easy solutions to these problems.

Aside from inefficiency in the bureaucracy, government's allocative effect on the economy is often harmful. Tariffs, many water resource projects, rent control laws, and the principal regulatory activities of organizations such as the Civil Aeronautics Board and the Interstate Commerce Commission are all strongly condemned by most economists.[23]

Two decades ago many economists optimistically imagined a federal government that would selectively intervene in the economy to correct for market imperfections once the principles of public finance were better developed and disseminated.[24] Few today have such a vision. A recent survey of top economists with past high-level government experience found that most national policy proposals were developed to deal with political necessities and under tremendous time pressures. Careful analysis of the proposals was rare.[25]

Thus, even when economists believe that a good case can be made for government intervention, they have come to realize that the intervention will not necessarily be the kind they envision or could defend. Some economists, for example, think that the government should announce a price somewhat above the world price of oil at which it will purchase synthetic fuel in the future. This might help make the United States less dependent on foreign oil. It could do so by assuring companies that they could develop technologies free of the fear that OPEC could rob them of their fruits at any time by reducing its price to a level still well above the OPEC cost of production but below the cost of synfuels production. But in fact the current synfuels program does not rely on a price guarantee. Instead, it provides inefficient subsidies for doing what companies would do anyway, if it were worth doing, and loan guarantees that would bail out companies in cases of bad management as well as OPEC price cutting.[26] Once in place such subsidies are very hard to end. Even in a period of declining oil prices and extreme fiscal pressures Congress would not abandon a $4.5 billion synfuels plant in Kentucky.[27] A different problem arose when government tried to reduce the time it would take markets to adjust to shortages of skilled personnel. The subsidies for teaching, medicine, and dentistry continued past the point where predicted future "shortages" had become "surpluses."[28]

Economists' critiques of government-directed reindustrialization proposals further reveal their skepticism about government's ability to improve on the market on most allocation questions. New "industrial policies" were a part of the domestic programs of several of the leading candidates for the 1984 Democratic presidential nomination. But the industrial policy idea began before the most recent campaign. Near the end of his term President Carter set up several tripartite business, labor, and government committees as a "permanent partnership" for restoring the fortunes of slumping industries such as steel and automobiles. And as early as 1981, then California governor Jerry Brown, the AFL-CIO, and the congressional Black Caucus were all supporting proposals for an active government role in directing long-term investment decisions. Speaking for the Black Caucus, the Reverend Walter Fauntroy said that the answer to our economic problems was to "undertake a comprehensive restructuring of the economy, to rethink the whole idea of who will make what."[29]

Like its predecessor "supply-side economics," industrial policy is not a well-defined idea. Many economists would support some elements of proposed industrial policies such as shifting current income taxation to consumption taxation (discussed further in chapter 6). Few of the proposed industrial policies call for the ambitious "comprehensive restructuring" that Fauntroy supports. Still, the most talked about proposals do involve substantial new government involvement in directing capital investment toward some firms or industries and away from others.[30]

Most economists oppose such proposals. They argue that the European experience has been "terrible,"[31] "conspicuously unsuccessful."[32] Targeted industries such as aircraft in Great Britain, computers in France, and the nuclear industry in Germany have done poorly. In any case, these countries' performance provides no model for the United States. Over the last decade all of them have had higher increases in unemployment and lower increases in GNP growth than we have had.[33] Japan's growth rate has clearly been superior to ours. But studies find that government investment there goes mainly to urban and regional development, environmental protection, and the economy's infrastructure. Brookings Institution analyst Philip Trezise concludes that "the amounts directed to specific industrial sectors...are quite small, almost trivial."[34] Lifelong Democrat and Carter economic adviser Alfred Kahn similarly notes that "the most successful Japanese industries, such as consumer electronics and automobiles, have had only very limited government support."[35] The Japanese government's tax policies (discussed further in chap. 6) provide far greater incentives for savings and investment than ours do. Some economists think that *that* "industrial policy" helps explain Japan's high growth rate.[36] Others emphasize "the quality of Japanese firms – their managers and workers."[37]

Yale economist Richard Nelson notes that private technological innovation is largely unpredictable. Many seemingly promising developments do not pan out. Other important breakthroughs were unexpected and not supported by most experts in the field.[38] Nelson finds that "in most of the technically progressive industries, like chemicals and electronics, most of the bad bets were rather quickly abandoned, particularly if someone else was coming up with a better solution, and good new ideas generally had a variety of paths to get their case heard." On the other hand,

military R&D programs since the mid-50's, the civil reactor programs, and the supersonic transport experience are in sad contrast. In all of these areas the early batting average has been dismal. However, there has been a tendency to stick with the game plan despite mounting evidence that it is not a good one.

Nelson suspects that a central plan for technological advance would make things worse because such advance is not

a clearly plannable activity. In fact, it is an activity characterized as much by false starts, missed opportunities, and lucky breaks as by brilliant insights and clever strategic decisions. Only in hindsight does the right approach seem obvious; before the fact, it is far from clear which of a bewildering array of options will prove most fruitful or even feasible.

Nelson favors an active government role in support of basic research and applied knowledge of widespread interest (where nonappropriable public-good benefits may be present). But he opposes support for development of particular products that government believes will be commercial winners. Nelson finds that the historical record for such government ventures is "unequivocal. Unequivocally negative."[39]

Economist Robert Samuelson argues that precisely because technological change is so unpredictable, the market may be best equipped to promote it:

The much maligned "market" is simply a shorthand way of describing a system that allows diversity; that allows firms and people to guess what will work best....It is the threat of failure and prospect of reward, the uncertainty, that drives the constant search for improved products.[40]

Samuelson and others argue that it is not possible, intellectually, for government to pick industrial winners. They also argue that even if it were possible intellectually, it would not be possible politically. The Model Cities Program and the Economic Development Administration were both meant to provide selective assistance to targeted areas. But the 6 test sites for model cities soon became 150, and the Economic Development Administration's aid to economically depressed counties soon went to 87.5 percent of *all* U.S. counties. When our political process has discriminated among winning and losing industries, it has usually favored losers because they are established industries upon which more voters depend. Nearly half the members of Congress are members of the Steel Caucus. Only a handful identify with bioengineering or the microchip industry. Thus, as Alfred Kahn has said, there is a "grave danger" that Carter-like industrial revitalization policies

will provide a vehicle for business and labour to exert their concerted influence to enlist the government as a great protector, subsidizer and carteliser; to suppress competition domestically; to limit imports; to obtain government loan guarantees and other bailouts; to ward off the competitive retributions – unemployment and bankruptcies – that used to follow excessive wage and price increases and managerial ineptitude.

Kahn believes that we should strongly resist "this kind of bureaucratisation of the entire economy and ensconcement of exploitation and mediocrity" that occurred in this country under Roosevelt's National Recovery Administration.[41]

Most of the prominent theoreticians of industrial policies are not economists. Of those who are economists only Lester Thurow might be called a mainstream economist. His views on industrial policy are clearly in the minority even among prominent Democratic, liberal economists. Kahn and Nelson fit that description. So also do Walter Heller, William Nordhaus, and Charles Schultze. Heller is concerned about Democratic presidential candidates' searching for "novelty rather than soundness." Nordhaus, mentioned as an academic resource by both Gary Hart's and Walter Mondale's aides, believes that "the clearest difference between the Democratic candidates and Reagan" concerns government intervention through industrial policy. "On this [issue]," Nordhaus is "on the side of the President." And Schultze has recently said, "I'd like to get all these Democratic candidates off this industrial policy kick, which I think is absolute nonsense." Schultze believes that though the United States has economic problems, "an inability to make the necessary transition from old industries to newer, growing ones is not one of them."[42]

Noneconomists are likely to be slow to believe that the vast majority of mainstream economists could be so skeptical about the efficiency of government allocation of resources. Economists are rarely anarchists. They do want an active government role in setting up the legal framework for the market system, in providing for significant public goods, in correcting for important externalities and other market imperfections. Many mainstream economists also want an active government on macrostabilization questions and on redistributing income to the poor. In a laissez-faire economy the consensus among economists would be for more government intervention. But in America of the 1980s it is not. Economists have been in the forefront of the fight for deregulation of industry and have been nearly unanimous in advocating less intrusive ways of dealing with the pollution problem. Both their knowledge of the harm that has been done by a too active government role in the past and their concerns about inherent government efficiency problems make economists much slower than most to advocate government involvement.

Again, the best evidence of this appears in the views of those mainstream economists who are well to the left of center in the profession, those associated with the liberal wing of the Democratic party. These economists have some differences with other economists, but the differences with other noneconomist liberals are at least as great. Kenneth Arrow, for example, has recently written an article entitled "Two Cheers for Regulation." He opposes Milton Friedman's call for a reduction in the scope of government. But a careful reading of the article shows that Arrow actually calls for a greater government role in allocation matters for only one area, chemical handling and waste disposal. At the same time he urges less direct regulation of railroads and energy, some relaxation and redirection of efforts for occupational safety, and a less intrusive government role on pollution matters generally.[43] Similarly, Lester Thurow wants a government investment role, and both he and the late Arthur Okun want more government aid for those with low incomes. But, in their best-selling books neither is enthusiastic about government's allocative efficiency potential. Thurow opposes wage and price controls. He supports a much more modest government antitrust role and an end to the government monopoly on delivering the mail. He believes some unnecessary rules and regulations are now "strangling our economy," and he favors "stripping industrial rules and regulations down to the bare essentials."[44] Okun argues for most new federal initiatives to come through "check writing and extending the rules of fair play, rather than programs that require the federal government to produce and deliver complex services."[45]

RENEWED RESPECT FOR IMPERFECT MARKETS

O.K., fine, markets work well, but government is inefficient. You've explained Milton Friedman's "Chicago school" economics. If only there were small firms and perfect competition and everything worked so well in the real world. What about John Kenneth Galbraith? What about profits? Government can afford to be a little less efficient and still come out ahead because it doesn't have to make a profit. What about the monopolistic power and obscenely high profits of the big oil companies? Is it efficient for Mobil Oil to buy Montgomery Ward? Is that the best way to increase our energy supply? Is it efficient for U.S. Steel to buy Marathon Oil? Is that the best way to modernize the obsolete technology that plagues the U.S. steel industry? Sure, large government bureaucracies can be pretty inefficient at times, but so can large corporate bureaucracies. The private sector makes just as many blunders as the public sector. We just don't read as much about them. It will make still more without active government guidance.

When I explain economists' views on government and markets in class, students respond with comments of this kind. But, as the preceding quotations from liberal economists suggest, the skepticism about government efficiency is not confined to Chicago school economists. The respect for markets, as one finds them in the real world, is at least as common in the profession.

Imagine a profit-seeking businessman. Economists, unlike much of academe, find him pleasant to contemplate. The economist imagines the businessman to be just as greedy as his colleagues do, perhaps even more so. But today's economist, like Adam Smith, thinks that though the profit-seeking businessman does not intend to promote the public interest, by an "invisible hand" he promotes it nonetheless.[46] Higher prices and higher profits induced pencil manufacturers to give the consumer more of what he wanted, and losses made the toothpick manufacturer willing to make available added resources so that the pencil manufacturer could do so. If the consumer demand for pencils remains strong, above-normal prices and profits will lead new firms to start making pencils. This added production plus the increase by the old firms will in turn lead to lower prices and a profit rate from pencils no higher than in other industries. This "normal profit" is the return to investors for being willing to defer consumption (save) and take risks. The risk taking and deferred consumption (capital) permits investment and resulting increases in worker productivity and wages that spread benefits throughout society. Only persistently higher than normal profits not explained by greater than normal risk or firm efficiency trouble economists.

In 1975 the median college student thought the average large national corporation received a 45 percent return on its business. He thought a fair profit level would be 25 percent. In fact, the real after-tax rate of return of nonfinancial corporations (both as a percentage of assets and of receipts) is under 6 percent and was lower in the 1970s than in the 1960s.[47] Even this 6 percent return is not a cost of doing business that government might avoid if it provided the same good or service. Additional increments of government spending are usually paid by debt (federal spending is 55 percent of total public spending), and those who lend this capital also expect a return (a "profit"). The tax-free interest on municipal bonds that makes municipalities' borrowing costs lower than industry's does so only by forsaking an equivalent amount of taxes, which means other taxes must eventually be raised.[48]

Even the most criticized of the profit seekers, the middlemen and speculators, escape the economist's wrath. Middlemen are a further development of the wealth-increasing division of labor. If they do not provide services worth their costs, retailers that do not use them will put out of business both the middlemen and the retailers they supply. Speculation is condemned if it is part of an attempt to monopolize or "corner" a market. But usually it serves a socially useful function and helps stabilize prices for both consumer and producer. When bad weather hurts next year's coffee crop, congressmen howl at the "manipulation" of the market that leads to sharp rises in prices for coffee *this* year as speculators compete with retailers for the available supply. But speculators hurt consumers this year only by helping them next. They buy coffee only because they think prices will be significantly higher next year than this. If they are right, the higher price means consumers will value the coffee next year even more than this year. Without the speculators third cups this year might be available only at the expense of seconds next, and the price swings between the two years would be far greater.[49]

As for Galbraith, he is not an influential figure in economics. There is no Galbraithian school of economists in the sense that there is a Chicago school. At least half a dozen of Galbraith's propositions have been tested by other economists and found to be unsupported by the evidence.[50] Galbraith ignores these findings and continues to produce well-written books for a popular audience.[51]

Economists grant that private bureaucracies are often as large as public ones, and they do not doubt that inefficiencies exist in many private firms just as they do in the public sector. But even the largest firms in the most concentrated industries face severe consequences if they do not attract enough consumers to keep profits up. When the recession, high interest rates, high new car prices, and consumer dissatisfaction with Detroit's products combined to make consumers less interested in buying domestically built automobiles, the big three automakers were forced to make drastic, unpleasant changes in the way they did business. Chrysler, for example, reduced its costs so much that by 1982 it needed to sell only 1.2 million cars to break even, whereas in 1980 it needed sales of 2.4 million. To achieve this Chrysler reduced its salaried staff from 44,000 to 22,000 in a period of two years. During the same period Ford sliced its North American salaried work force by 25 percent.[52] Government agencies are not often able to respond to changes in demand as rapidly, especially at the federal level.

Monopoly has long been an important concern of economists. A profit-maximizing monopolist will restrict output to keep his price up. As a result, consumers will not get as much of the monopolist's products as they want even though they are willing to cover the costs of production. Pure monopolies are almost always regulated. The real issue is what to do about markets in which firms have substantial market power and compete with others only imperfectly.

In recent decades our largest firms have become more important in the economy. In 1947 the hundred largest firms contributed 23 percent of the total value added in U.S. manufacturing. In 1972 the top hundred firms contributed 33 percent. But manufacturing, the most concentrated sector of the economy, represents a significantly smaller percentage of gross national product than it did in 1947. Moreover, most of the increase in concentration in manufacturing came about before 1954, and there has been no change in manufacturing concentration since 1963 despite the large wave of conglomerate mergers in the 1960s. (This is possible because new companies form and grow rapidly.) More relevant to economists' concern with competition is the concentration in particular markets. It is declining. In 1963, 33.1 percent of total manufacturing income came from industries in which the four largest sellers had 50 percent or more of the business. In 1972, 29 percent came from such industries.[53] A more recent study using new data finds that between 1958 and 1980, the U.S. economy as a whole became markedly more competitive.[54]

Most economists think that the concentration figures underestimate competitive forces in the economy. The figures ignore foreign competition. They ignore competition across the usually defined markets, for example, motorized campers with vacation resorts and luxury cars with stereo equipment. They also ignore the dynamic nature of the competitive process, which cannot be grasped through a snapshot taken at any given time.

Over the last two decades economists have become relatively less interested in stimulating still more competition through active government antitrust efforts.[55] This trend is explained by new theory, by new evidence, and by some negative assessments of past government antitrust policy.

Economists today frequently emphasize that mergers and diversification can improve efficiency and even stimulate competition. For example, mergers can discipline inefficient managers. Firms that other managers think should be doing better with their assets and opportunities are prime candidates for takeovers.[56]

Elementary theory can show that a profit-seeking monopolist who reduces his costs of production will increase production and reduce price, thus passing some new benefits on to consumers. If greater concentration reduces costs, therefore, we may all benefit from permitting it, even if prices are set somewhat above the, now lower, opportunity cost of production.[57] There is some evidence that concentration does reduce costs in those industries where it occurs. One recent study finds that increased concentration creates less suboptimal capacity by merging firms that are too small to take account of economies of scale.[58] Two others find that increases in industry concentration are significantly correlated with reduced unit costs and product prices.[59] Still another study finds greater differentials between the profit rates of large and small firms in concentrated industries than in unconcentrated industries. This strongly suggests that the larger firms in concentrated industries are relatively low-cost firms.[60]

This evidence of efficiency gains to balance anticompetitive costs of concentration helps explain why economists now look more sanguinely at the imperfect competition that characterizes so many of our markets. Just as one finds prominent liberal economists expressing concern about government efficiency, so one finds them praising our capitalist system. Charles Schultze decries the poor public understanding of our market system. Though acknowledging that "the day-to-day behavior of the economic system does not match the text book world of market adjustment," he nonetheless argues that this day-to-day behavior provides a "misleading" picture of the system's "social efficacy." "Given time" our economic system responds with "incredible efficiency" to the price signals that society sends out.[61] Similarly, Arthur Okun has said, "While every market economy has fallen far short of the competitive ideal, the market has proved to be an efficient organizer of production in practice as well as theory."[62]

In part, many economists' skepticism about government's ability to improve much upon the performance of imperfect markets comes from their assessment of recent experience with economic regulation and antitrust policy. In the 1970s fares on interstate routes regulated by the Civil Aeronautics Board were more than 70 percent higher than on equivalent intrastate Texas and California routes, even though the market concentration ratios on these latter routes were quite high. On the Los Angeles to San Francisco route, one of the best serviced, two companies had about 70 percent of the business. Yet even this relatively low level of competition and the threat of more if prices went up kept air fares well below government-regulated interstate levels.[63]

One recent study finds that antitrust policy is an important cause of the increase in competition in the U.S. economy.[64] But in recent years criticism of antitrust policy has been more common than such praise. The Justice Department and the Federal Trade Commission have not generally chosen to prosecute in those industries where potential gains would be greatest, and many actions brought cannot be justified.[65] Even those cases brought in industries with high concentration ratings have seemed less important in retrospect. While the government's monopolization case was pending against Alcoa (1937–51), its share of the aluminum industry fell from 90 percent to 55 percent. While the case against IBM was pending (1969–82), the industry went through two generations of computers, foreign competition increased, and minicomputers able to handle almost all computing tasks were developed and marketed by many smaller firms. Similarly, since the introduction of the government's case against American Telephone and Telegraph in 1972, communications satellites and other developments have transformed its market.[66]

Most economists would still support vigorous prosecution of collusive price fixing and of mergers by close competitors that facilitate cartelization by significantly reducing the number of sellers. There is not a consensus for much else. Though some economists still favor breaking up firms in the most concentrated industries, the trend in antitrust economics is clearly toward advocating a more relaxed policy. For example, University of Wisconsin economist Leonard Weiss previously advocated challenging most substantial horizontal mergers among viable firms in even moderately concentrated markets. Because of the aforementioned efficiency results, he now favors contesting only those mergers that "increase the two-firm concentration ratio above 35 or the four-firm ratio above 50" *and* that "affect firms that rank first or second in the market or would rank first or second after the merger." Weiss notes that according to these criteria, "many of the horizontal merger cases that reached the Supreme Court in the 1960's were decided too strictly."[67]

Of course, one might prefer small businesses to large ones for reasons that have nothing to do with the cost of products. Huge firms may command undue political influence, and small, locally based independent entrepreneurs may provide important external benefits to their community. I am sympathetic to these concerns, and these externalities will be discussed in Chapter 10. They do not, however, substantially alter conclusions here, since tax changes could promote a small-business objective more effectively and without the costs of a very active antitrust policy.[68]

Perhaps business does make as many resource allocation blunders as government does. But most economists do not think so, and they offer substantial theory and evidence to support their belief. In an important sense the previous section's discussion of antitrust bends over backward to be fair to government, for it assumes that government is at least trying to weaken monopoly power and restraints of trade. But, as a large economic literature notes, much legislation concerning tariffs, unions, and franchising or licensing (in areas like banking, trucking, and taxicabs) suggests the contrary. As one authority has said, "The fabric of restraint woven by government is so extensive that private restraints may seem trivial in comparison."[69]

Economists retreat not at all when confronted by congressional cries about the perfidy of U.S. Steel's buying Marathon Oil or Mobil's buying Montgomery Ward.[70] They do not doubt that many mergers are mistakes. They even argue that our tax laws artificially encourage too many mergers.[71] But the market disciplines those who make the worst mistakes.[72] And U.S. Steel should want to look elsewhere for investments. Steel is a declining industry.[73] If well managed, such industries will want to diversify, and they will not always replace "obsolete" technology. It is precisely because governments are likely to resist this sort of efficient, long-term trend that economists want them to remain uninvolved. Economists will also know that Mobil's buying Montgomery Ward was an aberration – one that has not been successful and thus is not likely to be imitated. The oil industry is plowing most of its profits back into energy exploration and production just as it said it would.[74] But even if it were not, economists would be unconcerned. Investment should go where future profits will be highest because that is where consumer demand will be going unmet. At some point oil exploration will not meet the profit test for the oil companies, and they will diversify in their interest and ours.

Many oil companies are very big. But the oil industry is not unusually concentrated, and it is not becoming more concentrated. The top four firms control about 31 percent of domestic refining capacity. By way of comparison the big four in automobiles have 93 percent of the market; in tires and tubes, 73; in cigarettes, 84; in radio and television sets, 49; in farm machinery, 47; in soaps and detergents, 62; in organic chemicals, 43.[75]

How does one explain the Federal Trade Commission's case (recently dismissed) against the industry and the special congressional concern on both sides of the aisle about oil companies' market power? One scholar calls the petroleum litigation a "patently political response to overt Congressional pressure and to public frustration over rising gas prices."[76] Senator Gary Hart says no. He acknowledges that no single firm "has an unusually large share of the market." But he notes that the top *eighteen* firms control 80 percent of the refining capacity. "In the minds of many" this is enough to create "a shared monopoly."[77]

Many economists fear such minds.[78] They note that if the oil companies have unusual power, it is being used in an unusual way since over time their rate of return has not been higher than that of nonoil corporations. Most economists believe that government involvement in energy has done far more harm than good.[79] The energy price controls of the 1970s subsidized and thus increased the importation of OPEC oil. They created long lines, black-market resales by "high-priority" users and larger, less visible inefficiencies. By comparison the market approach – deregulated, higher prices – has increased supplies somewhat and brought enormous conservation gains.[80] Deregulation has, however, been slow in coming. In part this is because of public and congressional misunderstanding of the distribution and magnitude of gains and losses from price controls. That misunderstanding is better discussed as part of a broader look at economists' views on equity.

6

ECONOMISTS AND EQUITY

The previous chapter explains why economists give the market high marks as a mechanism for allocating resources. Some in society may be harmed when others engage in market transactions. Obviously those making buggy whips did not gain when Henry Ford sold his model Ts. But in the absence of imperfections the market achieves potential Pareto improvements, those where gainers gain more than losers lose. Henry Ford and all those who bought his cars would have been able to compensate the buggy whip makers for their losses and still be better off themselves.

But what should we think if, as is usually the case, the compensation does not take place? Though the market responds to the dollar votes of consumers, many feel that those votes are not equitably distributed. The person who buys the pencils (or bread) is sometimes the most eager to have them, but sometimes he is just the richest. Willingness to pay depends in part on ability to pay. If downtown renewal developers want to buy land now owned by landlords providing low-income housing, any agreement on a sale price suggests an efficient outcome in which the developers speaking for the new occupants are willing to pay more for the new use than the low-income residents were willing to pay the landlord to preserve their housing. Similarly when the costs of an inner-city neighborhood health center exceed the benefits, the project is inefficient. But perhaps the developers should be stopped and the health center supported once one considers equity.

Those critical of the economic approach to public policy often accuse economists of being preoccupied with economic efficiency and neglectful of equity. Economists are more confident that they draw on their expertise when they discuss efficiency than when they discuss equity. They are thus more comfortable talking about efficiency, and they do consider efficiency more often. Nevertheless, they talk about equity and the distribution of income a great deal. They have provocative views about the best way to achieve an equity objective and about the tension between the goals of economic efficiency and growth on the one hand and a more equal distribution of income on the other. On some equity questions they have reached a remarkable consensus, but on other, larger, ones there are huge gaps in or differences over evidence and appropriate societal values. Even when fighting among themselves, though, economists tend to agree on the framework for debate, a framework that, I will later argue, cuts off discussion of some important questions.

The term "equity" brings to mind only some of the subjects covered by the older term "justice." But equity is itself too broad to describe the distribution of income questions that economists focus on. Even many such questions spark little interest among economists. They do not usually concern themselves with how the Frost Belt is doing as opposed to the Sun Belt; farmers versus other groups; veterans versus nonveterans; or poor widows versus poor wastrels. There is a lively debate about the extent to which, in the absence of government involvement, competitive market forces will break down unjust discrimination associated with race and sex. But economists most often focus on one particular distribution question: the relative shares of national resources controlled by broad income classes.

PARETO OPTIMAL REDISTRIBUTION

On the core value issue of how equally income should be distributed economists claim no more expertise than the average citizen. But they do think that they can explain why a certain amount of government coercion for redistribution purposes may actually be economically efficient. Redistribution to help the poor can be seen as a public good that private charity will provide in insufficient quantity from the point of view of both rich and poor. In the absence of public welfare programs, many of the nonpoor would favor societal efforts to reduce poverty. Some of these might feel that it was their duty to give through voluntary charities, and they would get personal satisfaction from doing so. Others, though, would realize that their personal contribution would not make a dent in the nation's poverty, and they would prefer that others gave to help the poor so that they could enjoy the benefits of a reduction in poverty without spending any of their own money. If too many people reasoned thus, less would be redistributed to the poor than the nonpoor wished. The nonpoor might, however, gladly give something if they knew their personal contribution would lead to more than a drop in the bucket. By requiring all who are similarly situated to give their fair share, government can ensure that the individual's sacrifice makes a difference. Thus, coercive government taxes may be the only way to get government programs the nonpoor desire and are willing to pay for.

The Pareto optimality argument for redistribution does not help one deal with today's issues. We already spend a good bit of money to help the poor.

There is no consensus among the nonpoor that more should be spent. Indeed, since public-opinion polls usually find "welfare" to be one of the most popular areas for budget cuts, it is clear that many of the nonpoor think that too much of their money goes to some of the poor. This does not mean that they are necessarily right. It just means that additional redistribution has ceased to be justifiable on efficiency grounds. Economists still allow for a possible societal judgment on equity grounds that the rich have more dollar votes than is fair. If we so decide, most economists are perfectly open to requiring the rich to give more to the poor than they choose to.

HOW EQUAL IS THE DISTRIBUTION OF INCOME AND WEALTH?

Economists agree that wealth is much more unequally distributed than income. For example, the top 1 percent are thought to have 18.9 percent of the total wealth and the top 1 percent have about 6 percent of after-tax money income. However, the distribution of wealth became more equal between the 1920s and the 1940s, and it has since become more equal still if one takes account of employee pension funds and the present value of future Social Security benefits (as the foregoing percentages do).[1]

Economists more often focus on levels and trends in income distribution than on levels and trends in wealth. In part this is because the data on wealth are much less accurate. But Arthur Okun also thought that there were good, substantive reasons for focusing on income. Income "provides the basic purchasing power for maintaining a standard of living; moreover, when property incomes are included, the income distribution reflects holdings of wealth."[2]

Probably the most frequently cited distribution-of-income data are those collected by the U.S. Bureau of the Census.[3] These show the top fifth of families getting about 41 percent of total U.S. income, while the bottom fifth get around 5 percent. Though there was a trend toward greater equality from 1929 to 1945, there has been little change since then.[4]

For a number of reasons, most economists argue that these figures exaggerate the degree of inequality in living standards and mask movement toward greater equality in recent decades. First, such snapshot figures can take no account of family life-cycle changes. Even if there were no lifetime inequality at all, at any point in time, both older and younger families would be expected to have lower incomes than middle-aged ones with experienced, productive workers. If one defines equality as equal incomes for all families that are at the same stage of their life cycle, inequality in the United States declines markedly. It declines further if one takes account of family size. Through time family units have become smaller. When we became wealthy enough that more young people could form their own households sooner, this led to more measured inequality in family income. Since more often than not income increases with family size, data on the distribution of income among families exaggerate real inequalities in living standards. One study shows that taking account of these life-cycle and family-size factors leads one to expect that, even with perfect equality in *life-cycle* income, measurements at any *one time* would show that the "poorest" 20 percent of families have only 12.9 percent of national income. This is because the "poorest" 20 percent would include a disproportionately large number of small families headed by young adults and the elderly. If we examined the income distribution when these young adults and the elderly were middle-aged, they would appear to be among the richest. After adjusting for these family-size and age factors, this same study shows that actual income inequality declined 23 percent between 1947 and 1972.[5]

The census data also exaggerate inequality because they look at pretax income, thus ignoring the effects of taxes, which, on balance, take a higher proportion of income from the rich than the poor.[6] Moreover, the data ignore all in-kind income. This cuts both ways. Fringe benefits like company cars and entertainment expenses disproportionately help those with above-average incomes. (Capital gains have averaged zero in a typical postwar year and are not an important factor.)[7] But the food and lodging of farmers and farm workers and the government transfers of housing, health care, and food stamps help mainly those with below average incomes. On balance most economists think that adjustments for in-kind income would reduce measured inequality and would show an increase in equality over recent decades.[8]

Though economists more often highlight these figures for relative distribution of income, they frequently also supply figures based on the officially defined poverty level. If one counts in-kind transfers, the gains here have been substantial. Several recent estimates show that between 2 and 6 percent of all persons were poor in the late 1970s, less than one-half the 1965 total.[9] Another study shows that if the transfers to the poor were not maldistributed among them, no one would be poor by the official definition.[10]

Most economists would agree that we have made real progress in combating poverty and that there has been some movement toward equalization in the distribution of relative incomes. But there is no consensus on an appropriate policy stance for the 1980s. A number of economists still see too much income inequality and want government to help reduce it further. Others are pleased by the equalization gains of the last two decades but think we have gone far enough. Still others think we have gone too far. But almost all would agree that there are important costs from government redistributive social welfare programs that do not appear in any government budget. Such programs interfere with the efficient allocation of resources, and they reduce economic growth. To understand how this occurs one must understand how a market system distributes income.

THE MARKET DISTRIBUTION OF INCOME

In a market system an individual's income depends on the payments received for others' use of his labor, land, and capital. The relative demand for these factors of production depends on the demand for the products that they help make. In the absence of market imperfections, income is determined by how much one's labor and owned resources add to market-valued goods and services. Competitive pressures push wages toward levels that reflect the marginal (last-hired) laborer's additional contribution to output – what that laborer adds by working here rather than elsewhere or not at all. Many businessmen would no doubt like to pay their employees only half of what they add to their firm's profitability. But employers would then face pressure from other businessmen who see extra profits for themselves if they hire the first firm's employees and pay them a little more but still less than their productivity warrants. And the new employers in turn face pressure from firms willing to pay a little more still.

The market income received is a result of both chance and choice. It depends on the sort of family or neighborhood one was born into and on one's intellectual and other capacities. It also depends on one's hard work and foresight. The talented and lazy probably will not have the income of the talented and hardworking, but they may do better than the untalented and hardworking. And they may do better than the talented and hardworking whose talent is valued little by others (e.g., a buggy whip maker).

To put it mildly, many of the income results of a market system do not seem fair. Even if we leave aside the playboy living on inherited wealth and look only at earned income, many disparities seem ludicrous. Everyone has his own candidates for the outrageously overpaid. Popular singers, movie stars, professional athletes, and corporate executives are common choices. Among those often listed as grossly underpaid are nurses, teachers, and child-care workers.

Partly as a result of court cases involving equal pay for comparable worth, newspapers are full of the subject these days. The news that Burt Reynolds would receive $5 million plus 10 percent of the gross for a recent movie inspired one attorney to write a *Washington Post* column. The attorney asked "who decided" that Reynolds' talents or Reggie Jackson's at hitting a baseball were worth more than a teacher's or a paramedic's. He proposed compensating people on the basis of the utility of the tasks they perform.[11] Some personnel experts are now at work on elaborate job comparability indexes that consider matters such as the "thinking challenge" of a job and how independently one must work.[12] Others have suggested setting a maximum legal salary, say $100,000. During the time he was a poorly paid ballet dancer, even young Ron Reagan entered the fray:

It angers me intellectually more than in any practical kind of way. I mean I just think that when people work hard it's worth more than the little bit that's paid [dancers].

Garbagemen make more, stagehands make more, everybody makes more – well why? They're not working as hard, they're not doing something that's as creative. There's just an obvious problem there – something is wrong.[13]

It is striking that there is almost no support for any of these reform measures among mainstream economists, even the most liberal among them. For example, Arthur Okun's core values are strongly egalitarian: "Abstracting from the costs and the consequences, I would prefer more equality of income to less and would like complete equality best of all." Yet Okun ultimately argues that all people, "rich and poor," should be permitted to "keep a significant part of any additional income they earn."[14]

Economists' attitudes are explained by their understanding that there is no way to ignore the market's distribution of income and still expect it to perform the functions of transmitting information and providing incentives that were discussed in Chapter 5. The insights of marginalism are relevant here. Child-care workers perform important work, at least as important as air-conditioning repairmen. But suppose there are fewer children who need to be cared for and more air conditioners that need to be fixed than there used to be. And suppose that more young people like the idea of caring for children than like the idea of repairing air conditioners. If we are not going to compel people to be air-conditioner repairmen rather than child-care workers, is it not necessary to find some other way to get people to change their occupational choices? Is there any practical way other than compensating the disappointed, who had hoped to be child-care workers, with a higher wage? Though the total utility provided by child-care workers may be as high as the total utility provided by air-conditioner repairmen, we need one more of the latter more than one more of the former. In a way is it not even just that those would-be child-care workers who agree to shift fields get something for their sacrifice?

Perhaps there is something wrong with a society that pays Burt Reynolds and Johnny Carson so much more than a top ballet performer. Consideration of the question would require exploring the consumer-sovereignty assumption, a task for Chapter 9. But the relative wages of the three are clearly not a sign of a market efficiency imperfection. Far more consumers like to watch Burt Reynolds and Johnny Carson than like to watch the ballet performer. Suppose there were a law setting the maximum salary at $100,000 per year. Carson might just spend a week in Las Vegas or cut back his time on the *Tonight Show* to once a month. But the ratings indicate that he is far more popular than the substitute hosts. Many people find the Carson show one of the high points of their day. In total these people would lose far more than Carson would if the maximum salary measure led him to leave the *Tonight Show*. Moreover, Carson's taxes would also be lower, so either other taxpayers would have to pay more or some beneficiaries of government programs would have to do without.

What of corporate salaries? Economists find an active market for top talent and a good bit of involuntary turnover of corporate management. The evidence about the determinants of managerial pay is not without conflict. But standard performance criteria are clearly important, and the most recent evidence finds that "a firm's profit picture (measured either by its reported earnings or by the market value of its common stock) is the most important factor in explaining variations in the salaries of corporate executives."[15]

Most economists would oppose an absolute limit on corporate salaries.[16] Consumers benefit from good managers who can keep costs and prices low. They benefit most when such managers run companies that make more products or more valued ones. But why should the president of a small Sun Belt firm already making $100,000 leave his friends and his hometown to take on the pressures, congestion, pollution, and cold accompanying a position with a large firm headquartered in New York or Detroit if his pay would be no different?

Mainstream economists believe that society should not devise salary scales based only on some abstract standard of fairness to various income classes or occupations. To try to do so while ignoring market-determined salaries and current shortages and surpluses of labor would cause an unworkable administrative morass and would greatly depress national income.[17] But as indicated earlier, most approve of less drastic adjustments to market distributions even though these too have (lesser) efficiency costs. A progressive income or consumption tax[18] and some sort of income supplement program for the poor enjoy widespread support. As explained in the following section, however, there is disagreement about whether the United States should go further than it already has with such measures.

TAXES AND THE INCENTIVE TO WORK AND INVEST

Any redistributive measures, even well-designed ones, have efficiency costs (using existing resources less well) and growth costs (slower increases in productive capacity).[19] If getting a job means losing one's Medicaid or most of one's welfare benefits, some people who would like to work and can find a job will not do so. They might be willing to sacrifice their leisure for a job that pays $3.60 an hour, and an employer may be glad to pay them such a wage. But if the net pay (after taking account of the reductions in government assistance, Social Security taxes, etc.) is much less than $3.60 per hour, they may choose leisure instead. This effect on the recipients of government aid also occurs in programs that serve both the poor and the nonpoor, such as unemployment compensation and disability insurance. Those unemployed who are covered by insurance are less active job seekers than those not covered, and on average they are unemployed about 23 percent longer. Disabled workers who receive tax-free benefits close to their previous wages remain disabled longer, and they help to explain the rise in disability payments from less than $10 billion in 1965 to more than $40 billion in 1977.[20]

There are also efficiency effects on those who are taxed to pay for redistributive programs. Most will not quit their jobs, but they may retire earlier or invest their money in less productive ways or avoid overtime or forgo moonlighting and a spouse's part-time job. All existing taxes have inefficiency effects, but the more even-handed general ones, such as income taxes and general expenditure taxes, have less than most.[21]

Recently there has been much discussion in the press about how federal welfare programs create dependency among the poor. This concern crosses the political spectrum from budget-conscious conservatives to inner-city blacks and New Left alumni like Sam Brown.[22] The effect of welfare measures on work effort has been discussed by economists since the British experience with the old poor law.[23] Today's economists believe that those receiving assistance would be more inclined to work if welfare programs were designed differently without, for example, the all-or-nothing provisions of programs such as Medicaid, which eliminates all benefits as soon as income passes a single cutoff point. But any program that aids the poor will reduce the work effort of some of them to some degree.

Probably most people would support a welfare program that provides an adequate standard of living, keeps costs low by concentrating benefits on the poorest, and to encourage work, reduces benefits by less than fifty cents for each dollar earned by those on welfare. Unfortunately, even the best-designed programs cannot meet all these objectives.[24] If benefits are to be concentrated on the poorest, then they must be reduced quickly as incomes increase beyond poverty levels, and there is thus little encouragement to work. If the benefits are reduced slowly as income rises and if the minimum benefit is close to the official poverty level, costs inevitably become enormous, and much of the aid goes to the lower middle class, not to the poorest. If costs and the benefit-reduction rate are both to be kept low, the basic benefit level must be far below the poverty level.

One characteristic of our existing system is a high benefit-reduction rate and thus a very low incentive to work. Though the benefit-reduction or marginal tax rate varies depending on the number of programs the poor family participates in, one careful study found that it averaged 63 percent.[25] Some economists fear that this rate, together with the increases in the quantity of redistributive programs since the mid-1960s, may explain a significant part of the 15 percent reduction in labor supply among low-income families between 1963 and 1973.[26]

One possible solution to the work incentive problem would be to focus antipoverty efforts on education and job training. This was the initial emphasis of the War on Poverty of the 1960s, and it was stressed heavily in the 1964 Economic Report of the President. Unfortunately, though there are recent exceptions,[27] most evaluations have found that these programs are costly and not very effective. Even the most successful have left many trainees far from self-sufficient.[28]

The government could, of course, agree to be the employer of last resort. Lester Thurow has proposed an elaborate public employment program.[29] But many economists, including some liberal ones like Charles Schultze,[30] are unenthusiastic. With jobs guaranteed at a fixed rate of pay, there is little incentive for workers to put forth their best efforts. Any program would induce some workers to seek jobs in the public sector though they are more productive in the private sector. Moreover, in many families, one parent would have an incentive to cut back his working hours until family income fell enough to make the other parent eligible for a public-sector job.[31]

We are thus left, in Okun's words, with "a particularly nasty [dilemma]. . .Generous aid [for dependent children] removes important economic incentives that discourage women from getting into dependent positions, and that discourages their men from putting them there. But stingy aid denies the right to survival to the children of these broken families."[32] Or to quote Thomas Schelling discussing a different program:

Offering 90 percent of normal pay can make unemployment irresistible for some and even a net profit for those who moonlight or work around the home. Providing only 40 percent over a protracted period makes living harsher than we want it to be. There is nothing to do but compromise. But a compromise that makes unemployment a grave hardship for some makes it a pleasant respite for others, and we cannot even be comfortable with the compromise.[33]

Many economists believe that concerns with work effort must not be allowed to end the progress we have made in recent years toward more equal income distribution. They want more redistribution, not less. They point out that for thirty years the pure market distribution of earnings has been becoming more unequal. Government redistributive efforts have made possible the equalization progress achieved.[34] Without further efforts inequalities may begin to increase.

These economists are also encouraged by the results of the federal government's elaborate income supplement experiments. The experiments gave cash supplements to random samples of low-income families in several cities for several years. These families' work responses and some other changes in behavior were recorded. The different experiments produced somewhat different results, but all showed that those receiving cash supplements did, on average, reduce their work effort somewhat. The labor supply reductions (in hours of work) for the most sophisticated experiment were about 9 percent for male heads of families; about 14 percent for female family heads; about 20 percent for wives; and 24 percent for young adults (ages sixteen to twenty-one). Economists who want to redistribute more money to low-income families think these reductions in work effort are modest and tolerable. They also point out that there were some nutritional and school performance gains among the children of families receiving cash supplements. These gains may in turn make the children more productive workers as adults.[35]

Other economists are not convinced that market forces alone can explain the greater inequality in the pure market distribution of earnings that the first group cites. Labor's share of national income as compared to the share of owners of capital has been increasing steadily for fifty years.[36] Within the labor component the salary premium for higher education has been falling, not rising. Thus, for example, the inflation-adjusted wage rate for domestic service has almost doubled over the last thirty years.[37] These economists wonder if increased numbers of young, part-time, and occasional workers do not explain the increased inequality in the market distribution of income.[38]

Some economists are worried, not reassured, by the declines in work effort that the income supplements induced among assisted families in the federal experiments.[39] They advance reasons why long-term, societywide effects of an income supplement program may be even greater. For example, there were greater reductions in work effort in the last years of one income experiment than in the first year.[40] As indicated later, these economists also stress the effects of redistribution on the work effort and investment patterns of taxpayers and through these on economic growth that benefits rich and poor alike.

If there is a consensus on anything, it is perhaps disapproval of the pattern of President Reagan's welfare cuts that penalized the working poor more than the nonworking poor.[41] Though there is some support among economists for work requirements,[42] there is also skepticism about the ability of any such requirements to overcome the new disincentives for work effort that the administration has provided. If one wishes, it is easy to succeed at not getting a job, not keeping it, or not doing it well. Economists are interested in programs that encourage the opposite behavior. Many support wage subsidies and earnings supplements that both increase income and encourage work. On the employers' side some economists favor tax credits to increase the demand for and the wages of low-skilled labor.[43]

The effect of high marginal tax rates on work effort of taxpayers is also much disputed. On average the poorest tenth of Americans pay 11 to 12 percent of their total income in taxes whereas the richest pay 36 to 38 percent. But for all Americans the marginal tax rate, the percentage taken on the last dollars earned, is much greater – at least 35 percent in all income classes. Though the top tenth pays 46 percent of each additional dollar earned, the bottom income classes pay a higher rate because their government benefit programs decrease as income increases.[44]

It is the higher marginal tax rates, not the average ones, that affect work choice decisions, and some economists oppose further redistribution measures because they think these rates are as high as they should be allowed to go.[45] The efficiency damage from taxes increases in proportion to the square of the marginal tax rate. For example, "the additional damage caused by raising the marginal tax rate from 50 percent to 60 percent is greater than all the damage caused when the tax rate is initially increased from zero to 33 percent."[46] Moreover, in order to avoid work-discouraging benefit-reduction rates higher than 50 percent, half of any income raised for additional redistributive measures would have to go to the lower middle class, not to the poor. Many in the lower middle class may not be genuinely poorer than the middle and upper middle class who pay for the transfers. (There are not enough rich to pay for these transfers.) The lower-middle-class families generally have fewer workers and thus enjoy more leisure. And they are younger on average and thus will have higher incomes in the future.

Other economists would acknowledge that income levels do not always reflect actual levels of well-being, but they think that they do so often enough so that redistributive measures do bring important equalization gains. Some also think the work effort problem is nonexistent at tax rates close to today's. In Lester Thurow's words, "Income effects (the need to work more to regain one's living standards) dominate substitution effects (the desire for more leisure because of lower take-home wage rates), and individuals work for a variety of other rewards – power, prestige, promotions, satisfaction."[47]

Though all agree that better studies are needed, those that exist do show only modest gains for labor supply from tax cuts. One MIT study found that the 30 percent income tax cut proposed by Congressman Jack Kemp (R-N.Y.) and Senator William Roth (R-Del.) would have increased husbands' hours of work by 2.7 percent and wives' by 9.4 percent.[48] Some economists, however, point out that there can be an effect on work intensity and quality without affecting the hours of work. These economists also note that many of the labor supply effects of higher taxes will not be seen in the short term. People may emigrate or retire earlier in future years. Or they may do different, less productive work. They may, for example, decide that extra education is not worth it, or that a pressured, risky life as an independent entrepreneur is not worth the small potential after-tax gains in added income.[49]

Liberal and conservative economists agree that high marginal tax rates have a greater effect on the demand for fringe benefits and other untaxed income than on the supply of labor. As Okun noted, "High tax rates are followed by attempts of ingenious men to beat them as surely as snow is followed by little boys on sleds."[50] One result is more bartering and "pay me in cash" transactions in the underground economy.[51] Another consequence is the unproductive use, from society's point of view, of lawyers to escape taxes. Still other results are the purchasing of planes and yachts and attendance at business conferences in the Caribbean financed by tax-deductible business expenses. Some average taxpayers have found ways to deduct their cars, travel, and entertainment by forming part-time distributorships with Amway and other corporations.[52] Liberal economists think even lower rates will not end many of these abuses, but they believe that tightening rules can help significantly.[53] Conservatives think that "the fact that relatively little revenue is collected at the highest marginal [tax] rates testify [*sic*] to their basic futility."[54]

An important component of the debate about high taxes and efficiency costs concerns the effect of taxes on economic growth. For economists growth is a wondrous thing. Both liberal and conservative economists think it far more important in explaining the material progress of ordinary people than labor unions[55] or political reform. From the conservative side Thomas Sowell says:

If you read many histories and hear many discussions of social issues, you get the idea that people are no longer in rags or hungry today because various noble reformers refused to accept such conditions and worked to alleviate them. Meanwhile, it was merely coincidental that the gross national product rose by 5 or 6 times over that same span. But if you really want to know why it is that the poor of the nineteenth century were in rags and those of the twentieth century typically are not, it is because a man named Singer perfected the sewing machine, putting factory-made clothing within the reach of great masses of people for the first time in history.[56]

Liberal Alfred Kahn seems to agree completely. Without growth

liberalism could never have achieved its victories. (The improvement since the 1930s in the material welfare of President Roosevelt's "one third of a nation" has been made possible far, far more by the material progress enjoyed by all three thirds than by the modest redistribution from the top two.)[57]

Though all the causes of high productivity (GNP per employee) growth rates are not well understood, there is agreement that a crucial element is investment that leads to capital formation.[58] When workers work with better equipment and machinery, they become more productive. Competition in the labor market then causes their real incomes to rise. Investment requires saving, and the rich save a far higher percentage of their incomes than the rest of us. Society as a whole reaps some of the benefits from savings of the rich (and of others). Economists of most persuasions think that there is much truth in the "trickle-down" or "filter-down" theory of prosperity. Paul Samuelson says that the theory, "so scorned by so many non-economists," has "a very important element of historical truth in it."[59] And Alfred Kahn asks his fellow (noneconomist) liberals to reconsider

their opposition to any and all policies whose method of producing social benefits can be characterized as "trickle down." The most powerful engine of productivity advance is technological progress, generated in large measure by expenditures on research and development and embodied in improved capital goods and managerial techniques; and it confers its benefits on all of us, precisely, by trickling down.[60]

Chapter 5 noted that over the last decade the U.S. economy had surpassed its major European rivals in GNP growth and employment gains. But GNP grew more quickly because of a higher increase in the proportion of our population that was working, not because of rapid gains in the productivity of previously employed workers. From 1960 to 1973, industrialized countries' productivity gains were very strongly correlated with the amount of nonresidential investment. During this period the United States invested 13.6 percent and GNP per employee grew 2.1 percent per year; the United Kingdom invested 12.2 percent and grew 2.8 percent; West Germany invested 20.0 percent and grew 5.4 percent; Japan invested 29.0 percent and grew 9.2 percent. Since 1975, the United States' net corporate investment (gross investment less depreciation) has been lower than from 1960 to 1974, and for several years productivity growth was essentially zero (though it has turned up again recently).[61] This has occurred even though the societal gains from investment in plant and equipment are far larger than most realize, probably about 11 percent in real inflation-adjusted dollars.[62]

Most economists agree that we have a serious growth problem and that we should save and invest more than we have in the past.[63] They also agree that public policy in countries like Japan and West Germany explicitly encourages savings through tax exemptions and outright subsidies to small savers[64] whereas our policies do the reverse. For example, interest on savings accounts in the United States was until recently kept very low by regulation, and this savings income is still taxed. Savers who invest in corporations are taxed twice: once through the corporate income tax and later through the tax on dividends and capital gains. On the other hand, borrowing is subsidized. Consumer debt and mortgage interest are tax-deductible expenses. These and other tax provisions make it especially attractive to invest in property rather than wealth-generating corporations. Even Social Security, financed through a pay-as-you-go system, provides no investment for growth, and yet it makes saving unnecessary for much of the population.

From the 1930s until quite recently economists did not worry much about savings. For Keynes savings were a problem in that they depressed spending and thus led to an underutilization of existing productive capacity. After the war growth seemed to occur automatically. Moreover, the accepted wisdom of the profession was that a higher rate of return on savings would not significantly affect the volume of funds available for investment.[65] Recent work by Stanford's Michael Boskin calls such thinking into question. His studies suggest that an increase of 50 percent in real after-tax rates of return would increase savings by 20–25 percent.[66] And the comparison of British and U.S. policies and results with those of Japan and Germany has been made by economists concerned about our antisavings tax policies.[67]

Growth depends not only on the volume of savings but also on its distribution. U.S. tax laws have encouraged investments in property and other durable consumption goods, in hard-to-trace gold and silver, and in various elaborate, inefficient tax shelters. These investments contribute little or nothing to growth. They also lower tax revenues. A very high tax on less taxable income may not yield more money than a somewhat lower tax on more taxable income.[68] Thus many economists supported the recent change to a maximum tax of 50 percent as opposed to 70 percent on investment income.[69] They thought that investments would become more productive and that little or no revenue would be lost.

Some evidence for the ability of lower taxes to lead to an increase in productive investment had come earlier from examining the effects of Congress's decision in 1978 to cut the maximum tax on capital gains to 28 percent. The argument in favor of the cut was that "high capital gains tax rates suppressed investments in stocks, especially of new high-technology firms. If people gambled to back these risky enterprises, they wanted the reward if the companies succeeded." The results through 1980 have been as follows: "The number of new firms selling stock to the public rose from 46 (and $250 million) in 1978 to 237 (and $1.4 billion) in 1980. At the same time, venture capital investments in firms too new and too small to go public increased from $440 million in 1978 to more than $1 billion in 1980."[70]

Some economists, however, think that these results are explained by factors other than the tax cut.[71] More generally, liberal economists think "regressive redistribution of income is neither necessary nor sufficient for economic...growth."[72] Some have wanted the tax on capital gains raised, not lowered.[73] They think that the best way to get more private investment is to reduce the federal deficit so that more lendable funds will be available to the private sector. If specific savings incentives are needed, these economists favor personal tax credits to encourage new saving by the middle class.[74]

Many liberal and conservative economists favor achieving lower marginal tax rates by eliminating many of the deductions and credits that reduce the tax base.[75] In the early 1980s, liberal and conservative economists also supported business tax cuts[76] though many believed that the particular tax cut measures proposed by President Reagan and passed by Congress produced effective tax rates that varied "capriciously and without rationale across industries."[77] Some economists favor instead a refundable tax credit for all investment in excess of depreciation.[78] Others prefer a simple cut in the basic corporate tax rate.[79]

In some measure the debate on taxes, equity, growth, and efficiency is a generational one. Younger economists worry somewhat more about efficiency, older ones about equity. Thus Yale law professor Boris Bittker sees the debate among economists as one between "Old Turks and young fogies – a generation of idealists in their sunset years, still inspired by the ethics of compassion adopted in their youth, and a rising generation of skeptics insisting on the prudent calculation of costs before embarking on new ventures or endorsing old ones."[80]

Bittker calls himself a "troubled Old Turk." That may fairly describe much of the economics profession. In a 1978 poll of 211 economists, 40 percent generally agreed with the statement "The distribution of income in the United States should be more equal." Another 31 percent "agreed with provisions" and only 29 percent "generally disagreed."[81] Yet a shift in the profession toward a relatively more conservative stance than a decade ago is widely acknowledged.

One sign of this is the influence within the profession of Martin Feldstein, a forty-four-year old conservative economist who until mid-1984 served as chairman of Ronald Reagan's Council of Economic Advisers. A recent study that determined the economists most often credited in the footnotes to other economists' work found Feldstein the leader by a wide margin. His liberal Harvard colleague Otto Eckstein calls Feldstein "probably the best economist under the age of 50 or 60."[82] Moreover, the profession is not just more conservative because of the growing stature of young, bright, conservative economists like Feldstein but also because old-line liberal economists have become relatively more conservative. Eckstein himself has said that "there is not much doubt left that a tax burden is discouraging participation in the labor force and affecting productivity adversely."[83] And Charles Schultze, a high-ranking official under presidents Kennedy, Johnson, and Carter, has been very concerned about the steady growth in marginal tax rates and in government's share of the economy. In late 1981 he was decrying the excesses of the Great Society and calling for new budget cuts.[84]

As mentioned earlier, liberal economists sometimes favor boosting savings by way of tax credit incentives aimed at the middle class. This may well be the appropriate "liberal" position because such tax credits can get us more funds for investment without reducing tax rates for the rich. But the poor save almost nothing, so the credits will be of no direct benefit to them. Moreover, in the short run, the credits reduce tax revenues available to re-distribute to the poor. And it is surely striking to see an economist like Gunnar Myrdal, an architect of the Swedish welfare state, opposing the whole idea of an income tax: "For the majority of people a high and progressively increasing marginal tax rate must decrease the willingness to work more than necessary...Through the lowering of the income tax, the irrational direction of investment from production to durable consumption goods would not be so severe." Like many economists, Myrdal has come to prefer a consumption tax, a tax that can be designed to be progressive and that by taxing "living standard instead of income...puts a premium on saving and capital accumulation," an advantage that "should be liked by most everyone, especially in these times."[85]

Economists who want to help the poor can sound moderate or even fairly conservative when concerned about sluggish growth because in James Tobin's words "the potential gains to the poor from full employment and growth" are "much larger, and much less socially and politically divisive than those from redistribution."[86] Though *The Zero Sum Society* is the title of Lester Thurow's recent book, most economists do not believe that society is like a zero sum game in which for every net gainer there must be a net loser.[87] To quote Yale's Tobin again, "One of the differences between economists and politicians is that politicians instinctively think that the economy is a zero-sum game, and maybe they feel more comfortable in a kind of brokerage function, whereas economists are at pains to explain that it's usually not a zero-sum game."[88]

Redistributing 1 percent more national income to the poor would increase their incomes by about 12 percent. It would also require increasing marginal tax rates by 10 percent for all families.[89] This would reduce the growth in productivity, which has been close to zero in recent years. But if economic growth were increased to the average level of 1947–77 and if poor families continued to share in its benefits as they have in the past, they would gain an increase of 12 percent in their real inflation-adjusted incomes every four or five years.[90]

WHO BENEFITS AND WHO LOSES

Focusing only on economists' differences in the face of conflict between efficiency and growth on the one hand and redistribution on the other does not do justice to their agreement on a number of important, though smaller, equity questions. First, they agree that it is important to find out who really benefits and who loses from existing and proposed policies. In the 1960s there was much talk about the importance of subsidies to the small struggling family farmer. Economists were able to show that two-thirds of farm subsidy benefits went to the top 16 percent of farmers who had incomes well above those of the average American family. Some important cuts in inefficient programs were made when better knowledge became available on these equity consequences.[91] In a recent article Alfred Kahn notes another example with a less happy outcome. Kahn had proposed limiting the amount of employers' contributions to health insurance that employees may exclude from their taxable income. Economists think that employers' tax-free contributions make medical insurance seem cheaper than it really is, and the resulting high levels of insurance help explain the spiraling costs of medical services. Kahn notes that his proposal was met with an indignant protest from a high Carter administration official who charged that he was "ask[ing] the poor to bear the brunt of our efforts to limit the painful inflation of medical costs." In fact, as Kahn noted, "It is mainly the better paid workers and executives, with incomes above the national average, who enjoy this fringe benefit – not the poor."[92]

In the Reagan administration Martin Feldstein joined the liberal Kahn in support of reforming the tax treatment of health insurance. He also advocated making all unemployment insurance benefits subject to the income tax. When word of this reform proposal leaked in the fall of 1982, the political uproar was deafening. President Reagan had to quickly disavow interest in the idea, which the press and congressmen of both parties dubbed "the Thanksgiving turkey." Yet as Princeton economist Alan Blinder has said, the proposal represented "a sound reform that probably commands the assent of the vast majority of economists."[93] The level of unemployment insurance benefits is related to the level of previous earnings. Higher-salaried employees get higher benefits, and they get them even if they are unemployed for only a few weeks and even if their spouses' income is quite high. Thus more than half the unemployment insurance benefits go to families with greater than median family incomes, and 15 percent of benefits go to families with incomes more than double the median level.[94]

The Feldstein proposal to tax benefits from unemployment insurance attracts the support of both camps of economists, those most concerned about equity and those most concerned about efficiency. The equity-oriented economists see that taxing unemployment benefits would alter the distribution of benefits in favor of low-income classes. The poorest unemployed would pay little or nothing under our progressive income tax laws, and the richest would pay a substantial amount. The efficiency-oriented economists see that the reform proposal would reduce the incentive to remain unemployed.[95] As Blinder puts it, "This is a case in which incentives are improved by cutting the benefits of the rich rather than the poor – a refreshing change from most supply-side prescriptions."[96]

As these examples show, many of the distributional consequences of government policies are not what they appear to be on the surface. Often this is because the policies shift incentives in subtle ways. For example, businesses required to pay certain benefits or taxes will adjust so as to shift the real burden elsewhere. Though congressmen spend much time deciding what proportion of Social Security and Medicare contributions should be paid by employers and what proportion by employees, their decisions probably have few significant economic effects. "Economists generally believe that a payroll tax nominally paid by the employer is ultimately borne by the worker in the form of lower wages than he would otherwise receive or in higher prices for what he buys."[97] Similarly, the incidence – that is, the distribution of real costs and benefits – of the corporation income tax is seen quite differently by politicians and the public on the one hand and economists on the other. Almost everyone in the political arena assumes that when they raise this tax, they have hurt the rich more than the poor. Economists find the subject incredibly complicated. After many studies there is still uncertainty about whether corporations shift all or part of the burden to consumers. But even if they shift none of it, the tax is thought to be a far less effective tax on the rich than the progressive income tax. There is wide agreement that the tax is, in Lester Thurow's words, "both unfair and inefficient." There is also widespread support for integrating the corporate and personal income taxes so that low-income taxpayers who own stock through their union pension funds do not pay a high tax rate on their share of corporate income.[98]

As the debate over the incidence of the corporate income tax shows, economists are not always certain who gains and who loses from government policies. But where we are quite unsure about incidence it is hard to make a case for allowing equity concerns to override efficiency benefits. And where economists can provide good information, it may help us resolve thorny issues. It also, of course, may not if the shifting of burdens is so complicated that the public cannot be made to understand and thus demagoguery by candidates remains politically profitable.

COMPENSATING LOSERS

Some equity concerns disappear once one has better information on who gains and who loses. Economists may be secretly pleased when such concerns are dissipated because then they can avoid some very thorny questions about compensating losers. Politics aside, it is hard to design compensation systems that seem fair to all concerned. When a steel plant closes down, some workers will find well-paying jobs in their own community, but only after some delay. Some will quickly find lower-paying jobs in their community. Some will find good-paying jobs in other communities that require them to incur the expense of a long commute. Some will have to move out of town, and still they will have to settle for a lower-paying job. Others may not find another job. And the losses will not be just among steel workers. There will also be losses to the steel company's suppliers and to the retail stores that served their workers. It would obviously be extremely difficult to identify all the short- and long-term losers and provide each with appropriate compensation.

Moreover, if government frequently intervenes with special programs to help those harmed by changes in, say, the steel or auto industries, people may begin to believe that the route to material success is through one's high standing with government officials rather than with consumers.[99] If unions can get special trade-adjustment assistance for their industry, why should they not try for a little more aid, for example, tariff protection, so they do not have to adjust at all?

The competition for special compensation is not just a zero sum game. It is a negative sum game. Even the fellow who wins as many as he loses, loses on balance both because of the unproductive time he, his lawyers, and lobbyists have spent playing the game and because government so often deals with the equity concern by stopping efficient moves and creating inefficient programs (e.g., shoring up failing industries) rather than by simply compensating losers from the larger pie that greater efficiency has made possible. Moreover, in the real world the weakest and poorest are often the last rather than the first to get special consideration. And, as some of the most thoughtful economists know, the costs of the pulling and hauling go far beyond economics since the political fabric is strained when government makes more and more "explicit decisions about the fate of particular groups and communities."[100]

When compensation is needed, economists generally favor providing it to individuals, not to regions or industries. There has been much talk in recent years about regional equity and, in particular, about the problems of the Frost Belt states. Economists write little on the subject because they are uncomfortable with the whole concept of regional equity. Only individuals can do well or poorly, and many in the Frost Belt are doing just fine. Indeed, if per capita income is a fair indicator, the Frost Belt states are richer than the South. The South is growing faster, but from a much lower base.[101] Given the now higher cost of heating houses, it probably makes sense that more people live farther south than formerly. In any case, economists know that the market provides built-in mechanisms to keep regional disparities from becoming too great. If the South should become significantly richer than the Northeast, its politicians will soon be complaining about the businesses fleeing their region for cheap northern labor. [102]

Economists are even more skeptical of tariff protection or special subsidies for particular industries. Such measures can keep additional workers at their jobs in the steel and auto industries, but jobs elsewhere will be lost as other firms export less or other individuals pay for the subsidies rather than for other companies' products. Moreover, the aid to the industry benefits not just those who would otherwise have lost their jobs but also wealthy stockholders and those who remain employed at unionized, above-average wages. By keeping resources needed in growing industries tied up in declining ones, the policies are a source of great inefficiency. In Lester Thurow's words, each of the policies "imprisons us in a low productivity area. If we cannot learn to disinvest, we cannot compete in the modern growth race."[103]

Economists realize that they sound cold-hearted when they speak in this way about the losers from industrial change and about popular policies meant to assist them. But an increasing number of economists think that they must speak this way because economic growth necessitates a willingness to tolerate industrial change that makes some people worse off. Charles Schultze has said that an important advantage of the market as a means of social organization is "its 'devil take the hindmost' approach to questions of individual equity." Schultze explains as follows:

In any except a completely stagnant society, an efficient use of resources means constant change. From the standpoint of static efficiency the more completely and rapidly the economy shifts production to meet changes in consumer tastes, production technologies, resource availability, or locational advantages, the greater the efficiency. From a dynamic standpoint the greater the advances in technology and the faster they are adopted, the greater the efficiency. While these changes on balance generate gains for society in the form of higher living standards, almost every one of them deprives some firms and individuals of income, often temporarily and for only a few, but sometimes permanently and for large numbers.[104]

Neither Schultze nor most other economists favor a completely laissez-faire approach to the problems of industrial dislocation. There is considerable support among economists for compensation schemes for those who would be hurt because of a sudden change in public policy. For example, there would be large efficiency gains if more taxicabs were allowed to operate in New York City and if more trucks could provide services in interstate commerce. However, many taxi and truck owners paid tens of thousands of dollars or more to obtain taxi medallions or trucking certificates. They would suffer large capital losses if others could operate without such medallions or certificates. Some economists have suggested resolving the equity versus efficiency dilemma by giving all New York City taxi drivers an additional medallion with the right to sell it. And there was support among economists for the provision of the 1981 tax act that permitted the owners of motor carrier certificates to write off as tax credits the decline in the value of their certificates consequent to trucking deregulation.[105] Similarly, where an outright elimination of a long-standing subsidy to producers is not possible or advisable, economists want to encourage disinvestment by allowing the subsidy to be transferable by its recipients. Rather than fight farmers in the arid but growing West over their irrigation water subsidies, we could simply let them sell their water for other more highly valued nonagricultural uses.[106]

All these compensation schemes are designed to overcome opposition to efficient policies that nonetheless deprive some of long-standing benefits. Compensation schemes can also help overcome opposition to efficient public policies that impose new burdens on some. A perennial problem for public officials is where to put the power plant, the halfway house, the airport, the dump, the highway, or the oil refinery. The benefits of the projects are often far greater than the costs for the community as a whole, but not for the neighborhood that becomes the facility's home. Economists suggest compensating the losers for their losses so that the equity problem disappears and projects yielding net benefits are not forsaken. Some have proposed auctioning off these facilities to those communities that would settle for the lowest amount of compensation.[107]

Though many economists support compensation schemes like these just mentioned, some have expressed disappointment with the results of other compensation programs. For example, trade adjustment assistance, with its special grants to displaced workers, was once supported by many economists as a way to ease the transition from declining industries while not interfering with free trade. But now many economists believe that the $3 billion program "may make matters worse by encouraging workers to delay retraining or relocating." Robert Samuelson now proposes either abolishing trade adjustment assistance entirely or limiting it to retraining and relocation grants. More generally, Samuelson and Mancur Olson believe that accommodating people's desires for stability and absolute economic security is "the surest formula" for economic failure.[108] There is increasing sentiment among economists for compensating losers only through general policies. Charles Schultze describes this alternative in the following way:

Rather than compensate for each change, use the tax-and-transfer system to ensure that the cumulative effect of all the changes is an income distribution that meets society's standards of fairness and equity.[109]

EQUITY AND THE PRICE MECHANISM

Economists oppose a whole host of politically popular equity measures that involve interference with flexible market-clearing prices. Rent controls, minimum wage laws, and energy price controls are all thought to be of substantial benefit to those with low incomes. Economists wonder. Many upper-middle-income apartment dwellers pay controlled rents.[110] Moreover, though low-income families in controlled apartments gain under rent controls, other low-income families looking for housing lose. A recent poll shows that 98 percent of economists agree that "a ceiling on rents reduces the quantity and quality of housing available."[111] When shortages exist, the poorest citizens will be well represented among those doing without or managing with lower quality. Rent controls also encourage landlords to maintain their profit margins by neglecting maintenance. When property values and the tax base then decline, the poor, especially dependent on public services, are particularly hard hit.

Of those whose wages are boosted by the minimum wage more are teenagers from middle-class families than primary earners from low-income families.[112] Of the total wage income gains from the minimum wage, 47 percent go to families in the top half nationally in terms of income.[113] Minimum wage laws also leave unemployed the workers with the very lowest productivity who are not worth the minimum wage to any employer. Poorly educated, inexperienced workers are thus deprived of the opportunity to improve their productivity through job experience. Moreover, by creating a surplus of labor, minimum wage laws make discrimination costless. In 1948, when the minimum wage was only forty cents an hour, black youth were more likely than white youth to be in the labor force, and they had a lower unemployment rate. Today their unemployment rate is four times higher than in 1948 and twice as high as white youth's. In 1956, when the minimum wage was increased by one-third, nonwhite teenage unemployment increased from 13 percent to more than 24 percent.[114]

Among the greatest beneficiaries of oil price controls were the refiners of oil, who could sell more of their product when they could buy their crude oil at low, controlled prices.[115] Lower-income families spend a somewhat higher proportion of their income on energy than do higher-income families, but the difference is "quite moderate when indirect purchases of energy (that is, energy incorporated in goods) are included."[116]

It is striking that there is almost no support for any of these price control measures even among the most equity-conscious economists. Thus, for example, Kenneth Arrow tried to give equity its due on the petroleum price controls issue by weighting dollar benefits and costs by the income level of the recipient. He assumed that the value of a dollar was inversely proportional to the present income of the recipient. In other words, it is half as valuable to give a dollar to an individual with an income of $20,000 as it is to give a dollar to an individual with an income of $10,000. Arrow found that the efficiency gains (more valued output produced in lower-cost ways) were large enough that decontrol was justified even if one used such weighted dollars and even if no windfall profits tax were passed.[117]

At about the time Arrow wrote, former Senator Henry Jackson (D-Wash.) and others were in a congressional conference committee trying to strike a balance, as Jackson put it, between the interests of consumers and the interests of producers. Economists care first and foremost about consumers' welfare, and they are unconcerned about the welfare of particular firms. Yet they believed that consumers would benefit most in the long run from what Jackson called the producer position (i.e., decontrol).

Once one absorbs a little economics, few public-policy debates appear as one-sided as do those over these price control issues. Proponents of the measures offer ignorance of their actual effects, empty moralisms, and wishful thinking. In 1974 the District of Columbia began rent control as a "temporary" measure until the vacancy rate rose. In 1979 the district housing director said, "Everybody would like to phase [rent control] out. But we need to increase housing production first." What progress had been made on this between 1973 and 1979? Rental units in the district had declined by almost 7 percent.[118] As a local economist said of one of those who wanted rent control, "Until the housing shortage is relieved," he "might as well have said that he intends to hit himself on the head until it stops hurting."[119] In the original act the district council included many provisions that made it unlikely that landlords could earn the 7 percent the council deemed a fair rate of return. But more fundamentally, even a full 7 percent would not ensure that funds for new housing would be forthcoming. With national and international markets available, investors are surely not bound by local determinations of a fair rate of return.

But Sister Bernardine Karge of Catholics Concerned for the Elderly says that "the real [rent control] issue is greed."[120] And my two local state representatives say, on the minimum wage, "I do not think it is too much to require that able bodied men and women be paid [the new state minimum]" and "we will have to hope that the small percentage that lose their jobs ... are able to find another soon."[121]

The real issue is, in large measure, ignorance. Economists like to look for rational, hidden interests at work. The anti-growth upper middle class has narrowly self-interested reasons for wanting rent control laws so effective at stopping construction that might cause crowding in their neighborhoods. And skilled union laborers know that the minimum wage raises both the demand for their services and their wages by making their competitors, unskilled labor, more expensive and thus less attractive to employers.[122] These effects are present, but they do not explain Sister Karge's beliefs or those of my intelligent, public-spirited representatives. Ignorance of economics goes a long way toward doing so. What economists know does not travel far in the groves of academe, much less beyond. My representative thinks that the percentage who lose their jobs is small. But one recent study shows that if the minimum wage increases pay and costs by 11 percent, it reduces employment among sixteen- and seventeen-year olds by 27 percent and among eighteen- and nineteen-year-olds by 15 percent.[123] In 1971, ninety-nine witnesses in the House and seventy-seven in the Senate testified on the minimum wage. Of the total, only one was a mainstream economist. More typical were representatives of the International Ladies Garment Workers Union, the Amalgamated Meat Cutters and the National Council of Churches on one side and the South Carolina Restaurant Association and the Menswear Retailers of America on the other. It is easy to see why congressmen might see the issue as a simple question of equity between business and labor.

Economics as a discipline has weaknesses, but one of them is not a lack of understanding of how markets work. If economists are convinced that these price control measures are more costly, less effective, and less equitable than alternatives such as wage subsidies or housing vouchers, many others could be convinced as well if they knew what economists knew.[124]

HOW TO REDISTRIBUTE: IN KIND VERSUS IN CASH

If a society wants to help its members with low incomes, it can give them food, medical care, housing, transportation, and the like. Or it can give them cash. Most economists favor giving cash. In the poll of economists cited earlier, the proposition "Cash payments are superior to transfers-in-kind" enjoyed overwhelming support: 68 percent "generally agreed"; 24 percent "agreed with provisions"; and only 8 percent "generally disagreed."[125]

The general public's views are very different. In 1969, a sample of Americans was asked if they would support a guaranteed income plan with a minimum set at $3,200. Substantial majorities were opposed. Even among those who themselves had incomes under $3,000 a year, 44 percent were opposed and only 43 percent were in favor.[126] By way of contrast, cuts in most in-kind programs are unpopular. When President Nixon proposed such cuts in 1973, over 60 percent opposed him on Job Corps and Head Start, over 70 percent objected to cuts in hospital and school lunch aid, and 92 percent thought the elderly should not have to pay more of the costs of medicine.[127] Some economists have speculated that the public's preference for in-kind transfers stems from tangible external costs (such as crime, disease, and delinquency) that they can avoid if the poor have better housing, medical care, and the like. Others have thought it more likely that the well-off simply want to avoid the psychic suffering that occurs when they see how the poor live. Still others think the nonpoor are paternalistic altruists who think they know what the poor need better than the poor themselves do. Whatever the reason, if the public's preferences for in-kind aid are fairly strong, consumer sovereignty and economic efficiency suggest the need for in-kind subsidies so as to take account of these external benefits for the nonpoor when the poor consume specific goods and services.

One does occasionally hear economists making this argument.[128] And some forms of in-kind aid such as medical care and education enjoy fairly wide support in the profession.[129] But for most economists, support for many in-kind measures is grudging or nonexistent. Even supporters of in-kind aid seem to prefer in-cash assistance but think the public will support only in-kind aid. The latter then becomes a desired second-best measure – better than no redistribution at all.[130]

One cannot understand the consensus among economists on this issue without some discussion of their evaluations of particular in-kind programs. Economists have found, for example, that public housing costs anywhere from 10 percent to 100 percent more than equivalent private units. They also find that most beneficiaries of housing programs value their units at much less than the cash equivalent of the units' fair market value.[131] This last observation is not surprising since the whole point of the in-kind subsidy is to induce the poor to consume more housing than they would choose, given their income level. Still, from the point of view of the poor, the housing subsidies are much less valuable than an equivalent amount of cash would be. The special benefits to the nonpoor of in-kind aid would have to be large, if the inefficient use of resources from the point of view of the poor is to be outweighed. After adding the consumption inefficiencies (from the point of view of the poor) and the costly production inefficiencies of public housing, one recent study estimates that the average recipient of housing assistance would be perfectly willing to have the subsidy cease if he received an unrestricted cash grant costing taxpayers only 61 percent of the cost of the housing subsidy. Or, by spending the same amount of money, a switch to cash grants could increase the perceived benefits to subsidized families by 66 percent.[132]

The housing programs are also quite inequitable. The neediest often get less assistance than those with higher incomes. Families in equivalent circumstances do not get equivalent assistance. Moreover, the subsidized housing is frequently better than the typical housing of families just above the upper income limit for eligibility.[133]

Many of the production inefficiencies and inequities could be eliminated by replacing all current subsidy programs with a housing allowance. The allowance would consist of a cash grant given to all low-income families on the condition that they occupy housing meeting certain standards. The Experimental Housing Allowance Program has tested this voucher idea and found that, contrary to critics' expectations,[134] competitive pressures kept landlords from simply pocketing the money without providing better housing.[135] Almost all economists who support any kind of special housing assistance at all support some variant of a housing allowance program.[136]

This support for a voucher approach to housing might lead one to think that the food stamp voucher program is a favorite of economists. It is not. They point out that the administrative costs are higher than they would be for a straight cash-transfer program. Moreover, to the extent that the subsidy induces the poor to consume more food than they want to, given their income, the stamps do not give a dollar's worth of benefit to recipients for every dollar of cost to taxpayers. Tobin, as well as more conservative economists, concludes that food stamps are simply "an inferior currency."[137]

The literature on food stamps is not surprising if one reads the pro-housing voucher studies carefully. These studies show that even though the vouchers are much better than current programs, the benefits, as perceived by recipients, are well under the dollar cost to taxpayers.

It is only a slight exaggeration to say that most mainstream economists have silently united on a grand strategy. First, they will convince the rest of us that vouchers, which let competitive market forces work for efficiency and allow some freedom of choice to consumers, are preferable to all in-kind programs in which government provides services directly. Then, with the interim goal achieved, they will point out that for many families the vouchers do not increase consumption of housing and food any more than a straight cash grant would.[138] Moreover, the administrative costs are higher and the inequities from a lack of perfect meshing of programs are greater with the multiple in-kind programs. And since in any case 88 percent of poor people's income goes to basic needs – food, housing, medical care, transportation, and clothing – why not just cash everything out and put an end to the inefficiencies and inequities?[139]

James Tobin nicely contrasts the layman's and the economist's perspectives on these issues:

While concerned laymen who observe people with shabby housing or too little to eat instinctively want to provide them with decent housing and adequate food, economists instinctively want to provide them with more cash income. Then they can buy the housing and food if they want to, and if they choose not to, the presumption is that they have a better use for the money. To those who complain about the unequal distribution of shelter or of food, our first response . . . is that they should look at the distribution of wealth and income. If the social critics approve that distribution, then they should accept its implications, including the unequal distribution of specific commodities. If they don't like it, then they should attack the generalized inequality rather than the specific inequality.[140]

CONCLUSION

Noneconomists can learn much from the economic literature on equity. By reminding us of the allocative function of wages and profits and of the effect of high marginal tax rates on work, on savings, and on economic growth, economists set certain reasonable boundaries to intelligent debate about income redistribution. Moreover, by figuring the magnitude and incidence of gains and losses from policy measures, they help to eliminate some equity concerns and channel others in more fruitful directions. The presumption against compensating losing regions or producers seems justified. So does that against interfering with flexible market-clearing prices in pursuit of equity goals. And in spite of the reservations voiced later in this chapter about economists' opposition to almost all in-kind transfers, there can be no doubt that these have been overused in recent years.

As indicated at the start of this chapter, the most common criticism of the economic approach to public policy is that it overemphasizes efficiency and neglects equity. After reading economists' criticisms of several social welfare programs, many of my students have concluded that the whole profession is cold and uncaring. They look at the many areas where the poor have much less than they have, and they want to close the gap in one area after the other. For example, if they learn that some low-income people have great difficulty getting into town from rural areas, they approve of the federally funded Jaunt Program, which serves the "rural and special transportation needs" of our outlying counties.

Economists would oppose Jaunt. They would think it silly to set up a separate, federally funded transportation system with administrators at several levels to serve such a need. The costs per passenger mile traveled are extremely high. More important, those served have many needs. Since the funds for social welfare programs are limited, attempts to make dramatic improvements in the poor's access to some goods or services inevitably mean that the poor will fall far short of adequacy in others. In 1981, there were 550 separate grant programs to the states and localities.[141] Each required administrators to run them. They thus helped contribute to a situation in which white-collar professionals received far more of the money spent for social welfare programs than did the poor.[142]

The fact that most economists want a smaller government doing fewer things does not necessarily mean that they want a conservative government or one without power to help the poor. A government that did little more than take money from the rich and give it to the poor might nonetheless be quite powerful and quite radical.

I see only two ways in which the economic framework and economic studies might be seen as biased toward conservative positions. First, even comprehensive statements by liberal economists, such as Okun and Thurow, speak only of the domestic distribution of income. Such statements ignore the far greater inequalities worldwide. Second, through discussion of many specific inequalities that the poor put up with, the nonpoor are constantly and dramatically reminded of the plight of those with low incomes. Ending most in-kind programs, as economists wish to, would eliminate the educative function of the debate and of the programs themselves. The public's willingness to support social welfare programs might then be reduced. As Steven Kelman has noted, the advocate of cash transfers is

constantly urging people to stifle natural inclinations of sympathy for the plight of others. He urges them instead to avoid taking account of equity in the given areas where it most naturally arises in people's minds – and instead, if they are interested, in some other time and place, to work for a cash transfer to the unfortunate. The result would be a sort of "I gave at the office" mentality, where people give and then don't think about the disadvantaged for the rest of the year.[143]

Kelman's is a powerful argument. But if the economist's mode of reasoning has such an effect, it is surely an unintended one. Remember that economists are usually quick to disregard the nonpoor's preferences for in-kind aid, in large measure because they want to raise the poor's sense of well-being further than in-kind transfers allow. Moreover, most economists prefer to frame discussion in terms of the distribution of income shares rather than in terms of an official poverty level or any other minimum living standard set in absolute terms.[144] By so doing, they help ensure that the relative plight of those with low income will always be a public issue and will not die away as growth continues and the "war on poverty" is won.

From the point of view of the public this whole focus on the distribution of income seems radical, not conservative. Wilbur Cohen has noted that despite economists' interest, there was little congressional discussion of redistributing income or a negative income tax in the 1960s. He explained that "very few members of Congress want to discuss it in those terms because for their constituents that is socialism."[145] So it seems. In 1981, 75 percent of a sample of Americans were opposed to placing a $100,000 limit on income that can be earned. By a margin of 57 percent to 33 percent, those with incomes under $5,000 also expressed opposition.[146] In 1976 a Harris survey asked if those polled wanted the "federal government to try to make a fairer distribution of the wealth of the country." By using "fairer" rather than "more equal" and "wealth" not "income" the question seemed designed to produce favorable responses. Yet 47 percent said no and 38 percent yes.[147]

Americans support programs that provide a minimally acceptable standard of living for those who cannot help themselves. They believe that taxpayers should contribute more to such programs if they have a greater ability to do so. But with these qualifications, they believe that people have a right to keep what they earn.[148]

The public's views seem quite faithful to those of the Founding Fathers. As *Federalist Paper* number 10 reminds us, the founders thought "the protection of different and unequal faculties of acquiring property," "the first object of government." The founders in turn followed Locke, who believed that "every man has a property in his own person; this nobody has any right to but himself. The labor of his body and the work of his hands, we may say, are properly his."[149]

In the contemporary context this thought sounds conservative. It has had no effect on the way most economists examine equity questions. They are intellectual descendants not of Locke, but of Bentham, who took special delight in ridiculing natural rights. Bentham feared that belief in such rights would prevent progressive, utility-based legislation.[150] Most economists fear the same. When necessary, they want to be able to rearrange property rights so that more efficient outcomes are obtained.[151] Moreover, though they cannot prove that the poor get more utility from added dollars than the rich, most believe that they do.[152] And they want to try to maximize utility. Remember the 1978 poll showing (in the wake of the redistributive efforts of the previous decade and before the Reagan Administration's cuts) a majority preference for more equality in the distribution of income.

As Irving Kristol has noted, the very term "distribution of income" "casts a pall of suspicion over existing inequalities, implying as it does that incomes are not personally *earned* but somehow *received* as the end product of ... political-economic machinations."[153] The Founding Fathers saw the right to property – the fruits of one's labor – as based on natural law. Most economists, on the other hand, grant society the right to determine what is a fair share of income for all individuals within it. For the economists, not rights, but only a much-debated, inconclusive concern with efficiency should restrain society from dividing up the fruits of an individual's labor in any way it sees fit. That is not a conservative point of view. Nor does it seem to me superior to that of the founders and the general public.

As Marc Plattner has argued, the politicization of the distribution issue in the absence of any fundamental belief in the right to keep what one earns is likely to lead to self-interested ballots more often than charitable ones. Moreover, the "uncertainty about the safety of one's wealth and the prospects of one's future income ... would be bound to have a deleterious effect not only on incentives but also on the general feeling of political and economic security enjoyed by the citizenry."[154]

Economists frequently give no more deference to worthiness among the poor than to property rights among the nonpoor. When designing programs for those with low incomes, they tend to resist any attempts to distinguish among widows or veterans on the one hand and the lazy or dissolute on the other.[155] When I was at the U.S. Bureau of the Budget in the 1960s, I was struck by the antagonism of economists toward all veterans programs. As one memorandum said, "Special housing goals for veterans simply because they are veterans is not a sufficient goal. It does not fill an unmet need, as veterans today are at no more disadvantage in home buying than any other citizen."[156] Economists would be even more adamant on the subject today, now that the volunteer army pays an "appropriate" competitive wage. Here the economist's belief that recipients always prefer cash to in-kind benefits fails him. People do not join the Marines because the pay is good. The organization will not perform its function as well if they ever do. Veterans want and deserve the special praise and recognition, the honor that categorical programs help provide. They cannot buy that honor. We should not "cash out" the Iwo Jima memorial.

Economists resist rights, worthiness, absolute thresholds for poverty, and in-kind programs based on "minimum standards." In part they resist because marginalism teaches them to resist all absolutes. More fundamentally, they resist because of their theory of social welfare – that revised utilitarianism that focuses on outcomes as judged by consumers. A full discussion of the consumer-sovereignty assumption must be postponed until Chapter 9, but an assessment of the economic work on equity requires a preliminary examination here.

As Thurow notes, "At the heart of the economist's love affair with cash transfers is the doctrine of absolute consumer sovereignty."[157] This doctrine explains why economists have so little interest in aspects of in-kind voucher programs that noneconomists think crucial. Economists comment on the lack of good evidence on the nutritional effect of the food stamp program.[158] But no Ph.D. dissertation in economics ever sets out to investigate the subject.[159] Browning and Browning's text explains why.

> Any improvement in food consumption and nutrition comes at the expense of a reduction in consumption of other goods, which might include housing, medical care, education, clothing, drugs, or alcohol. In any event, the other goods sacrificed are considered more valuable to the recipient than the food or nutrition gained. Why should an improvement in nutrition be considered desirable if the recipient is worse off than with a cash transfer? That is the basic question, irrespective of whether nutrition is improved or not.[160]

Similarly, Richard Zeckhauser has been quite critical of in-kind efforts to reduce life-threatening risks facing the poor. He sees the poor's fundamental problem as low income and views our safety and health efforts as a means of "salving the conscience of the middle class at the expense of the welfare of the poor."[161]

If economists had more open minds on the consumer-sovereignty assumption, they would be more curious about the explanation for a startling series of facts. Despite extraordinary outreach efforts, less than one-half of eligible households participated in the Experimental Housing Allowance Program. Similarly, in 1977 fewer than half of all eligible households were participating in the food stamp program. And the supplemental security income cash program for the elderly poor attracted only 60 percent participation.[162]

Who are these nonparticipants? Are they self-reliant people who are doing better than we might think possible and who want no part of "welfare" and government bureaucrats? Or are large numbers senile, mentally ill, alcoholic, drug addicted, ignorant, or totally demoralized – people who cannot cope sufficiently to take advantage of a voucher program? Economists rarely ask these questions. They seem puzzled by the low participation rates.[163] They would expect an awfully high demand for free goods. But most do not really seem troubled. Few seem to think they ought to go out to see how the nonparticipants are really living. Fieldwork among the economic experts on these programs is almost nonexistent.[164] Instead, the typical new improved study develops a more ingenious methodology for manipulating existing data. It seeks to develop a more accurate estimate of just how much cash the minority of the poor who are program participants would need to make them as well off as they are with the current in-kind program.

Even among those who do participate in voucher or cash programs, there will be people not helped in any significant way. Among noneconomists there is recognition of cultural pathologies among large numbers of the poor.[165] These are not likely to be overcome by housing vouchers or negative income taxes. A more equal distribution of income will do the able-bodied poor little good if it means that they are more firmly in the grip of dependency.

Most economists shudder at such paternalism. If the poor have more cash, they command more resources. They have more of what Thomas Hobbes called power, "present means to obtain some future apparent good."[166] Cash to an economist is a multipurpose means that is almost as universally useful as power was to Hobbes. With cash the poor can get more of what they want. They are thus better off. Even the hard case of the guy who sacrifices nutrition for drugs and alcohol is not in fact a hard case. As the Brownings say, he would be "worse off" with the nutrition.

Socrates would argue that some "apparent" goods (e.g., drugs for a drug addict) are not real goods. He would also argue that cash is not a crucial means to many important goods. If one seeks wisdom, for example, he needs most of all not money, but means such as native intelligence, self-discipline, and access to good teachers (or today perhaps a public library). One cannot know what power is, what means one needs, until one knows what the good things in life are.[167] Economists do not rebut Socrates. Like Callicles in the *Gorgias*, they try to ignore him. No one knows what the good things in life are. That is for each individual to decide. But cash will best help each get what he wants.[168]

It is important to understand that when the economist is concerned about work effort, he is not concerned about what dependency does to the poor. If a high benefit-reduction rate keeps a poor person who would like to work from doing so, that is cause for concern. But if high welfare benefits induce a poor person to quit his job or not to want one in the first place, whatever the tax rate, then he is better off on welfare without the job. The work effort problem exists because the nonpoor are unhappy that they now must pay to support him.[169]

Noneconomists, unchained to the consumer-sovereignty assumption, can see the problem differently. They see dependency as degrading, humiliating, and dehumanizing.[170] And "whenever a person's sense of control over his own life is expanded; whenever he sees himself as the source of his own pleasures and security, his pride increases, his self-esteem increases."[171] His capacity for caring for others and for living a good life increases proportionately.

Though economics has progressed in many ways through the years, it has forgotten as much as it has learned about the problem of poverty. Adam Smith could see that the problem was not fundamentally one of inadequate income. The poor had the "necessities of nature" and a little more besides. But they were ashamed of how others saw them.[172] More cash payments will not make the shame go away.[173]

I do not pretend to expertise on the poverty problem. I am sure that there are no simple answers. I understand that work is not a realistic possibility for many of the poor. Moreover, the economic critique of many existing in-kind programs is quite persuasive. And I understand that in-kind aid with strings attached can sometimes create dependency, not fight it. But if one were willing to see dependency as a tragedy for the dependent rather than a rational choice, in-kind programs that build up the dependent able-bodied poor's basic skills and their confidence in their ability to find and hold a job might be more attractive. So might subsidized, enriched day-care programs.[174] A humane, dependency-fighting policy might mix such programs with less income-equalizing in-cash aid, not more.[175] The economist's framework for discussing equity does not allow for serious consideration of such matters. Thus, despite economists' prominent role in proposing alternatives to existing programs and despite the good sense of many of their suggestions, the discipline is unlikely to make major contributions to solving one of our principal domestic problems – pockets of dependency and poverty in a land of plenty.

7

EXTERNALITIES AND THE
GOVERNMENT AGENDA

For those concerned with public policy none of the concepts in the economist's kit is more important than externality. Externalities are the most pervasive kind of market imperfection that may justify government intervention. When economists discuss "the desirable scope of government," the externality concept is at the center of their analysis.[1] When a government role can be justified, economists also use the externality concept to determine what level of government should take responsibility.

WHY EXTERNALITIES MAY NOT JUSTIFY GOVERNMENT
INTERVENTION

In Chapter 5 externalities were defined as nonpriced effects on third parties that are not transmitted through the price system and that arise as an incidental by-product of another person's or firm's activity. As explained there, externalities are everywhere. External benefits can be caused by education or by newly planted flowers; external costs are produced by serious air pollution or by crabgrass.

The parallel concept of government failure helps explain why economists do not think widespread externalities justify widespread government intervention. Other elements from the theoretical literature on externalities also support a cautious approach to government intervention to correct for externalities.

First, when property rights are clearly defined and small numbers of people are involved, private action may take account of externalities without government involvement. For example, if a retailer thinks a run-down neighboring store hurts his business, he can buy it out or subsidize the refurbishing. Or if a townhouse developer thinks potential buyers' concerns about noise from or external maintenance of the development's other units will suppress his houses' value, he can build quieter units or arrange for cooperative provision of exterior painting and landscaping.[2]

Second, many effects on third parties, both beneficial and harmful, are transmitted through the price system and are not real externalities as economists define them. Real externalities occur when the market's price system inefficiently breaks down, that is, when it does not take account of some people's preferences. When a factory dumps harmful pollutants in the river, an inefficient externality is present since neither the factory's managers nor the customers who buy the firm's product take into account the preferences of downstream water users. The cost to downstream users has no effect on profits or product price. The market's price system slips up. On the other hand, when a manufacturer harms competitors by expanding output and thus forcing down prices, this effect on competitors is not inefficient and is thus not an externality. The effect is transmitted through the price system, in the form of lower prices, not outside it. If the manufacturer who had expanded production were forced to cut back and raise prices again to take account of the adverse effect his actions had had on rival businesses, customers would lose at least a dollar for every one the rival businesses gained.[3] When Henry Ford put buggy whip manufacturers out of business, the effect on them was quite serious, but there was no inefficiency because Ford and his customers gained more than the buggy whip manufacturers lost. Changes in tastes and technology are constantly having both beneficial and harmful effects on employers, employees, stockholders, and even consumers (e.g., when a big popular chain restaurant with many potential customers buys out a small, struggling eatery with a loyal clientele). Most of these effects are captured by the price system and are not externalities as economists define them.[4]

Third, externalities that are in principle relevant may not justify government intervention in the case at hand. Third parties are affected adversely by noise and positively by education. But we already have noise ordinances and education subsidies that take account of these externalities to some degree. Perhaps the marginal benefits of further efforts along these lines are smaller than the marginal costs.

Finally, government intervention can rarely be justified to take account of small externalities. Many homeowners are bothered by the effect of their neighbors' crabgrass on their own lawns. Some of these homeowners buy weed killers and spend unpleasant summer afternoons killing crabgrass that would not be so prevalent if their neighbors were more attentive to their own lawns. But some of those neighbors could not care less about crabgrass. If a law were passed requiring them to rid their lawns of crabgrass, *they* would feel unnecessarily put upon. And there would be costs to the public for the inspectors and courts necessary to enforce the law. Government intervention to correct for an externality can be justified only if the benefits of adjusting for the externality exceed the costs of doing so. And estimates about these benefits and costs should not assume ideal implementation untouched by the government failure problem discussed in Chapter 5.[5]

EXTERNALITIES AND THE DESIRABLE SCOPE OF GOVERNMENT

In some cases the externality concept provides fairly clear guidance about the need for government involvement. It can, for example, show the inadequacy of reliance on voluntary action as the means for cleaning up pollution and securing obedience to pollution standards. In recent years, the Chemical Manufacturers Association has advertised widely in an effort to convince the public that government does not need to force the industry to clean up the environment because the chemical industry is already doing everything it can to keep it clean. In one newspaper advertisement, Ken Ficek, a water specialist with the chemical industry, is pictured smiling while his wife and two children fish in the background. Ken tells readers that he is working to control water pollution in two ways. First, he helps develop chemicals used by municipalities and industries to purify drinking water and treat wastewater. Second, he is working to make sure that the water his own company discharges is "safe for our rivers." Ken tells readers that the chemical industry has 10,000 specialists whose sole job is controlling pollution and that he himself has been working to combat pollution for twenty years. He notes that the industry has already spent $15.3 billion on projects to protect the environment. Ken's fundamental message is simple: The owners and employees in the chemical industry are concerned about the same things we the public are, because they too must live in the environment they create:

I work at improving water quality all over the country. And here in my own neighborhood . . . the job we're doing is improving the environment for all of us.[6]

According to Ken, because "all of us" want a clean environment, it is not necessary for government to compel industry to clean up. Industry will clean up voluntarily because its interests are our interests. (Note Ken's comment that he was working hard on water quality twenty years ago, long before the major federal water-quality legislation was passed.)

Anne Gorsuch Burford, the first administrator of the Environmental Protection Agency under President Reagan, seemed persuaded by Ken's argument. She and her top aides continually emphasized volunteerism. In 1982 her agency was commended by the president's Task Force on Private-Sector Initiatives for its emphasis on "voluntary compliance with environmental laws." Even in the wake of his forced resignation in March of 1983, Burford's general counsel, Robert Perry, was telling the press, "It's ultimately voluntary compliance that is going to clean up this nation."[7]

Anne Gorsuch Burford's successor, William Ruckelshaus, is unpersuaded by Ken's argument. Ruckelshaus says there is "no way in the world" that voluntarism can work because if even one firm does not comply (and therefore achieves lower prices by avoiding the costs of compliance) other competitive firms will not be able to comply either.

The only way the free enterprise system can work is if there is a framework for competition that roughly provides the same kind of requirement on everybody to protect the free externalities of air and water and land . . . So there has to be a regulatory program, and it has to be an effective national regulatory program.[8]

The externality concept suggests that we should side with Ruckelshaus rather than Burford and Ken Ficek. The owners of chemical firms and their employees do not have the same interests as the rest of us. Many of the chemicals dumped in "our rivers" will end up in other people's neighborhoods far from the homes of chemical industry employees. But even if all the pollution caused by the chemicals remained in the communities surrounding the chemical plants, the plants' owners and employees would have different interests than others in the community. As Ken Ficek notes, everyone, chemical plant employees and their neighbors, would share in the benefits of cleaner water. But the costs of cleaning up would be far higher for owners and employees than for their neighbors. If chemical firms devote major efforts to reducing the pollution resulting from their manufacturing processes, their costs will increase significantly. The price of their products will thus rise, and demand for those products will fall. Profits in the industry will then fall as well. Some employees will lose their jobs as business declines, and others may lose their raises. If allowed to decide for themselves ("voluntarism"), the chemical companies may conclude that the costs of certain pollution-control efforts – costs borne mainly by their management, stockholders, employees (and customers) – exceed the benefits. But most of the total costs of pollution and the gains from ending it accrue to those with no connection to the industry; that is, they are external effects on third parties whose interests are likely to be ignored in the decision-making process. If one considers the benefits of reducing pollution to the entire community, the pollution-control efforts might well be efficient and justified.

Well before Ann Gorsuch Burford took office, there was ample evidence of what simple reflection on the externality concept would have suggested – that voluntarism will not get the pollution abatement job done. In the early 1960s the auto companies assured the public that they wanted to move faster on emissions controls, but the problem was difficult. In 1963 California got tired of waiting. It set up a board to examine and certify proposed emission-control systems. It also passed a law requiring exhaust systems on all new cars sold in California one year after the state certified that two practical systems were available at reasonable cost. This law gave equipment manufacturers new incentives. By June of 1964 the state certified four devices, all made by independent parts manufacturers. Emissions-control devices would thus be required for the 1966 model cars.

As economist Lawrence White has noted,

The results were startling. Three months earlier, in March 1964, the automobile companies had told the state that the 1967 model year was the earliest that they could install emissions control devices. (It is worth noting that a decade earlier they had told government officials that devices might be installed as early as 1958.) The June certification miraculously speeded their technological development programs. In August 1964 they announced that, after all, they would be able to install exhaust devices on their 1966 model cars – devices of their own manufacture.[9]

External costs that (sometimes) necessitate government intervention also occur with traffic congestion. My students occasionally argue that there is no market failure with traffic congestion because the person who drives at eight in the morning rather than ten is surely made aware of the costs of congestion. But again the driver considers only the costs to himself. He knows, for example, that it may take him twenty minutes longer to drive at rush hour, but he does not consider that if he does drive at eight (and thereby *adds* to the congestion), it may take hundreds or even thousands of other cars on the road three seconds longer as well. Typically, the total congestion costs flowing from the individual's decision to drive are, in aggregate, far greater to the many others affected than to the driver in question. If congestion becomes severe, government intervention is necessary to correct for these external costs.

How government should intervene remains an open question. Highway officials often argue that by showing their willingness to continue driving when roads are congested, the people are telling us that they want more roads. Economists are not so sure. They usually prefer schemes to make people consider the external costs of rush-hour driving such as selling special expensive stickers that cars must display on certain highways during heavy-traffic hours. This may cure the congestion. If congestion continues despite high sticker fees – high enough to pay for a new road and to cover the environmental costs of constructing and using it – then a new road should be built.[10]

Knowledge of the appropriate limits to the externality justification for government involvement can also help one reject special pleas for involvement that rely on bogus externalities. Without using the economists' terminology, general aviation[11] interest groups have, in effect, used the positive side of the externality concept when arguing that benefits to the nonflying public justify continuing their aviation facilities subsidy. The benefits listed have included gains to complementary industries and thus GNP, to defense capability in time of war, to mail service, and to disaster-relief operations.

Throughout the last two decades government economists have argued that none of these benefits could possibly justify existing policy that makes the general public pay over 80 percent of the costs the Federal Aviation Administration incurs in support of general aviation. Some of the nonflying public does benefit from the availability of airmail and fresh Hawaiian fruit, but those who enjoy these benefits should expect to pay for them. (There are no external benefits for you when I eat Hawaiian fruit or send my mother an airmail letter.) Though the Hawaiian fruit producers have a bigger market because of air travel, the local ice cream manufacturer has a smaller one. Both contribute to GNP, and neither should expect transportation subsidies that prevent consumers from making choices based on prices reflecting the opportunity costs of production.[12]

The general public does benefit from having a fully operational airport and airway system available in the event of war. But as one government economist has said,

There is no reason to believe that such benefits differ sufficiently in either substance or amounts from the secondary benefits of a host of other industries, such as steel, chemicals, and electronics – none of which have part of their costs of doing business paid from the general tax revenues of the federal government.[13]

Moreover, we already have an extensive aviation system. When considering a subsidized, *further* expansion of aviation, we should think only of the consequent defense and disaster-relief benefits to the nonflying public that would *not* be available in the absence of the subsidy. These *marginal* benefits are almost certainly quite small, perhaps less than the additional external costs of noise pollution to which many nonflyers would be subjected.[14]

Supporters of subsidies for railroad passenger travel also point to presumed externalities as their justification. Throughout the last decade the Interstate Commerce Commission and many congressmen have criticized the Department of Transportation when it proposed the abandonment of routes along which Amtrak was typically taking in only one dollar of revenue for every five dollars of cost. In 1978 the ICC said that public opposition to proposed cutbacks "has helped demonstrate that human needs, which transcend the simple criteria of profit and loss, may indicate a demand for continued intercity rail passenger service even if that means more federal funding."[15] On other occasions the ICC has been more specific, claiming general public benefits from reduced energy consumption, highway congestion, and automotive air pollution. For particular routes they have been more specific still. It is argued that service between Chicago and San Francisco should be preserved because trains pass through the Feather River Canyon, and the spectacular scenery there makes the trains a unique national asset. Trains to the Tampa-St. Petersburg area are essential because it has "a large number of elderly and retired people who are especially dependent upon rail service." And service to Mexico City is important to our good neighbor policy toward Latin America.[16]

The externality concept helps us sift through these arguments. Public outcry at the loss of service is not necessarily a sign that a criterion of profit and loss must be missing something. The outcry only shows that the people who use the trains would benefit from continuation of the service when they pay 20 percent of the cost. If most of these would still benefit even if they paid far more, Amtrak would have raised fares long ago. Some of the current passengers might be willing to pay five times as much, but this is not conclusive either. Most failing businesses have some customers right up to the time they close their doors. They just do not have enough of them to cover their costs.

Reductions in energy consumption, in congestion, and in pollution all yield benefits to those who do not travel by train. The externality, however, results not from the positive side effects of train travel, but from avoiding the negative side effects of other modes of travel that consume more energy, produce more congestion, or pollute more. If we subsidize train travel as a means of reducing energy consumption, congestion, and pollution, we will end up with an inefficiently large percentage of society's resources in the railroad industry since fares will be lower than the marginal costs of providing the services. This suggests that the appropriate policy is not a subsidy, but rather a tax on the adverse side effects of travel.

Even as a second-best policy, current subsidies to Amtrak cannot be justified on these externality grounds. A Congressional Budget Office study finds that passenger trains outside the Northeast corridor are less energy efficient than automobiles and far less efficient than buses. The most heavily subsidized trains are outside the Northeast corridor, and they do little to reduce highway congestion. And the potential for pollution reduction is small since even a doubling of intercity railroad travel would leave trains with less than 1 percent of total intercity travel. The pollution-reduction gains to the rest of us if others more often traveled by train would surely not be four times greater than the benefits received by the train travelers themselves.

The concern about the scenery in the Feather River Canyon does not point to an externality. The scenic benefits of the canyon will not disappear if the trains do. Moreover, it is those on the train, not the rest of us, who benefit from the beautiful scenery. This should help Amtrak sell tickets. Yet, it still cannot compete with planes, which get people where they are going much faster and, subsidies aside, at far less cost.

Some of my students are at first quite sympathetic to those retirees in Tampa-St. Petersburg who are "especially dependent" on rail service. But even an advocate of some in-kind transfers can find little reason to defend this subsidy. The subsidy (over $100 per passenger for travel from New York) benefits everyone, young and old, rich and poor. Most people on the trains are not elderly. Most of the elderly on them are not poor. Our poorest citizens rarely retire to Florida and then travel frequently by interstate train. Those who do are not "especially dependent" as long as buses are also available. Some minimum level of food, shelter, and medical care may now be the birthright of every American. But if we keep opportunity costs in mind I think we will draw the line before we reach subsidized train service to Tampa-St. Petersburg.

To a noneconomist the good neighbor policy to Latin America may seem the flimsiest justification of all. But here we have an externality (assuming ill will in Mexico if train service is discontinued). Everyone benefits from good relationships with Mexico, not just those citizens who travel there by train. When considering whether to continue the train, an economist would want to know how great the needed subsidy was. Then he might ask the State Department if it could think of alternative measures that would do as much for relations with Mexico and cost less. If it could, the subsidy would not be justified. If it could not, some judgment would have to be made about whether the opportunity costs of the subsidy or the costs in relations with Mexico were greater.[17]

The externality concept gives useful guidance about the need for government intervention in the aforementioned cases. But in a large number of cases its teaching is less clear. It is easy to show that the problem of market failure is far greater for environmental pollution than for occupational safety. Most of the benefits from reduced pollution go to those outside the firm, whereas most of the benefits from better occupational safety go to the firm's own employees.[18] But just because the externality case for an environmental agency is stronger than the case for an occupational safety administration does not mean that the case for the latter cannot be made. Even if one ignores friends and relatives, others are affected by the higher health and life insurance premiums that result from inadequate occupational safety measures. Also, some feel psychic pain from deaths and injuries incurred on the job by strangers.

Similar ambiguity often arises if one looks at the case for various measures within an agency. A better case can be made for requiring automobiles to have features such as dual brake systems or good tires than for requiring them to have collapsible steering wheels. Drivers and pedestrians outside the car are helped by the former, but not the latter. Indeed if the collapsible steering wheel leads to more aggressive driving,[19] there may be negative externalities for other drivers and pedestrians.

There will, however, also be positive externalities like those associated with occupational safety programs. Economists are likely to point to more appropriate policies to take account of these sorts of pervasive financial and psychic externalities. Some have argued, for example, in favor of more severe penalties for speeding and steeper taxes on alcohol.[20] Others have mentioned the loss of liberty that occurs when we let financial external costs (such as higher health insurance premiums) justify coercing people into doing what they do not believe is in their interest (e.g., buying collapsible steering wheels or eating more vegetables).[21] Still the externality case for making collapsible steering wheels mandatory cannot be conclusively refuted. It may help to know that it is less urgent than other measures, but it cannot be ruled out.

Economists discussing agencies such as the Occupational Safety and Health Administration and the National Highway Traffic and Safety Administration tend to first show that the market will bring some safety improvements on its own. Because workers and consumers want safe jobs and safe cars, they will demand and get a certain measure of safety even without government involvement. After making this point, economists then mention the positive externalities discussed earlier. But, in part because the agencies seem certain to survive whatever the theoretical case for their existence, these discussions are often quite brief and inconclusive.[22] Accepting the decision to intervene, economists put most of their effort into suggesting better methods of intervention.

EXTERNALITIES AND FEDERALISM

Most economists who have thought about the question seem to support a federal system of government where national, regional, and local bodies share power. Though the traditional political reasons for preserving local power are sometimes mentioned, economists focus on the justification that flows from the externality or spillover concept. There are external benefits associated with street lights and police services and external costs associated with fires, noise, and litter. But few of the external benefits and costs flow beyond the local level. This suggests that they should be a local responsibility. Some communities will be more concerned with providing street lights and police services, others with combating noise and litter. Citizens will have different preferences for public goods, and they will tend to live in communities where others share their preferences. Their satisfaction will be higher than it would be if the national government were to provide uniform services for all communities.

Though localities should provide these services, others, such as water-quality management, provide benefits that spill over well beyond localities, and these should be furnished by state or regional administrations. Still other services such as national defense, space exploration, and cancer research should be provided for at the federal level.[23] Unlike mosquito spraying or water-quality management, the benefits of these public goods flow beyond any single region, state, or locality. But when deciding how much to spend on such functions, each subnational unit may consider only the benefits that accrue to its residents. The benefits to particular parts of the nation will be less than the total costs for many programs even though benefits to the nation as a whole will be greater. Thus, without provision by the federal government, too little is likely to be spent on all of these goods.

Incentives more than externalities explain why most economists think the national government should be responsible for redistributive welfare programs. A few economists note that people like to give to neighbors rather than strangers and argue that people's preferences about the desirable degree of redistribution differ among states and localities. They thus believe that all three levels should play some role in redistributive efforts.[24] But most economists argue that any substantial state or local effort will lead some of the rich to leave (to avoid high taxes) and some of the poor to enter the area (to gain higher benefit levels). To avoid such a decrease in average per capita income, subnational governments will have a tendency to keep the level of welfare programs lower than most citizens would wish them to be were it possible to neutralize the incentive effects.[25] The mobility that helped localities reach efficient outcomes for other services can prevent such outcomes for redistributive programs. Placing the responsibility for redistribution at the national level can neutralize most of these adverse incentive effects since only migration beyond national boundaries would then increase benefits or reduce burdens.

This scheme for the distribution of powers is complicated by the fact that few if any government services do not provide *some* benefits beyond city and state boundaries. Most of the benefits of police services are probably received by those in the localities that pay for them. But localities elsewhere can benefit if a city locks up a thief who would have visited them next, or they can incur costs if the first city's vigilance scares the thieves to their neighborhoods. Californians were surely harmed when, in retaliation for California's refusal to extradite a man wanted in South Dakota, the latter let ninety-three people charged with forgery, burglary, and theft move to California rather than be prosecuted.[26] And these more tangible externalities aside, there are people who feel psychic pain when reading about brutal crimes outside their city or state. Some of these would presumably pay something to reduce the number of such crimes.

When such jurisdictional spillovers seem minor, economists recommend ignoring them. Where only two or three jurisdictions are involved, voluntary agreements about services such as fire protection or metropolitan transportation may deal with the problem. But if the spillovers are significant and a number of jurisdictions are affected, a federal or state matching-grant program may help achieve efficiency without losing all the benefits of decentralized service provision. Economists usually suggest that the state or nation subsidize the benefit-generating, lower-level government in accordance with the value of their services to other jurisdictions. Thus if 70 percent of the benefits of a municipal waste-treatment plant accrue to those in the municipality, the municipality should pay 70 percent of the costs.[27]

Just as there is often room for reasonable disagreement about whether significant externalities exist, so there is often room for argument about whether significant benefits spill over beyond city and state boundaries. Still the precepts that flow from the externality concept can be of help in establishing what level of government should have responsibility for a government function.[28] For example, there is currently a public debate about what level should be responsible for dealing with environmental pollution. Externality analysis suggests that much depends on the type of pollution. It is hard to see how states or localities can deal with acid rain where the spillovers across state boundaries are massive, but the local nature of most types of noise pollution costs makes the existing federal-government role there hard to justify.[29]

CONCLUSION

The concept of externality can be very useful in helping expose the weaknesses of self-serving interest group positions on public-policy issues. Reflection on the concept sometimes suggests that we should reject arguments for reliance on voluntarism and market forces in the face of clear-cut external costs (e.g., pollution). Such reflection sometimes helps us see the fraudulent nature of pleas for subsidies based on bogus external benefits (e.g., air and rail transportation). Even when the externality concept cannot give us conclusive guidance about the appropriate role for government, it often can help us structure debate by clarifying exactly what is at issue.

Though the externality concept is terribly useful, it is also terribly troublesome. Because externalities are pervasive and often intangible, good judgment in separating the significant from the insignificant is essential. Chapters 9 and 10 will argue that the world view of many economists leads them to unduly constrict the policy relevance of the externality concept. These chapters will also argue that major public-policy errors can result.

8

BENEFIT-COST ANALYSIS

Benefit-cost (sometimes called cost-benefit) analysis is one of the best-known and most controversial tools in the economist's kit. It is common to see the government defending a proposed regulation by referring to a benefit-cost study. Business often attacks the regulation by producing a less favorable study of its own. And from the other side unions and Nader groups attack the proposed regulation as too lax, and they often go on to attack the whole concept of benefit-cost analysis. Frequently, however, these latter groups too feel compelled to at least comment upon the numbers in the government and business studies. Benefit-cost studies have become so much a part of our political process that even the Supreme Court makes reference to them when ruling on many regulatory questions.

Benefit-cost analysis was first used in government as a means of assessing proposed resource development projects. Since the 1930s it has been used to help determine both the size of federal water project agencies' budgets and the particular projects that should be undertaken. In the 1960s it was applied to many government programs and became part of the federal government's planning-programming-budgeting (PPB) system. Since 1974 it has been used by the former Council on Wage and Price Stability and by the Office of Management and Budget to assess proposed government regulations. In this connection a Reagan administration executive order issued in 1981 on procedures for regulatory review includes the most detailed requirements to date for economic analysis and the weighing of benefits, costs, and alternatives.[1]

On the whole the Congress has been more skeptical about benefit-cost analysis than recent presidents have been. In the 1970s several committees chastised the Nixon and Ford administrations for their use of benefit-cost analysis on health and safety programs.[2] In addition, certain laws have more or less precluded its use. For example, the Delaney Clause seems to forbid the weighing of costs and benefits by requiring a ban on any food additive found to induce cancer in human beings or laboratory animals. Similarly, the

Occupational Safety and Health Act of 1970 directs the secretary of labor to implement standards that attain the "highest degree of health and safety protection for the employee" – employment "free from recognized hazards likely to cause death or serious physical harm."[3] However, other legislation such as the Toxic Substances Control Act and the Consumer Product Safety Act requires the analysis of benefits, costs, and risks in formulating regulations. And there is now some support in Congress for regulatory reform legislation that would require agencies to consider the costs and benefits of new regulations.[4]

Benefit-cost analysis can be used to conduct evaluations of existing programs or to assess the probable results of proposed programs. When used for the latter purpose the analysis can be seen as the next step after an externality or other justification for possible government involvement has been established. The last chapter argued that there was in principle an externality justification for requiring that automobiles be equipped with features such as dual braking systems. Since those outside as well as those inside the car benefit, automobile consumers making choices in the private market may not achieve optimal results here. But after establishing that a significant externality exists, economists would still want to know if the benefits of dual braking systems to those in and out of the car exceeded their costs.

When an economist determines that a program's benefits exceed its costs, he in principle says nothing at all about the effect of the program on his own welfare. He instead makes a calculation that society as a whole gains according to the economic efficiency or potential Pareto optimality criterion discussed in Chapter 5. In other words, the gainers from the change gain enough that they could fully compensate the losers with money or goods and still have an improved situation themselves.

Benefit-cost analysis is thus an applied branch of welfare economics, and like welfare economics, it rests on the assumption that societal welfare is best achieved through consumer sovereignty. As one of the best-known benefit-cost texts puts it, "all . . . the economic data used in a cost-benefit analysis . . . is based on this principle of accepting as final only the individual's estimate of what a thing is worth to him at the time the decision is to be made."[5] The benefits of an environmental improvement are therefore determined either by individuals' willingness to pay to achieve it or by the monetary compensation they would need in order to be willing to voluntarily accept the adverse effects in the absence of the improvement. As a practical matter it usually does not make much difference which of these two approaches to estimating benefits is adopted.

As a method of estimating willingness to pay, a few economists would rely on polls or questionnaires. Most, however, believe that the results obtained from such methods are quite suspect. They argue that people are not used to answering questions about willingness to pay and that they have no positive incentive to think carefully and give accurate responses. Although polling is the only method available at times, economists usually prefer willingness-to-pay estimates based on actual consumer behavior.[6] Most benefit estimates link preferences for a publicly provided good to some related private good where consumers' reactions to price changes can be observed in the marketplace.

Determining benefits usually involves two steps. First, one estimates the effects of the government program, for example, number of lives or minutes of travel time saved. Then one values these effects in dollar terms. In estimating benefits (and costs), it is important to look at marginal, not average, figures. For example, when considering the expansion of the interstate highway system, decision makers should want to know not how many lives and minutes of travel time are saved per thousand miles of existing interstate, but how many would be saved with a thousand *additional* miles. Since interstate highways (or police or mobile heart units, etc.) are usually put first where they will do the most good, the marginal benefits of government program expansions will usually be less than the average benefits the program has yielded in the past.

Estimating costs in dollars can sometimes be difficult, as when business may be required to develop new technology to meet an antipollution standard. But frequently the costs of program expansion (e.g., another mobile heart unit, another airport radar system, another police unit, another mile of interstate) are fairly easily calculated. Estimating the benefits of government programs is usually the more problematic and controversial part of the economist's work, and it is that effort on which this chapter will focus. The next section very briefly outlines some methods economists have used to assess the principal benefits of several kinds of government programs. Later sections will examine the views of the critics of benefit-cost analysis.

ESTIMATING BENEFITS OF GOVERNMENT PROGRAMS

Air transportation

The federal government is responsible for reducing delays and preserving safety in the nation's airspace. One of the ways it can reduce delays is by installing better instrument landing systems in airports so that planes can land safely in bad weather and need not be diverted to other cities. By collecting information on weather patterns at various airports, analysts can calculate how many diversions improved landing systems could prevent.

A more common type of delay is that caused by congestion. There are various ways to deal with this problem, ranging from building new airports or runways to changing landing procedures or charging more for landing rights, especially at peak travel times. One important Federal Aviation Administration study compared the effect of various actions on delay by using queuing formulas and simulations. These techniques took account of a number of factors such as the effect on delay of changes in weather and of changes in the hourly distribution of demand.

A portion of the benefits from reductions in diversions and congestion can be given a dollar value by calculating the gains to airlines from reduced outlays on fuel, flight personnel, and aircraft maintenance. Also easily estimated are the hotel and restaurant expenses incurred by airline personnel and passengers due to diversions. How to value the time costs of congestion and diversion delay to passengers is the most difficult problem. Some economists have valued an hour of delay avoided at the after-tax passenger wage rate on the assumption that this is the price for which passengers in fact exchange an hour of their time. But there are many problems with assuming that this figure represents the costs incurred by those circling an airport. For example, some will be terrified and would want much more than their hourly wages to be compensated for their fear; others amused with drinks and magazines might incur no costs at all. Studies of motor travel have estimated the value of time by observing travel patterns on parallel toll and nontoll roads. There are a large number of such parallel toll and nontoll roads, and there is also a wide variation in the level of the tolls and in the amount of time one saves by using the toll road. The toll-per-minute-saved level at which statistics suggest that half the drivers will use the toll road is thought to furnish an empirical indication of the amount that an average motor passenger would pay to save a minute, or, via simple multiplication, any other unit of time. In today's deregulated air transportation environment similar studies may be possible by checking consumer preferences for slower, cheaper airplanes compared to faster, more expensive ones. In the absence of such studies the use of a less adequate estimate such as a wage-rate figure or an income-adjusted motor time one is necessary.

For new airport safety equipment, modeling and simulations are necessary to estimate effectiveness. But for older equipment one can learn much from a careful analysis of past performance. For example, one FAA study compared the accident rates for an eight-year period of the 151 medium-activity airports that had traffic control towers and the 261 medium-activity airports that did not.[7]

The most important effect of safety measures is the saving of lives, and the most controversial feature in all of benefit-cost analysis is the attempt to put a dollar value on human life. Several recent studies have used data on the wage premiums paid for risky jobs as an indicator of how much money people must be paid to be willing to accept the risk of death. One study looked at death rates in thirty-seven hazardous occupations, such as lumbermen and plant guards. After controlling for factors such as education, race, experience, unionization, and region, the authors found a clear, systematic tendency for wage rates to rise with increased risk. It appeared that it took about a $200 wage premium per year to induce a thousand of these workers each to accept an extra death risk of .001 per year. If one assumes a linear relationship, this implies a value for life of $200,000.[8] Workers engaged in the hazardous occupations studied, earned, on average, less than the average U.S. worker. Another economist has thus adjusted the $200,000 figure to take account of the higher wage (and thus presumably the higher willingness to pay for risk reduction) of the average U.S. worker. This economist has also tried to take account of some relevant external benefits of risk reduction such as the lower life and health insurance premiums for others when worker deaths are reduced. He estimates a value for life of $303,000 in 1978 dollars.[9]

Health and safety regulation

There is great variation in the quality of the data available to health and safety analysts trying to determine the effectiveness of proposed regulations. In the case of occupational hazards like cotton dust or drugs like diethylstilbestrol (DES), there is clear evidence of past harmful effects to humans. In many other cases (e.g., saccharin) there is no human epidemiological evidence of harm. For these latter cases, the analyst must extrapolate from the effects of the additive on laboratory animals at relatively high doses to the effects on them at low doses. Then, assuming that it is valid to extrapolate between species, one must extrapolate from rats to humans. The desire to be cautious usually leads analysts to assume that, after adjusting for differences in species' body weight, small levels of the additive will cause proportionate human harm (the linear dose-response, no-threshold approach). However, some scientists believe that the human immune system can counteract small doses, and they would predict low-dose harm only at levels 100 times greater than most studies estimate.

Even in cases in which there is clear evidence of harm to humans many uncertainties remain. There is rarely good evidence on how harm varies as exposure levels change. And good data on crucial parameters are often unavailable even when they should be fairly easy to obtain. For example, OSHA has estimated that 467,000 workers are at risk from cotton dust. But Bureau of Labor statistics data suggest that only about 273,000 workers were exposed in 1971, and since then the industry had declined by 10 percent and promises to decline further due to the movement toward synthetics.[10] Similarly, the data on the number of injuries attributable to lawnmowers are incomplete, and estimates of the effect of proposed regulations on current injuries are often based on little more than guesses.

At the valuing stage, the lifesaving problem is similar to that faced by air transportation analysts. For injuries or nonfatal illnesses, medical costs, lost productivity, and the societal costs of earlier retirement are often estimated. The costs of pain and suffering are sometimes added by multiplying the quantifiable costs by some arbitrary factor. An alternative injury or nonfatal illness cost-estimating procedure looks to the results of legal settlements.[11]

The environment

To estimate the health effects of environmental pollution one can use laboratory data, careful analysis of special groups, or general population studies that correlate mortality rates with air pollution levels after controlling for a wide range of socioeconomic and other variables. The value of reducing these effects can be estimated using methods like those described earlier. Nonhealth effects are also extremely important. Acid rain, for example, corrodes metals, erodes limestone, and damages paints, fabrics, and plastics. It also lowers the reproductive capacity of fish and reduces the yields of crops and timber. The costs of lower yields and of more frequent painting or replacement of materials (and thus the monetary gains from reduced pollution that lowers these costs) are fairly easily determined. For smog reduction or wilderness preservation surveys might be used to determine willingness to pay for improved visibility or for preservation of states of nature that could be destroyed by construction projects.

An alternative way to estimate the value of reduced damage to materials and vegetation and of greater visibility is to look at how property values vary across a single urban area (or among urban areas) with differences in air pollution levels. As expected, economists find that after controlling for other variables such as accessibility to employment centers and structural and neighborhood characteristics, property values are higher where pollution is lower. Aside from the usual statistical problems, one remaining uncertainty with this procedure is whether the value of health improvements is also captured in the property value results. Some kinds of health effects (e.g., eye irritation and shortness of breath) are easily perceived and presumably are reflected in property values. But several major pollutants are colorless and odorless. The effects of these and other pollutants on long-term health may not be well known to those buying residential property in polluted areas. But because most people are aware of some of these effects, simply adding reduced mortality benefits to the property-value-differential ones will bring about some double counting.[12]

Job training programs

The benefits of job training programs accrue both to those enrolled and to the rest of society. Those enrolled gain through higher post-training earnings and, perhaps, through intangible self-image gains from reduced dependence on government charity, on drugs or alcohol, and on unlawful income. The rest of society gains through use of goods and services produced during training, through increased taxes generated by trainees' post-program income, through lower costs for welfare, drug, and alcoholism programs, and through the intangible psychic gains of helping the disadvantaged make their way in the world.

Recently analysts have also attempted to take into account and to measure the decreases in crime rates that tend to be associated with expanded job training programs – reductions in personal injuries, in property damage, in stolen property, and in criminal justice system costs. These benefits of lower crime have proven substantial during the period of enrollment in live-in training programs such as the Job Corps.

The greatest uncertainty in benefit estimates of the job training programs stems from difficulties in finding a good control group so that the effects of the program can be isolated from other explanatory variables. This uncertainty affects the important estimates of earnings gains and lower costs of crime. Some studies use the older siblings of trainees or approved applicants who never enrolled as the control group. Others try to trace the employment and criminal history of a group of youths similar to the trainees in their age, sex, race, family background, school record, and so on. No matter how much care is taken to find comparable control groups, important differences may remain. For example, those who apply and then enroll may be more ambitious than those who apply but do not enroll. Alternatively, those who apply but do not enroll may be the more talented and ambitious who have found jobs elsewhere before the program starts. Though social experiments that randomly assign subjects to training and control groups are expensive, they can overcome many of these difficulties.[13]

CRITICISMS OF BENEFIT-COST ANALYSIS

Critics of benefit-cost analysis argue either that it offends important principles of equity or ethics or that actual benefit and cost estimates are too biased or uncertain to be of any use. Critics concerned with equity often point to the problem discussed in Chapter 6. A program passes the benefit-cost, economic-efficiency test if the gainers gain enough from the project so they *could* fully compensate losers for their losses and still be better off with the project than without it. Who gains and who loses is irrelevant, and it makes no difference whether the compensation is actual or just hypothetically possible. A project yielding $100 worth of benefits for the rich is efficient even if $99 worth of costs is imposed on the poor. Since willingness to pay depends on ability to pay in such cases, the poor may lose much more than the rich in real welfare. Thus in the words of Naderite Mark Green, "Society might desire regulation where the calculable costs exceed the calculable benefits because of the standard's redistributive effect: say the costs are shifted from hard-pressed workers to relatively well-off stockholders."[14]

Critics often link equity with respect for human rights and human life. Thus Steven Kelman says:

The notion of human rights involves the idea that people may make certain claims to be treated in certain ways even if the sum of benefits achieved thereby does not outweigh the sum of costs. It is this view that underlies the statement that "workers have a right to a safe and healthy work place" and the expectation that OSHA's decision will reflect that judgment . . .

When officials are deciding what level of pollution will harm certain vulnerable people – such as asthmatics or the elderly – while not harming others, one issue involved may be the right of those people not to be sacrificed on the altar of somewhat higher living standards for the rest of us.[15]

Even when equity is not a special issue, many are repelled by any explicit linkage of human life costs and dollar benefits. Chapter 2 quotes former senator Williams's view that trading off safety and economic growth is "unconscionable" and Congressman Obey's feeling that "economic costs are irrelevant" when human life is in question. Although not going quite as far as Obey, two thoughtful critics of analysis have voiced similar sentiments. Fred Hapgood sees that benefit-cost analysis might make us healthier and safer, but he thinks the costs to our ethical sensibilities and ethical self-confidence outweigh these gains.[16] Steven Kelman notes that the very act of placing a price on a nonmarketed thing such as human life can reduce that thing's perceived value.[17]

Though benefit-cost critics have a particular aversion to linking dollar values with lifesaving programs, the environment has also been singled out as a special good that cannot or should not be priced. Thus, after suggesting that life could never be satisfactorily priced, William Ophuls puts "irreversible development that forecloses future options" in the same category.[18]

The pragmatic objections to benefit-cost analysis focus on the great uncertainty in estimates. A congressional subcommittee's report on regulation and benefit-cost analysis approvingly quotes the National Cancer Advisory Board: "Quantitative extrapolation from animal studies for the purposes of evaluating human risks entails large uncertainties at the present time." In another section the congressional report points to uncertainties even in areas where complex human biological processes are not at issue:

Data for the cost side of the benefit/cost ledger have been elusive at best; e.g., NHTSA's [National Highway Traffic Safety Administration's] proposed passive restraint rule, with cost estimates ranging from $31 to $405 . . . The benefits side of the ledger . . . presents almost insuperable difficulties. Agreement on an approach to valuing human life is unlikely because the effort involves subjective judgments.[19]

Given uncertainty, when saving lives or ecology is at issue, many regulators, congressmen, consumer advocates, and environmentalists argue for taking no chances. Three Environmental Protection Administration regulators favor resolving the uncertainty of mixed evidence by assuming that a risk of cancer actually exists: "Although the risks may or may not exist, it is rational to treat them as real."[20] A Consumers Union study of proposed lawn mower regulations conducted for the Consumer Product Safety Commission finds that the costs of the most significant standards exceed the benefits based on the union's "low" and "medium" estimates of benefits but not on its "high" estimate. Though the medium estimate presumably represents the Consumers Union's best guess, it supports the standards because "consumers may be averse to the injury risks connected with present lawn mowers."[21] Similarly, the FAA's aforementioned study of airport towers carefully estimated the effectiveness and benefits of towers and then, in light of uncertainty, simply doubled all the benefits as a "safety factor."[22]

As for the risk aversion of ecologists, a thoughtful writer describes it as follows:

If the population climbing a fish ladder drops annually an average of 5 percent over several seasons, the ecologist will not agree that one could infer the number of years it would take for the population to drop to one-fourth, because a later drop could be abrupt. "No one knows the minimal oceanic population necessary for the survival of the species." The ecologist thus spreads a pall of ominous uncertainty over the entire enterprise of environmental planning.[23]

Aside from the uncertainty problem many regulatory agency personnel and their supporters are convinced that benefit-cost analysis is an unjustified invention of those opposed to regulation in principle. The congressional subcommittee report discussed earlier calls benefit-cost analysis a technique "advocated by those who seek a cutback in federal regulations."[24] A like-minded critic says:

[Risk benefit analysis is] the invention of those who do not wish to regulate, or to be regulated, and . . . its primary use in governmental decision-making is to avoid taking action which is necessary or desirable in order to truly protect the health of the public or the integrity of the environment.[25]

Mark Green notes that it is the regulated industry that controls the information about the costs of proposed regulations. As a result the benefit-cost studies are "ideological documents designed to prove preconceived notions" – a linchpin of the "business propaganda that is trying to make citizens hate their government." "To believe that business-dominated cost-benefit studies should control regulatory decisions is about as sophisticated as arguing that one party to a lawsuit should also be the judge."[26]

A CRITIQUE OF THE CRITICISMS

The case against benefit-cost analysis on the grounds that it is biased against regulation or inherently probusiness is extremely weak. Undeniably business is the source of much of the raw data that lead to estimates of cost of compliance. In addition, both business's and the EPA's benefit-cost studies have overestimated the actual costs of business compliance with regulations more often than they have underestimated them.[27] Many business-produced analyses are biased. But many economic studies are funded by government, by nonprofit institutions, by foundations, and by universities, not by business. Moreover, there is an adversary process in analysis, and the bias works both ways. Quantitative studies done by or for regulatory agencies tend to neglect some costs to consumers, such as the degraded vehicle performance caused by antipollution equipment. They also tend to inflate benefits. For example, proposed regulations would add anywhere from 30 to 74 percent to the cost of walk-behind power lawn mowers. The higher price leads to a decline in sales. Instead of treating the higher price as a cost to consumers who no longer obtain power mowers, a Consumers Union study done for the Consumer Product Safety Commission treats the lost sales as an added *benefit* since with fewer power mowers sold, there will be even fewer accidents from the use of such mowers.[28]

Moreover, there is a proregulation bias in the way consumer advocates describe the results of benefit-cost analysis. In the course of arguing that studies are biased against regulation, Mark Green cites some that have yielded unusually favorable results. When these studies give a range of benefit figures, Green often takes a number from the top end. He also makes much of Lave and Seskin's findings that the *total* benefits of environmental regulation exceed the *total* costs while ignoring Lave's findings that the *marginal* costs of many of the toughest features of the regulations far exceed the *marginal* benefits.[29]

Green would have us believe that his quarrel is with businesses and with a few of their "retained economists,"[30] but it is really with economists more generally – liberals and conservatives, Democrats and Republicans. Most economists are pragmatists, not ideologues. When general aviation business interests want a continuation of their air traffic control subsidies, economists oppose them. When businesses argue for the achievement of environmental goals through volunteerism or through tax write-offs for the purchase of pollution-abatement equipment, economists oppose them. When businesses urge weaker OSHA standards for asbestos and weaker EPA standards for sulfur oxides or airborne particulates, most economists informed enough to have an opinion oppose them. When in 1984 the Ethyl Corporation bitterly attacked an EPA benefit-cost study that recommended far more stringent regulatory standards for leaded additives in gasoline, government economists in the Office of Management and Budget and elsewhere strongly supported the study and its conclusions.[31] There are, of course, many cases where economists have supported business in their opposition to proposed regulations. Economists are often most visible in the regulatory process on those occasions – when they oppose some proposed regulation. But one must remember that they are dealing with regulations proposed by single-mission agencies headed by administrators who are very rarely as interested in other agencies' goals as in their own.

Often when economists oppose a regulation, they are opposing only its stringency, not regulation in principle. For example, though the costs of the automotive pollution standards through 1979 were substantial, perhaps $700 per car, economist Lawrence White nonetheless finds that the benefits were even greater. But for the 1980 and 1981 standards he estimates that the costs exceed the benefits. White also notes that even if the 1980 and 1981 pollutant reductions were worth their costs, it would be cheaper to achieve these reductions by being tougher on industries that emit the same pollutants and easier on motor vehicles.

Consumer advocates like Mark Green often see themselves as defenders of both the environment and the poor. White and other economists, however, see a tension between the two causes. Though on average poor and rich neighborhoods show similar improvements from air pollution reduction programs, the rich are willing to pay far more for these improvements. On the other hand, the poor, whose automotive transportation costs absorb a larger fraction of their incomes, incur a disproportionate share of the costs.[32]

It would be wonderful if urban air were as clean as rural air. But the real issues are less grand, and both opportunity cost and marginalism are relevant. One such issue is whether the standard for ozone should be .10 parts per million or .12 parts per million. Neither standard would provide exceptionally clean air, but the more stringent standard would cost more than $500 million more. In 1979 the EPA first proposed the .10 standard, but under pressure from business and Carter administration economists (who wanted a standard of about .18) they finally settled on .12. Even among those suffering from asthma, bronchitis, and emphysema, there is no evidence of significant, irreversible health effects from ozone in concentrations as low as .12 parts per million. (The health effects are mainly discomfort.) Moreover, the .12 standard provides cleaner air than this – air that meets the .10 standard – almost all the time. Yet the cost savings from the weaker (.12) standard are large enough to make possible a payment of $2,180 per hour of exposure to above .10 air to all those with pollution-sensitive ailments.[33] To be sure, those without pollution-sensitive ailments would also gain aesthetic pleasure from the marginally cleaner air the .10 standard would provide. But the aesthetic difference between .12 parts per million air and .10 air is not very great. Moreover, in the long run consumers, not business, will pay most of the costs of cleaner air. Thus, when economists emphasize the benefits and costs of regulatory measures, as with ozone, they speak for consumers' interests even when their calculations have the incidental effect of supporting some of business's interests as well.

There is great uncertainty in many analyses – uncertainty about the potential effectiveness of programs and about how to value that effectiveness. Economists sometimes acknowledge this, and they continually make technical criticisms of particular studies. However, doing away with benefit-cost analysis will not eliminate the uncertainty. As Alan Williams has argued, the limitations of benefit-cost analysis should not be made "the excuse for not abandoning old practices which have even more defects, on the curious notion that we should only change over if a *perfect* product is offered in place of the imperfect one we are already using."[34] By explicitly testing to see how results vary for different values of uncertain variables, a procedure known as sensitivity analysis, benefit-cost analysis teaches the nature and significance of the uncertainty. The more complicated the problem and the more uncertain the variables involved, the more likely are bad decisions in the absence of analysis.

Though there is often great uncertainty about the benefits and costs of the newer forms of regulation, the range of plausible values is not unbounded. If one compares studies done by businesses with those done by groups like the Consumers Union, the degree of uncertainty seems huge. But though still a problem, uncertainty seems more manageable if one compares studies done by competent economists. For example, after carefully reviewing a large number of studies that valued air pollution reductions on the basis of variations in property values, Myrick Freeman found that "the numerical values reported are generally plausible and broadly consistent both within cities as derived from different studies and between cities."[35] Allen Kneese has also reported consistency between pollution-reduction benefit estimates he has obtained using a property value approach and those he obtained surveying willingness to pay.[36]

Sometimes even extremely imprecise results are precise enough to be very helpful. For example, though most studies of willingness to pay estimate values for life of $200,000 to $1 million, some studies estimate values up to $3 or $4 million.[37] This fairly wide variation in results is still precise enough to suggest skepticism about the OSHA standards costing tens or hundreds of millions of dollars per death averted[38] (e.g., arsenic and benzene) and to suggest support for the asbestos standard where costs per life saved are less than $200,000.

Even when important values are left completely unquantified, an analysis can sometimes provide clear recommendations. Job training studies, for example, rarely estimate values for the psychological costs of crime. Yet crime victims report increased nervousness, difficulty sleeping, anger, shame, helplessness, frustration, and depression. They experience a decrease in positive feelings such as joy and contentment. Not just the victims but many of their friends, relatives, and neighbors, and the Good Samaritans who come to their aid, express a similar decrease in their emotional well-being.[39] These costs may outweigh the tangible costs of property damage, stolen property, and personal injury that the typical benefit-cost study quantifies. Yet reductions in these latter costs together with other quantified job training benefits are sometimes enough by themselves to make total program benefits exceed costs even without considering unquantified benefits.

If the quantified costs exceed the quantified benefits, however, the treatment of important unquantified benefits can be crucial. Although some economists warn against ignoring intangible factors or treating benefit-cost results as a mechanical decision-making formula,[40] others sometimes make these errors. But unquantified factors do not always argue in favor of government programs. As Chapter 6 argues, every tax imposes efficiency costs on the economy. Thus, in addition to the usually calculated costs of government programs, there are other costs from the very act of raising the taxes to pay for the programs. Edgar and Jacqueline Browning have estimated that the marginal costs of raising public funds are in the range of 20 to 30 percent of the tax revenue collected. This suggests that ''any expenditure program which does not generate benefits of at least 20 to 30 percent more than direct costs is inefficient.''[41] However, no benefit-cost studies ever consider these costs of raising revenue.

Regulatory programs involve other unquantified costs. First, business leadership may shift from product entrepreneurs to regulatory entrepreneurs

adept mainly at manipulating the legislators and bureaucrats who regulate economic turf. These *regulatory entrepreneurs*, it is true, can often achieve more for the firm's proverbial bottom line than even the best efforts of *product entrepreneurs*. Unfortunately, that ingenuity adds little to our nation's productive capacity.[42]

Second, regulation limits freedom by forbidding cost versus safety trade-offs that businesses and consumers might want to make. Third, regulation provides an incentive for political corruption. Former Maryland governor Marvin Mandel, for example, was convicted for letting personal gain influence his regulatory policies concerning the length of time that various race tracks may stay open.[43]

An argument could be made that uncertainty about whether benefits exceed costs should count against government regulation, not for it. It is precisely because they are uncertain about the accuracy of their efforts to deduce consumer preferences for publicly provided goods from expenditures for related private goods or from polls that many economists are reluctant to abandon the more precise calculation of the market where consumers' expenditures make their willingness to pay more clear. Uncertainty also helps explain economists' frequent support for user charges for government programs. Such charges give more precise information on consumers' willingness to pay than could any benefit-cost study. How much are the Department of Agriculture's reports on various crops worth to subscribers? The department recently began to charge for the reports and found that only 10 percent of subscribers were willing to pay for them. A department spokesman is said to have been surprised at the small number of complaints about the policy change.[44] Is it unclear whether most consumers would benefit or lose from some proposed auto safety measure? Why not leave the matter to the market, perhaps supplemented by government information about accident probabilities and the effectiveness of the safety devices. Consumers who are risk averse and drive a lot can buy a particular device, and those with other preferences and habits can save money by not purchasing it. If consumers are informed and a significant number are willing to pay the costs of the device, some car manufacturers will offer it as an option or as standard equipment on some models.

The view that government should take no chances when life is at issue was criticized at length in Chapter 2. Opportunity costs matter even here. Economists are wrong if they do not see that the strain on and loss of confidence in democratic institutions should be added to the lives lost when estimating the costs of a nuclear power plant or drug or food additive disaster. But it is not rational to assume the worst every time uncertainty arises. A siege mentality contributed to the swine flu vaccine fiasco.[45] We cannot eliminate all risky situations. We have to give some attention to the likelihood of the worst outcome as well as its magnitude. To do otherwise is to ignore totally the costs of assuming the worst – in the case of nuclear power, for example, the deaths of miners and asthmatics if coal replaces nuclear power.

If Kelman's asthmatics live in a particularly polluted area, they probably pay less for their apartment or home. If workers have a particularly risky job, they get paid more than their peers doing other work. It may seem unfair to ask asthmatics to move to less polluted neighborhoods or cities if the risk becomes too great, but if this alleviates the situation at a tiny fraction of the cost of a technological solution, is it fair to ask the rest of the population to adopt the technological solution instead?

Kelman and Hapgood are right to worry that publicly placing a price on a human life may reduce its perceived value and threaten our ethical self-confidence. Kelman at least would support cost-effectiveness analysis, which compares the cost to save a life across various programs but, unlike benefit-cost analysis, does not try to place a dollar value on these lives. One could use such cost-effectiveness analyses to save as many lives as possible until funds disappear. This process, however, would avoid decisions that place a dollar value on lives only if one makes the unrealistic assumption that the lifesaving budget is fixed and cannot be increased by higher taxes or by transfers of funds from nonlifesaving programs. But once one relaxes this assumption, one must confront the fact that lifesaving programs that are not quite effective enough to be funded in the current lifesaving budget would be effective enough if that budget were larger. By not increasing the budget (and we must always draw the line somewhere), we are in effect saying that saving, say, Y lives is not worth an increase in taxes of X amount. We are thus implicitly saying that a life is worth less than X/Y dollars.

Economists carry out most cost-effectiveness studies. By establishing the relative effectiveness of programs, they usually add more to the policy process than is added by taking the further step of valuing that effectiveness.[46] But often a program does more than just save lives. Reducing air pollution, for example, also means easier breathing, more comfortable eyes, better visibility, fewer unpleasant odors, healthier plants and animals, cleaner, longer-lasting materials, and much more besides. As Lave argues, it can be hard to make sense out of such a collection of items.[47] Valuing the effects may help a policy maker put such a list in some perspective. Moreover, a policy maker should pay some attention to consumer preferences for risk reduction, and thus economists should be encouraged in their efforts to add to cost-effectiveness analysis by developing willingness-to-pay benefit estimates. For reasons given in Chapter 9, current estimates cannot be used as a decision rule when establishing spending levels on lifesaving programs, but they also should not be irrelevant.[48]

As argued elsewhere, government officials are unwilling to acknowledge publicly that lives are being lost because the costs of saving them are too high.[49] This indicates that it is very demoralizing to value life collectively and publicly. Publicized valuing would weaken our ethical self-confidence, and this could make us feel more callous and cynical about ourselves and our government. A reduced respect for life could result. Because I share Kelman and Hapgood's general concerns, I see nothing to be gained from politicizing the issue. We should neither encourage the Democratic and Republican parties to include in their platforms competing values for a human life, nor encourage the Congress to pass a law telling program managers just what a life is worth this year. No Congress would pay attention to such advice in any case. Since politicians know their public better than economists or philosophers, that should tell us something about the possible costs of complete openness in this area.[50]

But there are also costs – in lives and in the quality of life – of continuing to muddle through wastefully in the way Chapter 2 described. Thus the middle way seems best. Do the analyses so that politicians and administrators can refer to them when making the unavoidably difficult judgments in this area, but expect no candid public debate. Such debate would prove no more helpful here than it would when determining which cities should be abandoned in the wake of certain nuclear war scenarios. Good political rhetoric rarely presents unadorned all that the politician believes or all that lies behind his difficult choices. Such rhetoric should not be scorned because by calming public passions, it often helps us live well together.[51]

The equity issue surrounding benefit-cost analysis goes beyond particular cases where some people face extra life risk. Critics oppose reliance on willingness-to-pay results because the dependence of those results on ability to pay makes them unfair to the poor. This concern, however, does not apply to benefit-cost analysis of many types of programs. When deciding whether to build projects like a prison or state office building, one can often assume that relative to their tax burden, the poor gain about as much as the rich. Moreover, equity considerations many times only strengthen efficiency conclusions. White found this to be the case in his analysis of the motor vehicle pollution standards. Another example: the grazing fees on federal lands are set at an inefficiently low level, and wealthy owners of large ranches benefit most from this inefficient policy.[52]

As argued in Chapter 6,[53] a number of apparent equity problems seem less important after carefully assessing who gains and who loses. Mark Green's statement about hard-pressed workers and well-off stockholders provides further evidence of misunderstandings about incidence. Most of the costs of business safety regulation fall on consumers. Workers (with lower wages and less demand for their services)[54] share those that remain with stockholders.

In those cases where there are net benefits to society as a whole but the poor lose, it may be possible to compensate the poor for their losses. If the poor experience net gains but society as a whole loses, a cash transfer rather than the inefficient program is sometimes the preferable policy. Economists frequently describe the distribution of benefits and costs so that policy makers can consider equity as well as efficiency. As Chapter 6 points out, economists consider increased equity a legitimate governmental function. Though the equity dimension has been neglected in some economic studies, the profession as a whole takes the issue quite seriously.

CONCLUSION

None of the general critiques of benefit-cost analysis are persuasive. To list all the technical problems in determining estimates of willingness to pay is to combat hopelessly the economists on ground where they are most comfortable. They make the same technical criticisms with greater confidence every day, but they understand that these application difficulties can never be decisive. If consumers' wishes are the appropriate standard for policy making, there is no reason to abandon consumer sovereignty for bad principles just because the latter are easier to apply. If the normative principles on which benefit-cost analysis rests are just and sufficient, the sensible course is to value the benefits of government programs at the best estimate of the people's willingness to pay for them.

The most common attacks at the level of principle also leave benefit-cost analysis standing. Costs and benefits remain relevant even when lifesaving programs are at issue. And though the economic-efficiency calculations take no explicit account of equity, the results obtained are frequently inoffensive to that principle. Moreover, economists are well aware that equity may be left out: They often present information on the equity dimension, and they frequently suggest ways to obtain equity and efficiency simultaneously.

Most of the critics of benefit-cost analysis are themselves willing to acknowledge that their attacks still leave such analysis standing as a guide to a wide range of policy questions. Thus Steven Kelman says that "for the common run of questions facing individuals and societies, it is possible to begin and end our judgment simply by finding out if the benefits of the contemplated act outweigh the costs."[55] And near the end of his strident attack on benefit-cost analysis Mark Green says, "Obviously, before implementing any proposed legislation, officials should attempt to estimate or at least specify the desired benefits, to minimize the costs of compliance and to consider alternative routes to the same goal."[56] The principal change Green offers from the usual economist's formulation is to substitute the phrase "desired benefits" for "expected benefits." It would be a fine world indeed if we more often got what we desired than what we expected, but it does not often work out that way.[57]

The three succeeding chapters will qualify further the qualified defense of benefit-cost analysis offered here. These chapters will argue that the world view of economists does lead to some biases in their assumptions about consumer preferences where these preferences are unclear and in the decisions economists make about which kinds of external effects are important. The chapters will argue that market-based estimates of willingness to pay are sometimes an inadequate indicator of people's real preferences, especially preferences concerning public policy. More fundamentally, they will argue that even the economist's cornerstone principle – the belief that the value of a policy alternative should be measured by aggregating the value each individual in the affected group would place on the consequences of the policy – is itself insufficient. The arguments made in these chapters do not, however, change the fundamental conclusions reached here. The most common criticisms of benefit-cost analysis are not persuasive. Moreover, in today's political process, filled with tunnel-vision advocates of many kinds, the economists with their benefit-cost studies do more good than harm.

likes cost-benefit analyses

Part III

THE LIMITS OF ECONOMICS

9

THE ECONOMIST'S CONSUMER AND
INDIVIDUAL WELL-BEING

All of evaluative economics assumes that individual welfare is best achieved through consumer sovereignty. Consumers size up their alternatives and make those choices that are the most likely to maximize their utility. But do not some consumers aspire to preferences different from their current ones? Do they not regret certain habitual and compulsive choices? Are not consumers even more frequently uncertain about what choices will further their welfare? Do they not need fuller information if they are to make intelligent choices?

THE ECONOMICS OF INFORMATION

Economists direct those interested in the last two of these questions to the economics of information. Those writing in this growing field emphasize the many ways the market provides information to help consumers learn what goods and services will satisfy their tastes. Manufacturers advertise their low prices or the attractive features and comparative advantages of their company's products. Clues about quality come from the brand names of successful companies with good reputations they are interested in preserving, or from the presence of an item in department stores known for the quality of their merchandise. Product warranties and magazines like *Consumer Reports* also aid the less knowledgeable, risk-averse consumer.[1]

Despite the many available sources of information, consumers are never perfectly informed. But economists argue that they should not want to be. There are costs in time and money of both producing and consuming information. Imperfectly informed consumers thus seek more information only if they judge that the expected value of the information will exceed the costs of acquiring it. Nonetheless many consumers do comparison shop. They check the sale prices given in advertisements. In addition, 35 percent of those buying clothes dryers visit two or more stores, and 91 percent of people check the laundering and care instructions in a garment before buying. These careful shoppers generate competitive pressures that help keep prices reasonable for less-informed, nonsearching consumers as well.[2]

Though competitive pressures induce firms to provide much relevant information, they do not easily yield some important kinds of safety information. American automobile manufacturers have not often publicized the superior crashworthiness of domestically produced automobiles because they fear that reminding consumers of the dangers of driving will hurt them as well as the Japanese manufacturers. Similarly, the Brown and Williamson Tobacco Corporation rejected its advertising agency's proposal to promote Fact cigarettes as offering greater protection from gases linked to heart disease. An internal Brown and Williamson document argued that advertising the low-gas benefit would be of little strategic value "until the problem of gas becomes public knowledge through government investigation or media coverage." When the ad agency persisted, the tobacco company later emphatically rejected the idea. It believed that talking about cigarette gases would be counterproductive because it "would require overt references to the alleged cardiovascular ill effects of smoking."[3]

When the competitive market will not provide information important to consumers, a good case for government involvement can be made. By publicizing the dangers of cigarette tar and nicotine and by establishing standardized testing procedures for measuring the amounts of these substances, the federal government injected an important new competitive factor into cigarette marketing. Individual firms may not have sufficient incentives to develop tests for important product characteristics because they realize that many consumers will assume that their testing procedures are biased.

Information is a public, collective-consumption good. If one person obtains information on the comparative features of competitive brands or the prices for the same product at different stores, he is not harmed if other customers use this information also. This makes it hard for private organizations that provide consumer information to cover their costs. If consumer groups developed a price index that rates supermarkets on their overall prices, they could not sell this information at its full value. Many who would pay for the information could obtain it free from newspapers or by word of mouth. Similarly, many who consult *Consumer Reports* when making a major purchase have never subscribed to the magazine. This helps explain why it can test only some of the models available for almost all product lines. Because information is a public good, a case can be made for government testing agencies, government provision of information, required disclosure of certain product characteristics, and other forms of government intervention in the market.

Goverment provision of information deserves some credit for the decline in smoking as well as for the lower tar and nicotine levels in the cigarettes that are smoked. The Environmental Protection Agency's standardized miles-per-gallon tests and publicity requirements have clearly made it easier for consumers to assess the fuel economy of automobiles. And the now mandatory appliance energy labels, which give the range of estimated energy costs for other similar models as well as for the brand the customer is looking at, should provide important information on product performance that otherwise would not have have been available either before or after the sale.

There are many factors to consider when examining a new government information policy. One might first ask if the private sector has been given time to deal with the problem. When a Food and Drug Administration panel of experts recommended a sunscreen protection factor (SPF) efficacy-rating system and suggested it be made mandatory, a rule was proposed that never became final. However, in the wake of substantial media attention to the panel's finding of adverse effects of sun tanning on skin, the industry voluntarily implemented a rating and labeling system and many new products entered the market, several of which were accompanied by intensive advertising that explained the SPF rating system and the skin type for which each SPF value was most appropriate.[4]

It is also important to try to avoid perverse unintended effects on consumers and producers. Unless great care is taken comparative performance information could lead consumers to make false distinctions between product classes. The EPA's required warnings about local water that falls below standards may turn users to the use of bottled water not subject to any standards or testing.[5] Similarly, radiation warnings on microwave ovens could suggest that gas ovens, which do not contain leakage or explosion warnings, are safer.[6] Further, government grading standards (excellent, good, etc.) may discourage innovation by providing little incentive for product improvement once firms have met the minimum standard for the top grade.[7]

A further consideration in determining whether government should supply information involves judgment about the likelihood consumers will attend to the information provided. Millions of dollars have been spent on many different programs designed to increase seat belt use, yet only about 12 percent of Americans currently use seat belts, about half the rate that used belts in 1974.[8] Since light bulbs of the same wattage have different light output (lumens) and average life, in 1970 the Federal Trade Commission required packages to conspicuously disclose lumen and average-life data on the packages. Four years after the disclosures began, however, few consumers knew what lumens meant, and only 1 of 168 customers surveyed mentioned lumens as a pertinent factor in selecting light bulbs.[9] Finally, there are the results of an experiment conducted by a bank that had doubts that the detailed electronic funds-transfer disclosure statement, required by law, really provided useful information to consumers. The bank recently inserted in the midst of the disclosure statement a sentence offering ten dollars to anyone writing the words "Regulation E" on a postcard and sending it to the bank. Out of 115,000 recipients of the statement not one responded.[10]

When estimating the costs and benefits of intervention, we should not forget the problems of government failure discussed in Chapter 5. In principle it may make sense to ask the Department of Agriculture to grade food quality.[11] But the actual standards developed on a product-by-product basis are so confusing as to be almost useless. For dried peas the top quality is number 1, but for lima beans "U.S. No. 1" is only second best and for other canned products it is third. For canned peas "choice" is better than "prime," but for beef "prime" is better than "choice." Even if consumers could understand the system, they might not find it all that helpful. "In a laboratory choice situation which made different quality steaks available to subjects at the *same* price – the 'best to buy' first choices of consumers did not follow the grade level hierarchies: 22% chose the Prime, 44% chose the Choice, and 34% selected the Good steak as best."[12] Far more harmful than the chaos in the U.S.D.A. rating scales have been state licensing laws, which were originally justified as a way of protecting unknowledgeable consumers from charlatans. Several studies have shown that most of these laws restrict competition, hinder innovation, and raise costs without improving quality.[13]

Within the last few years there have been a host of controversies over government information policy. Should labeling of sodium content in food remain voluntary or become mandatory? Should special consumer advisory inserts be required in prescription drugs? Should funeral parlors be required to make price lists available and give out price information over the phone? Should stickers listing all known defects be required on used cars? Should the government promulgate tire tread-wear ratings? Should the government continue to publish *The Car Book* containing information on fuel efficiency, crashworthiness, and maintenance costs for different models?

The growing literature on the economics of information has been very theoretical for the most part, and it has not yielded useful benefit-cost studies on questions like these. For example, one article that purported to make "welfare comparisons of policies concerning information and regulation" concluded by noting that "proper evaluation requires considerable information on consumer tastes which is difficult to acquire, not only in practice but even in principle."[14]

Almost all economists would agree that in order to preserve advertising as a reliable source of information we must have some laws against false advertising.[15] But many economists would disagree with Federal Trade Commission chairman James Miller's current efforts to severely limit the kind of deceptive advertising that the government may challenge.

Almost all economists would agree also that if government is to intervene in the market, information programs that allow for differences in consumer circumstances and tastes are generally to be preferred to mandatory standards. With energy labeling, for example, "consumers in the North can spend more of their money on highly efficient furnaces, while consumers in the South spend more of theirs on air conditioners. Large families can buy efficient clothes dryers and water heaters, while cheaper [less energy-efficient] ones are installed in small homes. A cheap, if inefficient, refrigerator can be found for intermittent use."[16] Mandatory energy-efficiency standards do not provide for this sort of flexibility. On safety characteristics as well, most economists believe that consumers should not be denied the chance to choose less expensive, but somewhat riskier products.

Still, even on this fairly narrow question of the type of government intervention some economists think product bans are sometimes justified. The light bulb case showed that simple label warnings are often ignored. Indeed, in one mock test, of the very small percentage of customers who saw a label noting that the U.S. Public Health Service had determined that protein supplements are unnecessary for most Americans, about as many thought the label said people do need the supplements as thought it said they do not.[17] Steven Kelman reminds us just how little we know of the safety characteristics of a whole range of products:

The reader may ask himself if he would feel confident identifying which one of the four following substances that may be present in food is far more risky than the other three: calcium hexametaphosphate, methyl paraben, sodium benzoate, and trichloroethylene. Or he may ask himself how confident he would feel making decisions about what safety features to buy in order to guard against power lawnmower accidents or to protect against a radio exploding or electrocuting him. If he does know, how confident does he feel that he understands the risks associated with various levels of the substance? Is five parts per million of benzene hexachloride a lot or a little? If the bacteria count in frozen egg is one million per gram, should we be alarmed?[18]

Detailed labels or information packets for all risky products would add to their price and require substantial amounts of consumer time if they were read at all. Thus an economist, Richard Nelson, draws the same conclusion as Kelman, the critic of economics:

All of us might jointly agree that writing and reading long complete labels is too costly as a general matter. We might agree that safety in a regime of incomplete and quickly read labels requires certain product restrictions, the cost of which is offset by a lower cost general signalling system.[19]

There is substantial agreement among economists that the case for an active government information or standard policy is strongest when most consumers' preferences are fairly similar, when the product is not purchased often, when it is costly for consumers to get adequate information from private sources, and when the damage from mistakes is great.[20] There is also agreement, even among relative activists such as Nelson, that if an agency gets involved in product regulation at all, it "might have a propensity to over-regulate."[21] But the differences on policy are great. In 1982 I asked several Washington economists about their views on *The Car Book*. Though these economists were in almost complete agreement on issues like air pollution or transportation deregulation, they were sharply split on whether the government should have continued to publish *The Car Book*.[22] On issues like this some economists emphasize the public-good nature of information and the demonstrated successes of some past government programs. They want a more active government role.[23] Others emphasize the vast quantities of information provided by an unregulated market and past government information-provision failures. They think government is doing too much already.[24]

ADVERTISING, PRODUCER SOVEREIGNTY, AND CHANGING TASTES

Most of the literature on the economics of information assumes consumers with clear, stable preferences but inadequate knowledge of what will best satisfy them. It thus does not come to grips with the criticisms made by those who think many consumer preferences are placed in consumers' psyches by producers trying to find markets for their products. Former senator George McGovern, for example, has argued that advertising can "brainwash the consumer . . . No one was ever born, for example, with a taste for huge gas-guzzling automobiles. That is one of so many created demands."[25] Ralph Nader has made the same point by quoting the late Senator Philip Hart's estimate that $200 billion spent by consumers in 1969 (of total expenditures of $780 billion) purchased nothing of value. Nader states that "economists for the most part have failed to . . . show how corporations . . . have been able to divert scarce resources to uses that have little human benefit or are positively harmful."[26]

McGovern and Nader's point is like that made by Thorstein Veblen at the turn of the century when he argued that much consumption was motivated by habit, a desire to emulate, or preoccupation with conspicuous display and did not serve human life.[27] Before Veblen, Marx argued that

under private property . . . every person speculates on creating a *new* need in another, so as to drive him to a fresh sacrifice, to place him in a new dependence and to seduce him into a new mode of *gratification* . . . The extension of products and needs falls into *contriving* and ever-*calculating* subservience to inhuman, refined, unnatural and imaginary appetites.[28]

And before Marx, Rousseau argued that the bloated passions of modern man are not natural and that they alienate man from his true self.[29]

The best-known contemporary spokesman for this line of thought is John Kenneth Galbraith. Galbraith argues that the consumer-sovereignty assumption, central to all of evaluative economics, is completely unrealistic. He distinguishes between what he variously describes as "physical needs" or "original" wants and "psychic satisfactions" or "contrived" wants. In an affluent society such as ours, increases in income serve mainly to gratify the psychic or contrived wants. These wants are often created by the advertising and salesmanship of the very producers who then satisfy them. Thus, increases in production to meet these contrived wants should not have a very high priority.

Galbraith sees a world in which producers, not consumers, are sovereign.

The individual's wants, though superficially they may seem to originate with him, are ultimately at the behest of the mechanism that supplies them. In the practical manifestation of this accommodation, the producing firm controls its own prices in the market. And it goes beyond this control to persuade the consumer to the appropriate responding behavior. And it also selects and designs products with a view to what can be so priced and made subject to such persuasion.

Galbraith asks if General Motors "is the proper agency to decide the proper level of consumption for its products." He argues that advertising produces "an extremely powerful and sustained propaganda on the importance of goods. No similar case is made on behalf of artistic, educational or other humane achievement."

Galbraith says that mainstream economists think that a slightly qualified form of consumer sovereignty is also operative in the public sector. But in reality producers reign:

For important classes of products and services – weapons systems, space probes and travel, a supersonic transport – decisions are taken not by the individual citizen and voter and transmitted to the state. They are taken by the producers of public services . . . The Congress and the public are then persuaded or commanded to acceptance of these decisions.[30]

The development in the argument on this important subject, from Rousseau to Galbraith, provides no evidence for human progress. It is surely wrong to suggest that economists argue that consumer sovereignty operates in the public sector. The whole government-failure literature discussed in Chapter 5 shows the contrary. Fortunately, however, Galbraith's villainous producers are not quite so influential with governments as to be able to "command" acceptance of their decisions. Those he dislikes are no more powerful than other producers whom Galbraith fails to condemn because he values their product more. The would-be producers of a domestic supersonic transport airplane would have loved to have had the political clout of, say, the education lobby.

Aircraft manufacturers aside, many other private-sector producers have not proven as powerful as Galbraith claims. In light of their difficulties in the late 1970s, who today can believe that General Motors "decide[s] the proper level of consumption for its products"? More generally, among those new products regarded by American management as technical successes, far less than half survive market testing to be launched commercially, and more than half of those launched are considered failures and withdrawn by management within one year.[31] In any case, if producers could really control demand, there would be no need to go to the large expense of developing new products. Galbraith believes that advertising creates stability for producers, but a study done to test this proposition found no correlation between advertising intensity and stability of an industry's sales and employment.[32] Only one of 1909's top eighteen firms [Exxon] is on today's list. Among the giant firms in that year were United States Cotton Oil, American Ice, Baldwin Locomotive, and United Shoe Machinery. These names alone recall industrial changes beyond the control of any firm that have transformed American industry. A more skillful marketing department would not have changed the fate of the early twentieth-century giants.

Galbraith says that firms choose products with a view to what lends itself to persuasion. But this is another way of saying that not everything does. And all else being equal, profit-seeking firms should prefer to produce products people will buy with just a little persuasion rather than incurring added cost by producing products people will buy only after a lot of persuasion.

Galbraith sees a market bias against artistic and educational achievement. There is, however, no reason to expect such bias with respect to many of their manifestations. One can charge admission to see either great art or mud wrestling. It is no more expensive to print a book of poetry or history than one of pornography. It is surely less expensive to film a Shakespearean production than a James Bond thriller. One not particularly admirable quality of most capitalists is that they are quite willing to sell almost anything if it will make more money. James Bond movies are better attended than Shakespearean productions precisely because it takes much more costly persuasion to get a significant number of people to go to the latter. Indeed, those few producers who try such persuasion sometimes misrepresent a bit in an effort to appeal to "original" human passions. A decade ago the *Los Angeles Times* contained a large advertisement for the American premier of a new production of *Julius Caesar* starring Sir John Gielgud among others. The advertisement pictured Abraham Lincoln, Martin Luther King, and John and Robert Kennedy together with a large hand holding a dagger. The copy read, "They were treacherous . . . those who murdered Abe, John, Martin, and Bobby but no more treacherous or twisted than those who plotted the assassination of JULIUS CAESAR."

It is precisely those tastes for the high culture that Galbraith most values that are the least well described as "physical needs" or "original wants." It takes more than the usual amount of persuasion or education before one acquires such tastes. It takes more effort to convince people that Brutus is interesting even though he was not the James Earl Ray of his day. Galbraith would place very little value on tastes that do not "arise in spontaneous consumer need" and on those where the demand "would not exist were it not contrived."[33] By such criteria even the works of Galbraith might be undervalued.

The modern goods that have done the most to transform the American way of life – goods such as automobiles, television, and air conditioning – are also widely desired in countries without extensive advertising. People in the Soviet Union "now strive at all costs to acquire household appliances, electronic goods and especially a . . . car." Families in India and Pakistan are wild about television, and they particularly like the "Mary Tyler Moore Show."[34] Moreover, repeated tests in the marketplace have shown that most consumers do not want a car that simply gives cheap, reliable transportation. They want style, power, and comfort as well.[35] In hindsight it is easy to criticize Detroit for not providing the more fuel-efficient cars that consumers demanded after the second oil shortage in the late 1970s. But one should not forget the surplus of unwanted subcompacts it produced after the first crisis in the mid-1970s. Moreover, by the early 1980s there seemed to be a shift in consumer demand back toward larger, roomier cars.

Most contemporary economists are qualified supporters of advertising. They find that although advertising can help create monopoly power, it can also help break down such power. Moreover, heavy advertising for new products can make possible economies of scale in production and distribution and thus lead to lower prices. Even for mature products advertising can help medium-size firms achieve scale economies. There are cases in which advertising seems to raise costs to consumers, for example, aspirin, detergents, and breakfast cereals. But many empirical studies have found cases in which it has reduced prices. By "preselling" customers advertising makes low-service, low-price discount stores possible. When heavy advertising of toys began in the 1970s, retailer prices and profit margins went down as sales increased. Separate studies of the gasoline, eyeglass, and prescription drug industries have found lower prices where more advertising prevailed.[36]

Granted the uses of advertising and the weaknesses in much of Galbraith's argument, an important point made by Galbraith and others has yet to be addressed. Much advertising seeks not just to inform, but to persuade. It seeks to persuade us that we will not get the attractive date and joyous friends until we have bought the mouthwash, the Löwenbräu beer, or the fancy car. A commercial society generally, and advertising in particular, provides one-sided propaganda for the view that the route to happiness is through money and what it can buy. By creating desires for some products we will never be able to afford, it makes some of us feel anxious and inadequate. As Ezra Mishan has noted, even if a man pays little attention to most advertisements

their cumulative effect over time in teasing his senses and tapping repeatedly at his greeds, his vanity, his lusts and ambitions, can hardly leave his character unaffected . . . [B]y drawing his attention daily to the mundane and material, by hinting continually that the big prizes in life are the things that only money can buy, the influences of advertising and popular journalism conspire to leave a man restless and discontented with his lot.

Mishan thus argues, "If private enterprise has the freedom to expend resources in influencing the tastes of the public in the interest of larger profits, and if so far it has on balance been successful in influencing them for the worse, there can be surely no objection to noncommercial attempts to influence them for the better."[37]

There is a small mainstream economic literature on the problem of changing tastes. An early article by Sidney Schoeffler acknowledges that when tastes change, economics can say nothing about whether consumer sovereignty with the first set of tastes or with the second achieves a higher level of well-being. Schoeffler also acknowledges that tastes change all the time since "any given governmental action or policy tends to remold the preference maps of the individuals in society." He asks biologists for help. An "absolute ordering would very likely have to be derived from *physiological* measurements of some sort, possibly, for example, from the 'size' of chemical disequilibrium within the body of the person. We have no choice but to await the future findings of biological science on this point."[38]

Since biologists had failed to find a chemical nirvana, a decade later Richard Weckstein approached the problem in a different way. Weckstein simply accepted the core of the Galbraith-Mishan point: By raising aspirations faster than income a commercial society may reduce real welfare even as it increases income. Weckstein suggested that welfare increases whenever the aspiration–income gap is reduced but he offered no way to measure the gap. Nor did any policy recommendations flow from his analysis.[39]

With regard to changing tastes, the approach that has gained the most support among economists solves the problem by defining it away. Kelvin Lancaster argues that utility is derived from the characteristics of goods, not from the goods themselves.

In this model, the whole process is extraordinarily simple. A new product simply means addition of one or more activities to the consumption technology. Given the technology (or the relevant portion of it) and given the intrinsic characteristic of the activity associated with the new good, we simply insert it in the technology, *and we can predict* the consequences.

Lancaster goes on to state that when a consumer replaces an old good with a new one, a welfare improvement occurs because the consumer can now more efficiently "reach his preferred combination of characteristics."[40]

Lancaster provides no illustrations of how his model might be used to make predictions, and if one tries to make such predictions it is easy to see why. Where does a personal computer fit into the "consumption technology"? Many consumers might buy one primarily for the video games. Some of these consumers might see the computer as preferable to Monopoly, others to a stereo, still others to the movies. An entirely different set of consumers may see the computer as an educational device for their children, whereas a third set sees the computer as an improvement over their filing cabinet. All of these consumers would define the characteristic that the computer adds in a different way. Moreover, the person who purchases a personal computer may not be better off simply because it became available. He may have previously had all he really wanted in life except a video disk recorder, which he planned to buy himself for Christmas. He now wants a computer too, but cannot afford both. He finally decides to buy the computer but regrets not having the video disk recorder, and he might have felt more content with his lot if he had never known that the computer existed. His neighbor who cannot afford *either* the computer or the video disk recorder but now wants both may also lose something from the existence of the new product and its vigorous promotion.

The larger issues of a possible information bias or welfare loss because of heavy advertising of goods and services receive little attention in the mainstream economic literature.[41] That literature interprets all events in the world in a way that does not threaten the fundamental assumptions of economics. Thus the typical economist is quick to say that what appears to be a change in a person's tastes may just be a shift toward the purchase of a new product that better suits his unchanged, fundamental preferences. If a person frequently purchasing *old* product A suddenly stops and begins frequently purchasing old product B instead (e.g., tickets to Shakespeare instead of mud wrestling), economists argue that he now has more information and experience and thus can more *"accurately"* order his purchases *"in accordance with unchanged underlying propensities"* (emphasis in the original).[42] If one insists that tastes themselves sometimes change, not just information or the characteristics of goods, economists may grudgingly acknowledge as much, but they are quick to add that one of the virtues of a free-market system is that it provides incentives for a rapid and full response by suppliers to meet such changes in tastes.

SUBJECTIVISM, SELFISHNESS, AND MATERIALISM

Chapter 5 pointed out that welfare economics has no room for any policy standards that limit or guide human preference. The last chapter explained that all data in benefit-cost analyses are based on the "principle of accepting as final only the individual's estimate of what a thing is worth to him at the time the decision is to be made."[43]

This radical individualism and subjectivism could easily lead to nihilism. If the good and the right can be judged only by individual feeling, then there is no objective basis for advocating any policy standard, including an individualistic one like consumer sovereignty.[44] But economists somehow avoid this slippery slope. They do not remain agnostic when someone like Mishan says that commercial propaganda emphasizing the "mundane and material" should be balanced by noncommercial attempts to influence tastes "for the better." Most who comment on remarks like Mishan's strongly object to them. Thus Robert Solow says, "It is a very fine line between analytical statements about the creation of wants by advertising and elaborate indications that one believes one's own tastes to be superior to those of the middle classes."[45] And William Baumol states, "I must sharply disagree with the implications of Scitovsky's view, for at its worst it offers unrestricted license to the bluenoses and those who would impose on myself and others their own standards of good taste and good behaviour."[46]

In a volume that resulted from the work of a study group composed primarily of theologians and other noneconomists, William Vickrey seems at least properly troubled by the problem:

> Advertising almost inevitably . . . produces changes in the fundamental preferences of the individual himself . . .
>
> . . . What is the place, in the broad scale of values, of activity designed to change the opinions, preferences, and ideals of individuals? We can hardly rest content to leave the decisions, as to how much effort is to be devoted to various kinds of educational and propaganda effort, to be determined by the financial support of those who are interested, either commercially or emotionally. This would imply that the ability of an idea or a program to command financial support would be the prime measure of the importance attached to its propagation. Such a proposition seems morally indefensible as an absolute standard, and defensible as a practical standard only in the absence of alternatives. But no alternative seems available, unless it is to lump this with other social values to be determined in part or in whole by methods outside the sphere of economics.[47]

Probably more common than Vickrey's ambivalence is Dean Worcester's conclusion that "too little time is likely to be devoted to advertising and to entertainment because government authorities, which may or may not be responsive to consumer interests, insist on a larger than optimal amount of public service programs."[48] Similarly, Robert Ayanian concludes a critique of Galbraith by saying, "Clearly the vast majority of advertising in American society is for goods that the American people both want and need."[49]

Why are economists so defensive when someone suggests that commercial advertising may leave many consumers with an exaggerated opinion of the importance of goods and services to human happiness? There are a number of reasons for this. First, potential professional recruits very quickly learn that in evaluative economics the best thing that can be said about a policy is that consumers want it. Most of those who find this world view uncongenial are likely to choose other professions. Thus economics has a disproportionately large number of people who subscribe to a consumer-sovereignty standard for public policy.

Second, those in the profession also learn that if consumer tastes can be assumed to be stable and real, economists can show themselves to be quite useful to policy makers. On the other hand, if an economist abandons this assumption, he calls into question the value of the competitive market and of many of his own professional tools. If we trust consumer sovereignty, we should be very concerned when economists locate inefficiencies, but if consumers' tastes are distorted and unbalanced because of one-sided propaganda, economic efficiency becomes much less important. Indeed, its very meaning becomes ambiguous. Two thoughtful mainstream economists have called the treatment of consumer tastes "the Achilles heel of neoclassical economics."[50] It is thus not surprising that economists protect this weak spot with such vigor.

Third, as Gordon Tullock has said, "Most economists having observed the functioning of the market and government for some time tend to think that most people, most of the time, have a demand curve, the overwhelmingly largest component of which is their own selfish desires."[51] And many believe that the most important of these selfish desires involves generating income and obtaining what it can buy.

Kenneth Arrow says that an economist sees himself as "the guardian of rationality, the ascriber of rationality to others, and the prescriber of rationality to the social world."[52] But economists do not really think reason is very powerful. It cannot, for example, determine the good things in life. The good things depend on each individual's idiosyncratic preferences. If idiosyncratic preferences move us, reason cannot be their source, for reason is not idiosyncratic. Passions could be, however. James Buchanan and Gordon Tullock have argued, as David Hume does, that "man's reason is the slave to his passions."[53]

Most economists would want to avoid grand pronouncements on human nature such as Buchanan and Tullock's. But by frequently assuming that we are narrowly selfish, many economists express silent agreement with their views. There are many signs of such assumptions.[54] Chapter 6 commented on the tendency to attribute the continued existence of minimum wage laws to the shadowy workings of narrow self-interest. The extraordinary effort to explain away facts that do not fit a selfish world view is also relevant. There is, for example, considerable evidence that narrow self-interest cannot explain a large part of voting behavior. Upper-income voters frequently vote for expenditures that will provide them few direct benefits. Those with the lowest incomes are evenly split over a guaranteed income plan that would raise their incomes; though they would seem to be the principal beneficiaries, southerners are especially opposed to such a plan.[55] A number of economists have wrestled with these findings. Buchanan cites new tax-incidence studies that are somewhat "less damaging" to the self-interested assumption.[56] Davis and Jackson suggest that those in the South may not be aware of the real effects of the policy, and they comment as follows: "Somehow it seems more rational to be opposed to something if one is not aware that it will result in personal benefits."[57]

Economists sometimes suggest that apparently altruistic behavior may just be a more refined kind of selfishness – the desire to feel good about oneself by helping others.[58] But economists realize that this explanation defines self-interest in such a way that it could explain any conceivable behavior.[59] So some search for a less exalted, narrower form of selfishness. William Breit points out that malevolence toward the rich could explain desires for redistribution as easily as does pity for the poor. But though he discusses this and other possible explanations, he seems most attracted to the theory that the middle class want to take from the rich to give to the poor out of a self-interested desire to avoid "rioting, looting, burning and other crimes."[60] Bruce Bolnick points out that philanthropic activity enables one to avoid costs such as social pressures, psychic unpleasantness, and religious pangs of conscience. He thinks the "apparent irrationality" of philanthropy can be seen as an attempt to avoid these sorts of costs.[61]

Chapter 5 said that welfare economics was concerned with anything any individual values enough to be willing to give up something for it. It was thus not, in principle, preoccupied with money and the things it can buy. In practice, however, economists do overemphasize the importance of money both as a human motive and as a source of happiness. Macroeconomics is, of course, almost solely concerned with money measures like inflation and gross national product. But microeconomics is also largely concerned with exploring and illustrating the power of money. It shows that money is a better unit of value than the layman thinks because it can buy more than narrowly defined goods and services. For example, by accepting lower pay, a low-income worker can, in effect, buy a safer job, and by buying property nearer the ocean, his West Coast cousin can purchase cleaner air. Economists are more interested in real income per capita than in better housing or nutrition for the poor because they know that money can buy those two goods and much more besides. The usefulness of the economic-incentive insight rests on the power of money to move mankind. And in the marketplace, which is where the economist almost always sees us, money is powerful indeed.

Microeconomics can be most powerful if money is central to mankind. Because profits are central for businessmen, economists can make useful predictions about their response to a rise in price. If preferences for government programs could also be explained by monetary gain, voting behavior could be predicted. And as will soon be illustrated, the assumption that monetary gain is what people care about makes it far easier to estimate the benefits and costs of many government programs. On the other hand, if people vote for programs they think are in the public interest or support programs that provide direct benefits to others rather than themselves, predictions and benefit-cost calculations become very difficult without finding out what people now think is in the public interest or who they now think deserves special assistance.[62]

Gordon Tullock wants to see if burglars have made "a sensible career choice." He can do so if he assumes, as he does, that money *should* be central to people and that they should feel the same about illegal income as they do about legal income. Sometimes "conscience" or "reputation" costs of crime are mentioned as unquantifiable factors, but they rarely affect economists' conclusions. For a crime like tax evasion Tullock thinks these costs can be ignored entirely. He gives a formula setting forth "the conditions for an individual's decision as to whether or not he should attempt to evade the tax on a particular portion of his income." The formula "indicates that if the likelihood of detection times the penalty he must pay on being detected is less than the standard [tax] rate, he would be wise to attempt evasion."[63]

If one can assume that money is what people care about, one can get fairly good estimates of the external effects of some government programs. For example, a recent article in the prestigious *American Economic Review* had one central point: The existing willingness-to-pay estimates for the value of life are inadequate because they ignore the external effects of lifesaving programs on others. But the author did not have in mind a psychic pleasure that people feel when they know a fellow citizen's life has been saved. No such effect was mentioned at all. What W. B. Arthur had in mind was the following:

Willingness to pay, as currently interpreted, would approve an advance in life from seventy to eighty years if those affected and their kin were willing to pay the cost of the increase. Forgotten, however, is that prolongation of life is not costless, to wider society: those who live longer, consume longer, and this extra consumption must be financed by the production of those at younger labor force ages. Proper accounting, we would suspect, should include intergenerational transfer costs, felt in this case as a heavier Social Security burden on the young.

Arthur sees an important question of equity here:

Where altered mortality risks strike the population unevenly, or the mortality change comes suddenly . . . some people may reap the benefits of increased life and production, while others bear the consumption costs. For example, a sudden mortality improvement can be a windfall to the elderly – they enjoy extra years while escaping the corresponding extra support of the generation that went before.[64]

John Morrall provides reasoning similar to Arthur's in his analysis of OSHA. Morrall is open to the argument that people besides the victims and their families would like to prevent occupational deaths and injuries. He is open because he finds that others do pay more for Social Security, welfare, workers' compensation, Medicare, and Medicaid in the wake of such deaths and injuries. Morrall even points out some interesting "policy implications." Since the costs to others of nonfatal respiratory disease among cotton-textile workers are greater than the costs of fatal accidents among construction workers, society may have "a greater financial interest" in reducing the former. What about nonfinancial interests – the psychic pain suffered by the kindhearted from learning about preventable deaths on the job? Some noneconomists have thought these external costs significant. But Morrall concludes that "it remains to be shown that the quantitative significance of such beliefs

[is] important relative to the feelings of the direct beneficiaries of occupational health and safety programs (the workers) and the financial stake that the public has in reducing the social costs of occupational illnesses and injuries.'' For his own part Morrall thinks these psychic external effects either ''trivial or ambigous [sic].''[65]

THE POVERTY OF THE ECONOMIST'S WORLD VIEW

Let us look again at Mishan's views: Commercial advertising teases our senses and taps repeatedly at our greed, vanity, and lusts; because business propaganda emphasizes the mundane and the material, it should be balanced by noncommercial attempts to influence tastes, for the better.

As argued earlier, advertising performs some useful services. Moreover, even when it changes tastes it may be beneficial. Tibor Scitovsky argues that variety and fresh sources of stimulation are important elements in human happiness. Advertising of new goods can help meet this need.[66]

Granting all in its favor, a commercial society does have the effect that Mishan says it does. Business advertises barbecue grills and ''Dallas'' more often than it does history books and Shakespeare, not because it is inherently biased against high culture, but because more persuasion, and thus more money, is needed to induce people to buy the latter. Nonetheless, the effect is constant propaganda emphasizing the mundane. And because business can make money only by selling goods or services, it necessarily urges the importance of the essential means to achieve these goods and services, namely, money.

If polls asking individuals to evaluate their own happiness are reliable, real (inflation-adjusted) increases in national income do not make a society's people feel happier. To be sure, in any given country those with higher incomes are more likely to report that they are ''very happy.'' But by and large the people living in richer countries do not feel happier than those living in poorer countries. Moreover, though average inflation-adjusted, after-tax income had increased by 70 percent between the late 1940s and 1970, the average American's self-reported level of happiness had hardly changed at all. Some scholars have thus suggested that we are on a ''hedonic treadmill'' where the ''upward shift in perceived needs tends to offset the positive effect of income growth.''[67]

Though most economists are aware of these findings, their implications are almost completely ignored in the welfare economics and public finance literature. Alan Blinder does briefly mention them in his lengthy discussion of the level of economic well-being. Blinder believes that people with greater income are ''happier on an absolute scale,'' but when answering survey questions, they tend to rate their happiness ''relative to that of their contemporaries.''[68] Perhaps so, but this should be a troubling argument for any economist believing in a standard for well-being that is based on subjective sense of satisfaction. In any case, the findings suggest that a society interested in increasing the happiness of its citizens would be wise to avoid putting all its eggs in the money basket.

What else is important to the happiness of most Americans? A job where one's work matters to society. If it is a job in which one gives pleasure or relieves pain for others and receives their obviously sincere thanks (a good doctor, teacher, baker, or air conditioning repairman) or one that provides important challenges and a sense of accomplishment when they are met, better still. A loving, stable family living in a friendly, supportive community free of serious drug or crime problems and bitter ethnic or political differences; a good school system; some rich associations outside the family: good friends, rewarding participation in the life of a church or synagogue, a civic association, or an athletic team. Most of all, a sense that one is liked, loved, and respected.[69]

Most efforts at persuading adult Americans about what is important are made by profit-seeking businesses. Average Americans encounter their advertising on television and in newspapers a number of times every day. These advertisments tell us that we will be happier if we buy a product or service. They rarely if ever tell us that we will be happier if we spend more time with our family, friends, church groups, or civic associations, or if we have a lower-paying but more satisfying job. One could say that there is an important market imperfection here. No one has a strong financial interest in reminding us about the importance of some of the most important things in life.[70]

The best friends are old friends. Friendships require time – both in years and unhurried leisure. Mishan argues that "long familiarity with personages and places is a source of deep gratification."[71] If so, perhaps we should more often forget the higher-paying promotion in another city. But advertising coaxes us to take it. Then we can afford both the computer and the video disk recorder. If family and friends are more important sources of happiness, however, perhaps we should forget both the computer and the video recorder. When our most important pleasures come from machines, our ties to people cannot be very strong. More time with friends and family might make sense.

If work, family, friends, church, and associations are more likely sources of happiness than money, the person who seeks happiness may have to take a broader view of self-interest. For example, someone who is narrowly selfish is incapable of sharing, and without sharing there can be no friendship.[72] As Ronald Sharp has argued, the commercial model does not fit an act of friendship since it

cannot be understood as spending and thus depleting some allegedly limited supply (of, say, favors, good will, emotion, or, more generally, friendship itself). It is, rather, an act of giving, in which there is no thought for increasing or decreasing one's own capital – even though, paradoxically, it will lead to increase. We do not use up our friendly emotions by feeling them; on the contrary, we intensify them. "There is nothing more productive of joy," says Cicero, "than the repayment of kindness or the sharing of interest."[73]

Imagine two situations. In the first a narrowly self-interested man nears death and establishes an athletic scholarship in his name at his alma mater. In the second a loved and respected track coach nears death, and those he coached join with university colleagues to establish an athletic scholarship in his name.[74] In the second situation those who contribute toward the fellowship feel good about finding a way to show their appreciation of a man who possesses so many admirable human qualities. Those who later receive the fellowship may receive some added pleasure from association with the name of such a universally respected man. And the track coach himself, together with his family, is likely to feel much better about this tribute to his life than will the narrowly self-interested man who, being selfish, will be able to think of little besides his impending demise.

Some economists seem unable to appreciate the pleasures that good will and good character bring to people. Gordon Tullock, for example, argues that we may have an interest in subjecting individuals to "indoctrination" so as to increase the "conscience" costs when they break the law. We should do so, however, only if this proves a "lower-cost method of reducing the crime rate than the use of policemen and prisons." Consider, however, the following: If a stranger returns, untouched, a missing wallet, we feel better than if a policeman returns it after catching a thief because in the first case we see some evidence that our environment is honest and friendly. The stranger himself, as well as others, may genuinely gain from such an honest act. This Tullock ignores. Indeed, the principal problem he sees with reliance on indoctrination is that "the badly indoctrinated" gain "a distinct advantage over the well indoctrinated."[75] By indicating that only "indoctrination" can make conscience costs take hold and by ignoring conscience costs when giving advice about when individuals should break the tax law, Tullock suggests that conscience costs are unnatural or irrational even if they are socially useful. But perhaps the pain of conscience is not unnatural for mankind, the animal that can blush. And perhaps the pleasure that comes from doing the right thing is natural for such a social animal. Aristotle's gentleman, for example, is not selfless. But he is "a man who wishes to live with himself; for he does so with pleasure, since the memories of his past acts are delightful." He perceives "his own goodness, and such perception is pleasant in itself."[76]

A respected economist, Julius Margolis, finds it useful to look at an elected official as a "small-scale unincorporated businessman." His "revenues" include "cash contributions to his electoral fund, cash contributions to his private account, contributions of time, indirect contributions via patronage of a business he controls, organizational support, and public esteem." In Margolis's subsequent discussion of various kinds of "payoffs," "public esteem" fades from view. And he ignores entirely the "private satisfactions in getting a 'good job done' or molding the government to conform to his values" since "there are few craftsmen who work solely for the joys of their products."[77]

Margolis may accurately portray many elected officials. But some in local government subject themselves to much unpleasantness for little pay or apparent satisfaction other than that of getting a "good job done." Richard Fenno's exhaustive research shows that many congressmen seek out certain committee assignments mainly because they want to influence public policy.[78] The recent eulogies for the late Senator Henry Jackson (D-Wash.) spoke of his decency, professionalism, idealism, and clarity of purpose. They also noted that he lived modestly. "He never took a dime for a speech. The money went directly, and quietly, to a scholarship fund."[79] Again such people need not be completely selfless. The local officials may want to be remembered as the track coach was, and the congressman may seek the admiration of his peers and an honorable place in future history books.

Recent polls show that 75 percent of Americans "frequently feel that God loves them, and approximately one-half engage in prayer and attend religious services."[80] Presumably many of these believe in a heaven and hell. They might think that more than social pressure and pangs of conscience make philanthropy rational.

Chapter 5 pointed out that economists have noticed that narrowly self-interested motives cannot explain the decision to vote since a single vote almost never changes an outcome. More puzzling to them still are the cases described in this chapter of people who take the time to vote and then vote against their financial interest. Also unexplained are experiments that have not supported a strong version of the free-rider hypothesis. In these experiments, large groups of people are given tokens they can invest either in an individual exchange that returns 1 cent per token to the individual investing, or in a group exchange that returns 2.2 cents per token but divides these earnings among everyone in the group regardless of who invests. In other words, in the group exchange, the subject receives a share of the return on his own investment (if any) and the same share of the return on the investment in the group exchange made by the other group members. Most economists would predict that a self-interested individual would put nothing in the group exchange because this behavior maximizes benefits to himself. (Most of the [greater] gross benefits from his investing in the group exchange would go to other members of the group. Moreover, those who do not invest in the group exchange nonetheless share in the proceeds from investments made in that exchange by others, i.e., they get a "free ride.") But, in fact, in a number of experiments people have voluntarily contributed substantial resources – usually between 40 and 60 percent – to the group exchange (i.e., the public good). Many in the experiments have also said that a "fair" person would contribute even more than they did. The only notable exception has been a group of entering graduate students in economics. They contributed only 20 percent to the group exchange, found the concept of fairness alien, and were only half as likely to indicate that they were concerned with fairness in making their decision.[81]

When Davis and Jackson found voters who voted against policies that would provide "personal benefits," defined as monetary gain, they attributed this to voters' ignorance of actual policy effects. Similarly Rapaport and Chammah have commented on the lack of intelligence of the typical subject in the free-rider experiments. "Evidently the run-of-the-mill players are not strategically sophisticated enough to have figured out that strategy DD [the selfish strategy] is the only rationally defensible strategy, and this intellectual short-coming saves them from losing."[82] In light of these reactions, one suspects that if W. B. Arthur were to be told that most workers feel remorse when they learn that more old people have died, he too would see a problem of consumer ignorance. If his article is to be believed he would have to hold that the workers would feel differently if made aware of the "consumption support costs" they would save if the existing "windfall to the elderly" were eliminated. But in fact, polls show little support for cuts in Social Security benefits. Many of the poll respondents are workers, and a large number of them must be aware of the connection between the level of Social Security tax they pay and the level of benefits for the elderly. There is, moreover, no real connection between high benefits for the elderly now and high benefits for today's workers when they retire twenty or thirty years later. More spending now leaves less in the fund later, and policies can be changed at any time Congress chooses. In any case I doubt that many *fully informed* workers feel a net gain when a chartered plane carrying senior citizens goes down in flames. My guess is that if most Americans became persuaded that the costs of Social Security must be cut, they would favor a later retirement age or smaller retirement checks rather than cancellation of otherwise justifiable lifesaving programs because we begrudge the elderly the "consumption cost" benefits to which they are legally entitled.

Arthur's article needs a satirist more than it does a counterargument. But the fact that he wrote it is less worrisome than the fact that the editors of the *American Economic Review* thought it important and worth publishing. When most of us read Dickens, we see Scrooge as contemptible but also pitiable. He has no close family and no friends. No one likes or respects him. He is not a happy man. But much of the economic literature reviewed here suggests that he was in fact a model maximizer. Or at least he would have been if he had shown more interest in consuming some of his loot.

People who think that the best things in life are free are not likely to become economists. People who think money matters and narrow self-interest makes sense are more likely to become economists. Through their training economists learn that they and their discipline can be more powerful if money and self-interest matter even more than they first thought. The free-rider experiments show that economists have a different world view than the rest of us. They think it a more rational one. Though it seems obvious that commercial advertising presents a distorted view of the route to happiness, money and narrow self-interest cannot explain what it leaves out. Information policies that might correct distortions challenge the world view of many economists and the professional self-interest of most of them. Thus, arguments like Mishan's are unlikely to get a fair hearing in the profession.

WHICH PREFERENCES?

Socrates saw powerful bodily desires at war with reason in the souls of most men. In the well-ordered soul, its spirited part, the home of anger and shame, helped reason gain control over animal passions so that man could know the higher, uniquely human pleasures.[83] Social scientists today are likely to find this view quaint and archaic. But substitute "mind" for "soul," and some elements of it become perfectly compatible with the latest scientific research. A Columbia University scientist, Robert Jastrow, puts it this way:

It is as if two mentalities resided in the same body. One mentality is ruled by emotional states that have evolved as a part of age-old programs for survival, and the seat of this mentality is in the old-mammal centers of the brain, beneath the cerebral cortex. The other mentality is ruled by reason, and resides in the cerebral cortex . . .

In man, the cerebral cortex, or new brain, is usually master over the old brain; its instructions can override the strongest instincts towards eating, procreation or flight from danger. But the reptile and the old mammal still lie within us; sometimes they work with the highest centers of the brain, and sometimes against them; and now and then, when there is competition between the two mentalities, and the discipline of reason momentarily weakens, they spring out and take command.[84]

Economists usually assume that we have a single, integrated set of preferences about private and public goods and that it is found most accurately by examining decisions made in the marketplace. But brain research aside, we often do seem to be at war with ourselves, and when we reflect on the conflict we usually decide that reasoned resolution is our better half and the temptations of appetite or animal passion the worse. Our better half may sometimes side with the higher passions. It may tell us to act out of love or compassion rather than selfish calculation. But since our reflective selves approve of many such acts, they merely show that reason may be more than narrow calculation.

Many who regularly indulge themselves with food, alcohol, cigarettes, drugs, gambling, incest, prostitution, or pornography hate themselves for doing so and would love to be able to stop. Consider gambling. Gamblers Anonymous estimates that there are between seven and ten million compulsive gamblers in the United States. Many gamblers acknowledge that they are ruining their lives and those of their families. One reformed addict recalls that he had "no time" to drive his wife to the hospital on the day she miscarried. But he had time to drive to the race track that night. "I'd go from Arlington to Charles Town at 90 miles an hour just to make the eighth and ninth races. It would take me six to nine months to pay a bill that was due in 30 days."[85]

For many of these people there is no reason to think that outside intervention would violate consumer sovereignty if the relevant consumer is the reflective, higher side. One father who carried on an incestuous relationship with his daughter for two years says, "I knew it was wrong. When I was finished, I hated myself. I said I would never do it again, but I had no will power."[86] Cigarette smoking is a less dramatic vice, but most of its practitioners clearly see it as a vice. Surveys in England and the United States show that a majority of smokers have tried to stop.[87] An informal survey I conducted as a graduate student showed that most would not mind some financial coercion to encourage them to stop. I asked fifty smokers (in Ithaca and Philadelphia) the following question:

If it were determined that the Federal Government had to raise a certain amount of revenue, and the choice was between raising the income tax or raising the cigarette tax, and either increase would bring in the same amount of total revenue from the population as a whole, which tax would you prefer to be raised?

Thirty of the smokers preferred to raise the cigarette tax, eleven the income tax, and nine had no preference. Among the twenty-two heavy smokers (those smoking more than ten packs per week), eleven chose the cigarette tax, eight the income tax, and three had no preference. Ten of the cigarette-tax supporters volunteered some reasons, and they are revealing. Four said that if cigarettes are taxed, "then I'll quit" or "people will quit." The other six made comments like the following: "It's a habit I can do without. It won't hurt to cut down." "You don't have to pay." "You always contemplate that you will stop." "It's my fault; I might stop."[88]

Another compulsion a large number of people would love to be rid of is their tendency to spend more money than they have. Irving Kristol recalls his youth "when the only thing more reprehensible than buying on the installment plan was selling on the installment plan; it encouraged 'fecklessness.' "[89] Those days have passed. Though there are businesses that give advice to those deeply in debt, it does not resemble the counsel a good friend would give. Several years ago when the prime rate was 16.5 percent, a radio station in our little city carried a finance company's advertisement for their bill-payer's consolidation loans. The company promised to send customers away with hundreds of dollars in cash. It concluded, "You deserve that vacation you've always dreamed about."

Though business produces most often and most quickly those things that people will buy with little or no persuasion, this does lead to overemphasis on goods. Yet we seem to regret our susceptibility to the allure of material goods. Eighty-four percent of Americans believe that most people "buy a lot more than they need," and 49 percent believe that they themselves do. By a 79 to 17 percent margin, the public would place a greater emphasis on "teaching people how to live more with basic essentials" rather than on "reaching higher standards of living." By 76 to 17 percent, a sizable majority would stress "learning to get our pleasure out of nonmaterial experiences" rather than "satisfying our needs for more goods and services."[90]

The term "self-satisfied" is one of reproach. Many people, and most of those we admire, are not entirely happy with the preferences they "reveal" through their behavior. They aspire to be better friends, better parents, better teachers. They want to improve themselves through anything from losing weight to spending more time reading or traveling instead of watching television. The average American spends almost ninety minutes a day watching television. But surveys of viewers show that many are bored. The author of one of the surveys calls a large minority of viewers "compulsive." They were asked,

"When you're watching T.V. do you ever feel you'd rather do something else but just can't tear yourself away?" and, "About how often do you feel that way?" Twenty-four per cent answered, "Occasionally," another 12.5 per cent, "Almost always." Yet they continue watching.[91]

Even in the area of tastes all is not simply a matter of differing natures and arbitrary, inexplicable variations in preference (though much may be). In some cases there will be significant differences about whether it is fair to describe certain tastes as "low," "crude," "brutish," or "vicious" or about whether other tastes deserve praise such as "high," "civilized," "educated," or "enlightened." But in many cases there will be no such differences. There is little doubt about which set of words most of us would rather have applied to our tastes; and there are no disagreements in which A says a certain taste is "brutish and vicious" while B maintains that it is "enlightened" and "civilized."[92]

Many of us wish that we had different tastes. We make remarks such as "I wish I could appreciate classical music" or "I wish I could learn to like Shakespeare." The word "learn" is significant. When we make such statements, we usually think that we could come to appreciate the activity if we knew more about it. We may have a friend who likes classical music. We readily acknowledge that she knows more about music than we do and that this is at least part of the reason she likes it more. She as quickly acknowledges that someone else knows more than she. This sort of agreement comes about because when two people listen to music or discuss a book it is sometimes clear to one of them that the other sees or hears things that he misses. The new knowledge makes possible greater appreciation and pleasure.

When we send our children to a liberal arts college, it is often with the hope that they will learn to appreciate what we would like to appreciate, but cannot. When we call someone "cultured," it is because that person has certain tastes that depend in part on his nature but also in part on what he knows. If experts on literature were asked to name one hundred books every "liberally educated person" should have read, there would be important differences. But some books would appear on almost everyone's list. Those who have read and learned to appreciate them are likely to gain not only aesthetic enjoyment but also knowledge that will enrich their friends and family as well as themselves.

It takes knowledge to appreciate all kinds of activities, common as well as cultured. Friends like to go to a fancy Chinese restaurant with John because, knowing their general tastes, he can pick out a meal they will like better than they can themselves. If they want to see a baseball game, they go with Chris because he knows why the third baseman moved a little to the right with a tie score, two out, and nobody on in the bottom of the tenth. They go backpacking with Nicholas because he notices and can explain more than they, and Nicholas in turn looks forward to trips with Rebecca because she knows more than he.

Agreement on a fixed hierarchy among differing activities with their accompanying pleasures is less likely than agreement among practitioners of a single activity. Natures and capacities differ, and no one can know all the contenders well enough to be able to rank the activities with confidence. But the absence of total chaos in the usage of words like "crude" and "civilized" can save us from the nihilism involved in assuming that all choices are equal. As Leo Strauss has argued in another context, "If we cannot decide which of two mountains whose peaks are hidden by clouds is higher than the other, cannot we decide that a mountain is higher than a molehill?"[93]

This section has argued that a man's behavior does not necessarily indicate his preferences if "preferences" means what he thinks is best for himself or will maximize his well-being. Behavior seen in the market may be even further removed from what the man believes is best for the community. As pointed out earlier, many voters vote against their financial self-interest. There are also reported cases such as that of a union member who did not like to go to dances with blacks but thought nonetheless that all union members, including blacks, should be invited to the union's dances.[94] There no doubt are people who purchase liquor, pornography, or the services of prostitutes who think that the community, if not they themselves, would be better off if those products and services were not available. They may vote against their local availability. Though a strong proponent of markets, James Buchanan has nonetheless acknowledged that

the sense of participation in social choice may exert important effects on the behavior of the individual. It seems probable that the representative individual will act in accordance with a different preference scale when he realizes that he is choosing for the group rather than merely for himself . . . [H]is identification will tend to be broadened, and his "values" will be more likely to influence his ordering of alternatives, whereas in market choice his "tastes" may determine his decision.[95]

If we want to learn about people's views on public policy, we may often have to look to voting or polls rather than deduce values from market analogues of public goods. The preceding chapter showed, however, that the strong preference among economists is for the market analogue. Though in theoretical discussions one sometimes finds an acknowledgment such as Buchanan's,[96] Sen is correct when he says that "much of the empirical work on preference patterns seems to be based on the conviction that behavior is the only source of information on a person's preferences."[97] Indeed, this bias is so great that when Freeman discusses polling approaches to environmental improvement benefits, he *defines* an "accurate response to a question about willingness to pay" as one that is "consistent with the underlying preference ordering or utility function and with the behavior that would be revealed if the public good could be ordered in a market where exclusion was possible."[98]

This bias can lead to large mistakes in the treatment of preferences for goods where appetite fights reason. For example, economists' discussion of the cigarette tax often acknowledges its possible justification because of external financial costs to others through higher publicly subsidized medical costs and health insurance premiums. But a tax as high as the present one can probably not be justified on externality grounds alone.[99] Thus the standard economic mode of analysis must see the present high tax as both discriminatory against smokers (many of whom are poor) and inefficient because of the high tax wedge driven between the costs of production and the market price. This wedge induces some consumers who would "like" to consume more cigarettes to shift instead some or all of their purchases to other less pleasurable goods and services. However, polls showing that most smokers want to quit reveal that only a part of them that they wish to tame "likes" cigarettes. Moreover, my informal poll shows that by a margin of almost three to one smokers like to be "discriminated" against with respect to their habit. Because they think they and others might be led to give up their compulsive habit, smokers would rather pay higher taxes if the higher taxes are connected with their habit.

As indicated earlier, economists usually meet proposals for noncommercial efforts to improve tastes with calls to take to the barricades against the bluenoses. In addition to the factors mentioned then, the strong professional attachment to revealed preference helps explain this. The idea that human beings have complex natures and might want to improve their revealed tastes even in the absence of a badgering bluenose is strongly resisted if acknowledged at all. John Stuart Mill made a long and interesting argument for the distinction between high and low pleasures. In the course of his argument he states that "men often, from infirmity of character, make their election for the nearer good, though they know it to be the less valuable."[100] But mainstream economists are quick to reject this part of their inheritance from a

distinguished ancestor. Martin Bronfenbrenner has quoted the long passage
of Mill's in which this sentence is found and has suggested that it is an
"exquisite and labored amalgam of priggish condescension, intellectual snob-
bery, and what Bentham would call *ipse dixitism*."[101]

Robert Samuelson, a young moderate whose writing often reflects a professional middle ground, has come out for the abolition of the national endow-
ments for both the arts and the humanities along with the Corporation for
Public Broadcasting. In total these agencies spend less than $500 million per
year but Samuelson doubts that we "need the government to subsidize high-
brow entertainment – theater, ballet, opera and television drama . . . Let
people decide for themselves whether they want to be entertained by the
Pittsburgh Steelers or the local symphony."[102] On the position that people
will enjoy life more if they are educated to appreciate the higher pleasures,
Roger Bolton's exhaustive study of the economics and financing of higher
education says only the following:

Another non-earnings benefit which some might claim is that the educated person
"enjoys life more." What this really means is that the educated person enjoys the
life of the typical educated person more than a non-educated person would. The
statement that being educated permits one to enjoy life more is empty of empirically
verifiable content, since we cannot measure enjoyment very well. Casual empiricism
suggests that the educated person certainly lives differently, and allocates his consumption expenditures differently, but that he may not really enjoy life any more.[103]

POLICY IMPLICATIONS

"Elitists" is the term economists often use in conversation to attack exponents
of views such as I voice here. At the level of invective the appropriate retort
would brand the economists "philistines." Much I have quoted from economists' writings would surely be admissible evidence in support of such a
charge. Still, one cannot ignore the potential for abuse that economists point
to. We do wish to avoid giving "unrestricted license to the bluenoses and
those who would impose on myself and others their own standards of good
taste and good behavior." Businesses should be able to advertise freely for
a wide range of goods and services, including those some may think frivolous,
such as designer jeans and cars with tail fins. And choices about the place of
these goods and services in our lives must remain ours to make as individuals.

Our governments, however, should not think it illegitimate to try to influence tastes and behavior. They are not made up of unrepresentative groups
of bluenoses and elitists. They are elected by the people. There is every reason
to think that the people would encourage their governments to continue to
combat harmful, compulsive behavior such as drug addiction, alcoholism,
and cigarette smoking. Indeed, many of those involved in such compulsive
behavior would themselves encourage this. Because most smokers have tried
to stop, they probably wish they had never started. Cigarette advertising that

attracts new victims and reminds current smokers of vices their reasonable, reflective side would like to put behind them should be tightly regulated. There is some evidence that antismoking television spots are effective, and they should probably be expanded.[104]

Government also has a role in the process of teaching us how to "get our pleasures out of nonmaterial experiences," a change in outlook toward which a very substantial majority of Americans think we should be working. Perhaps we could help combat the current information bias toward sellable goods and services as the route to happiness with some combination of more public-service advertising and selective financial incentives. The family could be strengthened through generous tax credits for those who care for a handicapped child or an elderly parent in their home. Organizations that perform an important helping role, such as Alcoholics Anonymous and voluntary social welfare agencies, could be assisted through subsidized advertising on television and through matching grants or subsidized loans.

Government should also continue to support high achievement in science and the arts. One means of doing so is to encourage public appreciation of their products through organizations like the Corporation for Public Broadcasting and the National Endowment for the Humanities. It takes more knowledge, or what Scitovsky has called "consumption skills," to appreciate Shakespeare than it takes to appreciate the latest pulp novel. The same is true of much science, music, and history. Yet these endeavors stretch us; they awaken our natural curiosity and help us to escape unwitting bondage to the authoritative opinions of our time and place. They are higher, more distinctively human, pleasures, but also harder and less enticing initially. Thus some subsidization is warranted. Much that we support in education silently acknowledges as much. As the late Charles Frankel has argued, in free societies governments cannot be the only moral and aesthetic arbiters, but they "cannot escape being an arbiter, and an influential one." People need enough knowledge so that their choices can be significant; they need the intelligent power to choose.

In practice, then, an enlightened public welfare policy need not consist in the coercive imposition on a community of a point of view. It need not consist in this even where it concerns itself explicitly, as I believe it should, with aesthetic issues or with the protection and projection of standards of taste and achievement cherished only by a minority. Such a policy is simply an effort to restore perspective and balance; it is an effort to ensure that the better will not suffer because few know that it exists. For you cannot be said to know what you are choosing unless you know the alternatives, and there is no way of escaping Philistia unless you know there are other countries.[105]

Respect for and appreciation of natural beauty and wildlife are also worth encouraging if the public's interest should wane.[106] Environmentalists too frequently neglect opportunity costs and preach alarmism. But in their willingness to see us make nature our playground, raw material for our vagrant passions to dispose of as we will, economists can seem equally extreme. For example, William Baxter says, "The word 'Nature' has no normative connotation . . . I have no interest in preserving penguins for their own sake . . . Every man is entitled to his own definition of Walden Pond, but there is no definition that has any superiority over another, except by reference to the selfish needs of the human race."[107]

An alternative view sees us as a part of nature with an obligation to live in harmony and balance with it. Nature is one of our teachers. Running deer and breathtaking mountains remind us of the limits of human power. Such sights are awe-inspiring. They teach the existence of a reality more fundamental than the burning issues and passions of the day. At the same time they remind us of our special place in nature and thus combat nihilism. By creating a sense of duty beyond self, awe-inspiring nature can heighten respect for fundamental human rights and constitutionalism, both of which are dependent on a kind of self-denial.[108]

AVOIDING CONTROVERSY THROUGH "SCIENTIFIC" NEUTRALITY

When an eighteen-year-old argues that his concern for preserving nature is more than just an idiosyncratic subjective preference, economists are likely to show more patience than with adult elitists. The eighteen-year-old will be introduced to the fundamental difference between facts and values. For example, very early in their economics text, Lipsey and Steiner distinguish between positive statements "basically about matters of fact" and normative statements "based on, a value judgment." These authors are particularly good here and throughout the text in showing that many value judgments rest on factual assumptions that can be investigated. (For example, many people think rent control is good *because* it provides more decent housing for poor people.) However, Lipsey and Steiner give an example of a value disagreement where "reasonable people" would simply have "to agree to disagree." The text says that though one person may believe that we should be charitable to all human beings including the inhabitants of China, someone else may say, "You ought not to be charitable toward the Chinese because my moral principles dictate that you should be charitable only toward Christians." Lipsey and Steiner say, "If both sides insist on holding to their views on charity, even if both are perfectly reasonable, there is no civilized way of forcing either to admit error."[109]

But why would the second person say one should be charitable only to Christians? Presumably because he is himself a Christian, and he understands his views on charity to be a correct interpretation of Christ's will. If this is so, the next step should be an examination of the teachings of Christ. These teachings may show no support for the view that people should be charitable only toward Christians at which point reasonable people would not agree to disagree, but would agree that the second person's value judgment was unreasonable.

Though this value disagreement may be resolved easily, others may depend on the real status of a belief such as "Jesus Christ is the son of God." Is this a positive (factual) or normative (value) statement? Some might say that it is clearly normative since much of the world does not believe it is true. But Lipsey and Steiner say that for statements to be called positive ones "it is only necessary to be able to imagine evidence that could show them to be wrong." One need not have the evidence at the time the statement is made. But surely one could imagine such evidence for the statement about God and Jesus. God could appear to us all, perform appropriate miracles, and declare Jesus a fraud.

Most economists simply assume that the fact–value distinction was adequately demonstrated by positivist philosophers of an earlier era.[110] Often the fact that people disagree abut fundamental moral questions is thought to be evidence enough that reason cannot settle such disagreements. For example, because Gordon Tullock was writing a whole book on the logic of the law, he thought he should say a word about natural law. He mentions Plato, Aristotle, St. Thomas Aquinas, and William James and simply announces that "any critical examination of these works indicates that their authors have made mistakes in logic that escaped their notice because they were morally convinced of the truth of their results." Tullock says that we have knowledge of different cultures with different moral systems, and thus natural law is not convincing because believers in such law should expect to find "a uniform ethical code for the world as a whole."[111]

Tullock does not cite anyone who has demonstrated the mistakes in logic made by Plato, Aristotle, Aquinas, and James. He himself gives no illustrations of logical mistakes, and he has since as much as acknowledged that he has never critically examined these works and found such mistakes. This seems a safe deduction since he has told other readers that his knowledge of older political economists like Locke and Bentham came "largely" from secondary sources.[112] It is hard to imagine his carefully perusing Aquinas if he has not studied Bentham. And Tullock surely could not have read Aristotle and still believed that Aristotle was unaware of vast differences in various countries' ethical and political systems. Such differences settle nothing, however, since "knowledge of the indefinitely large variety of notions of right and wrong is so far from being incompatible with the idea of natural right that it is the essential condition for the emergence of that idea: realization of the variety of notions of right is *the* incentive for the quest for natural right."[113]

This is not the appropriate place, and I am surely not the appropriate person, to attempt to resolve these important timeless questions. What is relevant is that economists rarely think about them. When they do, they sometimes show ignorance of earlier philosophic argument (Tullock) and sometimes cut off fruitful discussion too quickly by declaring that reason cannot help us judge between competing value positions (Lipsey and Steiner). Amartya Sen, an economist who is nonetheless one of the discipline's most thoughtful critics, argues that a value judgment can be called basic only if it is supposed to apply under all conceivable circumstances. Most value judgments are nonbasic and can be addressed by evidence and argument. Moreover, though some value judgments are demonstrably nonbasic, none is demonstrably basic. Jones might always produce an argument or a hypothetical situation that would convince Smith that what Smith thought was a basic value for him was in fact nonbasic. Thus Sen concludes, "It seems impossible to rule out the possibility of fruitful scientific discussion on value judgments."[114]

Economists hope to avoid all these thorny problems by simply taking preferences as they find them. The underlying belief seems to be that one can avoid controversial value judgments if one refuses to make value judgments. But this procedure does not avoid controversial value judgments. Suppose that W. B. Arthur does find a large number of young workers who believe that their welfare increases when old people die. Suppose also that we are doing a benefit-cost analysis of a health program especially effective in reducing the risk of death for those between sixty-five and seventy-five. It is a fairly expensive program, but it looks as if the willingness to pay of the elderly, together with that of their friends, family, and kind-hearted members of the public at large, is great enough to pay for the medical costs. Adding the Social Security tax losses that Arthur mentions, however, makes costs exceed benefits and abandonment of the program ensues. Is this not controversial? Suppose the losers from the life extension are not Social Security taxpayers but instead greedy heirs despondent over measures that lengthen the lives of their eventual benefactors; or white racists who feel psychic costs from the benefits of a sickle-cell anemia program. Should one conclude that lifesaving programs that are in the public interest from the point of view of all but certain heirs and racists might cease to be in the public interest if those heirs and racists were sufficiently greedy or prejudiced? Perhaps some of the heirs and racists themselves would acknowledge that their gains from others' deaths should not influence a public policy that might lead to those deaths. For example, some people might believe that their welfare would go up if their rich uncles died and yet not wish for them to die. And some who might wish that their rich uncles would die might quite consistently think that such wishes should not be entitled to public recognition.

Criminal justice programs provide another case in which the failure to make value judgments is far more controversial that willingness to do so. Chapter 8 briefly described a benefit-cost analysis of the Job Corps Program. What was not described was the study's methodology for determining the benefits to society from reductions in the amount of stolen property. The reduction of stolen property was considered

a benefit to those other than Corpsmembers, but part of its value should be viewed as a cost to Corpsmembers, who no longer receive the income from stealing. The social benefit of a reduction in stolen property (the difference between the Corpsmember's cost and everybody else's benefit) is the decrease in property value associated with the operations of fences, the damage to stolen property, and the loss of legal titles.[115]

In other words, it is only because stolen goods are "hot" or damaged and thus not worth as much to criminals as to victims that there are any societal costs at all from stolen property.[116] A theft of money, for example, produces no costs for these benefit-cost economists. In Charlottesville, Virginia, a blind man has had his wallet stolen three times in three months. The losses to him would be seen as balanced by the gains to the thief.[117]

The authors of the Job Corps study are not members of the Mafia. Other applied studies have treated this issue in the same way, and their methodology enjoys the support of some of the best economic theorists.[118] The applied methodologies are presented in a matter-of-fact manner without the slightest hint that they might be controversial. These economists are doing what they were taught to do: treat preferences in an "even-handed," nonjudgmental manner. But most of the rest of the world will think that one who tries to adopt a nonjudgmental, amoral perspective when looking at an immoral act necessarily becomes an accomplice to the crime. Jeffrey Sedgwick has noted the older term for a criminal, an "outlaw." One who breaks the law puts himself outside the law and, for so long as he does so, outside society.[119] The gains to outlaws from their illicit activities can thus safely be ignored when judging society's welfare.

To be sure, some economists are embarrassed by what their model produces in the criminal justice field. Richard Nelson, for example, correctly notes that this view of the costs of crime will seem "clearly absurd" to most of us. But Nelson offers only a few brief sentences setting forth his "biases" on legitimate interests.[120] On the more general issue of illegitimate tastes Ezra Mishan's benefit-cost text has a "note" in the back in which he suggests that one should exclude from calculations losses because of envy of other's good fortune or because of displeasure at association with members of other ethnic groups. Mishan argues that an implicit ethical constitution should sometimes take precedence over utility calculations. Yet even an economist as willing and able as Mishan to make judgments about the quality of tastes is unwilling to let his thoughts in the note influence the body of the text. When Mishan discusses valuing lifesaving programs, for example, he mentions, without so much as a reference to his note, the need to include the preferences of those who would gain financially or psychically when others die.[121]

CONCLUSION

The mainstream economic literature on information and changing tastes avoids the most important questions and provides little useful policy guidance on the narrower ones that are addressed. For reasons given at the beginning of this chapter, most economists would acknowledge that government provision of information can be a useful supplement to market mechanisms in some areas. But general rules such as "intervene when it is costly for consumers to get adequate information from private sources" or "intervene when the damage from mistakes is great" do not provide much useful guidance. Economists probably do not go beyond such general rules because when they attempt to do so, they find that even the narrowest questions soon lead to larger ones with which they do not feel equipped to deal.

Whether one thinks consumers are adequately informed about some aspects of their lives inevitably depends on what one thinks should be important to a thoughtful consumer. How important is the free-rider problem that makes it hard to make a profit by selling lists comparing grocery store prices on a whole range of items? Much depends on how important money is to human happiness. If it is important, then it might make sense for government to provide comparative price information and for consumers to know it well. If it is less important and if the larger information problem is the market's overemphasis on money and goods, then such a price list could just encourage consumers to pay still more attention to money and goods as a source of happiness. What should one conclude about the unwillingness of consumers to wear seat belts? By now most drivers should know that they are safer in a seat belt, so perhaps government's information role can be abandoned. But perhaps people do not *really know* how much safer they are; perhaps they will not really *understand* until they are forced to see films that show the blood and broken bones, the grief-stricken families and such. Or if this is a case of passion and convenience overwhelming better judgment, one might favor mandated air bags in all cars. In the final analysis, an issue like seat belts/air bags forces a judgment about how important a fear of violent death in an automobile should be to a thoughtful individual.

Economists cannot really make a judgment about market performance without addressing such difficult, value-laden questions. To fail to address them does not mean one remains neutral because such failure represents an implicit decision against government intervention.[122] Controversy cannot be avoided. To do their applied work economists find they have to take a position on questions such as whether financial or psychic externalities are more important, that is, on whether we are materialistic and narrowly self-interested. And one does not remain neutral by deducing preferences for public policy from market transactions, by objecting to any government role in taste formation, or by effectively sanctioning theft.

As explained earlier, economists such as Marx and Veblen would have sharp differences with the usual assumptions of evaluative economics. Of much more significance, however, are the differences that earlier mainstream market economists would have with today's mainstream market economists. John Stuart Mill thought free government should try to elevate public tastes. This policy position stemmed from his belief that a lack of mental cultivation was the second most important "cause which makes life unsatisfactory." The only more important cause was "selfishness."[123] If Mill be thought not quite mainstream, the founder of modern economics, Adam Smith, can be consulted. Smith was concerned that the manufacturing process of his day could leave the ordinary worker

stupid and ignorant . . . not only incapable of relishing or bearing a part in any rational conversation, but of conceiving any generous, noble, or tender sentiment, and consequently of forming any just judgment concerning many even of the ordinary duties of private life . . .

. . . A man without the proper use of the intellectual faculties of a man, is, if possible, more contemptible than even a coward, and seems to be mutilated and deformed in a still more essential part of the character of human nature. Though the state was to derive no advantage from the instruction of the inferior ranks of people, it would still deserve its attention that they should not be altogether uninstructed.[124]

If Smith be thought archaic, hear Alfred Marshall, a successor to Mill who is generally considered the "father of neoclassicism." Marshall believed that "the power of rightly using such income and opportunities, as a family has, is in itself wealth of the highest order, and of a kind that is rare in all classes." He maintained that "the discussion of the influence on general well-being which is exerted by the mode in which each individual spends his income is one of the most important of those applications of economic science to the art of living." Marshall encouraged "wisely ordered magnificence," philanthropic expenditures on objects such as public parks and art collections. Such expenditures at once "free from any taint of personal vanity on the one side and envy on the other" would make available "an abundance of the higher forms of enjoyment for collective use."[125]

Marshall's great contemporary, P. H. Wicksteed, distinguished tastes further by noting that certain kinds of pleasures increased the capacity for future enjoyment. Intellectual, literary, artistic, and scientific enjoyment demand at some point "painful effort and discipline." But with greater study one's pursuit of these activities increases "hedonistic capacity," which is not true of most other activities. Like Marshall, Wicksteed believed that individual welfare could be increased if people could be induced to change their expenditure patterns. He noted, though, that commercial activity often brought about change of the wrong kind: The "action of the economic forces, unguided and unchecked, naturally favours the growth not only of a class of ministers to vice, but of a class of persons who live by enabling people to get another drop out of the squeezed orange of today's capacity for enjoyment, reckless of its reactions upon tomorrow."[126]

Still later, A. C. Pigou's pioneering *Economics of Welfare* argued that consumption patterns could exercise either an "elevating" or a "debasing" influence. He unabashedly declared the satisfactions connected with literature and art "ethically superior to those connected with the primary needs." A man "attuned to the beautiful in nature or art, whose character is simple and sincere, whose passions are controlled and sympathies developed" was "himself an important element in the ethical value of the world."[127]

Finally, consider the views of Frank Knight, an influential teacher at the University of Chicago in the 1930s and 1940s and a staunch proponent of free markets. Knight is particularly insightful about our aspiration for different, higher wants.

The chief thing which the common-sense individual actually wants is not satisfactions for the wants which he has, but more and *better* wants. The things which he strives to get in the most immediate sense are far more what he thinks he ought to want than what his untutored preferences prompt. This feeling for what one *should* want, in contrast with actual desire, is stronger in the unthinking than in those sophisticated by education. It is the latter who argues himself into the "tolerant" (economic) attitude of *de gustibus non disputandum*.

. . . the true achievement is the refinement and elevation of the plane of desire, the cultivation of taste. And let us reiterate that all this is true *to the person acting*, not simply to the outsider, philosophizing after the event.

Knight was concerned about the effects of advertising and salesmanship on people's tastes.

Ethically, the creation of the right wants is more important than want-satisfaction. With regard to the facts in the case, we may observe that business is interested in the fact of change in wants more than in the character of the change, and presumably effects chiefly those changes which can be brought about more easily and cheaply. Our general moral teaching would indicate that it is easier to corrupt human nature than to improve it, and observation of the taste-forming tendencies of modern marketing methods tends perhaps to confirm the view and to substantiate a negative verdict on individualistic activity of this sort.

Among the important adverse effects of salesmanship and economic rivalry is their tendency to work against the appreciation of the "free goods." They thus tend to undermine the "fairly established consensus that happiness depends more on spiritual resourcefulness, and a joyous appreciation of the costless things of life, especially affection for one's fellow creatures, than it does on material satisfaction."[128]

By quoting at length these great figures of the past, I do not mean to suggest that they would necessarily agree in all respects with each other or with what is argued here. Nor do I mean to suggest that no economists today combine an appreciation for capitalism and markets with a profound understanding of their weaknesses. Careful readers of this book will be aware of my debt to men such as Kenneth Boulding, E. J. Mishan, Amartya Sen, Tibor Scitovsky, and Leland Yeager. But the views of these men are not at all typical of today's profession. Economists of the past thought it was part of their task to remind their readers that there are high and low pleasures, that many of the high ones require reason and the sometimes-painful acquisition of knowledge, that we aspire to tastes better than our current ones, and that such aspirations are sometimes hindered by profit-seeking businesses that cater to vices and over-emphasize the importance of what money can buy. Today's economists are more likely to feel a professional obligation to combat such sentiments than to support them.

These striking differences reflect changes in the nature of the discipline and the way it educates its practitioners. Economics today is much more technical and much more insular. The older economists read widely beyond economics, and they felt the need to respond when one such as Thomas Carlyle said they were professing a "pig philosophy."[129] Because they were both broader and deeper, the older economists were less likely to forget that economic man is not the total man.

Today's graduate student in economics rarely studies any subject besides recent economics and mathematics. He is unlikely to know that even those contemporary philosophers who are utilitarian are more likely to side with Mill and praise the "incomparably more fecund" higher pleasures than they are to side with Bentham with his unwillingness to distinguish high from low.[130] He is also unlikely to know that the great economists of the past held views like those quoted earlier. Courses in the history of economic thought or political economy do not lead to the best jobs, and they attract few students. As Kenneth Boulding has noted, "It is fashionable indeed to decry the history of thought as a luxury in these days of econometrics, to proclaim that it is of no greater significance than, shall we say, the history of mathematics." Boulding argues that this attitude limits graduate students "to the fashions of the present" and confines them in "a tight little intellectual box from which there is no escape."[131] Despite Boulding's warnings the trend toward an increasingly narrow and technical education has continued. Even Boulding and the four other contemporary economists praised earlier will not be con-temporary much longer. Their average age is sixty-five, and their younger counterparts are not in sight. The profession now seems to attract those with a narrowly self-interested view of mankind, and much economic work depends on that view.

Earlier chapters made frequent use of the results of technical studies so I would not wish to deny there have been fruits from recent developments in the discipline. Nonetheless, much of what is interesting in economics requires little technique and is not really new. A large percentage of economic articles make one important and understandable point in ordinary prose and then dress it up with pages of formulas. One need not "progress" beyond Smith to learn to appreciate markets and the power of economic incentives. In the *Wealth of Nations* one can even find a rough outline of the contemporary discipline's views on the roles for the market, national government, and local government.

This chapter has argued that many economists' narrow view of man keeps them from raising questions that are intrinsically important to the discipline. But it has also argued that this narrow outlook prevents economists from finding convincing answers to some questions they themselves raise. These weaknesses are not likely to be remedied until economists relearn some of what their forebears knew, but which they now ignore or deny. One of the most pernicious effects of current efforts to make economics more "scientific" is the accompanying tendency to ridicule all beliefs that are "empty of empirically verifiable content."[132] The older economists knew that good politics can settle for less certainty than that. The inability to demonstrate conclusively the truth of a belief does not mean that both it and its opposite are equally likely to be true. The following chapter will show how the narrow scientism pervasive in the discipline distorts the perspective of economists in their treatment of externalities.

10

A SECOND LOOK AT EXTERNALITIES

In principle, the economic policy framework should be able to incorporate many of the concerns voiced in the previous chapter even if only by the back door. The welfare-economic principles do not allow one to see some pleasures as higher or more intrinsically satisfying than others. They thus do not allow for government intervention to induce individuals to change their behavior in a direction that seems likely to make them happier. Welfare economics does, however, allow for government encouragement of activities that bring pleasure to third parties and government discouragement of activities that bring third parties pain. Families that spend more time together are less likely to produce juvenile delinquents. Individuals who spend more time with friends or civic associations are likely to bring others pleasure. So too will those who learn more and who thus will be better citizens, cleverer inventors, or simply more interesting conversationalists as a result of their increased knowledge of history, literature, politics, or science. On the other hand, those addicted to cigarettes, alcohol, and drugs will increase for others the costs of crime and health insurance. Pornography and prostitution may weaken the family and lead to physical abuse and psychic pain for women not directly involved. And although the costs to the victims of crimes may deserve no more weight, in the welfare economist's calculus, than the benefits to the successful perpetrators, that calculus also would have to take into account the psychic pain experienced by third parties when criminals gain in this way, and these psychic costs alone may outweigh the gains to the criminal.[1]

Though some economists would acknowledge substantial costs to third parties from cigarette, alcohol, and drug addiction, the other externalities are ignored.[2] Earlier chapters have suggested reasons for this neglect. Most of these externalities call into question models and views of the world that emphasize money and narrow self-interest. They also complicate empirical work since clear recommendations are less likely if intangible externalities are significant. Moreover, economists probably sense that their technical education leaves them poorly equipped to weigh the significance of these effects on others.

There are also more defensible reasons for deemphasizing these sorts of externalities. An expansive view of externalities would necessarily lead to more decisions by governments that are frequently plagued by inefficiency and fewer by markets that perform important, if limited, functions well. This chapter will also explore another public-spirited reason offered by some economists who would narrowly circumscribe externalities: a concern for individual liberty. The chapter will argue, however, that the cramped view of externalities that most economists adopt ignores many considerations that are important to public welfare even as welfare economics itself defines it.

ILLEGITIMATE AND MEDDLESOME TASTES

As indicated in the last chapter, the body of Ezra Mishan's cost-benefit text treats malevolent and other questionable tastes as the equals of others. However, Mishan argues in a note to his text in favor of excluding tastes such as envy from benefit-cost calculations. In that note and elsewhere Mishan maintains that there are ethical propositions that command such widespread assent that they may be considered as forming part of a "virtual constitution."

Thus, notwithstanding that all members of society agree that an individual is the best judge of his own welfare, society may not wish to admit a Pareto improvement by reference to utility alone which otherwise affronts in any particular the moral sense of society.[3]

Mishan acknowledges that

the sort of welfare economics proposed here which defines a person's welfare in terms of his experience of welfare and yet at the same time, in defining social welfare, invokes value judgments that at certain points may conflict with the experience of welfare, does run the risk of serving social ethics rather than social welfare. But it is a risk we have to take if our welfare propositions are to have the sanction of the constitution.[4]

In the aforementioned note, Mishan suggests excluding from consideration all interdependent psychic utilities, not just the pleasure the malevolent get from others' bad fortune, but also the pleasure the benevolent get from others' good fortune. Later in the same section, however, he says that the composition of the ethical constitution must be determined on the basis of "what men of good will regard as reasonable." Still elsewhere, his suggested standard for the ethical constitution is "a consensus in the particular society."[5]

Though envy of one's neighbor's goods is proscribed by one of the Ten Commandments, even this part of Mishan's argument has not commanded widespread assent among economists. In a well-received book, James Duesenberry has suggested the need to take account of the effect on poorer neighbors when high-income people decide to work, earn, and spend more.

Since Duesenberry thinks the poor are harmed psychologically by additional expenditures by the rich, but the rich probably feel no worse when the poor consume more, he and others have also seen envy as an argument in favor of redistribution of income.[6] This literature, together with the more voluminous literature that sees benevolence to the poor as a public good justifying redistribution,[7] shows quite clearly that many economists would disagree with Mishan's suggestion that interdependent psychic utilities should be excluded from social-welfare calculations. Indeed, the preceding chapter's discussion of economists who have included benefits to criminals in their benefit-cost analyses indicates that applied economists have not been inclined to constrain utility calculations by an ethical constitution of any kind.

Nevertheless, there are indications in the theoretical literature that others share some of Mishan's concerns. Merewitz and Sosnick suggest focusing on externality cases where there has been an "absolute deterioration" in position "such as reduced incomes."[8] This is similar to Mishan's proposal that we look for a "palpable impact" on an individual's circumstances.[9] Both would agree with Friedrich Hayek's view that no account should be taken of psychic pain caused by "the mere dislike of what is being done by others."[10]

Well beyond libertarian circles one finds economists who are worried by the threats to individual liberty implied by an unconstrained application of the externality concept. Both Kenneth Arrow and Amartya Sen have suggested that we may want to preserve some sphere of personal activity where the preferences of others are irrelevant.[11] If Jones should be so hypersensitive as to feel pain because of the color of Smith's walls, we may want to tell Jones that such matters are none of his business. In a recent article Leland Yeager clearly states the principle that Sen and Arrow only hint at:

The very conception of a liberal society calls for distinguishing among the particular tastes of individuals, according some tastes more and some tastes less respect . . .

In contrast with a totalitarian or a tribal society in which people see externalities all over the place and in which government or tradition therefore controls the individual's life in detail, a liberal society narrows the range of supposed externalities dignified by social policy.[12]

It is not clear what percentage of the economics profession would subscribe to these views on meddlesome tastes. Sen's argument has led to much commentary, most of it critical.[13] Many economists would insist that no principles should constrain consumers' wills. In the presence of externalities, Hillinger and Lapham cannot even "conceive" of any " 'principle of liberalism' which would govern what actions are to be left to individuals independently of the majority preference of the individuals concerned."[14] Still, when informally commenting on particular policies rather than paying homage to their theoretical touchstone, consumer sovereignty, many economists do indicate disapproval of other people's tastes. It is usually because they find these tastes meddlesome. The policy areas most often involved are the laws surrounding activities dubbed by economists and others as "crimes without victims."

"CRIMES WITHOUT VICTIMS"

In the corridors of academe and in publications here and there many economists voice their strong opposition to laws outlawing gambling, recreational drugs, homosexuality, prostitution, and pornography. Thus, for example, Dean Worcester has briefly commented on the "sorry record" of "criminalization of the nonprescription narcotic industry."[15] Miller and North's discussion of recreational drugs is somewhat more extended. Like Worcester they link such policies to the failures of Prohibition. Laws can make pursuits illegal, but since desires remain, black markets appear. With them come organized crime and payoffs to police. Though Miller and North end their discussion of the "economics of euphoria" by denying that their analysis is an argument for the legalization of euphorics, it nevertheless reads like such an argument. The authors assert that "there are also benefits" of current laws, but they list only costs: crime, corruption, needlessly high prices, dangerously low quality. Miller and North's analysis of prostitution is similar, though they add the increased incidence of venereal disease to the list of costs of criminalization. Their lighthearted chapter on the "ladies of the night" begins by suggesting that a campaign in France to relegalize prostitution shows that the current prohibitions "have not proved too satisfactory."[16]

Sometimes those who object to these "crimes without victims" are portrayed in various unflattering ways. Thus Milton Spencer's economics text says that those who argue against legalized gambling are in the tradition that "assumes that a small group of determined people have the right to decide what a far larger group should or should not do."[17] Gordon Tullock's characterization of those who oppose decriminalized prostitution and pornography is more subdued. He does, however, suggest that such people are "puritans" and that the only costs they incur are to their "moral feelings."[18] He and James Buchanan also believe that laws on these matters would be "significantly weaker" if proponents had to pay to eliminate the behavior in others that they condemn as immoral.[19]

For some of these crimes there may be no substantial third-party victims, but it is remarkable that none of this economic commentary mentions persons external to the commercial transactions who may indeed be victimized. Take pornography as an example. The 1970 U.S. *Report of the Commission on Obscenity and Pornography* concluded that pornography was a victimless crime, but that report has been widely criticized. In the 1960s Denmark gradually abolished all laws against pornography. The early reports indicated that sex crimes had gone down, but later more careful reports found that "the incidence of rape did not decline but in all likelihood increased."[20] In the

United States research has shown that rapists are fifteen times more likely than others to have been exposed to hard-core pornographic photos before the age of eleven.[21] Other studies show that cities with a large number of pornography outlets tend to have disproportionately high rape rates, that rapists are frequently found to possess pornography, and that wife batterers are often devotees of pornographic literature. One big-city police commissioner, who also holds a Ph.D. in sociology with a specialization in sex roles, has said, "Often we find that the man is trying to enact a scene in some pornographic pictures."[22]

Since publication of the commission's report in 1970, the violence in pornography has increased significantly. Researchers have documented this even for popular publications such as *Playboy* and *Penthouse*.[23] But pornography comes much worse. The recent British commission on obscenity reported that it had been "totally unprepared" for the films it encountered showing "highly explicit depictions of mutilation, savagery, menace and humiliation."[24] At least 15 percent of commercial pornographic imagery is explicitly violent, and it is available in many supermarkets.[25]

Recent research findings of experimental social psychologists show that there is reason to be especially concerned about the effects of pornography in which a rape victim is portrayed as becoming involuntarily sexually aroused by the assault. Both self-reports and measures of penile tumescence show that such pornography yields sexual-arousal levels as high as or higher than those stimulated by depictions of sexual acts between mutually consenting participants. Moreover, men exposed to such "positive-outcome" violent pornography are more likely than others to believe that women in general derive some pleasure from being raped.[26]

A recent field experiment avoided the artificial context of these laboratory studies but came to similarly troubling conclusions. Over 100 college students were recruited to participate in a study ostensibly concerned with reviewing movies. On two different evenings some "reviewers" watched the movies *Swept Away* and *The Getaway*, both of which show women as victims of aggression within erotic as well as nonerotic incidents, while another group watched neutral feature-length movies. Members of the classes from which subjects had been recruited but who had not signed up for the experiment were used as a comparison group. Several days after the movies had been shown a sexual-attitude survey was administered in all the classes from which the "movie reviewers" had been drawn. Subjects were not aware that there was any connection between the survey and the movies. Embedded within many other items in the survey were questions assessing acceptance of violence against women and of myths such as the belief that rapes often end up being sexually enjoyable for the victims. "Results indicated that exposure to films portraying aggressive sexuality as having positive consequences significantly increased male, but not female, subjects' acceptance of interpersonal violence against women and tended to increase males' acceptance of rape myths."[27]

As Irving Kristol has noted, those who argue that "no one was ever corrupted by a book" must also argue that no one was ever improved by one. If art and education are morally relevant, then "the ways we use our minds and imaginations do shape our characters and help define us as persons."[28] The standard theme of a whole genre of paperback novelettes concerns women who, through a combination of seduction and compulsion, come to desire their own subjection. A frequent variation of the theme shows the woman being beaten into submission while desiring and inviting this treatment.[29] It would surely be surprising if none of the men who frequently read such literature came to believe it accurately portrays women's desires and began to act on such beliefs.

THE IMPORTANCE OF RIGHTS

Civil libertarians will want to remind us of the right to free speech and the dangers of embarking on the "slippery slope" of censorship. If a sadomasochistic book is censored today, what is to prevent the works of D. H. Lawrence from being banned tomorrow? It is surely true that difficult decisions will have to be made in close cases. But almost everyone would agree that a line must be drawn somewhere, for example, pornography picturing children and roadside billboards portraying scenes from a sadomasochistic novel. Those who would ban pictures of children simulating fornication but not pictures of children eating Wheaties acknowledge that pornography can be recognized and can cause harm.[30] To make such judgments they too must weigh conflicting claims.[31]

It is interesting that Lawrence himself criticized pornography as an attempt "to do dirt on [sex] . . . [It is an] insult to a vital human relationship."[32] Lawrence contended that he was writing literature, not pornography. In contrast, many authors of pornography have no illusions about the literary quality of what they write. One author has said, "I was unable to do any 'real' writing because plot, characterization, imagery, allusion, tragedy and comedy are all taboo in porn, and I had gotten out of the habit of paying attention to them." When another author was asked how he felt about the commercial success of his soft-core pornographic novel, he said, "Well, I think we all felt mildly depressed . . . depressed that it got such a reception."[33]

Irving Kristol has argued that the worst of the evils of censorship can be avoided through a liberal enforcment policy.[34] Pornography could be illegal but available under the counter to anyone who wants it enough to make an effort to get it. Under such a regime the pervasive external costs would be much lower. In this connection the results of an informal poll of half a dozen psychiatrists are of interest. Almost all of them made a distinction between the reading of pornography, as unlikely to be per se harmful, and the permitting of the reading of pornography, which was conceived as potentially destructive. The child is protected in his reading of pornography by the knowledge that it is pornographic, that is, disapproved. It is outside of parental standards and not a part of his identification processes. To openly permit implies parental approval and even suggests seductive encouragement. If this is so of parental approval, it is equally so of societal approval – another potent influence on the developing ego.[35]

The civil libertarian focuses on individual rights. As argued in Chapter 6, for the most part economists do not have much to say about the substance of rights – such as the right to the fruits of one's labor. Their standard is people's preferences pure and simple. Tullock, for example, makes no distinction between the views of those in this country who want to see commercial television portray blacks in a manner reducing white prejudice and the views of many South Africans who want to do the reverse: "The fact that we approve of one and disapprove of the other indicates that we have a certain set of preferences. It does not indicate that there is a difference in kind between them or that both of them are not efforts to generate externalities."[36]

A philosophy of nothing beyond preferences would allow envy and mal-evolence to count. It might lead to restrictions on annoying political speech. It would presumably banish from public view those people with hideous deformities who regularly draw taunts from the public.[37] It would recognize no principle preventing others from controlling an individual's behavior in any area of life. As the earlier quotations from Hillinger and Lapham reveal, despite its individualistic surface, this pure welfare-economic philosophy does not read like a philosophy of liberty.

Those economists who are concerned about envious and meddlesome tastes correctly want to draw back from the policy consequences of a rigorous application of evaluative economic principles. It would be a mistake, however, to think that the problem can be solved by counting only externalities that have an easily recognizable "palpable" or "tangible" effect on others.[38] Because economic models so often assume fixed preferences, it is too easy for economists on all sides of the issue of meddlesomeness to assume as well that legalized pornography can cause no significant external effects.[39] Those who object to pornography are seen as busybodies whose moral feelings may be slightly bruised. Their preferences would not be counted if an ethical constitution excluded meddlesome tastes nor would they be decisive if the minor pain they incur were balanced against the real losses of those who will be deprived of the pornographic literature. But pornography may change tastes. Even if we ignore subtle effects, there is evidence that it leads to violence against women.[40]

Ironically, economists here go wrong because they refuse to take public preferences about pornography at their face value. In 1977, 45 percent of Americans polled thought that their community's standards regarding the sale of sexually explicit material should be stricter, 6 percent thought they should be less strict, and 35 percent thought they should be kept the same (14 percent had no opinion). Even among those who had themselves seen an x-rated movie 31 percent were for stricter standards, and only 10 percent thought that they should be less strict.[41]

A plausible case for the harmful effects of pornography can be made. Most people tend to take their moral bearings from what they see around them. If a society refuses to use the law to defend its standards of decency, it cannot long preserve those standards. There will always be a market for hard-core pornography, and if those who sell it can do so as easily as those who sell soap, it will be everywhere. When indecency becomes legal and pervasive, it ceases to seem indecent. Economists should be especially slow to demand rigorous proof of tangible damage before taking seriously subjectively felt external costs.

To demand clear evidence of palpable or tangible effects on others before banning an activity would mean legalizing gladiator contests. Tullock comes close to advocating as much when he argues that people should be free to join a " 'violence' club" in which they could fight, or even "duel" if they so wished.[42] If violence clubs are unobjectionable, it is hard to see why watching their activities should be. Perhaps we should also permit entrepreneurs to charge admission to watch others commit suicide.[43] One can almost hear Tullock trying to cut through our Old World prejudice by patiently explaining that the guy would probably commit suicide anyway, and this way some good will come out of it; he can provide for his family and show some people a good time.

If only a tangible cost to other humans can justify outlawing an activity, there is also no justification for the laws against cock and dog fights. A few states permit such fights, and in many more they are conducted illegally. For followers of dog fights there is even an underground newsletter, *Pit Dogs*. It keeps devotees up-to-date with pictures and reports like the following.

One hour and a half. Scout working a down dog for 15 minutes, occasionally stopping to lick, then going back to chewing Buck. Mike starts encouraging the dog to kill Buck . . .

Queenie's front legs gone now and her time to go, but she goes across like a dog should . . . She reminds me of a seal walking, her front legs just flapping.[44]

Tullock seems quite open to restrictions on people's freedom because their appearance and dress offend others. He uses the example of some unbathed hippies in Rome who gather around the Spanish Steps creating an eyesore in one of the most beautiful spots in the city.[45] If you see something unpleasant, it apparently becomes tangible enough to be recognized as an externality even if what is unpleasant is only ungroomed human beings. But objections to a violence club that you only know about are not legitimate. "If both parties to a fight, duel, or brawl obtain pleasure from it, there is no welfare reason why outsiders should interfere.''[46] History, however, suggests some good reasons why one could object to legalized duels: They have been associated with reduced respect for the law and increased domestic violence.[47]

What about the animal fights? Unlike the gladiator fights, they do not necessarily weaken respect for *human* life. They do appeal to brutal passions, and one could argue that if these passions are encouraged, they may lead to brutality toward humans as well. But we should not have to show such an effect in order to ban these fights. It should be enough that we do not want our children raised in a society where one of the legal forms of entertainment is watching animals die painfully and unnecessarily. Even the psychic pain felt by adults from the knowledge that animals are being cruelly destroyed (or blind men brutally robbed) should be justification enough. Some of the least "palpable" externalities are felt by those possessing public-spirited, praiseworthy sentiments. They should be entitled to public recognition.

The preceding chapter argued that consumer-information problems inevitably lead to the largest questions about human nature and the conditions for achieving happiness. Judgments about many externalities do so as well. If some people want to do what shocks others, one must decide if the latter are narrow-minded, meddlesome pests or farseeing defenders of civilization alert to the "slippery slope" of human degradation. A difficult balancing process is inevitable. We will want to preserve the right of individuals to a sphere of private action worthy of a freedom-loving nation, but we should not sanction tastes that threaten our humanity. As Joseph Cropsey has argued, consumer sovereignty, individualism, or the importance of each of us as a unique phenomenon cannot be the bulwark of human dignity. What dignifies human beings "proceeds from their common relation to nonhuman things . . . Their dignity is the attribute of their common nature, of what they possess jointly, not severally, and it inheres in what elevates them above nonhumanity rather than in what merely distinguishes them from each other."[48]

ETHICS, GOOD WILL, CIVILITY, AND OTHER POLITICAL BENEFITS

Chapter 9 showed that many economists think human behavior is motivated by narrowly selfish and materialistic ends. It also showed that these economists believe such behavior is perfectly rational from the point of view of the individual. Once one considers externalities, however, it becomes apparent that such behavior may not maximize societal welfare even if one defines societal welfare as economists themselves do. As was argued in Chapter 4, when self-interest fails, an economist's inclination is to rechannel it so it succeeds. For example, simple changes in the law can make it in a businessman's interest to clean up pollution rather than add to it.

Though in many cases such rechanneling is all that is needed to achieve efficient outcomes, frequently it is insufficient. In recent years a few economists have explored cases in which even rechanneled self-interest fails to maximize societal welfare. Such failures arise in a striking way when one party to a transaction has far better information than the other. Sellers of automobiles and houses know far more about their defects than do buyers, and physicians know much more about the treatment a patient needs than does the patient himself. Narrowly self-interested sellers of products such as these can exploit their superior knowledge to increase their incomes. As Kenneth Arrow has argued, effective codes of ethics can achieve greater societal efficiency by increasing buyer confidence and satisfaction, which in turn leads to more business for sellers.[49]

Self-interest fails efficiency, however, in a host of situations that cannot be explained by differences in knowledge possessed by buyers and sellers. Because externalities are so pervasive and so frequently expensive to correct for, laws can affect only a small fraction of them. Higher ethical standards together with greater good will and civility could increase societal well-being in most areas where externalities remain uncorrected. If people were more law-abiding, our roadsides would be cleaner, and, more important, much violence and fear would disappear from our lives. If only the currently law-abiding were more willing to report violators and step forward as witnesses, significant gains along these lines might be possible.[50] And there are many small things that collectively could make a big difference in the quality of our lives. Just imagine a world where almost everyone was helpful when your car broke down or when you asked for directions, where people greeted each other with friendly words and smiles, where few made noise in movies, libraries, or late at night, and where people almost always left public campsites and rest rooms as clean as they found them.

The handful of economists who have concerned themselves with these aspects of life have not been encouraged about the prospects for ethics and civility. The free-rider problem looms large. Whether I take the time to flush a toilet or go to court to testify about a crime I have seen will have little effect on the cleanliness of the public rest rooms I will use or the number of criminals I will encounter later. Someone will be better off, but since there are so many of us and since my behavior will at most encourage emulation by only a few others, it is unlikely that I will be better off if better off is equated with narrow self-interest. Moreover, as Leland Yeager notes, "The more prevalent and well-based is the belief that people are generally decent and honest, the greater is the chance that culprits have to benefit from the presumption that they too have these virtues."[51] James Buchanan joins Yeager in arguing that if the culprits become a significant minority, the majority, feeling exploited, will begin to imitate their behavior.[52]

Though the free-rider phenomenon has presumably existed through the ages, both Buchanan and Roland McKean suggest that its perverse effects are becoming more threatening. McKean gives a number of reasons to support such a conclusion. The new emphasis on individual fulfillment may make us more willing to behave as a free rider. The popularity of "situational" ethics makes one unsure of what can be expected from others and perhaps more willing to behave as a free rider. Client-centered psychological therapy may undermine "socially valuable feelings of guilt and obligation." In addition, as people have become more mobile, their neighbors, co-workers, and friends change more often. The support for ethical codes that comes from the approval or disapproval shown by friends or neighbors is thus less important. Finally, and in McKean's view, "probably most important of all,"

With increased literacy, sophistication, and contact with others, people may be increasingly aware of their free-rider positions and decreasingly credulous about the sanctity of religious doctrine, traditions, and behavioural tenets.[53]

In light of the pervasiveness of the inefficient externalities that exist in our society and these predictions that societal trends are making the problem worse, not better, one might expect to find economists proposing public policies that will help reinvigorate ethics, good will, and civility. One finds no such proposals.[54] To be sure, both Arrow and McKean make the general point that government policies can promote or hinder the effectiveness of informal codes.[55] And in Chapter 9 we saw that Tullock's book on the law includes a short section in which some sort of indoctrination to raise conscience costs is recommended if that should prove the least costly way to reduce crime. Yeager, though, takes pains to deemphasize government's role, preferring to rely instead on "informal, decentralized" support for ethical conduct.[56] But in light of McKean's analysis of societal trends, without governmental support, societal forces seem unlikely to make much progress. Finally, Buchanan's position is quite curious. On the one hand, he sees large benefits resulting from law abidingness and from internalized ethical codes. He even concludes an important book by despairing of the future of democracy if citizens are unwilling to constrain themselves by adhering to a "constitutional attitude."[57] Yet elsewhere he has said that problems of personal morality or of an individual's obligation to obey the law "do not belong properly in political theory" and that with full freedom to trade, "there is little need for the preacher."[58]

Though the solutions proposed by these economists seem inadequate given the magnitude of the problem they outline, they at least see the problem. As was suggested in both Chapter 4 and the preceding chapter, most economists are unlikely to see any serious problems with self-interest. Like Charles Schultze they believe that "harnessing the 'base' motive of material self-interest to promote the common good is perhaps the most important social invention mankind has yet achieved."[59] If problems remain these economists will tend to think they can be dealt with by tinkering with the way the old horse is harnessed. We could, for example, increase fines for those who leave dirty campsites, pay witnesses to crimes far more for their testimony, and perhaps give monetary rewards to those citizens with the biggest smiles and the most helpful attitudes.

So we could. But the higher fines would be ineffective without an expensive police force to inspect the campsites, and an ample bounty paid for court testimony might induce some to bear false witness against strangers. And perhaps the big smiles will seem less pleasing if we think their size is explained by a desire to win a contest rather than by a friendly, helpful nature.

Certainly we could avoid all these costs if people would behave in a civil, public-spirited, or friendly manner without the need for a newly crafted financial incentive.[60] Moreover, cost aside, there is evidence that good character is a far more effective cause of moral and law-abiding behavior than are financial or other types of legal incentives. The findings of criminologists about the relative importance of moral commitment and fear of punishment are relevant here. Matthew Silberman looked at the impact of a number of variables on the crime rate. He found that moral commitment explained most of the variance and that certainty of punishment was far less important. Another study attempted to assess the effects of a "sanction threat" and of a "conscience appeal" on compliance with income tax laws.

Taxpayers were randomly assigned to treatment and control groups. Before tax returns were submitted, one group was interviewed and asked questions suggesting the possibility that they might be punished if they misreported their incomes. A second group was reminded of their moral responsibility, while a third group was interviewed but asked none of the questions suggesting a "sanction threat" or a "conscience appeal." A fourth group was not interviewed. The "sanction appeal" and "conscience appeal" groups both reported significantly higher incomes than the control groups, but the appeal to conscience was found to produce greater reported income than the sanction threat.[61]

Punishment can educate and help create good habits so legal incentives cannot be forgotten even if we seek to build moral character.[62] But the relative advantages of character as a means to law abidingness are clear. Crime rates should be lower if people avoid crime because they think it wrong than if they avoid it because they fear detection. We cannot possibly check on everything. McKean relates a case in which a man, having smashed into a parked car, left the following note under its windshield. "People are watching me. They think I am writing down my name, address, and license number. I am not."[63] Such clever people will get away with most crimes they choose to commit. Thus, attention to ways of encouraging us to respond to the better sides of our natures may bring substantial increases in societal well-being.

Churches and synagogues may be important allies in this endeavor. Sociologists have found that traditional religion remains an influential force in American life. Though we have a large number of sects they tend to have common views about private and public morality. In the private sphere they support "monogamous marriage, family solidarity, the Ten Commandments, private charity, self-control, self-improvement, dutifulness and patience under suffering" and in the public sphere "patriotism, the authority of law, democracy and human rights."[64] Though institutions that support such virtues perform an important public service, today's Supreme Court says the First Amendment forbids our assisting them. Still, as we shall see in the next chapter, public-choice economists have not been slow to suggest constitutional revisions in other areas. Our churches' teaching seems to encourage behavior that generates external benefits while discouraging behavior that generates external costs. Economists might thus be expected to be in the forefront of those recommending a return to the founders' understanding of good constitutional law and public policy in this area: a mix of religious liberty and no official church on the one hand, and nondiscriminatory aid to religious institutions on the other.[65] Moreover, simple changes in the tax law could aid churches without offending the Court in any way. A large share of middle-class charitable giving goes to churches, and a provision allowing taxpayers to deduct their full amount of charitable contributions even if they take the standard deduction could increase church revenues significantly.[66]

The middle class also likes to give to community-based service organizations so the tax provision would aid these as well. Moreover, the amount of time and energy that individuals devote to charitable activities is strongly correlated with the amount of their financial aid to charities.[67] Though correlation does not prove causation, it is possible that new incentives that induce taxpayers to make new monetary contributions could lead the benefiting organizations to provide contributors with more information about the organizations' other needs and thus induce at least some additional contributions of time as well.

Once patterns of behavior that generate external costs or benefits have taken hold, they often mushroom in a way that can dramatically affect a community's way of life. Political scientists James Q. Wilson and George Kelling have noted that seemingly small signs of disorder – loud, ill-smelling drunks, rowdy teenagers, unrepaired broken windows, etc. – send signals that "no one cares" and weaken "mutual regard and the obligations of civility." Vandalism and crime often follow.[68] By the same token, goodwill and civility often increase rapidly once they make their presence felt.

Psychologists have found that if they set up situations calling for an altruistic response – for example, a woman looking helpless beside a broken-down car – more people will respond with offers of help if they have recently witnessed someone else behaving altruistically in a similar situation (i.e., because the experimenters put a man helping a woman to change a tire back down the road) than if they had not witnessed an altruistic act.[69]

Similarly, at my son's public elementary school an initially small parent-teaching-assistance program has mushroomed to the point where over ten parents volunteer every week for each class of under fifty students.

Even within the individual the use of goodwill often increases rather than decreases its supply. Over 6,000 people in our community of 100,000 perform volunteer work. One hundred participate in the "Meals on Wheels" Program, donating a few hours a week and driving expenses to take a hot meal to elderly people who cannot cook for themselves and who live alone. One suburban mother of small children explains her participation as follows:

You get so attached to the people on your route. As soon as I started it, I got hooked. Now I really look forward to it.

Another volunteer, seventy-four years old herself, says,

I have 18 stops to make and everybody wants to talk. Often, I'm the only person who stops by. If you could just see how grateful they are, you'd know why I've been doing this for two years.[70]

This program is a perfect example of the kind of in-kind redistributive program economists typically attack. The charge would go like this. "Why have a separate bureaucracy charged with one small thing – delivering hot meals to the elderly? What is so special about a *hot* meal, anyway? Why not give the elderly the money we spend on the program to do with as they wish. They can use the money to buy Stouffer's frozen dinners if they want a hot meal, and they will still have money left over."

This analysis misses something. The most important thing the volunteers bring the elderly is not the hot meal, but the human contact and the sense that someone cares. Volunteers can do this more convincingly than bureaucrats. More generally, more volunteers mean more public benefits can be secured without the inefficiency costs of bureaucracy and taxes. And if people get their pleasure from giving others pleasure, society obviously gains. If someone decides that he would rather volunteer than go to the movies, the economist must see both him and those assisted as better off – a clear Pareto improvement.[71]

Perhaps "Meals on Wheels" is inefficient because this synergistic effect could be more fruitfully attached to some other programmatic vehicle. But the externality concept should in general make economists eager to support policies – tax breaks, public-service television announcements, civic education in the schools, and government "starter" money for programs like "Meals on Wheels" – that seem likely to increase voluntarism. Here the question of rights, which complicated decisions to ban activities generating external costs, is not an issue. Modest amounts of public funds and a willingness to let government perform its civic-education function are all that is required. The taxpaying experiment suggests that a simple reminder of moral responsibility is often enough to increase public-spirited behavior.[72] Few people know of all the volunteer organizations in their community. Imaginative publicity about the accomplishments and pleasures of volunteerism might thus increase participation significantly.

Though a concern for encouraging behavior that generates external benefits would argue for support of religious and volunteer institutions, so too would concern about preserving political support for economically efficient capitalism. The most powerful charge against capitalism has always been that the selfishness at its base corrupts all of society, alienating us from each other and destroying all sense of community.[73] Those making this charge too often neglect the political benefits of capitalism. People seeking material gain are usually industrious and prudent. Moreover, private property acts as a shield against government coercion, and capitalism helps preserve liberty by spawning many economic interests, which in turn make it harder to form what the Founding Fathers called majority factions.[74] The charge against capitalism, however, points to a real danger, and economists, as supporters of capitalism, should be alert to chances to moderate its weaknesses by supporting community-building institutions.

Arthur Okun criticized his professional colleagues for considering only the economic-efficiency effects of mergers and ignoring their tendency to concentrate political power.[75] Though this effect may be important,[76] other political effects of business size are no less so. In larger businesses corporate executives are transferred frequently. These moves bring personal costs to the executives' families, and they also rob communities of much of the loyalty and leadership that executives of smaller, locally owned industries can provide. The large firms and the mergers that create them also more directly undermine political support for capitalism. As Joseph Schumpeter argued,

Even if the giant concerns were all managed so perfectly as to call forth applause from the angels in heaven, the political consequences of concentration would still be what they are. The political structure of a nation is profoundly affected by the elimination of a host of small and medium-sized firms the owner managers of which, together with their dependents, henchmen and connections, count quantitatively at the polls and have a hold on what we may term the foreman class that no management of a large unit can ever have; the very foundation of private property and free contracting wears away in a nation in which its most vital, most concrete, most meaningful types disappear from the moral horizon of the people.[77]

In part because the bourgeoisie was largely unaware of the threat to its existence, Schumpeter doubted that much could be done to slow the economic processes that were undermining the small producer. Congress, though, seems to be aware of the political benefits of small business. As one congressional report has said, "A healthy small business community helps to provide stability and moderation in the economy, in politics – in the broadest sense of that term – and in society in general."[78] Today's economists, however, take no account of this benefit, and most have not supported programs to aid small business. For example, Robert Samuelson says "efforts to assist small business as a class are no more virtuous than aiding large business as a class."[79] The Small Business Administration has not had a glorious record, and perhaps nothing can be done to give significant help to the small producer. But if

Schumpeter is right, long-term support for capitalism (and thus for economic efficiency) may require that we sacrifice some efficiency gains generated by large firms. Schumpeter saw that capitalism, though useful, commanded little "emotional attachment." If today's economists took account of this political problem, they might support measures, such as a revised corporate tax law, that would give greater assistance to small business – a potent source of emotional attachment to capitalism.[80]

A wide distribution in the ownership of property also builds support for capitalism at the same time that it creates conditions favorable to the preservation of free government. Jefferson was not the first political thinker to believe that the ownership of property gave people a stake in society and thus made them interested in "the support of law and order. And such men may safely and advantageously reserve to themselves a wholesome control over their public affairs." In Jefferson's view, the propertyless "mobs of great cities" would not have the self-restraint necessary to provide fertile soil for self-government.[81]

The form of property ownership that gives most contemporary Americans a clear emotional stake in private property is home ownership. Economists point out that the tax law's deduction for home mortgage interest gives the well-off more of an incentive to buy bigger homes or second homes than it motivates the lower middle class to buy a first home. Moreover, the resulting overinvestment in housing as opposed to industry hinders economic growth. The case for changing current law to eliminate the interest deduction for second homes (and a portion of it for luxury homes) is persuasive. But it is striking how often economists' discussions fail even to mention the political advantages of home ownership. Milton Friedman, for example, has said, "The right percentage (of home ownership) emerges in a free market in which housing is neither subsidized nor penalized."[82] At an oral examination a few years ago of a master's degree candidate whose thesis was on savings and loan institutions, the possible political-stability gains from home ownership were mentioned. The economist in attendance sneered and said, "Political stability is good for incumbents, I suppose."

The public-choice "political economists" are often no better than other economists when it comes to noticing subtle political benefits of the kind that concerned Schumpeter and Jefferson. The new political economy is quite technical. It often sets forth assumptions and hypotheses and then makes deductions. Its practitioners frequently have more in common with mathematicians and logicians than with political historians or students of contemporary politics. As a result, instead of seeking ways to build support for capitalism and democracy, they often unwittingly make proposals that will undermine them.

Gordon Tullock is one of the most respected of the new political economists. His recommendation for the legalization of duels has already been discussed.

He has also criticized the use of juries in civil cases.[83] In doing so Tullock takes no account of Tocqueville's view that the jury in civil cases is defensible not as a judicial institution but as a political one in which ordinary citizens are educated in the law and in their rights and duties and thus may become better citizens.

The jury, and more especially the civil jury, serves to communicate the spirit of the judges to the minds of all the citizens; and this spirit, with the habits which attend it, is the soundest preparation for free institutions. It imbues all classes with a respect for the thing judged and with the notion of right . . . every man learns to judge his neighbor as he would himself be judged . . . It invests each citizen with a kind of magistracy; it makes them all feel the duties which are bound to discharge towards society and the part which they take in its government. By obliging men to turn their attention to other affairs than their own, it rubs off that private selfishness which is the rust of society.

Tocqueville believes that "the practical intelligence and political good sense of the Americans are mainly attributable" to the long use they have made of that "gratuitous public school" which is the civil jury.[84]

In his approach to the jury, as throughout his book, Tullock assumes that progress in the law and in ethics comes from better reasoning about these subjects. He favors the discovery and establishment of an economically efficient law followed by the indoctrination of people with "a similar ethical code" that will support that law. Tullock wants a change in our ethical system so we will not be "stuck with a nonprogressive part of our society." He earlier notes that changes in the law require "relearning the law," and the time this takes would presumably be a cost of change in ethical systems just as it is in changes in law. But this relearning is presented as a purely intellectual endeavor and a relatively minor consideration.[85]

Tullock thus ignores Aristotle's argument that politics is not like other arts where better knowledge leads almost automatically to better results. Change in medicine or shoemaking is almost always for the better. When doctors found that antibiotics cured infection, they all very quickly started prescribing them. When shoemakers found that rubber soles lasted longer than leather ones, they all started offering them to their customers. But as Aristotle notes,

Change in an art is not like change in law; for law has no strength with respect to obedience apart from habit, and this is not created except over a period of time. Hence the easy alteration of existing laws in favor of new and different ones weakens the power of law itself.

Because of these considerations Aristotle thought it clear that "some errors [in law] should be let go."[86] Rousseau, who saw that it was the "antiquity of laws" that makes them "holy and venerable," would have agreed completely: "in growing accustomed to neglect old usages on the pretext of making improvements, great evils are often introduced to correct lesser ones."[87] James Madison in the *Federalist Papers*, no. 49 agrees as well. In opposing a plan to make constitutional revisions easier he notes that frequent constitutional appeals to the people would

> deprive the government of that veneration which time bestows on everything, and without which perhaps the wisest and freest governments would not possess the requisite stability . . . When the examples which fortify opinion are *ancient* as well as *numerous*, they are known to have a double effect. In a nation of philosophers, this consideration ought to be disregarded. A reverence for the laws would be sufficiently inculcated by the voice of an enlightened reason. But a nation of philosophers is as little to be expected as the philosophical race of kings wished for by Plato. And in every other nation, the most rational government will not find it a superfluous advantage to have the prejudices of the community on its side.[88]

There might be no cause for criticism if Tullock disagreed with this ancient wisdom and presented arguments in rebuttal. He gives no evidence, however, of ever having heard these arguments. And without considering them he writes an entire book proposing widespread changes in the law and ethics.

In ignoring subtle but important political effects, Tullock is not unique among today's political economists. James Buchanan, for example, has also discussed alternatives to the jury on the assumption that its only function is the judicial one of rendering a "truth judgment."[89] He has also had some kind words to say about organized crime. It is not that he thinks organized crime is good, but rather that disorganized crime is worse. Buchanan's main point is simple, yet ingenious and illuminating. In the production of things society values, monopoly is bad because it leads to artificially high prices and restrictions on output. But then, for things society opposes, such as prostitution or illicit drug use, monopoly (or organization) by leading to less output should be good. Buchanan cautions that he is not advocating a government policy of dealing with the syndicate. He merely suggests that there may be "social benefits from the monopoly organization of crime." Therefore, he gently admonishes "against the much-publicized crusades against organized crime at the expense of enforcement effort aimed at ordinary, competitive criminality."[90] But again, the whole analysis neglects a political factor of great importance. Unlike disorganized crime, organized crime is a competing power center that corrupts our police and politicians. These corrupting crimes, committed in order to gain the power to offer illicit services, threaten political legitimacy. The gains made by having the syndicate organize and thus restrict the market for prostitution and drugs may be more than counterbalanced by the political legitimacy and legislative costs when public servants are on the take.[91]

CONCLUSION

In Chapter 9 we saw that W. B. Arthur and John Morrall focused only on external financial costs and ignored psychic ones in their treatment of life-saving programs. This chapter has presented other areas in which economists have failed to consider less tangible externalities that in principle are important to the achievement of societal welfare as the economists themselves define it. Important external-cost-generating behavior is not discouraged, and important external-benefit-generating behavior is not encouraged. Some economists might try to defend themselves by narrowing the scope of economics and insisting that as practitioners of a discipline concerned for the most part with ordinary goods and services they cannot be expected to note all the benefits and costs of the type discussed here. But this defense is not really open to economists. When critics claim that they are concerned only with material things, the economists indignantly respond that this is untrue – they are concerned with all that the consumer is, including aesthetic, educational, and charitable desires. Welfare and benefit-cost economics adopt for themselves a grand scope, and economists have explicitly chosen to comment on meddlesome tastes and to explore the largest political questions. If they fail to consider important external effects and political benefits, they should expect to be criticized.

Moreover, economics has something to contribute to discussions about the issues raised in this chapter. Chapter 7 argued that the externality concept can be a useful device to help structure political debate. It could perform the same function in some of the areas explored here. For example, at the start of this chapter I argued that those who learn more history, literature, politics, or science benefit others by becoming, for example, better citizens, cleverer inventors, or simply more interesting conversationalists. On the other hand, those who study macrame or poodle grooming at the local community college or who check out a detective thriller from the public library provide few, if any, significant external benefits to others. The externality concept helps distinguish between activities that are fine and unobjectionable but essentially private concerns, like poodle grooming or macrame, and others that may yield important external benefits. The former do not deserve public subsidy; the latter may. The externality concept can usually only structure the debate, not provide clear answers. But it can reveal the weakness in the argument that sees strong patronage of subsidized macrame or detective thrillers as evidence that ''the public'' wants a continuation of the subsidy. And when learning that generates external benefits exists, the economist's concept of marginalism can serve as a reminder to ask how great the externality is and if added subsidization will significantly increase the amount of the learning.

Some economists have explored the externality questions as they bear on financial assistance for higher education.[92] However, perhaps the most illuminating (and provocative) use of the externality concept to explore these types of policy issues is contained in an article on libraries written by Edward Banfield, a political scientist.[93] This fact suggests that economists may not be best equipped to apply their own concept when important, intangible externalities are present. Given their technical education, economists will be uncomfortable exploring in depth arguments that may be "empty of empirically verifiable content." Thus, for example, in the course of his book, *The Economics of Education*, John Vaizey says, "I have tried . . . to satisfy the plea to pay attention to the 'immeasurable' benefits of education, though I must confess to an instinctive conviction that what cannot be measured may not exist."[94] Moreover, given their technical education and a world view that stresses the importance of narrow self-interest, many economists are likely to leave unrecognized situations in which important intangible externalities are present. If these are not to be ignored, broadly educated noneconomists may have to learn a little economics and then set to work on the problem.

11

REPRESENTATIVES, DELIBERATION, AND POLITICAL LEADERSHIP

ECONOMISTS' VIEWS

Welfare and benefit-cost economists make recommendations about good (i.e., consumer-preferred) policy. They have no explicit teaching about desirable characteristics of the policy process or of political institutions. Nonetheless there is an implicit teaching. Because externalities exist and preferences differ, some sort of political process that aggregates and weighs individuals' preferences is necessary. But consumers are assumed to have clear preferences. As E. J. Mishan has said, "All . . . the economic data used in a cost-benefit analysis, or any other allocative study, . . . is based on this principle of accepting as final only the individual's estimate of what a thing is worth to him at the time the decision is to be made."[1] Moreover, consumers not only know what they want, but they should get what they want. In William Baumol's words, "It is essential . . . that the pattern of public intervention be designed very explicitly in terms of the desires of the public."[2]

As Chapter 8 indicates, in applied-economic studies the desires of the public are determined by deducing preferences for government-provided goods from market decisions or, in the absence of such decisions, from public polls. This assumes that participation in discussion and deliberation prior to decision does nothing to improve public policy. It thus ignores one of the principal functions of and arguments for representative political bodies. Moreover, deliberation aside, welfare and benefit-cost economics leave no room for independent representatives or political leadership. By advocating that public policy be based on consumer "willingness to pay," welfare and benefit-cost economists silently assume the desirability of passive representatives;[3] if political judgment or leadership is needed at all, it is only to find the best tactical route for implementing the policy desires of today's consumers.

On these questions the explicit teaching of most public-choice political economists differs little from the implicit teaching of their benefit-cost cousins.

The good representative is a clerklike aggregator of consumers' preferences.[4] However, although benefit-cost economists seem to assume that there are some such representatives willing to implement the consumer-desired programs the economists' studies recommend, the public-choice economists seem certain that no such representatives exist. The public-choice economists believe that representatives seek personal economic and political benefits rather than broader public ones.[5] In the early public-choice literature it was sometimes suggested that the selfish desire for reelection would lead representatives to give their electorates more or less what they wanted.[6] But more recent articles emphasize that "rational" voter ignorance makes politicians' support of inefficient special-interest legislation politically profitable. It also allows representatives to feather their nests with money from interest groups seeking governmental favors.[7]

As mentioned earlier, one traditional argument for representative democracy focused on the potential for deliberation to produce better policy than would mere aggregation. Since public-choice economists assume that representatives are ruled by narrow self-interest, they do not believe that much if any deliberation (i.e., reasoning on the merits) takes place in representative assemblies.

In light of their views on the motives and products of representative assemblies it is not surprising that some public-choice economists have begun to wonder if bodies such as the U.S. Congress cannot be improved upon. Several have suggested that we rely much more on public referenda and less on legislative decisions. For example, more than a decade before he became chairman of the Federal Trade Commission, James Miller proposed a voting system that would make use of the home computers on the horizon to allow voters to directly register their decisions on public issues. When voters felt that they did not know enough to cast a knowledgeable vote on any particular issue, they could delegate proxy on that issue to someone else who they thought would vote as they would if they knew more.[8] Economists such as Gordon Tullock have supported Miller's proposal, and others have suggested different forms of referenda and "direct-democracy" devices.[9]

Some public-choice economists support more direct forms of democracy but believe that it would be tremendously costly for everyone to become informed enough to make Miller's system work well. Mueller, Tollison, and Willett, for example, note that though computers have reduced the costs of casting votes, technology has also increased the complexity of public issues. The total amount of time needed to enable the general public to cast votes based on reasonable levels of information is at least as high as in earlier eras. These three economists favor a representative system of government because, through the division of labor, it reduces the time costs of informed decisions. They propose, however, a more democratic form of representation, one where legislators would not be elected but chosen at random from the voting populace as a whole.[10]

THE POLITICAL FUNCTION OF CITIZENS

Despite their differences, both benefit-cost and public-choice economists seek a public policy determined less by elected representatives and more by ordinary Americans. As the *Federalist Papers* tell us, the Founding Fathers rejected direct forms of democracy because their reading of history and of human nature told them that direct democracy had not and would not produce stable, effective governments. The ancient republics of Greece and Italy "were continually agitated . . . kept in a state of perpetual vibration between the extremes of tyranny and anarchy." Though their "countenance" was more democratic than ours, their "soul" was more oligarchic. When decisions were made by the people as a whole, a skillful orator was able to appeal to the passions and "rule with as complete a sway as if a scepter had been placed in his single hand."

The founders believed that the people are everywhere prone to "irregular passions" and "temporary errors and delusions." Therefore, though "the republican principle demands that the deliberate sense of the Community should govern the conduct of those to whom they entrust the management of their affairs," it should not be interpreted to "require an unqualified complaisance to every sudden breeze of passion." Because the "interests" of the people are sometimes at variance with their "inclinations," it is advisable "to refine and enlarge the public views by passing them through the medium of a chosen body of citizens, whose wisdom may best discern the true interest of their country and whose patriotism and love of justice will be least likely to sacrifice it to temporary or partial considerations."[11]

Madison and Hamilton believed that the true friend of democracy would support representative institutions that could preserve democracy by guarding against its excesses.[12] Lincoln, who saw and condemned "wild and furious passions" and "worse than savage mobs," agreed completely.[13] Even Jefferson, though defending the right of the people to instruct their representatives and emphasizing popular control of government, supported nonetheless a government where the "natural aristocracy" held office. The people were "competent judges of human character," capable of electing the "good and wise." But the representative's independent judgment would be essential, for "the mass of individuals composing the society" are "unqualified for the management of affairs requiring intelligence above the common level."[14]

Jefferson did emphasize that there were "portions of self-government" for which the people were "best qualified" – "concerns . . . under their eye" such as "the care of their poor, their roads, police, elections, nomination of jurors, administration of justice in small cases," and such.[15] When Tocqueville visited America nearly half a century after the Constitution took effect, he applauded the widespread interest among the citizenry in filling the nearly "innumerable" offices concerned with these local problems. While warning against plebiscitary democracy at higher levels, he thought town meetings and other municipal institutions a bulwark of liberty. Tocqueville, however, supported public participation for reasons quite different from those of public-choice economists. Widespread participation was not meant to provide an outlet for narrow self-interest but rather a means of tempering it. Municipal government in American provided a way of "interesting the greatest possible number of persons in the Common weal." It gave people a taste for liberty at the same time that it taught them the art of self-government.[16]

Candid public discussion of the people's weaknesses is not a characteristic of twentieth-century politicians. In his inaugural address Jimmy Carter spoke to us as if we were gods.

You have given me a great responsibility – to stay close to you, to be worthy of you, and to exemplify what you are . . . Your strength can compensate for my weakness, and your wisdom can help to minimize my mistakes.[17]

But politicians aside, many knowledgeable people still publicly support the founders. Washington journalists, for example, see the weaknesses of both the people and of representatives. They talk to people on the campaign trail, read the public-opinion polls, and observe the workings of the Congress at close quarters. Though David Broder, Haynes Johnson, and George Will differ on many issues, all have warned against increased reliance on public-opinion polls and voter initiatives in the making of public policy.[18]

The results of polls testing the U.S. public's political knowledge lend support to the journalists' views. In the early 1980s only 37 percent of the people questioned knew that the United States and the Soviet Union were the two nations involved in the SALT talks. Only 47 percent knew that the United States, not the Soviet Union, was a member of NATO. Thirty percent answered both questions correctly, a larger percentage than those who could tell in what part of the world El Salvador is located (25 percent).[19] On domestic questions the results were not much better. Energy and environmental questions were much in the news during the Carter administration. Yet in 1980 only 37 percent of those polled knew what synthetic fuels were, and only 26 percent could identify acid rain. A full 52 percent said that a nuclear power plant could explode and cause a mushroom-shaped cloud like the one at Hiroshima. Another 16 percent were not sure.[20]

Tocqueville thought democracies had great difficulty in subduing "the desires of the moment with a view to the future." This vice was particularly dangerous to the conduct of foreign affairs and to the public finances. The more direct the democracy, the greater the danger.

The disastrous influence that popular authority may sometimes exercise upon the finances of a state was clearly seen in some of the democratic republics of antiquity, in which the public treasure was exhausted in order to relieve indigent citizens or to supply games and theatrical amusements for the populace.[21]

The president and Congress have not done wonders with the public finances in recent years. But irrational public pressures may explain much of the record. Certainly the public's views do not suggest that it would be more willing than Congress to sacrifice now for future benefits. The public, for example, has absorbed only the indulgent half of the Keynesian teaching. By 67 to 20 percent they favor tax cuts in "slow times to maintain prosperity by giving people more money to spend." But by 67 to 16 percent they reject the proposition that "one way to control inflation is to cut down consumer spending by raising taxes."[22] Similarly, when Carter pollsters checked for support for the administration's energy program, they found opposition to a decontrolled, higher price of oil, to the gasoline tax, and to the "gas guzzler" automobile tax. But the proposed tax credits for home insulation and solar power enjoyed strong support.[23]

REPRESENTATIVES, DELIBERATION, AND POLITICAL LEADERSHIP

Tullock says that "the traditional response of students of politics to the obvious ignorance of the voters has been to lecture the voters on their duty to learn more."[24] To the contrary, in our country at least, the traditional response has been representation. In the new science of politics expounded by Hamilton and Madison it was precisely this "scheme of representation" that "promise[d] the cure." As mentioned earlier, the founders expected elected representatives to be wiser and more virtuous than the average voter. In addition, the powerful offices created by the Constitution, with their fixed and fairly lengthy terms, would appeal to able men, those who "possess most wisdom to discern, and most virtue to pursue the common good of the society."[25]

The founders knew, of course, that "enlightened statesmen will not always be at the helm."[26] But they thought that the large commercial republic they established would encourage quite ordinary representatives to behave in a more statesmanlike manner. In small republics there are few factions and interests, and it is easy for a single faction to compose a majority and proceed to oppress the minority. In a large commercial republic, however, even within an individual congressional district, there are a large variety of limited and specific interests. To win an election, candidates

must appeal to diverse interests and win wide popular support. The ability to win such an election inclines the successful candidate toward the decent and moderate quality of representation which the system requires. Moreover, representatives from such districts need not be the captive of any one group but rather can find some elbowroom for statesmanship in the very confusion of factions.[27]

Even a representative from a district dominated by a single faction soon finds that he must cooperate with representatives with different constituencies if he is to obtain even a portion of what he wants. Thus, the large republic's legislative process encourages temperaments predisposed to consider the needs of others and the "permanent and aggregate interests of the Community."[28]

The founders thought that the "deliberate sense" of the community should guide democratic representatives.[29] But they did not think the "deliberate sense" could be known without deliberation. In 1796 James Madison said,

this House, in its legislative capacity, must exercise its reason, it must deliberate; for deliberation is implied in legislation.[30]

The deliberative process makes possible a "refin[ing] and enlarg[ing]" of the public views. As Woodrow Wilson later argued, such a process goes beyond mere bargaining among interests or aggregating preferences.

Common counsel is not aggregate counsel. It is not a sum in addition, counting heads. It is compounded out of many views in actual contact; it is a living thing made out of the vital substance of many minds, many personalities, many experiences; and it can be made up only by the vital contacts of actual conference, only in face to face debate, only by word of mouth and the direct clash of mind with mind.[31]

In Wilson's perspective such deliberation was important, not just because it produced better policy, but also because legislative discussion was an important source of "instruction and elevation of public opinion."[32] Such instruction and elevation were for Wilson the essence of political leadership, and this led him to emphasize a side of the statesman's art wholly outside the range of interest of most economists, namely, political rhetoric. The people possess fundamental values and aspirations, but the statesman must give these coherent direction by providing explicit ideas, policies, and programs. As one commentator notes, under such a system republican institutions and politicians become "molders of a public mind, not simply reflectors of popular demands . . . Such a democracy is both agent and educator of its citizens."[33]

Lincoln also found leadership and rhetoric crucial:

With public sentiment nothing can fail; without it, nothing can succeed. Consequently, he who moulds public sentiment goes deeper than he who enacts statutes or pronounces decisions. He makes statutes and decisions possible or impossible to be executed.[34]

Throughout his career Lincoln used his gift of speech to try to calm the public's unjust passions. In the 1830s, when lynchings of both slaves and abolitionists became commonplace, he sought to make a "reverence for the laws" the "political religion of the nation."[35] When the war neared its end, he fought vengeful passions with a policy of "malice toward none" and "charity for all."[36] And, of course, in his great debates with Stephen Douglas, Lincoln never ceased to remind his fellow citizens that consumer sovereignty or, as Douglas put it, popular sovereignty, was not a sufficient principle for public policy.[37] Lincoln noted that the principles of the Declaration of Independence required not only government by consent of the governed, but also respect for individuals' unalienable rights to life, liberty, and the pursuit of happiness.[38] He said that people outside the territories could not justly remain indifferent about whether citizens in the territories voted for or against slavery. To adopt a stand of moral indifference would be to enshrine in the body politic the pernicious doctrine that "there is no right principle of action but *self-interest.*"[39]

The beginning of this chapter noted that welfare and benefit-cost economists are concerned with the substance of policy rather than the policy process. But in fact, as we have seen, for them the substance of good policy is no more than whatever the consumers want. Lincoln spent much of his life fighting this doctrine. He believed that only a principled, substantive concern with substance could be sufficient. Good policy never ignores public opinion, but it also never ignores good ends. This means that strong public feelings and inclinations should sometimes be seen as danger signals rather than as guideposts for policy.

These views held by great American statesmen are not archaic. Some recent students of politics continue to emphasize the importance of deliberation in law making, of independent judgment in representation, and of leading and educating through public rhetoric.[40] A Nobel Prize-winning economist whose work on the economics of development is far removed from the literature discussed in this book defends such a perspective by noting that citizens judge a politician

only to a limited extent by his accordance with their preconceived ideas. Rather a great poltical leader is judged like a great composer: one looks to see what he has created.[41]

When V. O. Key Jr., published his landmark *Public Opinion and American Democracy* in 1961, he felt it necessary to respond to those such as Walter Lippmann who despaired of the future of democracy because of the influence on policy of ignorant mass opinion. Key was less pessimistic, not because he believed that the mass of the public was in fact well informed, but because he believed that the public was content with a role in which its electoral and other participation fixed only the "range of discretion within which government may act or within which debate at official levels may proceed." This left room to maneuver for the opinion leaders and political activists who behaved responsibly on the whole.[42]

Among recent politicians, John F. Kennedy seemed to go even further than Madison, Wilson, and Lincoln when discussing the appropriate independence of elected representatives.

We must on occasion lead, inform, correct *and even ignore constituent opinion*, if we are to exercise fully that judgment for which we were elected.[43] (emphasis added)

If representatives believe that it is legitimate to exercise independent judgment during their elected terms, outcomes may be different from those recommended by benefit-cost economists in a host of policy areas.[44] Consider lifesaving programs, for example. One economist has proposed allowing each taxpayer to decide how to divide his tax dollars among various government health programs.[45] But inevitably the media publicize the plight of some patient groups more than others. Those groups whose needs have been publicized in an effective way will already receive more private contributions than others equally as needy. Instead of correcting for the inadvertent injustice to those whose plight is not made known to benefactors, a public policy determined by consumer willingness to pay would accentuate it.

Policy toward lifesaving programs may also affect the good will and cohesion that exist among the citizenry. Tocqueville worried about the atomizing effect of American individualism and materialism because he believed that a society without cohesive qualities could not preserve political liberty. In his work on the value of life, Ezra Mishan calmly predicts that an atomizing process is under way: "The gradual loosening of emotional interdependence should cause the magnitude of the [psychic external costs of] bereavement . . . to decline."[46] W. B. Arthur's work assumes that the atomizing process has already progressed to the point where younger citizens' welfare improves when older citizens die earlier.[47] Should a political representative merely adjust his value for life downward if the people's preferences should change toward callousness or indifference in this way? Believing that a reverence for life and a concern for our fellow citizens are political goods in a democracy, he may instead want to try to extend the people's feelings and make them more public-regarding by, for example, promoting voluntarism or expanding and highlighting lifesaving programs.

CONCLUSION

Most economists seem to believe that the citizens' views on public policy should be decisive. For these economists everything depends on the political capability of ordinary citizens. This is paradoxical because economists realize that consumers often have poor knowledge of politics. Almost any microeconomist can cite cases in which consumers are clearly misinformed about the actual effects of popular price controls or environmental programs. Economists believe consumers' preferences are revealed most accurately in the market, and they thus prefer benefit estimates deduced from revealed preferences for a private good. But if these estimates are not available, and they very often are not, polling seems acceptable to many, if not most.[48] As suggested in Chapter 9, economists tend to insist that what some call ignorance others call wisdom. And by equating democracy with consumer sovereignty, they often come to believe that a good democrat has no alternative to plebiscitary democracy.

Chapter 5 showed why public-choice economists believe that political ignorance on the part of the public is rational and thus intractable. Some public-choice economists have suggested institutional reforms that address the problem, such as letting the private sector perform more government functions and decentralizing others.[49] These suggestions are helpful, but even their proponents would acknowledge that they address only a small part of the awesome information problem public-choice theory has revealed. Still, the intractability of the political-ignorance problem has not led public-choice economists to reassess the contemporary discipline's fundamental presuppositions. Like their colleagues, they have a personal commitment to and a professional stake in consumer sovereignty. And, as we have seen, they often favor more direct forms of democracy. I believe these forms would compound dramatically the risks posed by the political ignorance of ordinary citizens.

Tullock has suggested that voter initiatives and referenda may make it easier for the voter to make up his mind than the current system where a single vote must cover the entire scope of governmental activity. He thus concludes that such changes may actually ease the information problem for the voter.[50] But a single citizen's vote is no more likely to decide the outcome when being cast on initiatives than it is when voting for candidates. Thus, unless the initiative process makes politics seem much more interesting to the average voter, the ignorance outlined earlier will control policy without being transformed.

In states where the initiative and the referendum have been used, voters continue to exhibit only an intermittent interest in and rudimentary knowledge of politics. In California, for example, well-financed special interests usually spearhead the effort to get the petition signatures necessary to place initiatives on the ballot. One reporter tells of hurrying commuters in one subway station being pressed to sign three separate petitions at the bottom of a single escalator.[51] One California pollster later questioned those who had signed a petition on a complicated oil conservation measure.

Most of them couldn't remember signing the petitions, and of those who did the majority didn't in any way connect signing the petition with the oil controversy then raging through the state. And among the signers of the petition, about half were for the measure they qualified for the ballot and half against it![52]

Official handbooks intended to educate the citizenry on the initiative issues usually justify political scientist Raymond Wolfinger's description of them: "fifty or sixty pages of absolutely impenetrable prose." Wolfinger says that he does not read California's handbook, and he does not know anybody who does except to see who is for or against a proposition.[53] Though noting the popularity of the initiative process among the California citizenry, respected California pollster Mervin Field says the following about voters' knowledge of the issues:

Voters seldom have clearly defined opinions about most measures, even on the eve of voting. Many have a limited and even erroneous understanding of the issues and opinions of this type are often subject to quick change under the pressure of massive propaganda and emotional appeals.[54]

When voter knowledge of issues is rudimentary or nonexistent, James Miller's proposal to allow voters to give an expert their proxy would do little to remedy the knowledge problem. If, for example, voters know nothing about economics and if they have neither desire nor incentive to learn anything about it, they cannot be expected to choose in any meaningful sense among contending economic "experts." Those elected are likely to be entertaining demagogues who propagate one-sided Keynesianism or some other attractive doctrine. Our current political process sometimes produces such doctrines as well. But after elections presidents and congressmen have time to reassess them. And they generally turn to distinguished economists to help them do so. Men such as Alfred Kahn, Charles Schultze, and Martin Feldstein would not find it as easy to contribute to the political process under Miller's scheme.

Even if voters were as interested in politics as a typical congressman is, they would not be able to perform the legislative function as well through an initiative process. As representatives of a profession that propagates marginalism, economists should not need to be told of the importance of looking at the details when making decisions. Despite their reliance on the work of subcommittees, representatives frequently report that they have too little knowledge of the bills on which they must vote. The problem would obviously be compounded for citizens who must make a living in some other way.[55]

Perhaps the greatest weakness of initiatives as compared to our current system is their inability to build consensus.[56] Under the founders' system, candidates for office are reluctant to take policy positions that alienate significant minorities in their districts. After election, the legislative process leads to further communication and consensus building. The compromises that result usually mean that even those who oppose an enacted measure feel that some attention was paid to their views. Initiatives and referenda, on the other hand, tend to divide the population into warring camps. Fifty-one percent is enough to pass a measure, but as Lincoln emphasized, it often takes the goodwill and cooperation of far more than this if statutes are to be enforceable.

The proposal to select representatives by lot would provide for some sort of a legislative, integrative process. But some of the claimed advantages over the current system seem suspect. The hope is that representatives unable to seek reelection will be less supportive of local pork-barrel projects and less inclined to throw politically difficult issues to the executive branch for resolution. However, if randomly chosen representatives will someday return home, they will also want projects for their localities. And if the average tenure of a representative decreases, the executive branch may gain greater power. In the states legislative power is hindered by high legislative turnover.[57]

Under the randomly chosen representative system unelected legislative staff would probably gain more power than would either executives or legislators.

The typical representative would be like the average voter, little interested in politics. Thrown in the midst of a host of issues and complicated legal language, many would probably do what their staffs suggested they do. Since their terms would be fixed, there would be no electoral incentive to master the issues. Nor would representatives' incomes be affected by such mastery. They could, however, be affected by their votes on special-interest legislation. One suspects that representatives would be offered lucrative jobs later or other benefits in exchange for votes. The temptations for these representatives, used to lower salaries back home and deprived of any reelection incentive to behave themselves, would be great indeed. The proponents of the representative-by-lot system have noted these potential problems, but these institutional economists have no institutional solution. In an uncharacteristically vague way they simply say that "care would have to be taken to insulate the legislators from lobbying pressures and to see that they cast informed votes."[58]

Though the randomly chosen representative system is meant to give the average American more influence, in fact it would mean that typical Americans would have nothing at all to do with their government.[59] There would be no campaigns, no elections, no visits to the home district by the representative. The citizenry would not have an identified congressman to write. Representatives would have no incentive to attend to any mail received from ordinary citizens. Congressional scholars suggest that the citizenry wants access to, two-way communication with, and character or judgment ("a good person") from their representatives more than they want agreement with their incompletely formed policy preferences.[60] With a randomly chosen legislature, citizens would clearly get less of the first two than they now do. And one suspects that the average voter still thinks the representative he *selects* through an electoral process has a better-than-average character even if the voter does not think the representative belongs among the natural aristocracy.

This, of course, the public-choice economists deny. As the discussion of Margolis in Chapter 9 indicated, economists tend to see representatives as narrowly self-interested[61] – distributors of favors to groups that can get them reelected and collectors of cash contributions for themselves or of patronage for businesses in which they have an interest. More than a little of this sort of behavior goes on. But economists do not present systematic evidence supporting the adequacy or comprehensiveness of this view of representatives. Indeed, the most recent systematic study of the subject found, to the surprise of the economists who authored it, that ideology seemed to explain much more congressional voting than economic self-interest did.[62] Most public-choice economists, however, simply assume that representatives are narrowly self-interested like everyone else, and they then deduce that if they are rational they will behave in a way like that described by Margolis.

Congressional scholarship paints a more complicated picture. Some scholars do think that the desire for reelection explains most congressional behavior.[63] But others point out that many congressmen seek out particular committees because of their general policy concerns.[64] Representatives who seek power within Congress itself voluntarily leave committees that can help them get reelected for others that cannot, such as the House Rules Committee.[65] The rules and customs of the Congress often seem designed to constrain rather than service the reelection impulse. For example, "there is a custom of arranging subcommittees [of the House Appropriations Committee] so that members do not handle programs they have a direct interest in financing."[66]

There is also evidence that deliberation is important to Congress.[67] Bernard Asbell followed Edmund Muskie daily for more than a year to see how the Senate really worked. He found senators who insisted that real senatorial power was dependent on "doing your work and knowing what you're talking about." And for committees it depended on

a reputation for thoroughness, or comprehension, or reliability for fairness and accuracy, and for good judgment.

He found a lobbyist who was surprised at the nature of the recently opened subcommittee markup sessions:

The whole operation is much more subtle than I thought . . . I imagined, when they were behind closed doors, that the decisions would be much faster, You know, the chairman names the issue, everybody's already made up his mind or made his trades, and they vote. But its not like that. There's a real *process.*

With respect to lobbying, Asbell himself decided that 99 percent of it was not "parties, weekend hosting and passing plain white envelopes, but trying to persuade minds through facts and reason." Asbell also expressed surprise to find senatorial committee members open to arguments from across the aisle and clearly involved "in the difficult technical challenges of writing a clean air law."[68]

Economists rarely refer to any of this congressional literature. Their view of the representative comes mostly from deductions, not from data. Similarly, the voter-ignorance problem is treated in an abstract, conceptual way. Economists almost never note and reflect on poll results such as those cited earlier in the chapter. James Buchanan is one of the few public-choice economists who has systematically studied some poll results. He is also one of the few to emphasize new constitutional restrictions on social intervention rather than unimpeded popular rule.[69]

The founders and Tocqueville viewed direct democracy with great alarm because they studied the results where it had been tried. Economists do not interpret that history differently; they simply do not mention it. Lippmann and Key, as well as Madison and Tocqueville, saw the political ignorance and the strong passions of the people as powerful forces that could bring down democratic regimes. Economists rarely cite such authors and presumably do not read them. They see ignorance as an interesting analytical puzzle.

Madison discussed the instability and "calamities" resulting from the six-month terms for representatives in some of the states of his day.[70] Jefferson agreed, arguing that the strong state governments he desired to counterpoise federal power would necessitate fewer representatives serving longer terms.[71] James Miller, however, would have his proxy representatives recallable instantly.[72] And, without so much as a bow toward Madison or Jefferson, Amacher and Boyes argue for more frequent elections of representatives.[73]

They, together with Greene and Salavitabar, claim to have tested the Madisonian argument that representative democracies work better in large, heterogeneous jurisdictions than in small ones.[74] They note that contemporary economists have argued that decentralized, homogeneous governments, not the large heterogeneous ones, are the most responsive to voters. The test of both sets of authors consists in discovering what types of jurisdictions are most responsive to the voters' policy views. These authors find that representatives from large, heterogeneous jurisdictions do behave in a less responsive, more independent fashion. Thus the economists are declared right, and Madison wrong.

The Madison tested bears no relation to the original. He never claimed that representatives in large republics would be more responsive. Minorities could sleep more easily in large republics because representatives would *not* be so quickly responsive to a majority faction's whim. Madison's argument for a large republic was like that of Jefferson. In small societies the schisms are too "violent" and "convulsive." Only in large republics will "a majority be found in *its councils*," *free* from "local egoisms" and "particular interests" (emphasis added).[75]

The classic controversy in the literature on representation pits those who see representatives as delegates, mere agents, against those who see them as independent trustees.[76] Economists writing on representation give no sign that they know of the controversy. For Miller, the "ideal of representation" demands instant recall,[77] and for Amacher and Boyes, "less responsive" equals "less representative."[78] Economists writing in the benefit-cost literature seem to agree entirely. Thus, for example, Thomas Schelling has said that consumer sovereignty in public policy is derivable from the principle "No taxation without representation."[79] Economists claim to speak for the people. But the people themselves are not sure that they want to govern directly. When asked if congressmen should follow their own best judgment or the feelings and opinions of their district, the public is very closely divided. Sometimes the trustee view commands a majority; sometimes the delegate view predominates.[80]

Our current system of representation seems well suited to the public it represents. That public has only a little interest in and knowledge of the issues of politics. Students of voting, however, find some evidence that "voters do have knowledge about the issues that they themselves raise in canvassing their likes and dislikes of parties and candidates.'' Sometimes people vote on the basis of a candidate's (or a party's) stance on a policy issue important to them, but more often they vote on the basis of their assessment of a candidate's experience, integrity, judgment, or capacity for leadership.[81] Voters who, like John Stuart Mill, care more about the competence of candidates than about their issue stances are served well by a system that makes representatives accountable to the public but gives them considerable room to exercise their independent judgment during their term in office. Our system has worked fairly well for nearly two hundred years, and it enjoys "that veneration which time bestows on everything, and without which perhaps the wisest and freest governments would not possess the requisite stability." James Madison, the author of those words, promulgated a new science of politics only after reading the greatest theorists of free government, reflecting on contemporary and historical experience, and carefully considering all sides of relevant issues. The new science of politics promulgated by economists proposing constitutional restructuring of government falls well short of meeting those standards.

12

CONCLUSION

Economists spend most of their time studying human behavior in the marketplace. There they find that materialistic motives and narrow self-interest can explain almost all of what they observe and that with the help of free markets and flexible prices, these motives usually lead to the efficient production of valued goods and services. As economists have begun to study the world beyond the marketplace, they have brought the lessons learned from it with them. But those lessons do not always apply elsewhere. Economists sometimes notice this and are puzzled. They search for explanations for the "apparent irrationality" of philanthropy. They wonder why voters and non-economists participating in the free-rider experiments do not seek to maximize their individual incomes. Often they fall back on an explanation they resist strongly when critics of consumer sovereignty use it, namely, consumer ignorance. In evaluative work, however, what economists call consumer ignorance in these cases is assumed away. There, economists too often confidently equate an individual's policy preferences with his financial self-interest. By this criterion, all citizens who pay Social Security taxes are declared gainers when the elderly die earlier.

Although economists sometimes assume materialistic motives even when they are apparently absent, the citizenry seems to prefer that such motives sometimes be ignored even when they are present. Polls show that about half of Americans think they themselves buy more than they need, and three-quarters think we should learn to get our pleasure from nonmaterial experiences. Though some earlier economists thought aspirations for higher tastes significant, today's economists tend to ignore such aspirations. They hope to avoid the thorny value questions by taking tastes and preferences as they find them. But aspirations aside, treating preferences in a nonjudgmental way does not avoid controversy, for when weighing costs and benefits such treatment can sometimes make decisive the gains to the criminal from crime or the costs to the malevolent from lifesaving.

Even if money and narrow self-interest were the route to individual well-being, the well-being of society as a whole requires more. The most ingenious rechanneling of self-interest cannot overcome inefficiencies caused by free riders. Ethics, goodwill, and civility can do so. There is some evidence that reminders of one's civic responsibilities and examples of or experience with altruistic acts can change behavior for the better. But economists largely ignore such external-benefit-generating possibilities even though these benefits are important to the achievement of societal well-being as economists themselves define it.

Economists tend to ignore these types of externalities both because they call into question views of the world that emphasize money and self-interest and because they complicate empirical work. But perhaps the most important reason is the way the discipline educates its practitioners. Economists' technical education leaves them unlikely to look for intangible externalities and poorly equipped to weigh their significance if they should bump into them.

Policy economics today is in large part a mixture of deductive theory resting on very simple assumptions and empirical research based on data other people collect. Often these approaches produce helpful results, but sometimes they do not. Chapter 11 discusses the dangers of unhistorical abstract theorizing about constitutional structure, and Chapter 6 points out the weaknesses of welfare-policy conclusions based on previously assembled data that ignore the majority of the poor who do not participate in poverty programs.

Kenneth Boulding has suggested a reason why young economists rarely collect their own data: Today's graduate departments in economics rarely teach them how. Boulding also points out the dangers of forming conclusions about how the world works without ever confronting it directly:

The successes of economics should not blind us to the fact that its subject matter is a system far more complex than the systems which are studied by the natural scientists, for instance, and we must recognize that our most elegant models can be no more than the crudest of first approximations of the complex reality of the systems which they purport to represent. If we educate out of our students that almost bodily sense of what the real world is like even though we may see it through a glass darkly, a trait which was so characteristic of the great economists of the past, something of supreme value will be lost.[1]

As Boulding suggests, many of today's practitioners of the worldly science, even the policy analysts, are remarkably unworldly. Those who write on particular welfare programs seldom interview those who are eligible for assistance and try to develop for themselves a sense of how welfare recipients live. Moreover, few ever mention sociologists who have done so. Those who write on the largest political questions too often fail to approach their task with humility and trepidation, in full awareness of the high stakes involved. Their work rarely reflects on human nature or on the lessons of history. It does not ponder ''violent'' and ''convulsive'' schisms in politics, such as in

Northern Ireland or Lebanon, and ask what institutions best build consensus and support for law. It does not note Hitler's early popularity in Germany and discuss the case for supreme courts that look to standards beyond consumer sovereignty. Indeed, it rarely refers to political theorists who have reflected on these matters.

Knowledge of some subjects, like math, requires only a good theoretical mind. Knowledge of others, like love, requires experience. It may make sense to ask a twelve-year-old prodigy for help with a calculus problem, but a college student looks elsewhere for advice about problems with his girlfriend. Politics and public policy are more like love than math. Good answers to even general questions, such as how and when to restructure institutions, require judgment that can come only with experience of the regime in question and with some knowledge of history.

Most of the evaluative studies discussed in this book, whether on food stamps or constitutions, could have been carried out by an unusually bright schoolboy. Economists seem to think better policy and better economics will flow from better abstract theorizing and better technique. As discussed in Chapter 9, when Lancaster was confronted with the changing-tastes problem, he tried to solve it by simply creating a new definition. When Sidney Schoeffler faced it, he asked biologists to conduct experiments measuring the extent of chemical disequilibrium within the body. Schoeffler thought that through such a procedure, we could develop an "absolute ordering" of tastes, presumably even the *summum bonum*. Economists do need some help with these broader questions, but I do not think biologists are best equipped to provide it.

When looking for help, economists would do better to seek it in the same places the great economists of the past found it – in the humanities and social sciences. Joseph Schumpeter, for example, read widely in political theory, history, and literature. He read those who studied human beings in the round. He came to share Marx's view that capitalistic dynamism inflamed appetites, enlarged expectations, and undermined traditional social structures and values. This concerned Schumpeter for he believed that capitalism, though useful, is unlovely and incapable of producing emotional attachment. It badly needs the protective framework it constantly undermines. Schumpeter's broader perspective led him to notice subtle external benefits from institutions such as small business.[2] The writings of today's economists give no sign that they read beyond their discipline in the way Schumpeter did. Indeed, one rarely finds a footnote to Schumpeter himself.

The criticisms made in the last three chapters, however, should not overshadow the lessons economists taught us in earlier chapters. This book's central message is not antieconomics. I think economists should read more outside of economics, but most people should read more within it.[3]

First and foremost, economists teach us to respect markets. As Thomas Schelling has said, "Nothing distinguishes economists from other people as much as a belief in the market system."[4] Economists continue to think there is much truth in Adam Smith's view that though a businessman seeks only his own interest, the invisible hand of the market leads him to promote society's interest nonetheless. Indeed, economists are more certain than some businessmen that the profit-seeking entrepreneur promotes the public welfare regardless of his philanthropic activity. As Kenneth Boulding has said, economics "makes people appreciate the productivity of the commonplace, of exchange and finance, of bankers and businessmen."[5]

There is no reason to defer to economists' pronouncements about human nature or good constitutions, but markets are another matter. If economists possess expertise on anything, it is a knowledge of how markets work. They know that in the private sector firms' managers and owners reap the rewards when they efficiently respond to consumer demand. They suspect that governmental processes do not have as powerful mechanisms for promoting efficiency. Final proof of such a global judgment may always elude us. But Chapter 5 showed that it is not just theory; there is suggestive evidence that economists have properly evaluated the comparative efficiency of the two allocative mechanisms. To the skeptical but less knowledgeable noneconomist, it should be reassuring that this promarket judgment is shared by both liberal and conservative economists.

It is not, however, reassuring enough. Noneconomists almost always have reservations. They are troubled by profits, middlemen, speculators, and conglomerate mergers. I briefly responded to these concerns in Chapter 5. But my brief responses are not conclusive, for one can always find examples of private-sector blunders. The noneconomist wonders if government could not have prevented them. Or he sees exciting opportunities and wonders if government cannot somehow help take advantage of them. Of the private-sector blunders economists can only suggest that there will be fewer of them in the market than in government since those who commit them lose income. As for the public sector, economists usually say that government can improve the general climate for innovation but is incapable of identifying (and supporting) the products that will be commercial winners in the future. Here, for example, is Robert Samuelson on the microelectronics revolution:

Someone is bound to ask: What can government do to encourage the realization of the most promising possibilities? The answer is everything and nothing. Ten years ago, virtually no one foresaw today's microelectronics explosion. Today, no one can accurately predict the most productive uses of microelectronics a decade hence.

G.E.'s [automatically adjusting light sensor] bulb now is too expensive to support a mass consumer market. Who knows whether costs can be brought down sufficiently to change that? Government can't judge the choices effectively . . .

Paraphrasing Chairman Mao we ought to adopt the motto, let a hundred flowers bloom. We need hordes of firms searching for new applications and ways to lower costs and increase reliability.

Through its tax laws, government can help create a climate for risk-taking. It ought to prey on the greed in human nature and the industriousness in the American character. Otherwise, stand aside.[6]

But one more quotation from someone in the economic mainstream is not likely to convince the unconvinced. Economists realize this and throw up their hands. Albert Rees says that "much of the public hostility to our economic system comes from ignorance of it."[7] Charles Schultze declares that he is increasingly convinced that "no one but economists (and not all of them) really understands" how a market system works.[8] And Alain Enthoven says of economist's work in government,

The economic theory we are using is the theory most of us learned as sophomores. The reason Ph.D.'s are required [is] that many economists do not believe what they have learned until they have gone through graduate school.[9]

Arguments that say "You would agree with me if you knew more" insult one's readers and invite their scorn. But I can understand the temptation. Most people who systematically study the allocative problems of all societies and the way markets solve them, come away with increased respect for markets.[10] I ask only that my noneconomist readers test this proposition for themselves.

If economists are right about markets, greater respect for their allocative mechanisms will mean an increase in valued goods, services, or leisure. These are significant benefits in their own right, but perhaps not the most important ones efficiency brings. An economy that functions well can help foster political stability by building confidence in the system as a whole.[11] Increasing efficiency and facilitating expansion in the economy can make possible an improved standard of living for workers and the elderly, stronger defenses, and a cleaner environment too. Political differences are usually more manageable in such circumstances.

Much of the sound advice economists offer on more specific questions also flows from their knowledge of markets. From studying markets they learn that resources are scarce and our ends multiple. Thus to worry about costs is to care about benefits, benefits forgone in other sectors. Dedicated public professionals, eager to achieve their policy goals, sometimes need to be reminded of such opportunity costs. By studying markets economists also learn that spending decisions should not be determined by looking at the intrinsic importance of a function since they require a weighing of marginal cost and marginal benefit. Those setting public-sector priorities may need reminding. And of course markets show the power of material incentives to coordinate human activity in a productive way. Many of the new regulatory programs rely on detailed laws and regulations to achieve their objectives. Economists convincingly show that using economic incentives instead can give us cleaner air, safer workers, and far lower bills besides.

Though economists frequently fail to notice intangible political and social effects of policy measures, they are skilled at tracing subtle interrelationships within the economy that are altered by shifts in monetary incentives. This explains much of what they contribute on equity as well as on pollution. The need to use economic incentives to overcome labor surpluses and shortages tells us that although we may want to alter the market distribution of income, after-tax salaries should not be based only on some abstract standard of fairness to various income classes or occupations. An appreciation of economic incentives provides some assurance that regional disparities in income will not become too great. It also alerts us to the possibility that although we may require business to clean up the water or to pay for an employee's Social Security, someone else may ultimately bear the cost. And, finally, an understanding of incentives brings to light a host of adverse side effects of attempts to achieve equity objectives by controlling wages and prices. Such attempts are at the heart of what economists sometimes call their "non-agenda of government."[12] As Arthur Okun puts it,

Whatever the ideological stripe of an administration or Congressional body, its economists are likely to be among those least enthusiastic about agricultural programs based on contrived scarcity, ceilings on interest rates, rapid advances in the minimum wage . . . and other controls and constraints on prices or wages.

An appreciation of incentives explains this consensus. As Okun says of still another form of government price fixing, "Rent controls destroy incentives to maintain or rehabilitate property, and are thus an assured way to preserve slums."[13]

Study of the market also led to the development of the enormously useful concepts of externality and public or collective-consumption good. Economists first determined that competitive markets produced efficient outcomes because production in all sectors continued up to the point when the marginal costs of production equaled the benefits to the last consumer. But then Marshall and Pigou noted cases in which some societal costs of production were not reflected in firms' supply curves and in which some societal benefits were not reflected in consumers' demand curves. Useful work on market failure and on the functions of government soon followed.

Even the methodology of benefit-cost analysis is built on earlier work with markets. Costs are the opportunity costs of production, and benefits the willingness of consumers to pay. Moreover, quite frequently benefit-cost analysis evaluates programs that are deeply immersed in the market. Most of the so-called social regulation, for example, has profound effects on the economic system. We want clean air, safe products, and healthy workers, but we also want business to produce interesting and useful products at reasonable cost. Because of their study of industrial processes, economists are well equipped to help us determine the private-sector costs of our public-sector programs.

Economists know that the market is an efficient mechanism to allocate scarce resources to valued goods and services, and they know that material incentives are the fuel that makes the market work. Most of what economists contribute to public-policy deliberations can be traced to their knowledge of the utility of the mechanism and the power of the fuel. Their attachment to the mechanism and to the materialistic motive is thus quite understandable. But a healthy polity requires more than an efficient economy, and there is no automatic mechanism that will produce health in a polity as regularly as the market produces efficiency in the economy. A healthy polity must find a way to deal with powerful political passions that are not always as harmless as most market desires. It must promote institutions that build consensus and strengthen ethical standards. Rather than continually giving narrow self-interest its head, it must sometimes seek to make narrow self-interest less narrow. And it must find a way to compensate for the market's overemphasis on the things money can buy as the route to human happiness.

The analytical framework economists use to look at the world will not always point the way toward good public policy. Moreover, it will sometimes obscure important questions. But there is no superior methodology lurking in the mainstream of some other social science, and this book has not attempted to create one. Still, my criticisms are meant to be constructive. Public policy should improve if we are alert to economists' propensities and the types of errors they can lead to. For example, if a study attempts to draw welfare conclusions from the behavior of the dependent poor or of compulsive consumers such as cigarette smokers, we should look at it with a skeptical eye. More generally, the tendency of market-behavior estimates of benefits to give too much weight to narrowly self-interested preferences and too little to altruistic ones should be considered. If benefit estimates instead come from polling we should ask if there is reason to think consumers' preferences are stable and reasonably informed. If consumers are asked how much they would pay for more frequent trash collection, they can easily visualize what is at issue, and their preferences should carry great weight with representatives. Their preferences about a new missile system are likely to be less informed and more dependent on idiosyncratic changes in media coverage. Representatives should consequently be less bound by estimates of benefits that rely on such preferences.

We should not expect economic studies to reflect common views about high and low or unethical tastes. Their authors will not have open minds about programs that provide support for or encourage appreciation of high achievement in the arts and sciences, and they are likely to sanction routinely the preferences of criminals and others among the malevolent. When uncertainties abound they will tend to emphasize monetary benefits and ignore less tangible ones. Since their focus is on narrow self-interest, they will not think about the need to foster military courage through special forms of honor or about ways to encourage ethics, civility, and altruism through appeals to the better sides of our natures.

Those with technocratic minds, and some others as well, will be impatient with the imprecision of a suggestion that we consider such matters when we examine economists' work.[14] But we should never expect to achieve a mechanistic evaluation methodology that can crank out uncontroversial policy conclusions. Sometimes matters of great weight are hidden amidst narrowly economic questions. There is no litmus test that will distinguish all such cases for us. A person of learning and judgment – a Schumpeter – will notice more of these situations than the rest of us will. We cannot reproduce his judgment, but we can seek to reproduce his learning, and if we are successful, our judgment should improve as well.

Before closing I offer a guide to this book for some among those busy readers who may be thumbing through these last pages first. If you are a libertarian conservative, please read Part III. If you are an Americans for Democratic Action liberal, please read Parts I and II. This course seems best suited to test your ideas and mine and thus to provoke the spirited, friendly, serious debate that is an important sign of a healthy democracy.

To be sure, the mainstream-economist message presented in Parts I and II can enlighten some conservatives. They will learn that there are powerful arguments for a vigorous federal government role in environmental protection and assistance to the poor. They may come to see some merit in providing welfare assistance to the working poor. But conservatives will already have absorbed most of the mainstream message. They believe government is less efficient than the private sector. They dislike government controls on prices and wages. They stress the importance of savings, investment, and economic growth. They think the costs of many government regulatory programs far exceed the benefits. They support the market mechanism and the use of self-interest as a means to achieve public purposes.[15] But they, like economists, should confront the argument that a free, well-functioning market does not of itself produce a civilized society.

Americans for Democratic Action liberals, on the other hand, do not need to be reminded that private markets and material self-interest have their limitations. They may profit, however, from reflecting on the mainstream-economic consensus described in Parts I and II. The model platform for the Democratic party compiled by the Americans for Democratic Action in 1980 contained the following proposals: "an equitable system of controls not only on wages but on prices, rents, profits, interest rates and service fees"; "an economic planning system" that would "establish credit control, a national capital investment policy in accordance with national needs and the requirement that a large portion of profits be reinvested to up-date industrial plants"; an extension of "public control of future energy development," a section of the economy where "production and distribution are [currently] monopolistic"; "vigorous enforcement of the anti-trust laws" together with additional measures to curb the power of our biggest corporations who are acting "irresponsibly, placing profits before the welfare of the country and of their own employees''; opposition to the ''anti-people campaigns'' of those who ''demand emasculation'' of the Federal Trade Commission, the Occupational Safety and Health Administration, and the Food and Drug Administration; opposition to ''any further weakening of the Clean Air Act standards''; vigorous enforcement of the Clean Water Act and adequate levels of funding for the ''municipal and rural waste treatment program''; a natural resources and environmental quality policy guided by the philosophy that ''we can no longer afford to balance our diminishing natural environment against the demands of private economic growth''; universal comprehensive national health insurance that would entitle every American to the ''best possible health care''; ''the use of federal dollars'' to expand the supply of housing especially for the poor; and various other social welfare programmatic increases designed to meet ''human needs.''[16]

After the Democratic defeat in 1980 economist Alfred Kahn wrote an article whose ''main purpose'' was

to explain to the ADA kind of liberals, in whose number I used to consider myself, why we had better start figuring out what kinds of policies make sense in the 1980's, and specifically what preconceptions, slogans and remedies of the 1930's through the 1960's we are going to have to scrap.

Kahn asked that liberals recognize the need to restrain demand and encourage supply; that they recognize the importance of savings and investment for economic growth; that they be ''less ideological'' in their condemnation of economic power and thus more willing to condemn its exploitation by large labor unions; that they be more selective in supporting programs that help the poor and, in particular, that they stop supporting spending programs that help some poor but mainly the nonpoor; that they end their opposition to ''any and all policies whose method of producing social benefits can be characterized as 'trickle down' ''; that they stop reacting to ''the painful manifestations of the economics of scarcity'' with positions that are ''largely romantic in both rhetoric and substance'' – wage and price controls, an easier monetary policy, additional government expenditure programs.

What these proposals have in common is that every one of them in effect denies the existence of a scarcity problem; seeks merely to suppress its unpleasant symptoms; and by so doing would actually aggravate the disease, by artificially encouraging demand and interfering with the efficient expansion of supply.[17]

The *New Columbia Encyclopedia* defines pragmatism as ''a method of philosophy in which the truth of a proposition is measured by its correspondence with experimental results and by its practical outcome''; it insists on ''constant empirical verification of hypotheses.''[18] I think that many, probably most, economists would find that method of philosophy a fair description of what they seek to do. But then again the ADA also defines itself as an organization made up of ''issue-oriented, visionary pragmatists.''[19] Within the Democratic party there is a significant fight between ADA liberals and economist liberals over the correct understanding of liberal Democratic pragmatism. The theory and evidence that the economists rely on are clear. The pragmatic credentials of the ADA's positions are less clear. Perhaps this explains why the economists are making some headway among young liberals in the Senate. Paul Tsongas (D-Mass.) stresses investment and economic growth, and he opposes all types of price controls.[20] Long before his 1984 campaign for the presidency, Gary Hart (D-Colo.) was arguing for a domestic agenda that stressed "market-oriented solutions" to pollution and other problems rather than "the old New Deal" programmatic approach.[21] I believe the country will be better off if *this* trend to the economists continues. Kahn's article shows that – even without considering civil rights, civil liberties, defense, and foreign affairs – Democrats can absorb the persuasive part of the mainstream economic consensus and still find room for healthy combat with Republicans.

NOTES

1 See Albert Nichols and Richard Zeckhauser, "Government Comes to the Workplace: An Assessment of OSHA," *Public Interest* no. 49 (Fall 1977): 65.

1. INTRODUCTION

1 The first statement is that of Paul McCracken, former chairman of the Council of Economic Advisers. McCracken also noted that even on the council, most of his time was spent on microeconomic questions; see William Allen, "Economics, Economists and Economic Policy: Modern American Experiences," *History of Political Economy* 9 (1977): 70–3. The second statement was made by an unnamed Harvard economist; see Steven Kelman, *What Price Incentives? Economists and the Environment* (Boston: Auburn House, 1981), 11n.

2 See the works cited by Gerald Marwell and Ruth Ames, "Economists Free Ride, Does Anyone Else," *Journal of Public Economics* 15 (1981): 295–310; by Richard McKenzie and Gordon Tullock, *The New World of Economics* (Homewood, Ill.: Irwin, 1975 ed. ch. 12 and 1981 ed. ch. 8; and by Amitai Etzioni, *An Immodest Agenda* (New York: New Press, 1983), 15. Sociologist James Coleman's "Public Schools, Private Schools and the Public Interest," *Public Interest* no. 64 (Summer 1981): 19–30, is full of economic concepts. Also note the economic critic B. Barber's view that "because of its success, economics is looked to by some in the other social sciences the way physics has been looked to by some in biology"; "Absolutization of the Market," in Gerald Dworkin, Gordon Bermant, and Peter Brown, eds., *Markets and Morals* (Washington, D.C.: Hemisphere, 1977), 171.

3 Edmund Phelps has noted that "leaks from economics threaten to inundate the compartment of political science"; *Altruism, Morality, and Economic Theory* (New York: Russell Sage, 1975), 1.

4 In their well-known books, John Rawls (*A Theory of Justice*) and Robert Nozick (*Anarchy, State and Utopia*) disagree on almost everything, but the thought of both has been deeply influenced by their study of economics. See Marc Plattner's discussion, "The New Political Theory," *Public Interest* no. 40 (Summer 1975): 119–28.

5 See Vincent Ostrom, *The Intellectual Crisis in American Public Administration* (University: University of Alabama Press, 1973); Richard Nelson, *The Moon and the Ghetto* (New York: Norton, 1977), 44; Peter Self, *Econocrats and the Policy Process* (Boulder, Colo.: Westview, 1975), 187.

6 A survey of eight of the leading schools of public policy found that economics was required in more programs than any other discipline and that it was the only one to have at least four faculty representatives at each school; William Dunn, "A Comparison of Eight Schools of Public Policy," *Policy Studies Journal* 4 (1975): 68–72. A political scientist, Arnold Meltsner, has observed that "policy analysis continues to be dominated by economists or by those with an economic orientation"; *Policy Analysts in the Bureaucracy* (Berkeley: University of California Press, 1975), p. 15.

7 John Bunker, Benjamin Barnes, and Frederick Mosteller, *Costs, Risks and Benefits of Surgery* (New York: Oxford University Press, 1977), esp. xiii.

8 See Kelman, *What Price Incentives?* 1–11; Barber, "Absolutization of the Market," 16–17; Laurence Tribe, "Policy Science: Analysis or Ideology," *Philosophy and Public Affairs* 2 (1972): esp. 68–69; Stephen Elkin, "Political Science and the Analysis of Public Policy," *Public Policy* 22 (1975): 405; Benjamin Ward, *What's Wrong With Economics?* (New York: Basic Books, 1972), 89.

9 Arthur Okun, *The Political Economy of Prosperity* (Washington, D.C.: Brookings Institution, 1970), 1.

10 For the poll results finding consensus on micro (but not macro) questions, see J. R. Kearl, Clayne Pope, Gordon Whiting, and Larry Wimmer, "What Economists Think," *American Economic Review, Papers and Proceedings* 2 (May 1979): 28–37. Also see Milton Friedman, "Why Economists Disagree," in Friedman, ed., *Dollars and Deficits* (Englewood Cliffs, N.J.: Prentice-Hall, 1968), 1–5; Walter Heller, "Why Can't Those (#$+%!¶) Economists Ever Agree," *Congressional Record*, June 25, 1975, H-6, 203–5; Herbert Stein, "How to Introduce an Economist," *Fortune*, Nov. 30, 1981, 134–5.

11 Some of these, such as Galbraith, Robert Heilbroner, and Robert Lekachman, have considerable following among intellectuals though they have had almost no influence on mainstream economists.

12 Allen, "Economics, Economists and Economic Policy," has a number of quotations to this effect.

13 Economists quoted in Allen, "Economics, Economists and Economic Policy."

14 Some of the literature is discussed in ch. 11. Also see James Ceaser, "The Theory of Governance of the Reagan Administration," in Lester Salamon and Michael Lund eds., *The Reagan Presidency and the Governing of America* (Washington, D.C.: Urban Institute, in press); James Q. Wilson, "American Politics Then and Now," *Commentary* (Feb. 1979); and Wilson, ed., *The Politics of Regulation* (New York: Basic Books, 1980), esp. 112–14, 263–4, 272–4, 299, 384, 394; Theodore H. White, *In Search of History* (New York: Harper & Row, 1978), 4–5; *Washington Post*, Feb. 15, 1976, K-4. On the influence of economic ideas in particular see especially Martha Derthick and Paul Quirk, *The Politics of Deregulation* (Washington, D.C.: Brookings Institution, in press). Also John Morrall III, "OSHA After Ten Years" (working paper no. 13, American Enterprise Institute, Nov. 18, 1981), VI-13; Michael Malbin, "Congress, Policy Analysis and Natural Gas Deregulation," in Robert Goldwin, ed., *Bureaucrats, Policy Analysts, Statesmen: Who Leads?* (Washington, D.C.: American Enterprise Institute, 1980), 63–4. Also pertinent is the famous quotation from John M. Keynes: "The ideas of economists and political philosophers, both when they are right and when they are wrong, are more powerful than is commonly understood ... I am sure that the power of vested interests is vastly exaggerated compared with the gradual encroachment of ideas," *The General Theory of Employment, Interest, and Money* (New York: Harcourt, Brace, 1936), 283, as quoted in Richard Nelson, *The Moon and the Ghetto*, 17.

15 J. W. Anderson (a member of the editorial staff of the *Washington Post*), "The Power of a Book," *Washington Post*, April 18, 1983, A-10. Also see Robert Behn's assessment of the Brookings budget books in "The Budget Watchers," *Public Interest* no. 71 (Spring 1983): 148–53.

16 For more data on economists in high governmental positions see my "Economists and Policy Analysis," *Public Administration Review* (March–April 1978): 112–20.

17 *Cornell University Newsletter* 3 (Fall 1981): 1. In an interview with the author, Darius Gaskins, head of the Interstate Commerce Commission under President Carter, also stressed the usefulness of his economic training in his governmental work. In an article on the Civil Aeronautics Board under Kahn, political scientist Bradley Behrman says, "Kahn consciously attempted to run

CAB meetings as seminars that sought to identify the most economically efficient policy and *then* to consider how such a policy could be implemented without violating the law"; in Wilson, ed., 112. Also see Douglas Anderson, *Regulatory Politics and Electric Utilities* (Boston: Auburn House, 1981), ch. 4.

18 For a discussion of the differences between "political rationality" and "policy rationality" see my *Policy Analysis in the Federal Aviation Administration* (Lexington, Mass.: Lexington Books, 1974), ch. 1.

2. OPPORTUNITY COST

1 Kenneth Arrow, *The Limits of Organization* (New York: Norton, 1974), 17.

2 James J. Kilpatrick, "Worse Than the Publicity," *Charlottesville Daily Progress*, March 8, 1981, E-2. In fairness, Kilpatrick does say that it is better not to displace forty-nine men by buying the Caterpillar, but this judgment does not affect his views on efficiency and underemployment.

3 Richard Lipsey and Peter Steiner, *Economics* (New York: Harper & Row, 1978), 228. Lipsey and Steiner note that the "view that public control was needed to save an industry from the dead hand of third-rate, unenterprising private owners was commonly held about the British coal industry and was undoubtedly a factor leading to its nationalization in 1946." One British commission reported as follows: "It would be possible to say without exaggeration of the miners' leaders that they were the stupidest men in England; if we had not had frequent occasion to meet the owners." Economist Sir Roy Harrod saw it differently, arguing that the contrast between the rundown state of the mines in Wales and their advanced state in Derbyshire was explained by the Derbyshire's mines' impressive (coal) capacities, not their management's.

4 *Congressional Quarterly Almanac*, 1971, 135.

5 William Allen, "Economics, Economists and Economic Policy: Modern American Experiences," *History of Political Economy* 9 (1977): 70.

6 Allen Kneese and Charles Schultze, *Pollution, Prices and Public Policy* (Washington, D.C.: Brookings Institution, 1975), 22.

7 Kneese and Schultze, *Pollution, Prices and Public Policy*, 85, 90. The incentive approach will be discussed more fully in ch. 4.

8 Steven E. Rhoads, *Policy Analysis in the Federal Aviation Administration* (Lexington, Mass.: Lexington Books, 1974), 106.

9 Frank S. Levy, Arnold Meltsner, and Aaron Wildavsky, *Urban Outcomes* (Berkeley: University of California Press, 1974), 154–7, 238. For a discussion of how economists and engineers understand "efficiency" differently see Douglas Anderson, *Regulatory Politics and Electric Utilities* (Boston: Auburn House, 1981), esp. 100–1.

10 Richard R. Nelson, *The Moon and the Ghetto* (New York: Norton, 1977), 115–18, 150.

11 Gary E. Tagtmeyer, "Analysis of a Fire Department" (University of Virginia, May 28, 1976, Mimeo).

12 *Charlottesville Daily Progress*, Aug. 17, 1977, B-1.

13 *New York Times*, July 4, 1966, 40, as quoted in Edward Banfield, "Some Alternatives for the Public Library," in Banfield, ed., *Urban Government* (New York: Free Press of Glencoe, 1969), 645n.

14 Paul Abels, "The Managers are Coming! The Managers are Coming!" *Public Welfare* 31 (1973): 14–15.

15 *Charlottesville Daily Progress*, Feb. 25, 1980, B-2.

16 Fred Hapgood, "Risk-Benefit Analysis: Putting a Price on Life," *Atlantic Monthly*, Jan. 1979, reprinted in Steven E. Rhoads, ed., *Valuing Life: Public Policy Dilemmas* (Boulder, Colo.: Westview, 1980), 316.

17 Rhoads, *Policy Analysis in the Federal Aviation Administration*, 28n.

18 John Maher, *What is Economics?* (New York: Wiley, 1969), 45.

19 Eugene Bardach, "A Solution in Search of a Problem," *Commentary*, 1976, reprinted in George McKenna and Stanley Feingold, eds., *Taking Sides* (Guilford, Conn.: Dushkin, 1978), 310.

20 Kneese and Schultz, *Pollution, Prices and Public Policy*, 62–3.

21 Bernard Asbell, *The Senate Nobody Knows* (Baltimore: Johns Hopkins University Press, 1978), 376. For Ralph Nader's view that we should reduce pollution to the greatest extent possible see John C. Esposito, *Vanishing Air* (New York: Grossman, 1970), 67, 306–7, and Nader's foreword, ix.

22 Asbell, *The Senate Nobody Knows*, 330.

23 This effect appears to have occurred in the early 1980s. The stricter 1981 standards probably led to more pollution in 1981–4 than the less strict 1980 standards would have; Lawrence White, *The Regulation of Air Pollutant Emissions from Motor Vehicles* (Washington, D.C.: American Enterprise Institute, 1982), 83–4.

24 Asbell, *The Senate Nobody Knows*, 196.

25 *Washington Post*, Nov. 29, 1976, A-1.

26 *Washington Post*, July 31, 1974, A-3.

27 John Mendeloff, *Regulating Safety: An Economic and Political Analysis of Occupational Safety and Health Policy* (Cambridge, Mass.: MIT Press, 1979), 69.

28 Rhoads, *Policy Analysis in the Federal Aviation Administration*, 18–21, and *Valuing Life*, 2.

29 As quoted in Albert Nichols and Richard Zeckhauser, "OSHA after a Decade: A Time for Reason," in Leonard W. Weiss and Michael W. Klass, eds., *Case Studies in Regulation*, (Boston: Little, Brown, 1981), 212.

30 Public Law 91-596, 91st Congress, S.2193, Dec. 29, 1970, 4.

31 Steven Kelman, *Regulating America, Regulating Sweden: A Comparative Study of Occupational Safety and Health Policy* (Cambridge, Mass.: MIT Press, 1981), 89–93.

32 Undated testimony of Richard Wilson, "proposed standard for occupational exposure to benzene" before the Department of Labor, assistant secretary of labor for Occupational Safety and Health Administration (OSHA Docket no. H-059, Mimeo.).

33 Mark Green, "The Faked Case Against Regulation," *Washington Post*, Jan. 21, 1979, C-1.

34 For a discussion of the role of labor–management negotiations in improving occupational safety and health see L. S. Bacow, *Bargaining for Job Safety and Health* (Cambridge, Mass.: MIT Press, 1980).

35 Most of the studies are summarized and analyzed in Martin Bailey, *Measuring the Benefits of Life Saving* (Washington, D.C.: American Enterprise Institute, 1979).

36 W. Kip Viscusi, *Employment Hazards: An Investigation of Market Performance* (Cambridge, Mass.: Harvard University Press, 1979), ch. 14. Because businessmen must pay workers in risky jobs more than those in safe ones, they have a financial interest in making safety improvements where this can be done at reasonable cost. See Nichols and Zeckhauser, in Weiss and Klass, eds., esp. 206–7. Viscusi calculates that the total amount that U.S. firms pay workers in risk premiums is $70 billion a year, which is about 3,000 times as much as business pays in OSHA penalties; *Regulation* (May/June 1983): 42.

37 Wilson, testimony, OSHA Docket no. H-059, 21–6.

38 Bernard Cohen, "Society's Valuation of Life Saving in Radiation Protection and Other Contexts," *Health Physics* 38 (Jan. 1980): 33–51.

39 Richard Wilson, "Statement Submitted to the Environmental Protection Agency in connection with the Rulemaking Proceeding on a Proposed National Emissions Standard for Hazardous Air Pollutants; Benzene Emissons from Maleic Anhydride Plants" (EPA Docket no. OAQPS 79-3, Aug. 21, 1980, Mimeo.), 16.

40 See Rhoads, *Valuing Life*, 129.

41 Excessively strict safety standards sometimes save few if any additional lives despite their high costs. Highway safety again provides some useful examples. In 1967 interstate highway system design standards were made stricter in several ways. These changes raised the cost of building a mile of road by 13 percent. The added costs have meant that fewer miles of interstate highway can be built with a given amount of money. But noninterstate roads are far less safe than interstates, even those interstates built according to the less strict pre-1967 standards. It cannot be denied that if the standards had not been changed, some people traveling on the very safe interstate highways, built since 1967, would have been traveling on a less-safe interstate instead. Some of these would have died. But because fewer interstate miles per year are now built, some people now die on poor noninterstate roads who would have lived had the *relatively* safer pre-1967 type of interstate been built and available to them. Thus Herbert Mohring has speculated that the stricter safety standards may have led to more deaths than they prevented "Three Back-of-an-Envelope Evaluations of the Interstate Highway System," in James Miller, ed., *Perspectives on Federal Transportation Policy* (Washington, D.C.: American Enterprise Institute, 1975), 169–71.

The same sort of paradoxical outcome can occur as a result of some of the federal government's efforts to make motor vehicles safer. The Ford Motor Company has argued that it should not have been required to recall about 144,000 Mercury Capris with defective windshield wipers because government traffic figures show that there will be more accidents from 144,000 cars making a round trip from home to their Ford dealer than the government predicted would occur from the defective wipers. A student of mine who investigated the case found some small points to quarrel with in Ford's analysis, but concluded that Ford was probably correct in its conclusion; Sherman O. Halstead, Jr., "Risk Analysis of Motor Vehicle Defects and Recall Campaigns in the Capri Wiper Defect Case" (University of Virginia, May 23, 1981, Mimeo.).

Ford acknowledged that there was a defect, and perhaps competitive pressures to produce a reputation for quality and the threat of civil suits after accidents are not enough to force auto companies to produce the level of safety we want. If not, some sort of penalty for Ford and notification and/or compensation to owners might be called for. But surely we do not want a government highway safety agency to send a letter encouraging consumers to make a special repair trip to their Ford dealers to have a defect fixed if there is reason to think that more highway accidents will result from such a letter than if it had never been sent.

Government actions that prevent certain kinds of dangers while leading to other, perhaps greater, dangers occur in areas beyond highway safety. Many doctors, as well as economists, are concerned about the effect of Food and Drug Administration procedures that try to ensure that no harmful drugs are ever marketed. These procedures are far more elaborate than in other Western countries. They delay the introduction of lifesaving drugs, and by increasing costs to producers, they delay their discovery and development as well; Henry Grabowski and John Vernon, *The Regulation of Pharmaceuticals: Balancing the Benefits and Risks* (Washington, D.C.: American Enterprise Institute, 1983); William M. Wardell and Louis Lasagna, *Regulation and Drug Development* (Washington, D.C.: American Enterprise Institute, 1975). Also see Wardell and Lasagna's later articles in *Regulation*, e.g., Nov./Dec. 1979, and Sept./Oct. 1979. And after taking account of the dangers of nuclear energy, most serious studies find it far safer than the high-polluting alternative energy sources we will turn to in its absence. This was the conclusion of a mammoth 1979 study by Resources for the Future as well as that of two respected Harvard academics. The latter calculated that nuclear energy was one of the cheapest ways of producing power, was environmentally superior to the alternatives, and was far safer than coal, which kills miners and those sensitive to the air pollution its use produces. The Harvard study concluded that nuclear energy has so far saved 50,000 lives worldwide by replacing more dangerous energy sources in the countries involved; Sam H. Schurr and other staff of Resources for the Future, *Energy in America's Future* (Baltimore: Johns Hopkins University Press, 1979), 34–8, and R. V. Kline and Richard Wilson, "When the Oil Runs Out," *Washington Post*, Aug. 22, 1980, A-15.

More generally, Aaron Wildavsky has argued that what appear to be small lifesaving gains obtained at high cost may in fact not be gains at all. Wildavsky notes that in all countries at all times death rates go down as income goes up. Economic growth naturally leads to better nutrition, better working conditions, and a more secure and less wearing way of life. Studies have shown that social class is a more powerful predictor of mortality rates than risk of work. Efforts to reduce hazards for particular groups in particular ways often use scarce investment capital, and thus they reduce economic growth. Because a rising per capita income leads to lower death rates, such efforts may ultimately do less to save lives than would an overall improvement in the standard of living. "Richer is Safer," *Public Interest* no. 60 (Summer 1980): 23–39.

Declines in the growth rate affect not only private lifesaving activities but public ones as well. One reason why health care is a rising proportion of gross national product is that real gross national product is itself rising less fast than it used to. This has led to pressure to reduce the government's bill for health care. One sign of this pressure is the federal government's unwillingness to fund heart transplant operations costing less than $100,000 for all treatment and leading to a 50 percent chance of five or more years of life for middle-aged people who will die within months without the operation. This cost-conscious policy occurs at the same time that the government requires business to pay many times as much to save lives among workers facing risks far more tolerable.

42 Kelman, *Regulating America, Regulating Sweden*, esp. 58, 60, 73, 149.

43 See Steven E. Rhoads, "How Much Should We Spend to Save a Life?" *Public Interest* no. 51 (Spring 1978), reprinted in Rhoads, ed., *Valuing Life*, esp. 1–6, 303–6.

44 Reagan administration regulators came into office determined to make use of respirators to deal with problems such as cotton dust. They have since had to abandon the effort to allow textile plants to substitute respirators for expensive ventilation controls and have had only modest success with the respirator approach in other industries. See *National Journal*, Nov. 7, 1981, 1, 988, and *Washington Post*, Jan. 10, 1982, A-6 and June 8, 1983, 23.

45 Arthur H. Miller, "What Mandate? What Realignment?" *Washington Post*, June 28, 1981, D-1.

46 Seymour Martin Lipset and William Schneider find that well into 1981 the public wanted to cut spending generally but opposed cuts in almost all specific programs; *The Confidence Gap* (New York: Free Press, 1983), 182, 347–9. Also see the *Gallup Report*, Feb. 1981, 12; *Washington Post*, Sept. 5, 1981, 20, and Feb. 20, 1982, A-11; Council on Environmental Quality, *Public Opinion on Environmental Issues* (Washington, D.C., 1980); George H. Gallup, *The Gallup Poll, Public Opinion 1972–1975*, vol. 1, 43, 145, 298.

47 Eva Mueller, "Public Attitudes toward Fiscal Programs," *Quarterly Journal of Economics* 77 (May 1963): 210–35.

48 Kenneth Webb and Harry Hatry, *Obtaining Citizen Feedback* (Washington, D.C.: Urban Institute, 1973): 36–7.

49 *Washington Post*, Dec. 8, 1978, A-3.

50 Kneese and Schultze, *Pollution, Prices and Public Policy*, 21–2, 56.

51 Saul Pett, "Hizzonor' Keeps the Big Apple Hopping," *Charlottesville Daily Progress*, Dec. 4, 1980, C-3 and Edward Koch, "The Mandate Millstone," *Public Interest* no.61 (Fall 1980): 42.

52 *Washington Post*, Feb. 12, 1982, D-7.

53 Robert Samuelson, "Bailout Politics, Economics Collide," *Washington Post*, May 31, 1983, D-7.

3. MARGINALISM

1 A. H. Maslow, *Motivation and Personality* (New York: Harper & Row, 1954), ch. 5 and p. 107.

2 Richard McKenzie and Gordon Tullock, *The New World of Economics* (Homewood, Ill.: Irwin, 1981), 331–8.

3 See Kenneth Boulding, *Beyond Economics* (Ann Arbor: University of Michigan Press, 1970), 220.

4 Demand curves usually show the relationship between price (vertical axis) and quantity desired (horizontal axis). Though completely inelastic demand curves are vertical (or totally insensitive to price changes), almost all demand curves slope downward obliquely since at a lower price more will be consumed.

5 See Jack A. Meyer, *Health Care Cost Increases* (Washington, D.C.: American Enterprise Institute, 1979), 12.

6 Joseph Newhouse, Charles Phelps, and William B. Schwartz, "Policy Options and the Impact of National Health Insurance," *New England Journal of Medicine* 290 (1974): 1345–59. Reprinted in Richard Zeckhauser et al., *Benefit-Cost and Policy Analysis, 1974* (Chicago: Aldine, 1975). A more recent Rand Corporation study found that medical expenses were 50 percent higher for those with complete health insurance coverage. The study also suggested that cost sharing may not have an adverse effect on health; *Washington Post*, Dec. 17, 1981, 8.

7 Newhouse et al., "Policy Options."

8 Charles Fried, "Difficulties in the Economic Analysis of Rights," in Gerald Dworkin et al., *Markets and Morals* (Washington, D.C.: Hemisphere, 1977), 188–9.

9 This economic point of view is covered in more depth in ch. 6.

10 Fried, in Dworkin et al., eds., 191.

11 Michael Cooper, "Economics of Need: The Experience of the British Health Service," in Mark Perlman, ed., *The Economics of Health and Medical Care*, Proceedings of a Conference of the International Economic Association (New York: Wiley, 1973), 89–99, 105.

12 Cooper, in Perlman, ed., 91–3.

13 M. S. Feldstein, *Economic Analysis for Health Efficiency* (Amsterdam: North Holland, 1967), cited in Cooper.

14 Donald Gould, "Some Lives Cost Too Dear," *New Statesman*: 90 (Nov. 21, 1975): 634.

15 *Washington Post*, June 23, 1978, A-2.

16 See Miller and North's description of how this fire-fighting arrangement works where private business provides services under contract to Scottsdale, Ariz., in *The Economics of Public Issues* (New York: Harper & Row, 1980), ch. 15.

17 The FAA's policy-guidance process is discussed in more detail in Steven

E. Rhoads, "Policy Guidance for the FAA's Engineering and Development Programs" (Federal Aviation Administration, AVP-110, Aug. 8, 1974, Mimeo.). The quantitative objectives established by the FAA represented that agency's version of the federal government's Management By Objectives (MBO) system. This management tool, previously used in business and in some governments, was brought to the federal government by Richard Nixon. MBO systems that focus on end products are fine if an identified unit is responsible for the outcome and if it, for example, is asked to achieve as much as it did the preceding year with less money. MBO systems can also be useful tools for scheduling and following through on the particular tasks that must be acomplished to implement a program that will further an objective. Specific end-product or process objectives may even help a well-led bureaucracy do more than staff paper studies had suggested was possible. But an objective-setting process like the FAA's will not serve in these ways. No single FAA unit is responsible for meeting broad agency goals such as "reduce general aviation accidents by 10 percent." Moreover, even if there were a unit head who controlled all programs affecting general aviation, the FAA could not hold him accountable. Since little thought has been given to whether the funded programs affecting general aviation could reasonably be expected to reduce general aviation accidents by 10 percent, there is no way to know whether a manager achieving an 8 percent reduction should be praised or blamed.

The National Advisory Commission on Criminal Justice Standards and Goals has used a flawed goal- and priority-setting process like that of the FAA. See Jeffrey Sedgwick's discussion in "Welfare Economics and Criminal Justice Policy" (Ph. D. diss., University of Virginia, 1978), ch. 7.

18 Kenneth Boulding, "Economics as a Moral Science," in his *Economics as a Science* (New York: McGraw-Hill, 1970), 134.

19 Alexis de Tocqueville, *Democracy in America* (New York: Random House, 1945), p. 51.

20 Tocqueville, *Democracy in America*, 45.

21 John Rawls, *A Theory of Justice* (Cambridge, Mass.: Harvard University Press, 1971), 412. See also Allan Bloom's discussion "Justice: John Rawls vs. The Tradition of Political Philosophy," in *American Political Science Review* 69 (1975): esp. 659.

22 Bernard Asbell, *The Senate Nobody Knows* (Baltimore: Johns Hopkins University Press, 1978), 349.

23 See Allen Kneese and Charles Schultze, *Pollution, Prices and Public Policy* (Washington, D.C.: Brookings Institution, 1975), epilogue and 56 for an interesting discussion of the political feasibility of economic approaches to pollution policy. Also see Schultze's *The Public Use of Private Interest* (Washington, D.C.: Brookings Institution, 1977), 76–90.

24 Kneese and Schultze, *Pollution, Prices and Public Policy*, epilogue.

25 Hobart Rowen, *Washington Post*, March 12, 1981, A-21. One study found that economists believed economic journalism to be "inaccurate, biased, distorted, sensationalized, and unsophisticated." J. R. Kearl et al., "What Economists Think," *American Economic Review: Papers and Proceedings of the 91st Annual Meeting August, 1978* 69 (1979): 28–37.

26 See Charls E. Walker's discussion in *Washington Post*, June 1, 1981, A-11.

27 In addition to chapter 4 see Kneese and Schultze, *Pollution, Prices and Public Policy*, 62–3, 81, 87–9, 99. For an example of an academic economist's use of marginalism upon entering the political arena see Alfred Kahn, "Applications of Economics to an Imperfect World," *American Economic Review* 69 (1979): esp. 1–3. Also of special interest is Douglas Anderson's discussion of Kahn's use of marginalism in *Regulatory Politics and Electric Utilities* (Boston: Auburn House, 1981), ch. 4.

28 James Buchanan, "Economics and Its Scientific Neighbors," in Sherman Krupp, ed., *The Structure of Economic Science: Essays on Methodology* (Englewood Cliffs, N.J.: Prentice-Hall, 1966), 168.

29 John Maher, *What is Economics?* (New York: Wiley, 1969), 146–8.

30 McKenzie and Tullock, *New World of Economics*, ch. 2.

4. ECONOMIC INCENTIVES

1 Charles Schultze, *The Public Use of Private Interest* (Washington, D.C.: Brookings Institution, 1977), 1–16.

2 There is, however, some evidence that if the pollution goals are set extremely high and standards extremely strict, the efficiency gains from an incentive approach become smaller. See Department of Commerce, Office of the Secretary, *Regulatory Reform Seminar: Proceedings and Background Papers*, Oct. 17, 1978, 58–9. But compare M. T. Maloney and Bruce Yandle, "Cleaner Air at Lower Cost," *Regulation* (May/June 1980): 51.

3 Lester Lave and Gilbert Omenn, *Clearing the Air: Reforming the Clean Air Act* (Washington, D.C.: Brookings Institution, 1981), 1.

4 Robert W. Crandall, "Has Reagan Dropped the Ball?" *Regulation* (Sept./Oct. 1981): 17.

5 Lave and Omenn, *Clearing the Air*, 9. See also R. Shep Melnick, "Deadlines, Common Sense and Cynicism,'' *Brookings Review* (Fall 1983): 21–24.

6 Lawrence White, *The Regulation of Air Pollution Emissions from Motor Vehicles* (Washington, D.C.: American Enterprise Institute, 1982), esp. chs. 5, 8, 9.

7 Pollution and cost figures given in text, and later, are from Lave and Omenn, *Clearing the Air*, 19–21, 40–6; American Enterprise Institute, *The Clean Air Act: Proposals for Revision* (Washington, D.C.: American Enterprise Institute, 1981), 7–9; Larry Ruff, ''Federal Environmental Regulation,'' in Leonard Weiss and Michael Klass, eds., *Case Studies in Regulation* (Boston: Little, Brown, 1981), 247–52; Crandall, ''Has Reagan Dropped the Ball?'' 17, and Robert Crandall, *Controlling Industrial Pollution* (Washington, D.C.: Brookings Institution, 1983).

8 Robert Crandall, ''Environmental Protection Agency,'' *Regulation* (Nov./ Dec. 1980): 20.

9 Ruff, in Weiss and Klass, eds., 246.

10 Bernard Asbell, *The Senate Nobody Knows* (Baltimore: Johns Hopkins University Press, 1978), 318–26; see also 175, 188, 363.

11 Winston Harrington and Alan J. Krupnick, ''Stationary Source Pollution Policy and Choices for Reform,'' in Henry Peskin, Paul Portney, and Allen Kneese, eds., *Environmental Regulation and the U.S. Economy* (Baltimore: Resources for the Future, Johns Hopkins University Press, 1981), 111–14.

12 Ruff, in Weiss and Klass, eds., 254.

13 As quoted in Ruff, 254.

14 David Harrison, Jr., and Robert Leone, ''Federal Water Pollution Control Policy'' (Working paper no. 12, rev. Oct. 29, 1982), American Enterprise Institute, IV-25 and IV-26.

15 The Federal Water Pollution Control Act Amendments, as cited in Schultze, *Public Use of Private Interest*, 51–2.

16 *Washington Post*, May 10, 1981, A-1, and May 11, 1981, A-8.

17 Ruff, in Weiss and Klass, eds., 256–8.

18 Allen Kneese and Charles Schultze, *Pollution Prices and Public Policy* (Washington, D.C.: Brookings Institution, 1975), 89.

19 For a discussion of the strengths and weaknesses of inspection systems see White, *Regulation of Air Pollution Emissions*, ch. 9, and Edwin Mills and Lawrence White, ''Government Policies Toward Automotive Emissions Control,'' in Ann Friedlaender, ed., *Approaches to Controlling Air Pollution* (Cambridge, Mass.: MIT Press, 1978).

20 Lester Lave and Eugene Seskin, ''Death Rates and Air Quality,'' *Washington Post*, Nov. 12, 1978, B-7.

21 For more on this example see *National Journal*, Oct. 10, 1981, p. 1, 818.

22 Schultze, *Public Use of Private Interest*, 26–7.

23 Chapter 8 discusses ways in which this harm to society might be estimated.

24 For more on the advantages and disadvantages of the two methods see Crandall, *Controlling Industrial Pollution*, chs. 4, 10; Harrington and Krupnick, in Peskin et al., eds., 127–8; Lave and Omenn, *Clearing the Air*, 29; David Harrison, Jr., and Paul Portney, "Making Ready for the Clean Air Act," *Regulation* (March/April 1981): 31.

25 Singapore's congestion charge system, inaugurated in 1975, and the South Coast (California) Air Quality Management District's small-emission charge system, inaugurated in 1977, "have both been conspicuous for their smooth operation and lack of administrative problems"; Ward Elliott, "The Case for Smog Charges in the South Coast Basin" (Claremont McKenna College, Feb. 1983, Mimeo), 41. For additional technical discussion about the relationship between the tax scheme and economic efficiency see Dean Worcester, Jr., "A Note on the Postwar Literature on Externalities," *Journal of Economic Literature* (March 1972); F. Trenery Dolbear and commentators, "On the Theory of Optimum Externality," in Robert Staaf and Francis Tannian, eds., *Externalities: Theoretical Dimensions of Political Economy* (New York: Dunellen, 1974); Richard Musgrave and Peggy Musgrave, *Public Finance in Theory and Practice* (New York: McGraw-Hill, 1980), 753–65.

26 Harrison and Leone, "Federal Water Pollution Control Policy," IV-13, IV-14.

27 General Accounting Office, *A Market Approach to Air Pollution Control Could Reduce Compliance Costs without Jeopardizing Clean Air Goals* (Report no. PAD-82-15, March 23, 1982), esp. 25–6; Crandall, *Controlling Industrial Pollution*, ch. 3; Robert Crandall and Paul Portney, "The Free Market and Clean Air," *Washington Post*, Aug 20, 1981; Kneese and Schultze, p. 99.

28 Kneese and Schultze, *Pollution Prices and Public Policy*, 81–2, 88n, 90.

29 See, e.g., *Compensation for Pollution Damage* (Organization for Economic Cooperation and Development, 1981); Kneese and Schultze, *Pollution Prices and Public Policy*, 109–11; *Washington Post*, June 27, 1976, F-1.

30 Thomas Tietenberg, "Regulatory Reform in Air Pollution Control," in Robert Haveman and Julius Margolis, eds., *Public Expenditure and Policy Analysis* (Boston: Houghton Mifflin, 1983), 470. For problems and recent reforms see Harrington and Krupnick, in Peskin et al., eds., 123–7; *Washington Post*, Oct. 17, 1980, A-12, and Dec. 16, 1981, A-29; Lave, 23–5.

31 Harrington and Krupnick, in Peskin et al., eds., 122.

32 Lawrence Mosher, "Big Steel Says it Can't Afford to Make the Nation's Air Pure," *National Journal*, July 5, 1980, 1,088–92.

33 Maloney and Yandle, "Cleaner Air at Lower Cost," 51.

34 Harrington and Krupnick, in Peskin et al., eds., 123–7; Crandall, *Controlling Industrial Pollution*, 84.

35 Kneese and Schultze, *Pollution Prices and Public Policy*, 112–20; Schultze, *Public Use of Private Interest*, 72–4; Robert H. Haveman, "Efficiency and Equity in Natural Resource and Environmental Policy," *American Journal of Agricultural Economics* 55 (Dec. 1973); 868–78; Lester B. Lave, *The Strategy of Social Regulation* (Washington, D.C.: Brookings Institution, 1981), 133; "Regulatory Report," *National Journal*, Dec. 5, 1981, 2, 151. Also see Asbell, *The Senate Nobody Knows*, 340.

36 Actually, though they were opposed, business lobbyists knew little about the tax schemes economists recommended. See Steven Kelman, *What Price Incentives? Economists and the Environment* (Boston: Auburn House, 1981), 118–22. One study suggests that by shifting the burden to firms more able to meet it, the tax approach could ultimately cost business less than the standards approach even though, taken as a whole, business would clean up as much pollution as under the standards approach and have to pay taxes for effluents remaining besides (see Kneese and Schultze's discussion of the Delaware estuary study; *Pollution Prices and Public Policy*, esp. at 94). Still, the current approach puts special barriers in the path of new firms, a substantial advantage from the point of view of old firms; James Buchanan and Gordon Tullock, "Polluters' Profits and Political Response: Direct Controls vs. Taxes," *American Economic Review* 65 (1975); 139–47. For a discussion of industry opposition to the sulfur tax proposed by President Nixon see *National Journal*, Oct. 21, 1972, 1, 648 and Oct. 28, 1981, 1, 665. On business's more general opposition to pollution taxes see *Washington Post*, May 31, 1976, A-16.

37 *Washington Post*, May 12, 1978, L-15. Also see Feb. 7, 1979, A-2.

38 Kelman sees this objection to selling a "license to pollute" as central for many environmentalists (*What Price Incentives?* 44).

39 *Congressional Record*, U.S. Senate, vol. 117, pt. 30, Nov. 2, 1971, 38, 829.

40 See, e.g., Kneese and Schultze, *Pollution Prices and Public Policy*, 90.

41 Kelman, *What Price Incentives?* 44–53, 69–77, 112.

42 Kelman, *What Price Incentives?* 110–14.

43 Lave and Seskin, "Death Rates and Air Quality."

44 *Los Angeles Times*, Dec. 30, 1971.

45 *Washington Post*, Dec. 31, 1979, A-2.

46 Quoted in White, *Regulation of Air Pollution Emissions*, 22. Also note p. 76, where White shows that in 1973, William Ruckelshaus found that Chrysler had made a "good faith" effort to meet the pollution standards only after "placing decisive reliance" on the fact that if Ruckelshaus found otherwise he might have to force them to close down.

47 *Washington Post*, May 31, 1976, A-16.

48 Kelman, *What Price Incentives?* 117.

49 Kelman, esp. 32–9.

50 Schultze, *Public Use of Private Interest*, 17–18.

51 Kenneth Arrow, "Gifts and Exchanges," *Philosophy and Public Affairs* (1972): 343–62. For a critique of Arrow, see Peter Singer, "Altruism and Commerce: A Defense of Titmuss Against Arrow." *Philosophy and Public Affairs*, II (1973): 312–19.

52 Kelman, *What Price Incentives?* 55.

53 William Ophuls, *Ecology and the Politics of Scarcity* (San Francisco: Freeman, 1977), 175.

54 Kelman, *What Price Incentives?* 84, 114.

55 Asbell, *The Senate Nobody Knows*, 341.

56 *Congressional Record*, U.S. Senate, vol. 117, pt. 30, Nov. 2, 1971, 38, 830.

57 Kelman, *What Price Incentives?* 144–8.

58 Kelman, 10.

59 Albert L. Nichols and Richard Zeckhauser, "Government Comes to the Workplace: An Assessment of OSHA," *Public Interest* no. 49 (Fall 1977): 65.

60 For a fuller discussion of tax approaches to the worker safety problem see Nichols and Zeckhauser, "Government Comes to the Workplace," and Robert Stewart Smith, *The Occupational Safety and Health Act* (Washington, D.C.: American Enterprise Institute, 1976), esp. 78–83.

61 Gilbert White, *Strategies of American Water Management* (Ann Arbor: University of Michigan Press, 1969), cited in Robert K. Davis and Steven Hanke, "Pricing and Efficiency in Water Resource Management," in Arnold C. Harberger et al., eds., *Benefit Cost Analysis 1971* (Chicago: Aldine, 1972), 276. For an interesting discussion of economist Alfred Kahn's uses of incentives and marginalism in reforming New York State's electric utility rate structure see Douglas Anderson, *Regulatory Politics and Electric Utilities* (Boston: Auburn House, 1981), ch. 4. Telephone directory assistance is another case of a quasi-public service where scarce resources are wasted frivolously when provided free. In 1977 the Chesapeake and Potomac Telephone Co. found directory assistance calls fell 59 percent when a ten-cent charge was instituted for each assistance call beyond the first six per month; *Washington Post*, March 9, 1977, A-12.

62 Sam Peltzman, *Regulation of Automobile Safety* (Washington, D.C.: American Enterprise Institute, 1975), 19–23.

63 *Washington Post*, July 12, 1981, C-8.

64 Glenn Blomquist, "Traffic Safety Regulation by NHTSA" (Working paper no. 16, American Enterprise Institute Nov. 18, 1981), ch. 2, n.4.

65 In an effort to make the argument of this paragraph more forcefully, Richard McKenzie and Gordon Tullock ask if a driver would not drive more carefully if a dagger were mounted on the steering wheel, pointed at his chest; *The New World of Economics* (Homewood, Ill.: Irwin, 1981), 40n. Also see Peltzman and Richard Nelson's criticism of Peltzman's work (in working paper no. WC5-13 of Yale University's Institution for Social and Policy Studies). Despite his criticism, Nelson has told the author that the issue is "quantitative, not qualitative" and that he agrees with Peltzman that the Department of Transportation should give the incentive-to-riskier-driving effect some consideration when making automobile safety regulations. The past reliance on simple engineering studies has not done that. One cannot assume that if air bags will cut deaths from accidents of a certain type in half, deaths will be cut in half if air bags are required. If air bags are required, some people will feel somewhat more protected, will take more risks, and will have somewhat more accidents of that type.

This does not mean that safety measures are completely counterproductive, and we would save more lives by putting daggers on the steering wheels. Most studies find that vehicle occupants are on balance safer because of the safer cars they drive (i.e., the safer cars protect their health more than their riskier driving harms it). However, most studies find that pedestrians are now far less safe. For a review of the evidence see Blomquist, "Traffic Safety Regulation by NHTSA."

66 *Washington Post*, Nov. 28, 1980, A-22.

67 See G. Richard Biehl, "Handguns: What Really Counts," *Washington Post*, Dec. 21, 1980, C-7.

68 Antonio Martino, "Measuring Italy's Underground Economy," *Policy Review* no. 16 (Spring 1981): 87.

69 James J. Kilpatrick, "Getting Back to Anderson," *Charlottesville Daily Progress*, July 26, 1980, p. A-4.

70 See William Nordhaus and Alice Rivlin's discussion of this in *Regulatory Reform Seminar*, 60–1.

5. GOVERNMENT AND THE ECONOMY

1 For example, William Baumol expresses his concern about "bluenoses and those who would impose on myself and others their own standards of good taste and good behaviour.'' Baumol wants the pattern of public intervention in the economy ''designed very explicitly in terms of the desires of the public''; *Welfare Economics and the Theory of the State* (Cambridge, Mass.: Harvard University Press, 1965), 29. Pushpin is a children's game played with pins. Bentham's famous statement was, ''Prejudice apart, the game of push-pin is of equal value with the arts and sciences of music and poetry.''

2 John K. Galbraith, ''Economics as a System of Belief,'' in his *Economics, Peace and Laughter* (Boston: Houghton Mifflin, 1971), 82.

3 See, e.g., Steven E. Rhoads, *Policy Analysis in the Federal Aviation Administration* (Lexington, Mass.: Lexington Books, 1974), 121.

4 E. C. Pasour, Jr., and J. Bruce Bullock, ''Energy and Agriculture: Some Economic Issues,'' in *Agriculture and Energy* (New York: Academic Press, 1977).

5 Some economists do not like the potential Pareto improvement concept, and they would argue that economic efficiency is obtained only if the compensation of losers actually takes place and thus there are no losers. When benefit-cost studies talk of economic-efficiency benefits, however, they usually use the potential Pareto understanding of economic efficiency. Charles Schultze reflects this literature when he says, ''An efficient move is, by definition, one in which gains exceed losses''; *The Public Use of Private Interest* (Washington, D.C.: Brookings Institution, 1977), 22n. Edgar Browning and Jacqueline Browning's popular public-finance text also states that government expenditure and tax packages that make some citizens worse off may nonetheless be economically efficient; *Public Finance and the Price System*, 2d ed. (New York: Macmillan, 1983), 31–3. For more on Pareto optimality and economic efficiency see E.J. Mishan, *Cost-Benefit Analysis* (New York: Praeger, 1976) and Mark Blaug, *Economic Theory in Retrospect* (Cambridge: Cambridge University Press, 1978), 618–39.

6 K. J. Arrow and F. H. Hahn, *General Competitive Analysis* (San Francisco: Holden-Day, 1971), vi–vii.

7 Leonard E. Read, ''I, Pencil: My Family Tree,'' *Freeman*, Dec. 1958, as quoted in Milton Friedman and Rose Friedman, *Free to Choose* (New York: Avon Books, 1979), 3–5.

8 Friedman and Friedman, *Free to Choose*, 7. My discussion of ''The Pencil'' draws heavily on this work.

9 In their text Browning and Browning provide the following interesting example of free-rider behavior: ''In 1970 . . . General Motors tried to market pollution control devices for automobiles at $20 (installed) that could reduce the pollution emitted by 30 to 50 percent. . . . GM withdrew the device from the market because of low sales. This was simply the large-group free rider problem at work. Everyone might have been better off if all drivers used the device, but it was not in the interest of any single individual to purchase it because the overall level of air quality would not be noticeably improved as a result of his solitary action" (p. 28).

10 For more on government failure and public choice see Browning and Browning, *Public Finance and the Price System*, ch. 3; Ryan Amacher, Robert Tollison, and Thomas Willett, eds., *The Economic Approach to Public Policy* (Ithaca, N.Y.: Cornell University Press, 1976), pt. IV; Richard McKenzie and Gordon Tullock, *The New World of Economics*, 3d ed. (Homewood, Ill.: Irwin, 1981), ch. 11; Roland N. McKean, "Government and the Consumer," *Southern Economic Journal* 39 (1973): 481–9; and McKean, "Property Rights within Government, and Devices to Increase Governmental Efficiency," *Southern Economic Journal* 39 (1972): 177–86.

11 Note the inclusion of a "government failure" section in recent popular texts like those by Browning and Browning and Richard Lipsey and Peter Steiner, *Economics* (New York: Harper & Row, 1981).

12 E. S. Savas, "Refuse Collection," *Policy Analysis* III (Winter 1977): 49–74. Corroborative studies in three countries are summarized in E. S. Savas, "Public vs. Private Refuse Collection: A Critical Review of the Evidence," *Urban Analysis* 6 (1979): 1–13.

13 See the discussion of the study in the *Washington Post*, Oct. 10, 1975, A-1.

14 It would come as no surprise to public-choice scholars to learn that the potential savings had long been hidden from view by estimating distant employee retirement costs at less than one-third of the real figure; *Washington Post*, Aug. 24, 1976, A-4. Also on the federal contracting question see the *Washington Post*, April 11, 1981, A-2; Nov. 29, 1977, A-18; Nov. 22, 1977, D-7; Dec. 30, 1977, A-5. For a description of bureaucracy's attempt to preserve its monopoly on information by deliberately refusing to collect useful output information see the discussion of New York police response time in the *New York Times*, Jan. 10, 1978, B-1. Sometimes, however, the problem is politicians who block administrators seeking efficiency improvements. In 1978 a General Services Administration attempt to obtain competitive bidding on overhead projectors was blocked when eighty members of Congress received complaints from the projector industry and wrote the GSA; *Washington Post*, Aug. 25, 1978, A-9.

15 See Douglass North and Roger Miller, *The Economics of Public Issues* (New York: Harper & Row, 1980), ch. 15; Roger S. Ahlbrandt, Jr., "Efficiency in the Provision of Fire Services," *Public Choice* 18 (Fall 1973): 1–15; *Washington Post*, Oct. 11, 1981; also see on contracting and government efficiency Louis De Alessi, "An Economic Analysis of Government Ownership and Regulation: Theory and Evidence from the Electric Power Industry," *Public Choice* 19 (Fall 1979): 1–42; E. S. Savas, *Privatizing the Public Sector* (Chatham, N.J.: Chatham House, 1982); Donald Fisk, *Private Provision of Public Services: An Overview* (Washington, D.C.: Urban Institute, 1978); Robert Spann, "Public vs. Private Provision of Governmental Services," in T. E. Borcherding, ed., *Budgets and Bureaucrats: The Sources of Government Growth* (Durham, N.C.: Duke University Press, 1977); *Washington Post*, Nov. 5, 1980, B-1; Robert W. Poole, Jr., *Cutting Back City Hall* (New York: Universe, 1981); James Bennett and Manuel Johnson, *Better Government at Half the Cost: Private Provision of Public Services* (Aurora, Ill.: Green Hill, 1981). For a cautionary note on contracting, see a 1981 report by the National Tax Foundation (Sacramento).

Charles Goodsell has recently written what he calls "a public administration polemic" in which he argues that the studies on the comparative efficiency of government and business are mixed and inconclusive; *The Case for Bureaucracy* (Chatham, N.J.: Chatham House, 1983). Though Goodsell does discuss some early studies by economists, he cites none published after 1979. He also fails to cite any of the sources listed in this note. Some of these review the literature thoroughly, and all but one of these were published at least two years before Goodsell's book appeared.

16 Quoted in Charles Lindblom, *Politics and Markets* (New York: Basic Books, 1977), 69.

17 On the Soviet Union see the *Washington Post*, July 13, 1977, A-17; Nov. 2, 1981, A-1; Nov. 28, 1981, A-20; June 16, 1983, A-20; July 27, 1983, A-22; on Romania, *Washington Post*, March 25, 1978, A-9; on China, *Washington Post*, Oct. 3, 1981, A-1; Dec. 30, 1977, A-13; Dec. 10, 1975, E-3; Feb. 6, 1982, A-1; *New York Times*, Aug. 16, 1979, A-2; on Angola, *Washington Post*, Sept. 22, 1981; on Argentina, Feb. 4, 1982, A-18, and March 19, 1981, A-33.

18 *Washington Post*, Feb. 6, 1982, A-1.

19 *Washington Post*, Nov. 9, 1980, A-29. Also on Cuba see, *Washington Post*, Oct. 5, 1981, A-1; May 19, 1974, A-14; and *Los Angeles Times*, June 11, 1976, 1-A.

20 *Washington Post*, Nov. 15, 1981, C-7.

21 Robert D. Behn, "For U.S. '81 Outlays, There's No Tomorrow," *New York Times*, Sept. 30, 1981, 31.

22 *Washington Post*, Sept. 14, 1979, A-1.

23 Some of the results of these government policies are simply absurd. The ICC, for example, established such inefficient railroad price signals that the average U.S. boxcar traveled loaded only 7 percent of the time and covered only fifty miles a day. In California's naturally arid Imperial Valley irrigation water is so heavily subsidized that one of the favorite crops is watermelon; Charles Schultze, *Public Use of Private Interest*, 79.

24 See Roland McKean's discussion in "Divergences Between Individual and Total Costs Within Government," *American Economic Review* (May 1964): 54. Reprinted in Amacher et al., eds.

25 William Allen, "Economics, Economists and Economic Policy: Modern American Experiences," *History of Political Economy* 9 (1977): 52.

26 Schultze, *Private Use of Public Interest*, p. 41; Kenneth Arrow, "Two Cheers for Government Regulation," *Harpers* 262 (March 1981): 22; *Washington Post*, July 8, 1979, C-7; Feb. 6, 1981, A-14.

27 *Washington Post*, Jan. 27, 1982, A-2.

28 See Alex R. Maurizi, *Public Policy and the Dental Care Market* (Washington, D.C.: American Enterprise Institute, 1975); *Washington Post*, Nov. 15, 1980, A-18; for an economist who still favors using government subsidies to steer workers into needed fields see Robert J. Gordon, "Sweep Away the Dogma," *Washington Post*, Feb. 28, 1982, B-8.

29 *Washington Post*, March 23, 1981, A-15. For the AFL-CIO's and Governor Brown's views see *Washington Post*, Oct. 14, 1981, D-7, and Jan. 31, 1982, D-1. Also note Senator Edward Kennedy's support for credit controls channeling loan funds to "high-priority areas"; *Washington Post*, April 7, 1982, D-8.

30 Robert Reich, *The Next American Frontier* (New York: Times Books, 1983); Lester Thurow, *The Zero Sum Society* (New York: Penguin Books, 1981), esp. 96, 132, and "The Road to Lemon Socialism," *Newsweek*, April 25, 1983; Barry Bluestone and Bennett Harrison, *The Deindustrialization of America* (New York: Basic Books, 1982); Felix Rohatyn's positions are discussed in Jeremy Bernstein, "Profiles: Allocating Sacrifice," *New Yorker*, Jan. 23, 1983, 45–78. Over thirty industrial policy bills have been introduced in the 98th Congress. The Democratic Caucus of the U.S. Senate and the Democratic majority of the House Banking Committee's Subcommittee on Economic Stabilization have both endorsed industrial policy plans. The provisions of some of these bills and the ideas of the authors cited here are surveyed in Richard McKenzie, "National Industrial Policy: An Overview of the Debate" Heritage Foundation Backgrounder, July 12, 1983.

31 University of Pennsylvania economist Michael Wachter, as quoted in *Business Week*, July 4, 1983, 61.

32 Alfred Kahn, "The Relevance of Industrial Organization," in John V. Craven, ed., *Industrial Organization, Antitrust and Public Policy* (Boston: Kluwer-Nijhoff, 1983), 16.

33 Kahn, "The Relevance of Industrial Organization," 14; Robert Samuelson, "The Policy Peddlers," *Harpers* (June 1983): 62; Robert Crandall, "Can Industrial Policy Work?" *Washington Post Book World*, May 22, 1983, p. 8. Until recently Germany did have an impressive growth in labor productivity, as will be discussed in ch. 6.

34 Philip Trezise, "Industrial Policy is not the Major Reason for Japan's Success," *Brookings Review* (Spring 1983): 18.

35 Kahn, "Relevance of Industrial Organization," in Craven, ed., 16. Also see Amitai Etzioni, "The MITIzation of America?" *Public Interest* no. 72 (Summer 1983): 46–7. George Eads, "The Political Experience in Allocating Investment: Lessons from the United States and Elsewhere," in Michael Wachter and Susan Wachter, eds., *Toward a New U.S. Industrial Policy?* (Philadelphia: University of Pennsylvania Press, 1981): 472–9.

36 See Princeton economist Uwe Reinhardt, "Diagnosing the Great American Bellyache," *Princeton Alumni Weekly*, Feb. 22, 1982, 22.

37 Samuelson, "The Policy Peddlers," 62.

38 A recent case of this is North Sea oil. For years the North Sea was not considered a good bet for finding oil. In the 1960s a gas deposit found off Holland stimulated some interest. But after twenty-nine dry holes, eight of the nine exploration groups had abandoned their activities. The consensus among geologists was that there was no oil to be found. One group continued to explore, and we now know that the North Sea is a major oil province with sixteen billion barrels of reserves already discovered. Potential recoverable reserves are estimated at forty billion barrels or more.

Nelson and Richard Langlois give these other examples: "Strange as it now seems to us, aviation experts were once divided on the relative merits of the turboprop and turbojet engines as power plants for the aircraft of the future; and the computer industry was by no means unanimous that transistors – or later, integrated circuits – were to be the technology of the future"; "Industrial Innovation Policy: Lessons from American History," *Science*, Feb. 18, 1983, 815.

39 Richard R. Nelson, *The Moon and the Ghetto* (New York: Norton, 1977), 120; Nelson and Langlois, "Industrial Innovation Policy," 815, 817.

40 Samuelson, "The Policy Peddlers," 63.

41 Alfred Kahn, "America's Democrats: Can Liberalism Survive Inflation?" *Economist* March 7, 1981, 25; also see Etzioni (n.35), Samuelson (n.33), and Eads (n.35).

42 The first three quotes are from *Washington Post*, July 3, 1983, G-1, G-4; the last Schultze quote is from *Business Week*, July 4, 1983, 57. See as well Schultze's "Industrial Policy: A Dissent," *Brookings Review* (Fall 1983): 3–12. Liberal economists Joseph Pechman and Francis Bator have also been described as "dubious" about "whether industrial policy is more than a slogan"; *Washington Post*, June 10, 1983, D-8, D-11. It also seems unlikely that Arthur Okun would have supported the most common industrial policy proposals. In his well-known book, Okun noted that we expect taxpayer money to be treated with respect and caution, and he thus doubted that government could respond flexibly enough to organize economic activity in areas where experimentation and innovation are important; *Equality and Efficiency* (Washington, D.C.: Brookings Institution, 1975), 60–1.

43 Arrow, "Two Cheers for Government Regulation."

44 Thurow, *The Zero Sum Society*, esp. 8, 44, 127, 140, 144, 146–53, 210.

45 Okun, *Equality and Efficiency*, 117.

46 Adam Smith, *The Wealth of Nations*, book IV, ch. 2.

47 George H. Gallup, *The Gallup Poll, Public Opinion 1972–1975*, I, (Wilmington, Del.: Scholarly Resources), 494; *Congressional Record*, March 9, 1976, E-1, 133. Actual profit figures from Richard Caves, "The Structure of Industry" in Martin Feldstein, ed., *The American Economy in Transition* (Chicago: University of Chicago Press, 1980), 544, and Bruce Johnson, ed., *The Attack on Corporate America: The Corporate Issues Sourcebook* (New York: McGraw-Hill, 1978), 252–5.

In 1973 the Opinion Research Council found that a cross section of American adults believed that of the total of corporate earnings and employee costs summed together, employees received 25 percent and corporate owners, 75 percent. The true figures for that year were employees, 88 percent and owners, 12 percent. Poll and actual figures from Johnson, ed., *Attack on Corporate America*, p. 257. Also see Seymour Martin Lipset and William Schneider, *The Confidence Gap* (New York: Free Press, 1983), 176–83.

48 If the government spending is paid for by compulsory taxes rather than debt, it fares no better by the economists' standard of consumer sovereignty. Those who would have spent, not saved, the money taxed away would obviously require a higher-than-market return on their investment before they would agree to give up their private consumption. (Otherwise they would have planned to save their money, not spend it.)

49 On speculation see Armen Alchian and William Allen, *University Economics* (Belmont, Calif.: Wadsworth, 1972), ch. 10. For congressional concern about manipulation of the coffee market see the *Washington Post*, March 15, 1977, A-1. For Interior Department economists' devices for dealing with congressional misunderstanding of speculation see Christopher Leman and Robert Nelson, "Ten Commandments for Policy Economists," *Journal of Policy Analysis and Management* 1 (1981):102.

50 For criticisms of Galbraith see John Jewkes, *The Sources of Invention* (London: Macmillan Press, 1969); G. C. Allen, *Economic Fact and Fantasy* (London: Institute of Economic Affairs, 1967); Harold Demsetz, "Economics in the Industrial State – Discussion,'' *American Economic Review* 60 (1970): 481–4; Demsetz, ''Where is the New Industrial State?'' *Economic Inquiry* (March 1974); R. M. Solow, ''The New Industrialized State or Son of Affluence,'' *Public Interest* no. 9 (Fall 1967): 100–8; J. E. Meade, ''Is 'The New Industrial State' Inevitable?'' *Economic Journal* 78 (June 1968): 372–92. These studies are reviewed in Milton Friedman, *From Galbraith to Economic Freedom* (London: Institute of Economic Affairs, 1977). Also see Caves, in Feldstein, ed., 518.

51 Galbraith is discussed further in ch. 9.

52 *Washington Post*, May 23, 1982, F-2.

53 Caves, in Feldstein, ed., esp. 511, 515, 573.

54 William Shepherd, ''Causes of Increased Competition in the U.S. Economy, 1939–1980,'' *Review of Economics and Statistics* (Nov. 1982): 613–26. See Shepherd's exchange with Fred Smith in *Regulation* (May/June 1983): 2–4.

55 See Richard Posner's review of developments, ''The Chicago School of Antitrust Analysis,'' *University of Pennsylvania Law Review* 127 (1979): 925–48. Also see Leonard Weiss, ''The Structure-Conduct-Performance Paradigm and Anti-trust,'' *University of Pennsylvania Law Review* 127 (1979): 1,104–40.

56 See Kenneth G. Elzinga, ''The Goals of Anti-trust: Other than Competition and Efficiency, What Else Counts?'' *University of Pennsylvania Law Review* 125 (1977): 1,196, and Johnson, *Attack on Corporate America*, 216. The common accusation that money spent on mergers is wasted from the point of view of societal investment assumes that those receiving money for their companies' shares will not in turn invest it.

57 See Lipsey and Steiner, *Economics,* ch. 18.

58 Weiss, ''Structure-Conduct-Performance Paradigm,'' 1,117.

59 Sam Peltzman, ''The Gains and Losses from Industrial Concentration,'' *Journal of Law and Economics* 22 (1977): 191; Steven Lustgarten, *Productivity and Prices: The Consequences of Industrial Concentration* (Washington, D.C.: American Enterprise Institute, 1984).

60 Johnson, *Attack on Corporate America*, 245–51.

61 Schultze, ''Public Use of Private Interest,'' 76–9. Also see 25–6, 40.

62 Okun, *Equality and Efficiency*, 50–1. A 1978 survey of 211 randomly selected economists asked their reaction to thirty statements. The most striking areas of consensus were in the opposition to government ''interference with the price mechanism and exchange''; J. R. Kearl, Clayne Pope, Gordon Whiting, and Larry Wimmer, ''What Economists Think'' *American Economic Review: Papers and Proceedings* 69 (May 1979): 34. Also note Richard

Nelson's view that economists share an oral tradition in which the market as a force for initiative, resourcefulness, and energizing is more fully appreciated than in their written work; ''The Economic Problem and the Role of Competition'' (Paper presented to the Society of Government Economists, Sept. 17, 1976, Mimeo), cited in Charles Lindblom, *Politics and Markets* (New York: Basic Books, 1977), 75n.

63 See George Eads, ''Competition in the Domestic Airline Industry,'' in Almarin Phillips, ed., *Promoting Competition in Regulated Markets* (Washington, D.C.: Brookings Institution, 1975); for evidence on consumer savings since deregulation see Theodore Keeler, ''The Revolution in Airline Regulation,'' in Leonard Weiss and Michael Klass, eds., *Case Studies in Regulation* (Boston: Little, Brown, 1981), 53–85; John Meyer and Clinton V. Oster, *Airline Deregulation – The Early Experience* (Boston: Auburn House, 1981), and *Regulation* (March/April 1982): 52.

64 Shepherd, ''Causes of Increased Competition in the U.S. Economy.''

65 See, e.g., Johnson, *Attack on Corporate America*, 294–8, and Ernest Gellhorn, ''Two's A Crowd: The FTC's Redundant Antitrust Powers,'' *Regulation* (Nov./Dec. 1981): 32–42.

66 See Frank Easterbrook, ''Breaking Up is Hard to Do,'' *Regulation* (Nov./Dec. 1981), esp. 31. Also see Robert Samuelson, ''Some Cautious Words About Merger Mania,'' *Washington Post*, Dec. 1, 1981, D-6.

67 Weiss, ''Structure-Conduct-Performance Paradigm,'' 1,117–19. Also see Posner, ''Chicago School of Antitrust Analysis,'' 938; Joe Sims and William Blumenthal, ''The New Era in Antitrust,'' *Regulation* (July/Aug. 1982): 25–8; Yale Brozen, *Mergers in Perspective* (Washington, D.C.: American Enterprise Institute, 1982). In a letter Alfred Kahn expressed a ''mild demurrer'' to the implication in the first draft of this chapter that economists are ''virtually unanimous'' in ''their complacent view about mergers or the effectiveness of the market discipline on management supplied by the possibility of hostile takeovers. I agree unreservedly that you are describing the general trend in economics; and that the shift in the consensus view in the last twenty years in the various ways that you describe has indeed been striking. At the same time, I think there are an awful lot of us who wonder whether mergers are simply a reflection of the beneficent functioning of a market, so that one can safely assume that if company A is willing to pay a higher price for the stock of company B than the latter's reservation price, it must mean A's managers can make better use of the assets than B's management was able to do. I think almost all economists would say that's the place to begin, and are generally suspicious about the loosely expressed populist views to the contrary. And yet I think many of us also are sufficiently institutionalist to have been impressed by the Hayes and Abernathy articles in *The Harvard Business Review*...with the questions they raise about the motivations of company managements, their excessive recruitment from the ranks of lawyers, accountants and finance people, . . . we wonder whether the urge to merge may not reflect in some measure the possibly different motivations of managers from stockholders (in some degree, the things that the public choice people say about the motivations of political administrators and the inability of voters to judge them efficiently apply to corporate management, although, to be sure, the latter are subject to a profitability check). And we have a feeling that there is *something* to the often-expressed view that, with top corporate managers having an average five to seven year tenure in their jobs, they are inclined excessively to discount risky projects with a long-term payoff, for fear that the costs will be visible only during their tenancy and the benefits only after they leave – with the effect of the costs on reported profits hastening their departure. Observe the comparability with the situation of the legislator who has to stand for election every two years, and has difficulty therefore imposing costs within that limited span, even if in strictly economic terms they would be far outweighed by benefits that accrue sometime after the election.''

Kahn's arguments are powerful. He believes that the current merger movement is ''one manifestation of the institutional arrangements and business motivations that are in important measure responsible for the poor performance of the American economy today, and that we cannot. . . afford to take a complacent, permissive attitude toward mergers.'' ''The New Merger Wave'' (National Economic Research Associates *Topics* paper. The paper is based on testimony before the Committee on the Judiciary, Subcommittee on Monopolies and Commercial Law, U.S. House of Representatives, Aug. 26, 1981).

Still Kahn acknowledges that many mergers may produce real efficiencies, and he is not sure what the appropriate government policy should be: ''Perhaps the solution is a policy somewhere between permissiveness and blanket prohibition.'' Kahn suggests two possible ways to implement this policy. One would be a progressive tax on business size. The other would require that ''parties to very large mergers demonstrate the anticipated efficiencies, defined as improved productivity and more rapid technological advance.'' Kahn, however, suggests this latter possibility ''with great reluctance, since it flies in the face of my own conviction that even the private parties are typically incapable of assessing such prospects in advance, and a government reviewing agency is unlikely to do any better – except that it will be charged to apply a social rather than a private perspective to the assessment''; ''The New Merger Wave,'' 8.

I place this discussion here, rather than in the text, for two reasons. First, as Kahn is quick to acknowledge, his view is today in the minority among economists. The ''growing consensus'' and ''increasingly prevalent view'' are that the presumption should be ''in *favor* of such mergers as occur'';

"The New Merger Wave," 1. Second, Kahn's views qualify only slightly the main thesis of this chapter. Kahn, like most economists, has considerable respect for the basic efficiency of our market system, and as we have seen, he does not support the most talked about industrial policy proposals. Indeed, he has written that one of the most important current functions of industrial-organization economists is to warn of the dangers of such proposals; "The Relevance of Industrial Organization," 15–16.

This does not mean that Kahn's concerns are unimportant. Respect for the relative efficiency of imperfect markets should not blind us to the fact that they are imperfect. A large number of economists are concerned about the prevalence of paper entrepreneurs preoccupied with mergers, stock deals, commodity speculation, and tax avoidance. Robert Samuelson ("The Policy Peddlers") argues that a complicated tax code that too often creates private profit from transactions with no economic value helps explain this phenomenon. So too does inflation that encourages speculation while discouraging long-term investment. Samuelson thinks that government can do something to help by remedying the tax structure and inflation problems, but he believes that internal problems of management efficiency will be fixed by management itself if they are going to be fixed at all. He is encouraged by the fact that Abernathy, who coauthored the critique of American management that Kahn cites, has since coauthored a book in which he describes a "renewal" of American management in "full swing." The "commitment to competitive excellence" that Abernathy saw in visits to factories demonstrated "a spirit and level of performance every bit as impressive as that which we found in Japan"; William Abernathy, Kim Clark, and Alan Kantrow, *Industrial Renaissance* (New York: Basic Books, 1983), as quoted in Samuelson, "The Policy Peddlers."

68 See Elzinga, "The Goals of Anti-trust," 1,206, n. 58.

69 Phillip Areeda, *Antitrust Analysis* (Boston: Little, Brown, 1974), 26. Also note that Charles Lindblom, a political scientist and an economist, believes that monopoly is "a minor defect in popular control" compared to the defects of popular control through our political mechanisms (*Politics and Markets*, 149). Also see Kahn, "The Relevance of Industrial Organization," 15–16.

70 When Rep. John Lafalce (D-N.Y.), the chairman of the House Banking Committee's Subcommittee on Economic Stabilization, presented to the press the industrial policy proposal supported by the Democratic majority of his subcommittee, he was asked whether the proposed advisory council of business, labor, and government leaders might have opposed the U.S. Steel Corporation's 1982 purchase of Marathon Oil Co. and insisted instead upon greater investment in steelmaking. Lafalce said, "You got it"; *Washington Post*, Nov. 9, 1983, F-1. For additional congressional commentary along the same lines see Gary Hart and Harold Demsetz debating "Should Government

Deregulation Be Coupled with Deconcentration of Industry?'' in Bernard Siegen, ed., *Government Regulation and the Economy* (Lexington, Mass.: Lexington, 1980), 94, 96; and *Washington Post*, March 23, 1981, A-15, and March 29, 1981, B-3.

71 See Milton Friedman, *Capitalism and Freedom* (Chicago: University of Chicago Press, 1962), 130; and Roger Sherman, ''How Tax Policy Induces Conglomerate Mergers,'' *National Tax Journal* 25 (1972): 521.

72 For additional opposition to an active government antimerger policy see George Benston, *Conglomerate Mergers: Causes, Consequences and Remedies* (Washington, D.C.: American Enterprise Institute, 1980); and Robert Samuelson, ''Some Cautious Words about Merger Mania.''

73 Robert Crandall believes that there is little government or industry can or should do to prevent the gradual decline over time of the U.S. steel industry. Crandall finds that erosion in the U.S. competitive position in steel production is explained only in part by high and rising U.S. labor costs. Dramatic declines in the cost of shipping coal and iron ore greatly aided steel industries in Japan and elsewhere. The U.S. was and is powerless to impede these technological changes. New, modern U.S. steel mills are not the answer since the costs of producing steel in new mills would exceed both the costs of production in most existing U.S. plants and the costs of production in other countries; *The U.S. Steel Industry in Recurrent Crisis* (Washington, D.C.: Brookings Institution, 1981). Also see the *Washington Post*, Aug. 19, 1980, D-6, and Dec. 8, 1981, C-7.

74 See Art Pine, ''Big Oil: From the Wells to the Pits,'' *Washington Post*, April 5, 1981, F-1.

75 Lipsey and Steiner, *Economics*, 260. Also see *National Journal*, Jan. 2, 1982, 12–17.

76 Gellhorn, ''Two's a Crowd,'' 36–7; also see M. A. Adelman, ''Splitting the Oil Companies Won't Help,'' *Washington Post*, May 1, 1976. The aforementioned 211 randomly chosen economists polled in 1978 were asked if they ''agreed,'' ''agreed with provisions,'' or ''disagreed'' with thirty statements. The largest disagreement total (75 percent) came for the statement, ''The fundamental cause of the rise in oil prices of the past three years is the monopoly power of the large oil companies.'' Of the twenty-five full professors at seven leading graduate programs who responded, 96 percent disagreed. See Kearl et al., ''What Economists Think.''

77 Hart, in Siegen, ed., 93.

78 See, e.g., Demsetz's reply to Hart, in Siegan, ed., 104.

79 See Arrow, ''Two Cheers for Government Regulation,'' 22, for evidence of such a conclusion by a liberal economist with strong equity concerns. Also see Kenneth Arrow and Joseph Kalt, *Petroleum Price Regulation* (Washington, D.C.: American Enterprise Institute, 1979), and Alfred Kahn, "The Relevance of Industrial Organization," 10–12.

80 See the *Washington Post*, June 15, 1981, A-1, and Jan. 11, 1981, M-1. For evidence of earlier congressional doubts that rising prices could have any substantial effect on the use of oil products see the *Washington Post*, April 11, 1975, A-1 and Oct. 9, 1975, A-10.

6. ECONOMISTS AND EQUITY

1 Alan S. Blinder, "The Level and the Distribution of Economic Well-Being," in Martin Feldstein, ed., *The American Economy in Transition* (Chicago: University of Chicago Press, 1980), 465–8; Arthur Okun, *Equality and Efficiency* (Washington, D.C.: Brookings Institution, 1975), 66.

2 Okun, *Equality and Efficiency*, 66.

3 See, e.g., the *Washington Post*'s use of such data to conclude that "for the past three decades, the distribution of income in this country has been remarkably stable. The distance between rich and poor has neither grown nor shrunk" (June 28, 1981, D-6).

4 Paul Samuelson, *Economics* (New York: McGraw-Hill, 1980), 80–3; and Edgar K. Browning, *Redistribution and the Welfare State* (Washington, D.C.: American Enterprise Institute, 1975), 8–10.

5 Morton Paglin, "The Measurement and Trend of Inequality: A Basic Revision," *American Economic Review* 65 (1975): 598–609; Samuelson, *Economics*, 82; Laurence Lynn, Jr., "A Decade of Policy Developments in the Income Maintenance System," in Robert Haveman, ed., *A Decade of Federal Antipoverty Programs* (New York: Academic Press, 1977), 94–5.

6 See Edgar K. Browning and William R. Johnson, *The Distribution of the Tax Burden* (Washington, D.C.: American Enterprise Institute, 1979), and Blinder, in Feldstein, ed., 443; Okun, *Equality and Efficiency*, 102–3.

7 Blinder, in Feldstein, ed., 448.

8 See Blinder, in Feldstein, ed., 442–8, for a review of relevant studies.

9 A number of these studies are assessed in William Albrecht, "Welfare Reform," in Paul Sommers, ed., *Welfare Reform in America* (Boston: Kluwer-Nijhoff, 1982), esp. 21. Also see Blinder's discussion, in Feldstein, ed., 457–9; Robert Haveman, Introduction, in Haveman, ed., 8–10, 18.

10 Browning, *Redistribution and the Welfare System*, 18–25; also see Blinder's discussion, in Feldstein, ed., 443–5.

11 *Washington Post*, June 23, 1980, A-15.

12 *Washington Post*, July 14, 1981, A-2.

13 *Washington Post*, Feb. 4, 1981, K-7.

14 Okun, *Equality and Efficiency*, 47, 109.

15 See W. Mark Crain, "Can Corporate Executives Set Their Own Wages," in M. Bruce Johnson, ed., *The Attack on Corporate America* (New York: McGraw-Hill, 1978), 275. Also see Johnson, ed., 276–80. For a contrasting view that ignores the studies cited in Johnson, see consumer advocate Mark Green's "Richer Than All Their Tribe," *New Republic*, Jan. 6, 1982, 21–6. For a brief report on an economic study comparing star baseball players' salaries with their effect on attendance and profits see *Time*, Nov. 30, 1981, 69.

16 See, e.g., Okun, *Equality and Efficiency*, 55, 109.

17 See Okun, ch. 2.

18 A progressive income tax takes a higher percentage of income from people the larger their income. A progressive consumption tax takes a higher percentage from people the higher their consumption.

19 Alan Blinder makes this clear: "It has long been recognized that the market mechanism, if it is to function at peak efficiency, must operate on the survival-of-the-fittest principle. To squeeze the last ounce of productivity from society's resources, the market must be ruthless. It cannot show compassion. The winners in the economic game must receive the spoils, or else the incentive to become a winner will be dissipated and the strength of the market mechanism will be sapped.

This much is fact, or about as close to fact as we ever come in social science. What to do about it is another matter entirely." Blinder supports redistributing income through a negative income tax so as to keep the economic-efficiency losses as low as possible. He acknowledges that "no policy" can eliminate these losses entirely; "A Proposal for Supply-Side Economics That Doesn't Squeeze Out the Poor," *Washington Post*, June 15, 1982, A-21.

20 Edgar Browning and Jacquelene Browning, *Public Finance and the Price System* (New York: Macmillan, 1983), 153; *Washington Post*, Oct. 3, 1981, A-22. Also see Charles Meyer, *Social Security Disability Insurance: The Problems of Unexpected Growth* (Washington, D.C.: American Enterprise Institute, 1979).

21 This is because the general taxes induce less inefficient behavior on the part of consumers, workers, and investors. For example, a general expenditure tax drives a relatively small tax wedge between the prices of goods and services and the opportunity costs of their production, and thus it induces fewer inefficient consumer choices. If we were to raise all our government revenues through a very high general sales tax, people could buy less with their paychecks, and some people would work less than they would if their paychecks could buy goods whose prices were not inflated by the tax. But if we were to raise all our revenues through a still-higher tax on clothing only, we would distort not just the work vs. leisure choices, but also choices between clothing and food and clothing and entertainment. For example, a consumer might get more pleasure from a $4.00 shirt than a $4.00 trip to the movies, but if the shirt price (including the tax) is $8.00, he may go to the movies instead. But it costs society only $4.00 to make a shirt and the consumer would like to have one for that price. When he cannot get it and does not buy it, society's resources are not being used in a way that maximizes consumer satisfaction. Moreover, the tax on clothing alone would price out of the market consumers with far stronger preferences and higher willingness to pay (relative to costs) than would a broad-based tax. A 10 percent general sales tax would mean that a shirt and a movie ticket would each sell for $4.40. This means that some consumers willing to pay a little more (say $4.39) than the $4.00 cost of producing these items would not get them. But if all the tax were placed only on clothing at a 100 percent rate, then consumers with very strong preferences for shirts (i.e., willing to pay as much as $7.99 for one) compared to the cost of production would not get them because the artificially high price ($8.00) would lead them to purchase much less preferred things (say, a movie ticket for which they would pay a maximum of $4.39) instead.

22 Brown was the director of President Carter's Action Agency. For his views see the *Washington Post*, June 14, 1980, A-7; also Martin Kilson, "Black Social Classes and Intergenerational Poverty," *Public Interest* (Summer 1981): 58–78; and note a recent report of the National Urban League that warns that many government assistance programs "result in dependence, rather than independence," *Washington Post*, Aug. 9, 1980, A-9.

23 In his *Principles of Political Economy*, John Stuart Mill speaks of dealing with "the helplessness of the public" in a way that corrects it rather than increases and perpetuates it. He continues, "A good government will give all its aid in such a shape, as to encourage and nurture any rudiments it may find of a spirit of individual exertion" (book 5, ch. 11, para. 16). Also see A. C. Pigou, *The Economics of Welfare* (London: Macmillan, 1938), ch. X.

24 See Browning and Browning, *Public Finance and the Price System*, ch. 9.

25 Browning and Johnson, *Distribution of the Tax Burden*; for some discussion of higher estimates see Lynn, in Haveman, ed., 104.

26 Browning, *Redistribution and the Welfare System*, 25–6; Charles Murray, "The Two Wars Against Poverty: Economic Growth and the Great Society," *Public Interest* no. 69 (Fall 1982): 3–16.

27 David Long, Charles Mallar, and Craig Thornton, "Evaluating the Benefits and Costs of the Job Corps,'' *Policy Analysis and Management* 1 (Fall 1981): 55–76.

28 See the review of the evidence by Henry Levin, ''A Decade of Policy Developments in Improving Education and Training for Low-Income Populations,'' in Haveman, ed., 123–88. Also see Lester Thurow's comments in Haveman, ed., 119; Haveman, ed., 17; Browning, *Redistribution and the Welfare System*, 51–4; the statement of Henry Aaron, before the Subcommittee on Public Assistance of the Committee on Finance, U.S. Senate, Nov. 15, 16, 17, 1978; *Hearings on Welfare Research and Experimentation* (Washington, D.C.: GPO, 1978), 319; Lynn, in Haveman, ed., p. 116.

29 Lester Thurow, *The Zero Sum Society* (New York: Penguin Books, 1981), 200–11.

30 Schultze's congressional testimony was influential in weakening the public-employment provisions of the original version of the Humphrey-Hawkins bill. For excerpts from the testimony see the *Washington Post*, June 7, 1976, A-23.

31 See Browning and Browning's discussion, *Public Finance and the Price System*, 269–72; David Betson and David Greenberg find that public-service jobs would induce some workers to leave their private-sector jobs even if the public jobs paid only the minimum wage (''A Study of the Interaction between Cash Transfer Programs and Employment Programs,'' in Sommers, ed., 230–52.) Also see Larry Orr and Felicity Skidmore, ''The Evolution of the Work Issue in Welfare Reform,'' in Sommers, ed., esp. 182.

32 Okun, *Equality and Efficiency*, 111.

33 Thomas Schelling, ''Economic Reasoning and the Ethics of Policy,'' *Public Interest* no. 63 (Spring 1981): 43.

34 Thurow, *Zero Sum Society*, 19, 156–7; also see Lynn, in Haveman, ed., 95–6.

35 Henry Aaron's testimony cited in n. 28, this chapter. Also of interest is Okun, *Equality and Efficiency*, 97. For the experimental findings themselves see *Final Report of the Seattle-Denver Income Maintenance Experiment* (Washington: U.S. Government Printing Office, 1983).

36 Mark Blaug, *Economic Theory in Retrospect* (Cambridge: Cambridge University Press, 1978), 269.

37 Alan Blinder, in Feldstein, ed., notes the domestic service results (431).

38 See Lynn's discussion, in Haveman, ed., 95–6.

39 Robert Moffitt, ''The Effect of a Negative Income Tax on Work Effort,'' in Sommers, ed., 209–29. Also see Orr and Skidmore in Sommers.

40 Browning and Browning, *Public Finance and the Price System*, 260; *Final Report of the Seattle-Denver Income Maintenance Experiment*.

41 In the most recent edition of their text Richard Musgrave and Peggy Musgrave say that "it is widely agreed that [Aid for Dependent Children] benefits should be extended to the working poor"; *Public Finance in Theory and Practice* (New York: McGraw-Hill, 1980), 720. Also see Blinder, "A Proposal for Supply Side Economics."

42 Aaron, "Statement"; Moffitt, and Orr and Skidmore, in Sommers, ed.

43 See Robert Haveman, "Direct Job Creation," in Haveman, ed., 187–208; Betson and Greenberg and Orr and Skidmore, all in Sommers, ed. Also see Robert Haveman and John Palmer, eds., *Jobs for Disadvantaged Workers: The Economics of Employment Subsidies* (Washington, D.C.: Brookings Institution, 1982), esp. 10–11; Okun, *Equality and Efficiency*, 114.

44 Browning and Johnson, *Distribution of the Tax Burden.*

45 Concerns about the effect of high taxes on work effort antedate the birth of modern economics. See James Ring Adams, "Supply-Side Roots of the Founding Fathers," *Wall Street Journal*, Nov. 17, 1981, 26, and Richard Lipsey and Peter Steiner, *Economics* (New York: Harper & Row, 1981), 449.

46 Browning, *Redistribution and the Welfare State*, 101. This can be best understood by referring again to the explanation in n. 21. As an expenditure tax is increased, it drives a larger and larger wedge between the price of goods and services and the cost of production, thus inducing consumers with stronger and stronger preferences for the goods and services (relative to cost) to cease purchasing them. For example, someone who would choose to work an extra hour but not an extra hour plus three minutes, for a wage of $4.00 per hour so as to buy a shirt for $4.00 will not do it if a 10 percent sales tax makes the cost $4.40. But someone who, if necessary, would work an hour and a quarter at an hourly wage of $4.00 if he could buy a shirt with his wages (i.e., someone who has a stronger preference for the shirt vis à vis leisure) will not do so if the tax rate is 30 percent and thus the shirt sells for $5.20. Browning and Browning explain this more generally using a useful diagram; *Public Finance and the Price System*, 313–15.

47 Thurow, *Zero Sum Society*, 168. Also see Okun, *Equality and Efficiency*, 97–8.

48 Cited in Robert Samuelson, "Supply Side Theory Clashes with Reality," *Washington Post*, March 17, 1981, D-7. Also see Lipsey and Steiner, *Economics*, 339–40. For a discussion of some studies that found higher supply-of-labor responses to tax cuts see Robert Keleher, "Evidence Relating to Supply-Side Tax Policy," in Richard Fink, ed., *Supply Side Economics: A Critical Appraisal* (Frederick, Md.: University Publications of America, 1982), 265.

49 Edgar Browning, "How Much More Equality Can We Afford?" *Public Interest* no. 43 (Spring 1976): esp. 95; Keleher, in Fink, ed., 268–71.

50 Okun, *Equality and Efficiency*, 97.

51 See Carl Simon and Ann Witte, *Beating the System: The Underground Economy* (Boston: Auburn House, 1981). Simon and Witte find that the underground economy is about 10 percent as large as measured gross national product.

52 See Robert Samuelson, "The Tax Trap," *National Journal*, April 10, 1982, 641. One IRS study found that about 38 percent of all income earned by self-employed persons goes unreported; *Washington Post*, Dec. 31, 1981, A-15.

53 Okun, *Equality and Efficiency*, 97.

54 See George Schultz's comments in Feldstein, ed., 660–1.

55 Economic studies find that "most, if not all, of the gains of union labor are made at the expense of nonunionized workers, and not at the expense of earnings on capital"; Harry Johnson and Peter Mieszkowski, "The Effects of Unionization on the Distribution of Income: A General Equilibrium Approach," *Quarterly Journal of Economics* 84 (Nov. 1970): 560. Richard Freeman and James Medoff also note that "economists today generally treat unions as monopolies whose sole function is to raise wages. Since monopolistic wage increases are socially deleterious – in that they can be expected to induce both inefficiency and inequality – most economic studies implicitly or explicitly judge unions as having a negative impact on the economy." Freeman and Medoff think this standard view neglects the role unions play in giving workers a voice both at the workplace and in the political arena; *Public Interest* no. 57 (Fall 1979): 69–93. For other views see Leo Troy, C. Timothy Koeller, and Neil Sheflin, "The Three Faces of Unionism," *Policy Review* no. 14 (Fall 1980): 95–110; and the letters to the editor in *Policy Review* no. 18 (Fall 1981).

56 Sowell, "Thoughts and Details on Poverty," *Policy Review* no. 17 (Summer 1981): 20.

57 Alfred Kahn, "America's Democrats: Can Liberalism Survive Inflation?" *The Economist* March 7, 1981, 22. Also see Kenneth Boulding, "Economic Progress as a Goal of Economic Life," in A. Dudley Ward, ed., *Goals of Economic Life* (New York: Harper & Row, 1953), esp. 76.

58 Otto Eckstein and Robert Tannenwald call increased capital formation "an essential centerpiece of any program to renew productivity growth"; "Productivity and Capital Formation," in Michael Wachter and Susan Wachter, eds., *Toward a New U.S. Industrial Policy?* (Philadelphia: University of Pennsylvania Press, 1981), 142.

59 Milton Friedman and Paul Samuelson discuss, *The Economic Responsibility of Government* (College Station: Center for Education & Research in Free Enterprise, Texas A&M University, 1980), 24.

60 Kahn, "America's Democrats," 24.

61 See Princeton economist Uwe Reinhardt's "Diagnosing the Great American Bellyache," *Princeton Alumni Weekly*, Feb. 22, 1982, 22. Browning and Browning, *Public Finance and the Price System*, 432. Some investment estimates that focus on "gross fixed capital formation" show higher levels of investment for all countries, but the United States still lags behind most other industrialized countries according to this measure (e.g., over the last two decades the Japanese saved and invested 30-35 percent of GNP compared to the U.S.'s 17–20 percent). Charles Schultze, "Industrial Policy: A Dissent," *Brookings Review* (Fall 1983): 6.

62 Martin Feldstein, "The Retreat From Keynesian Economics," *Public Interest* no. 64 (Summer 1981): 100. Individuals, of course, cannot earn such a high return because of taxes, but those added tax revenues finance programs that benefit people too.

63 Browning and Browning, *Public Finance and the Price System*, 437–40; Reinhardt, "Diagnosing the Great American Bellyache," 22–5. Also note Lester Thurow's views: "We need for a time to have 100% of the tax cuts go into investment rather than having most go into consumption" (Christopher Conte, "The Doubts of Liberal Economists," *Wall Street Journal*, Feb. 27, 1981, 22); see also the support for more investment voiced by Walter Heller, Otto Eckstein, Laurence Klein, and James Tobin in Fink, ed., pp. 76–8, 242–3, 247, 342.

64 For example, in Japan every individual can receive several thousand dollars a year in tax-free interest income. There is a lower tax on dividends than in the United States and no tax on capital gains; *Los Angeles Times*, pt. IV, June 20, 1983, p. 4, and Thomas Humbert, "How to Cure America's Capital Anemia," *Heritage Foundation Backgrounder*, Aug. 26, 1983.

65 George F. Break, "Corporate Tax Integration: Radical Revisionism or Common Sense?" in Michael Boskin, ed., *Federal Tax Reform* (San Francisco: Institute for Contemporary Studies, 1978), esp. 72. Also see Okun, *Equality and Efficiency*, 98.

66 Michael Boskin, "Taxation, Savings and the Rate of Interest," *Journal of Political Economy* 86 (1978). Other recent studies are discussed in Keleher, in Fink, ed., 266, and Browning and Browning, *Public Finance and the Price System*, 436.

67 Reinhardt, "Diagnosing the Great American Bellyache." Katsuro Sakoh, "Industrial Policy: The Super Myth of Japan's Super Success," *Heritage Foundation Backgrounder*, July 13, 1983.

68 This is, of course, the idea behind the famous Laffer curve that has enjoyed almost no support among economists as a prediction of total revenue changes for a general tax cut but that is more plausible with respect to the high marginal tax rates of the very rich. See Browning's discussion in "How Much More Equality Can We Afford?" 109. Also see, Lipsey and Steiner, *Economics, 339.*

69 Michael Boskin, "Distributional Effects of the Reagan Program," in William Craig Stubblebine and Thomas Willett, eds., *Reaganomics* (San Francisco: Institute for Contemporary Studies, 1983), 194–5; Keleher, in Fink, ed., 268; *New York Times*, March 15, 1981, p. 17. For evidence of some noneconomist support for the measure from the liberal side of the political spectrum see the *Washington Post*, May 20, 1981, A-22, and March 18, 1981, A-21.

70 Robert Samuelson, "Once Upon a Supply Side Theory," *Washington Post*, Nov. 24, 1981, C-18. The tax also brought a short-term increase in annual revenues of $1.8 billion by encouraging the realization of capital gains.

71 See Robert Samuelson's discussion of Joseph Pechman's views in "Once Upon a Supply Side Theory."

72 Robert Solow and James Tobin, "Liberals Have to do More than Laugh," *Washington Post*, Jan. 10, 1982, C-7; Alan Blinder, "Capital Gains: Tax them Like Income," *Washington Post*, July 2, 1982, A-19.

73 Okun, *Equality and Efficiency*, 104. Also see Alan Blinder, "Searching for a Way Out of the Pitfalls of Reaganomics," *Washington Post*, March 2, 1982, A-17.

74 Joseph Pechman, "Taxes vs. Savings," *Washington Post*, June 14, 1981, C-7. Also Okun, *Equality and Efficiency*, 98–9, 105.

75 See Alan Blinder, "Searching for a Way Out"; Robert Samuelson, "Once Upon a Supply Side Theory"; Okun, *Equality and Efficiency*, 103–5; R. Samuelson, "Supply Side Theory Clashes with Reality."

76 The support for business tax cuts among prominent liberal economists was particularly strong. See the views of Walter Heller, Otto Eckstein, Laurence Klein, and James Tobin in Fink, ed., 76–8, 242–3, 247, 342.

77 The quoted words are Henry Aaron's in Stubblebine and Willett, eds., 201. Also see Heller in Fink, ed., 78.

78 Robert Eisner, "Tax Incentives – or Giveaways?" *Washington Post*, July 16, 1981, A-27.

79 See Robert Samuelson, "Tax Write-Off Bazaar May Worsen Problem," *Washington Post*, Aug. 18, 1981, D-8, and "Leasing Law Shows Tax System Confusion," *Washington Post*, Jan. 5, 1982, D-6. Also Arnold Harberger, "Tax Neutrality in Investment Incentives," in Henry Aaron and Michael Boskin, eds., *The Economics of Taxation* (Washington, D.C.: Brookings Institution, 1980), 299–313.

80 Boris Bittker, "Equity, Efficiency, and Income Tax Theory," in Aaron and Boskin, eds., 20–1.

81 J. R. Kearl, Clayne Pope, Gordon Whiting, Larry Wimmer, "What Economists Think," *American Economic Review: Papers and Proceedings* 69 (May 1979): 30.

82 The study on citations to economists is discussed in the *Washington Post*, Aug. 15, 1982, G-1. Eckstein is also quoted there.

83 Eckstein in Fink, ed., 243.

84 At the end of a 1981 interview with a reporter, Schultze commented on his own views by saying, "It doesn't sound very Democratic" (*Washington Post*, Oct. 18, 1981, F-3, and Dec. 30, 1981, D-10). Note also Henry Aaron's view that, in 1981, "almost everyone agreed...that the growth of public spending needed to be cut" (in Stubblebine and Willett, ed., 199). Based in part on his interviews with fifteen prominent economists James Dean concludes: "There is little question that in the last decade economists have swung markedly to the right"; "The Dissolution of the Keynesian Consensus," *Public Interest*, special issue (1980): 28–30. Also see Robert Samuelson "Europe's Elusive Prosperity," *Washington Post*, March 29, 1983, C-7.

85 Myrdal quoted in Bruce Bartlett, "Supply-Side Success Stories," *Reason* (July 1981): 51. For further discussion of a tax on consumption see Peter Mieszkowski, "The Advisability and Feasibility of an Expenditure Tax System," in Aaron and Boskin, eds., 179–202; Boskin, *Federal Tax Reform*, 234; Browning and Browning, *Public Finance and the Price System*, 447–50.

86 James Tobin, "On Limiting the Domain of Inequality," *Journal of Law and Economics* 13 (1970), reprinted in Ryan Amacher, Robert Tollison and Thomas Willet, ed., *The Economic Approach to Public Policy* (Ithaca, N.Y.: Cornell University Press, 1976), 276. Also see the views of Paul Samuelson: "Political action and intensifying the class struggle in an attempt to change the way the total social pie gets distributed – that may well only reduce the total for all and slow the rate of growth of the total pie, and yet may not fully succeed in changing the shares in what remains" (*Economics*, 82).

87 Thurow himself does not really believe that society faces a zero sum situation. He says there are solutions to our problems where "the plusses usually exceed the minuses," but some must suffer large economic losses. Thus our economy has "a substantial zero sum element" (*Zero Sum Society*, 10–11).

88 Tobin, quoted in William Allen, "Economics, Economists and Economic Policy: Modern American Experiences," *History of Political Economy* 9 (1977): 77.

89 Browning, "How Much More Equality Can We Afford?" 109–10.

90 Blinder, in Feldstein, ed., 432.

91 Economists still find that knowledge of perverse distributional consequences can help increase pressure to change inefficient policies. See the discussion of grazing fees on public lands in Christopher Leman and Robert Nelson, "Ten Commandments for Policy Analysts," *Policy Analysis and Management* 1 (1981): 107.

92 Kahn, "America's Democrats," 24.

93 "Taxing Unemployment Benefits is a *Good* Idea," *Washington Post*, Dec. 15, 1982, A-27. For other economist supporters see Charles Schultze cited in *Public Interest* no. 71 (Spring 1983): 151, and Robert Samuelson, *Washington Post*, Feb. 10, 1981, C-4.

94 Browning and Browning, *Public Finance and the Price System*, 145.

95 Daniel Hamermesh's review of more than a dozen studies shows "a substantial consensus that higher U.I. benefits do induce people to remain unemployed longer"; "Transfer Policy, Unemployment, and Labor Supply," in Robert Haveman and Julius Margolis, eds., *Public Expenditure and Policy Analysis* (Boston: Houghton Mifflin, 1983), 360.

96 Blinder, "Taxing Unemployment Benefits is a *Good* Idea,"

97 Charles Schultze, Edward Fried, Alice Rivlin, and Nancy Teeters, *Setting National Priorities: The 1973 Budget* (Washington, D.C.: Brookings Institution, 1972), 241n. Also see Browning and Browning, *Public Finance and the Price System*, 144, and Hamermesh, in Haveman and Margolis, eds., 360.

98 Thurow, *Zero Sum Society*, 96–102; Browning and Browning, *Public Finance and the Price System*, 384–6; Musgrave and Musgrave, *Public Finance in Theory and Practice*, 427–36; Break, in Boskin, ed., 55–73; An excellent summary of arguments against the corporate income tax is in Robert Samuelson, "Scrapping Business Tax A Reasonable Lunacy," *Washington Post*, Feb. 8, 1983, D-7.

After stating that he would probably kick himself for saying so, Ronald Reagan said in 1983 that the corporate tax was hard to justify. He probably did kick himself, since there was quite a political uproar. For example, House Speaker Tip O'Neill said Reagan's remark "showed his heart was still in the corporate boardroom" (*Washington Post*, Jan. 28, 1983, A-9). And Art Buchwald produced a hilarious column in which the president's "damage control team" considered options such as telling the press, "he was speaking for himself and not as President of the United States" (*Charlottesville Daily Progress*, Feb. 1, 1983).

99 Reinhardt fears that many firms have replaced product entrepreneurs with regulatory entrepreneurs adept mainly at manipulating legislators and bureaucrats; "Diagnosing the Great American Bellyache," 23.

100 Charles Schultze, *The Public Use of Private Interest* (Washington, D.C.: Brookings Institution, 1977), 75. On problems with compensation schemes see also Robert Goldfarb, "Compensating Victims of Policy Change," *Regulation* (Sept./Oct. 1980): 22–30. On the social waste from seeking government favors see Richard McKenzie and Gordon Tullock, *The New World of Economics*, 3d ed. (Homewood, Ill.: Irwin, 1981), ch. 15. Also see Reinhardt, "Diagnosing the Great American Bellyache," and Ryan Amacher, Robert Tollison, and Thomas Willett, "A Menu of Distributional Considerations," in their *The Economic Approach to Public Policy*, 246–75.

101 Using census data that exclude in-kind income the South's poverty rate in 1980 was 15.3 percent; the Northeast's was 11.3 percent; and the North Central States, 10.7 percent (*Washington Post*, April 23, 1982, A-1).

102 For a comparison of the economist's view that "migration is both natural and useful" with political perspectives see Robert A. Levine, "Policy Analysis and Economic Opportunity Programs," in *The Analysis and Evaluation of Public Expenditures: The PPB System, A Compendium of Papers* (submitted to the Subcommittee on Economy in Government, Joint Economic Committee, 1969), vol. III, 1,193. Also see the economists' views expressed on regional conflict and national policy in *Resources* (Washington, D.C.: Resources for the Future, July 1982), esp. 7, 12–13. Lester Thurow has said, "When a firm moves from Ohio to Texas, the nation as a whole does not suffer an economic disaster. Texas grows, the new workers get new, higher paid jobs, and those remaining in Ohio do not necessarily lose out in the long run" (Washington Post, Oct. 18, 1981, F-3).

103 Thurow, *Zero Sum Society*, 77; also see 145, 182–4, 210–11.

104 Schultze, *Public Use of Private Interest*, 21.

105 Thanks to Alfred Kahn for these last two examples.

106 *Resources* (Washington, D.C.: Resources for the Future, Oct. 1981), 8.

107 Michael O'Hare, " 'Not on My Block You Don't': Facility Siting and the Strategic Importance of Compensation," *Public Policy* 25 (1977): 407–58.

108 The quotations are from Robert Samuelson, "U.S. Fails to Treat Long-term Joblessness," *Washington Post*, Feb. 10, 1981, C-1, and " 'Bailout Politics,' Economics Collide," *Washington Post*, May 31, 1983, D-7. Olsen's views are in *The Rise and Decline of Nations* (New Haven, Conn.: Yale University Press, 1982).

109 *Public Use of Private Interest*, 22.

110 Edgar Olsen, "Questions and Some Answers About Rent Control: An Empirical Analysis of New York's Experience," in Olsen and Walter Block, eds., *Rent Control: Myths and Realities* (Vancouver: Frazier Institute 1981), 115.

111 J. R. Kearl et al., "What Economists Think," 30. Seventy-eight percent "generally agreed" and 20 percent agreed with provisions. The 2 percent who generally disagreed was the lowest percentage in this category for any of the thirty questions asked. The poll also asked for reactions to the statement "A minimum wage increases unemployment among young and unskilled workers." Sixty-eight percent generally agreed, 22 percent agreed with provisions, and 10 percent generally disagreed.

112 Christopher Jencks, "The Minimum Wage Controversy," *Working Papers* (March/April 1978): 12–14.

113 William R. Johnson and Edgar K. Browning, "Minimum Wages and the Distribution of Income," *Report of the Minimum Wage Study Commission*, vol. VII (Washington, D.C.: GPO, June 1981), Table 9. Also see Donald Parsons, *Poverty and the Minimum Wage* (Washington, D.C.: American Enterprise Institute, 1980).

114 Douglass North and Roger Miller, *The Economics of Public Issues* (New York: Harper & Row, 1983), 125.

115 Kenneth Arrow and Joseph Kalt, *Petroleum Price Regulation* (Washington, D.C.: American Enterprise Institute, 1979), 30–1.

116 Hans Landsberg, "Energy," in Joseph Pechman, ed., *Setting National Priorities: Agenda for the 1980s* (Washington, D.C.: Brookings Institution, 1980), 102.

117 Arrow and Kalt, *Petroleum Price Regulation*, esp. 39, 43. Glenn Loury conducted a study similar to Arrow and Kalt's and reached similar conclusions; "Efficiency and Equity Impacts of Natural Gas Deregulation," in Haveman and Margolis, eds., 301–23. For a further discussion of economists' attitudes on these price control policies see Schelling, "Economic Reasoning and the Ethics of Policy," 40–2.

118 *Washington Post*, Nov. 29, 1979, C-1.

119 Robert M. Dunn, Jr., "Policies that Don't Help the City's Poor," *Washington Post*, Aug. 26, 1978, A-19.

120 *Washington Post*, June 25, 1980, A-16. Economists wonder why the greedy who do not invest in rental property are not also asked to help pay for housing for low-income families. See Edgar Olsen, "Questions and Some Answers."

121 Personal correspondence with the author, Feb. and March, 1974. The state minimum passed then was $1.60 per hour.

122 See Barry Chiswick, "Employment Effects and Determinants of Minimum Wage Laws," in Simon Rottenberg, ed., *The Economics of Legal Minimum Wages* (Washington, D.C.: American Enterprise Institute, 1981), 514; Walter Williams, "Should the Minimum Wage Law be Abolished," in

Bernard Siegen, ed., *Government Regulation and the Economy* (Lexington: Mass.: Lexington Books, 1980), 28; Miller and North, *Economics of Public Issues*, 125–6. For a dissenting view that emphasizes voter ignorance see Edgar Browning, "More on the Appeal of Minimum Wage Laws," *Public Choice* 14 (Spring 1973): 91–3.

123 Finis Welch, *Minimum Wages: Issues and Evidence* (Washington, D.C.: American Enterprise Institute, 1978), 38. For another recent study finding that the minimum wage has a substantial effect on unemployment among low-skilled workers see John Peterson, *Minimum Wages: Measures and Industry Effects* (Washington, D.C.: American Enterprise Institute, 1981). For discussion of a study finding half the decline in black teenage employment since 1950 attributable to expanded coverage of the minimum wage law see *Public Interest* no. 67 (Spring 1982): 144–5. Also see Llad Phillips, "Some Aspects of the Social Pathological Behavioral Effects of Unemployment Among Young People," in Rottenberg, ed.

124 Only a few of the adverse effects of these policies are given in the text. Among some others: (1) Rent control laws encourage those whose families have grown and left home to stay in large apartments since costs are low and smaller apartments elsewhere are scarce; (2) even some of those remaining employed at the artificially elevated minimum wage may be hurt because employers may reduce expenditures on fringe benefits, training, and improved working conditions or require harder work or work at less convenient hours. Since there is a surplus of labor at the minimum wage it is easier for the employer to get away with such measures. For discussion and some evidence see Walter Wessels, *Minimum Wages, Fringe Benefits and Working Conditions* (Washington, D.C.: American Enterprise Institute, 1980); and Masanori Hashimoto, *Minimum Wages and On the Job Training* (Washington, D.C.: American Enterprise Institute, 1981). Hashimoto finds that the added income for those remaining employed at the higher minimum wage is outweighed by the losses in future earnings caused by diminished on-the-job training (52). Also see the assessment of two economists who are quite concerned about the equity dimensions of policy; Edward Gramlich and Michael Wolkoff. "A Procedure for Evaluating Income Distribution Programs," in Haveman and Margolis, eds., 183–204. More generally on economists on these equity and pricing issues see Schelling.

125 J. R. Kearl et al., "What Economists Think," 30.

126 *New York Times*, Jan. 25, 1969, 47, cited in James Rodgers, "Explaining Income Redistribution," in Harold Hochman and George Peterson, eds., *Redistribution Through Public Choice* (New York: Columbia University Press, 1974), 196.

127 See Harris poll results in the *Washington Post*, Feb. 26, 1973, A-6.

128 James Buchanan, "What Kind of Redistribution Do We Want?" *Economica* (May 1968): 185–90; Edgar O. Olsen, "A Normative Theory of Transfers," *Public Choice* 6 (Spring 1969): 39–58; H. H. Hochman and J. D. Rodgers, "Pareto Optimal Distribution," *American Economic Review* 59 (1969): 542–57.

129 See James Tobin, "On Limiting the Domain of Inequality," 290; Lester Thurow, "Government Expenditures: Cash or In-kind Aid," in Gerald Dworkin, Gordon Bermant, Peter Brown, eds., *Markets and Morals* (Washington, D.C.: Hemisphere, 1977); Okun, *Equality and Efficiency*, 70–1, 112.

130 Much of the applied literature on specific programs suggests this outlook. See, e.g., Jill Khadduri and Raymond Struyk, "Housing Vouchers for the Poor," *Policy Analysis and Management* 1 (Winter 1982): 201; John C. Weicher, "Urban Housing Policy," in Peter Mieszkowski and Mahlon Straszheim, eds., *Current Issues in Urban Economics* (Baltimore: Johns Hopkins University Press, 1979), 501. Also note that despite his support for in-kind aid, Okun still favored helping those with low income mainly through check writing, not delivery of services (*Equality and Efficiency*, 117; also see 16–17). Similarly, Thurow ends his defense of in-kind aid by stating that "the burden of proof should always lie on those advocating restricted grants." He suspects that "some" goods not given in-kind should be, but "many" now given in-kind should not be ("Government Expenditures: Cash or In-kind Aid," 104).

131 See Weicher's review of the evidence in Mieszkowski and Straszheim, eds. Also Khadduri and Struyk, "Housing Vouchers for the Poor."

132 Claire Hammond, "The Benefits of Subsidized Housing Programs" (Ph.D. diss., University of Virginia, 1982), ch. VI.

133 There is a nice discussion of the equity issues in Edgar Olsen, "Housing Programs and the Forgotten Taxpayer," *Public Interest* no. 66 (Winter 1982): 97–109. Also see Weicher, in Mieszkowski and Straszheim, eds., which includes a taxpayer's letter to his senator asking, "Can you explain to me why I should be taxed to help someone else buy a home that I myself could not afford to live in?" (480).

134 See Lynn's discussion in Haveman, ed., 111. Critics also seem to assume that increased demand from low-income people will not lead to any increases in production even in a market as competitive as housing. See congressmen's comments in the *Washington Post*, March 4, 1982, D-10, and the Becher letter to the *Washington Post*, Dec. 17, 1981, A-30. When low-income people start bidding for lower-middle-income housing, some people in this housing decide that at this price they might as well pay a little more for middle-income housing; the middle income people are then induced to move up also, putting pressure on upper-middle-income housing prices. Some upper-middle-income people then decide new housing is worth the now smaller price differential. When new housing is built, each income class begins to move up into the newly vacated old units. In any event we do not need new housing to get better housing. Added purchasing power by the poor could lead to more rehabilitation of existing units.

135 See the discussion of Rand Corp. research in *Regulation* (Nov./Dec. 1981): 53–4. Also see Khadduri and Struyk "Housing Vouchers for the Poor."

136 See Weicher's discussion of economists' views; Mieszkowski and Straszheim, eds., 501.

137 Tobin, "On Limiting the Domain of Inequality," 289. Also see Browning and Browning, *Public Finance and the Price System*, ch. 4; Kenneth Clarkson, *Food Stamps and Nutrition* (Washington, D.C.: American Enterprise Institute, 1975). Since 1979 food stamp recipients have not been required to purchase additional stamps as a condition for obtaining their free stamps. Moreover, the free stamps represent less than most poor families spend for food. Thus, the food stamp program does not now direct the purchases of most low-income families toward food any more than a cash grant would. Most economists support this revised program much more than the earlier one, which, by requiring the purchase of additional food, did distort the poor's consumption patterns away from the purchases that the poor thought would maximize their satisfaction. See Browning and Browning, 132–8.

138 One surprising finding of the housing studies was that a minority in the housing programs actually consumed *less* housing than they would have if they had received an equivalent subsidy in the form of an unrestricted cash grant. This is possible because housing, like education, is a "lumpy" good where it is hard for the consumer to supplement what the government gives him. If offered a subsidized two-bedroom apartment, some people will take it even though if given an equivalent cash subsidy, they would have rented a three-bedroom apartment. For further discussion see John Kraft and Edgar Olsen, "The Distribution of Benefits from Public Housing," in F. Thomas Juster, ed., *The Distribution of Economic Well Being* (New York: National Bureau of Economic Research, 1977), 58–60; and Browning and Browning, *Public Finance and the Price System*, 68–72.

139 Edgar Browning, "The Externality Argument for In-kind Transfers: Some Critical Remarks," *Kyklos* 28 (1975): 526–44. For evidence of this not-so-hidden agenda, see Thurow's view that "sometimes explicitly, and even more often implicitly, the Pareto optimality literature makes the judgment that a 'rational' donor should be interested only in the donee's utility"; in Dworkin et al., eds., 89. Also see Blinder, "A Proposal for Supply Side Economics," and Schelling: "The economist thinks the burden of proof belongs on those who want to give food stamps or subway tokens or eyeglasses to the poor and the elderly, not money'' (60). Even economists in the midst of a pro-voucher pitch never let one forget the possible superiority of a straight cash approach (see Khadduri and Struyk, ''Housing Vouchers for the Poor,'' 200–1 and Olsen, ''Housing Programs and the Forgotten Taxpayer,'' 107).

140 Tobin, ''On Limiting the Domain of Inequality,'' 277–8.

141 *Special Analyses, Budget of the United States Government, Fiscal Year 1982*, 255–6.

142 Michael Novak has noted that every black teenager in America could be employed forty hours a week year round for less than one-fourth the cost of CETA; cited in Thomas Sowell, ''The Welfare State is the Ultimate in 'Trickle-Down,' '' *Washington Post*, Dec. 6, 1981, C-7.

143 Steven Kelman, *What Price Incentives? Economists and the Environment* (Boston: Auburn House, 1981), 86.

144 Note the poll results discussed in this chapter in the section entitled ''Taxes and the Incentive to Work and Invest.'' Also, Douglass North and Roger Miller have said, ''[An absolute] definition of poverty is unsatisfactory since it is not the absolute but the relative level of income that causes poverty''; *The Economics of Public Issues* (New York: Harper & Row, 1980), 178.

145 Commenting in Haveman, ed., 192.

146 Everett Ladd, ''205 and Going Strong,'' *Public Opinion* 4 (1981): 10.

147 Cited in Mark Green, ''Richer than All Their Tribe,'' *New Republic*, Jan. 6, 1982, 26.

148 See Marc Plattner's discussion of the different principles behind redistributing income on the one hand and our traditional social welfare programs on the other; ''The Welfare State vs. the Redistributive State,'' *Public Interest* no. 55 (Spring 1979): 28–48.

149 John Locke, *The Second Treatise of Government* (Indianapolis: Bobbs-Merrill, 1952), ch. 5, p. 17.

150 See Tibor Machan, ''Wronging Rights,'' *Policy Review* no. 17 (Summer 1981): 41–45.

151 See Laurence Tribe, ''Policy Science: Analysis or Ideology?'' *Philosophy and Public Affairs* 2 (Fall 1972): esp. 86.

152 See, e.g., A. K. Sen, *Collective Choice and Social Welfare* (San Francisco: Holden-Day, 1970), 99.

153 Kristol acknowledges and paraphrases an argument of Peter Bauer's; *Two Cheers for Capitalism* (New York: Signet, 1978), 171. Also see 175–9.

154 Plattner, ''The Welfare State vs the Redistributive State,'' esp. 46–7.

155 Olsen, though sympathetic to some such distinctions, suggests that they are too difficult to make to be useful in program operation "Housing Programs and the Forgotten Tax Payer" (100). On the local level such distinctions would be easier to make. There are equity and efficiency reasons why it might be preferable to have eligibility decisions made nationally (see ch. 7), but the local option would be taken more seriously by economists if they were more concerned about worthiness.

156 Also see sociologist Robert Bell's complaint about U.S. Office of Management and Budget examiners who are wedded to the economic paradigm. In 1973 these examiners criticized the Department of Housing and Urban Development's proposed elderly housing program as "distorting resource allocation to [the] poverty population and later, despite repeated Congressional insistence on special aid to the elderly, proposed rescission of funds for this purpose" ("Professional Values and Organizational Decision-Making," *Administration and Society* (in press).

157 Thurow, in Dworkin et al., eds., 96.

158 See, e.g., Browning and Browning, *Public Finance and the Price System*, 140.

159 Note how cursory is the treatment in Barry Love, "An Economic Evaluation of the Food Stamp Program" (Ph.D. diss., University of Virginia, 1978). Also note Clarkson's (*Food Stamps and Nutrition*) strong negative conclusions, on the basis of very little evidence, about any nutrition impact of the existing program. I know of no economist who has done original research on the nutrition aspect of the food stamp program (despite his book's title, Clarkson does not conduct any) even though from the point of view of the nonpoor, it is probably the crucial parameter on which a final judgment should rest.

160 The quotation comes from the first (1979) edition of the Brownings' text (110–11). The second edition (1983) omits the provocative mention of the possibilities of drug and alcohol expenditures, but the underlying philosophy is unchanged.

161 Richard Zeckhauser, "Procedures for Valuing Lifes," *Public Policy* 23 (Fall 1975): 457.

162 Housing data from Raymond Struyk and Marc Bendick, Jr., "Housing Vouchers for the Poor," *Urban Institute Policy and Research Report* 10 (Winter 1980): 1–7. Food stamp and supplemental security income data from Browning and Browning, *Public Finance and the Price System*, 1979 ed., 114–15.

163 Browning and Browning, 1979 ed., 115.

164 Since first writing these words, I have encountered a passage in an essay by Kenneth Boulding that is very much to the point. Boulding believes that his profession's techniques have "exploited pretty fully the kind of data which is readily available and [are] now producing more and more analyses and less and less information." Boulding sees the need for "a revival of interest in economics in the improved collection of raw data," a task in which graduate school training has "actually retrogressed" in recent years; "Economics and the Future of Man," in Boulding, ed., *Economics as a Science* (New York: McGraw-Hill, 1970), 155–6.

165 Martin Kilson, a black Harvard political scientist who sees himself as "left or liberal" politically, finds "cultural or societal pathologies widely prevalent among lower class blacks. Lower class lifestyles among young men and women that are associated with the 'man-child' and 'woman-child' syndrome – above all, becoming mothers and fathers while still in one's teens – must be interdicted, constrained, and reversed" (see "Black Social Classes," esp. 70, 77). Also see Edward C. Banfield, *The Unheavenly City* (Boston: Little, Brown, 1970); and George Gilder, *Wealth and Poverty* (New York: Basic Books, 1981).

166 *Leviathan* (Indianapolis: Bobbs-Merrill, 1958), pt. I, ch. X.

167 This argument is made elsewhere, but is central to Plato's *Gorgias*.

168 Economists' overemphasis on cash and money is discussed at much greater length in ch. 9.

169 E. J. Mishan, *Cost-Benefit Analysis* (New York: Praeger, 1976), ch. 11.

170 In addition to the sources given in subsequent notes here and in n. 22, this chapter, see William Raspberry's column, *Washington Post*, June 30, 1980. Raspberry notes widespread support across the political spectrum for a work requirement for able-bodied welfare recipients. He himself favors such a requirement, not primarily because it will save taxpayers money, but because it will be better for welfare recipients ("the better care we take of people, the more helpless they become"). Raspberry quotes liberals concerned about the welfare "snare." For example, Willie Hardy, a District of Columbia councilwoman from one of Washington's poorest districts, has called for an end to public housing in its present form ("government-owned slave quarters"). Hardy says, "I just feel that all government [welfare] programs should have the common goal of rendering themselves [unnecessary] by giving individuals the opportunity to ultimately stand on their own."

171 Willard Gaylin, "In the Beginning: Helpless and Dependent," in David Rothman and Gaylin, eds., *Doing Good: The Limits of Benevolence* (New York: Pantheon Books, 1978), 30. Also see Steven Marcus's account of the British Poor Laws ("Their Brothers' Keepers: An Episode from English History," in Rothman and Gaylin).

172 Adam Smith, *The Theory of Moral Sentiments* (Indianapolis: Liberty Classics, 1976), pt I, sec. III, ch. 2.

173 Social scientists find that the primary source of human self-esteem is a sense of accomplishment; Robert Lane, "Government and Self Esteem," *Political Theory* 10 (1982): 5–31. On the subject of self-respect and welfare see Clifford Orwin's "Welfare and the New Dignity," *Public Interest* no. 71 (Spring 1983): 85–95.

174 See Peter Skerry, "The Charmed Life of Head Start," *Public Interest*, no. 73 (Fall 1983): 18–40.

175 After exploring the results of the British Poor Laws and of the reforms that followed them, Marcus concludes that "we can degrade people by caring for them; and we can degrade them by not caring for them" (65–6). See also Gilder, *Wealth and Poverty*. For a review of evidence suggesting that generous welfare can create dependency, see *Public Interest* no. 57 (Fall 1979): 109–13 and Murray, "The Two Wars against Poverty."

7. EXTERNALITIES AND THE GOVERNMENT AGENDA

1 The quotation is from the subtitle of a book by Gordon Tullock, *Private Wants, Public Means: An Economic Analysis of the Desirable Scope of Government* (New York: Basic Books, 1970). Tullock's "main analytical tool" is "the economics of externalities" (v). He says, "Traditionally, the decision between governmental provision of the good or service and private provision of the good or service has turned on rather irrational considerations." Tullock believes economics and in particular the externality concept provide "the necessary theory for making a genuinely scientific decision on this problem" (259). Though that claim is grander than most, this chapter will show that economists frequently use the externality concept to evaluate government involvement. For other examples besides those given here see my *Policy Analysis in the Federal Aviation Administration* (Lexington, Mass.: Lexington Books, 1974), 16, chs. 4–6, and citations on 141–2, nn. 55, 56. For another provocative example see Otto Davis and Andrew Whinston, "Economic Problems in Urban Renewal," in Edmund Phelps, ed., *Private Wants and Public Needs* (New York: Norton, 1965), 140–53.

2 The landmark article on the market's ability to take account of externalities is Ronald Coase, "The Problem of Social Cost," *Journal of Law and Economics* 3 (1960): 1–44.

3 Actually, as Tullock shows, customers would almost certainly lose more than businesses gained if the increase in production and the lower price were not permitted (see *Private Wants, Public Means*, ch. 7). Some economists call these economically efficient effects on others "pecuniary externalities," which they distinguish from the "real" or "technological," inefficient externalities. Other economists would reserve the term externality for real or technological third-party effects. Distinguishing "pecuniary" from "real" externalities can be difficult without substantial knowledge of economics. For more on the subject see Tullock, *Private Wants, Public Means*; Roland McKean, *Efficiency in Government Through Systems Analysis* (New York: Wiley, 1958), 136–49; and E. J. Mishan, *Cost-Benefit Analysis* (New York: Praeger, 1976), ch. 16.

4 They are efficient pecuniary third-party effects. See preceding note.

5 For more on this see James Buchanan and W. Craig Stubblebine, "Externality," *Economica* (Nov. 1962): 371–84; reprinted in Robert Staab and Francis Tannian, eds., *Externality: Theoretical Dimensions of Political Economy* (New York: Dunellen, 1974). Also see Roland McKean, "Property Rights within Government and Devices to Increase Governmental Efficiency," *Southern Economic Journal* 39 (1972): 177–86.

6 *Washington Post*, July 8, 1982, A-13. Repeated July 29, 1982, A-21.

7 *Washington Post*, June 3, 1983, A-19.

8 *Washington Post*, June 3, 1983, A-19.

9 Lawrence White, *The Regulation of Air Pollutant Emissions from Motor Vehicles* (Washington, D.C.: American Enterprise Institute, 1982), 14.

10 For more on pricing approaches to urban congestion see Damian Kulash, "Congestion Pricing: A Research Summary" (Paper 1212-99, Urban Institute, Washington, D.C., 1974); Donald Dewees, "Travel Cost, Transit, and Control of Urban Motoring," *Public Policy* 24 (Winter 1976): 59–80.

11 General aviation is a catchall designation encompassing all civil aviation not legally defined as commercial air carriers. It includes instructional, personal, business, and agricultural aircraft. Somewhat confusingly, it also includes some transport for hire, such as "air taxis" and certain charter and contract companies.

12 This bogus spillover GNP benefit of government expenditure is frequently used as a justification for programs. When a cut in the National Endowment for the Arts budget was proposed in 1981, Theodore Bickel warned of the economic effects on taxi drivers and restaurants (ABC radio news, February 14, 1981). What these businesses lose others will gain when the money is spent elsewhere. Also note Alfred Marcus's misuse of this sort of "benefit" in "Environmental Protection Agency," in James Q. Wilson, ed., *The Politics of Regulation*, (New York: Basic Books, 1980), 280.

13 Quoted in Rhoads, *Policy Analysis in the Federal Aviation Administration*, 43.

14 For a fuller discussion of economists' responses to general aviation arguments, see my *Policy Analysis in the Federal Aviation Administration*, esp. ch. 6. National defense is one of the arguments used to support proposed government-directed industrial policies that would assist "critical strategic" industries such as steel. Marginalism is at the core of economist Charles

Schultze's rebuttal: "The national defense/essential industry argument is usually presented in an all or nothing mode, as though, in the absence of import protection, the affected industry would disappear. In fact, what is almost always at stake is a much less dramatic change in the industry's fortunes, of a magnitude that is irrelevant to national defense. Whether, for example, the domestic steel industry meets 80 percent of the nation's peacetime needs, as it does now, or only 60 percent is of no significance to the nation's security"; "Industrial Policy: A Dissent," *Brookings Review* (Fall 1983): 9.

15 *Washington Post*, Oct. 1, 1978, A-5.

16 All these arguments except that pertaining to energy are taken from the *New York Times*, Dec. 30, 1970, 1, 29.

17 The rebuttal of the case for subsidized passenger trains is my own, but George Hilton also discusses a few of the general externalities claimed in *Amtrak* (Washington, D.C.: American Enterprise Institute, 1980), 62–7. Also see Robert Samuelson, "Rail System Would Be Star of Any Hall of Fame for Waste," *Washington Post*, July 4, 1978, D-6.

18 See ch. 2 for a fuller discussion of the market's treatment of occupational safety.

19 See ch. 4, nn. 61–5 and pertinent text.

20 See Christopher Zook, Francis Moore, and Richard Zeckhauser, " 'Catastrophic' Health Insurance: A Misguided Prescription?" *Public Interest* no. 62 (Winter 1981): 80.

21 Glenn Blomquist, "Traffic Safety Regulation by NHTSA" (Working paper no. 16 in government regulation, American Enterprise Institute, Washington, D.C., Nov. 18, 1981), ch. 3, p. 10.

22 See, e.g., Blomquist, "Traffic Safety Regulation by NHTSA"; and Albert Nichols and Richard Zeckhauser, "Government Comes to the Workplace: An Assessment of OSHA," *Public Interest* no. 49 (Fall 1977): 39–69.

23 In a letter Alfred Kahn has quite correctly pointed out that reasoning about externalities would lead one to believe that the functions should be provided supranationally. Most economists do not mention this possibility presumably because our supranational bodies have little power and because, as with income distribution and benefit-cost analysis, the profession seems to have accepted the convention that the nation is the most appropriate unit for analyzing welfare gains and losses.

24 See, e.g., Mark Pauly, "Income Redistribution as a Local Public Good," *Journal of Public Economics* 2 (1973): 35–58.

25 "When Florida first ran out of federal relief for its thousands of Haitian refugees, it notified each of them that they might find additional help from any of 10 other states. At the same time, Texas officials printed brochures with the warning that state welfare payments are the nation's second lowest, after Mississippi, and show no signs of rising"; (*Washington Post*, June 14, 1982, A-5).

26 *Washington Post*, June 14, 1982, A-5.

27 For a more extended discussion of externalities and federalism see George Break, *Financing Government in a Federal System* (Washington, D.C.: Brookings Institution, 1980), esp. ch. 3; Edgar Browning and Jacquelene Browning, *Public Finance and the Price System*, 2d ed. (New York: Macmillan, 1983), ch. 15. The Brownings suggest that the federal share under several matching grant programs is too high. For example, they doubt that 90 percent of the benefits of the federal interstate highway program go to nonstate residents. Similarly, they think it unlikely that 75 percent of the benefits from sewage waste-treatment systems go to nonresidents (480).

28 For an example from the policy literature of economists using externalities to help determine what unit of government should have program responsibility, see David Harrison, Jr., and Paul Portney, "Making Ready for the Clean Air Act," *Regulation* (March/April 1981): 24–31. The subject is also briefly treated in *Regulation* (March/April 1982): 54; *Regulation* (Jan./Feb. 1982): 3.

29 For one case in which federal subsidies have led local decision makers to spend money where "nobody in their right mind" would spend it, see the *Washington Post*, Jan. 4, 1982, 1, 4–6.

8. BENEFIT-COST ANALYSIS

1 For a discussion of the early benefit-cost work on water projects see Roland McKean, *Efficiency in Government Through Systems Analysis* (New York: Wiley, 1967), esp. 18–20. On more recent developments see Marvin Kosters and Jeffrey Eisenach, "Is Regulatory Relief Enough?" *Regulation* (March/April 1982): 20–7; and *National Journal* Jan. 16, 1982, 92–8.

2 Subcommittee on Oversight and Investigations of the Committee on Interstate and Foreign Commerce, *Federal Regulation and Regulatory Reform*, House of Representatives, 94th Congress, 2nd sess. (Washington, D.C.: Government Printing Office, 1976), esp. chs. 5, 15. Also see the *Washington Post*, Dec. 24, 1974, A-1.

3 Robert Smith, *The Occupational Safety and Health Act* (Washington D.C.: American Enterprise Institute, 1976), 15–17.

4 *National Journal*, Jan. 16, 1982, 92–8.

5 E. J. Mishan, *Cost-Benefit Analysis* (New York: Praeger, 1976), 318.

6 See, e.g., A. Myrick Freeman III, *The Benefits of Environmental Im-*

provement (Baltimore: John Hopkins University Press, 1979), and Martin J. Bailey, *Reducing Risks to Life* (Washington, D.C.: American Enterprise Institute 1980). For a more sympathetic treatment of surveys see Christopher Nash, ''The Theory of Social Cost Measurement,'' in Robert Haveman and Julius Margolis, eds., *Public Expenditure and Policy Analysis* (Boston: Houghton Mifflin, 1983), 76–7.

7 For more on the studies discussed here and on benefit-cost analysis in air transportation more generally see Steven E. Rhoads, *Policy Analysis in the Federal Aviation Administration* (Lexington, Mass.: Lexington Books, 1974).

8 Richard Thaler and Sherwin Rosen, ''The Value of Saving a Life: Evidence from the Labor Market,'' in Nester Terleckyj, ed., *Household Production and Consumption* (New York: National Bureau of Economic Research, Columbia University Press, 1975), 294.

9 Bailey, *Reducing Risks to Life*, 40.

10 John F. Morrall III, ''Cotton Dust: An Economist's View,'' in Robert Crandall and Lester Lave, eds., *The Scientific Basis of Health and Safety Regulation* (Washington, D.C.: Brookings Institution, 1981), 105.

11 For more on benefit-cost analysis on health and safety regulation see Lester Lave, *The Strategy of Social Regulation* (Washington, D.C.: Brookings Institution, 1981); Crandall and Lave, eds.; James C. Miller III and Bruce Yandle, *Benefit-Cost Analyses of Social Regulation* (Washington: Washington, D.C. American Enterprise Institute, 1979); John F. Morrall III, ''OSHA after Ten Years'' (Working paper in government regulation no. 13, American Enterprise Institute, Washington, D.C.: Nov. 18, 1981).

12 For a very readable and complete treatment of the benefits of clean air see Allen V. Kneese, ''Measuring the Benefits of Clean Air'' (Draft report for the Environmental Protection Administration, Feb. 1982, USEPA Grant No. R805059-010). A. Myrick Freeman III's *The Benefits of Environmental Improvement* is a complete but more theoretical treatment. Space does not permit coverage of methods that have been developed to assess the benefits of water pollution abatement. See Henry M. Peskin and Eugene P. Seskin, *Cost Benefit Analysis and Water Pollution Policy* (Washington, D. C.: Urban Institute, 1975). Miller and Yandle and Crandall and Lave both cover air or water pollution cases. Though not discussed here, the property-value approach has also been used to estimate the benefits of noise pollution reduction.

13 For a recent example of a benefit-cost analysis of a training program see David Long, Charles Mallar and Craig Thornton, ''Evaluating the Benefits and Costs of the Job Corps,'' *Journal of Policy Analysis and Management* 1 (Fall 1981): 55–76; also see Edward Gramlich, *Benefit-Cost Analysis of Government Programs* (Englewood Cliffs, N.J.: Prentice-Hall, 1981), ch. 9.

14 Mark Green, "The Faked Case against Regulation," *Washington Post,* Jan. 21, 1979, C-5.

15 Steven Kelman, "Cost-Benefit Analysis: An Ethical Critique," *Regulation* (Jan./Feb. 1981): 36.

16 Fred Hapgood, "Risk-Benefit Analysis: Putting a Price on Life," *Atlantic Monthly* (Jan. 1979), reprinted in Rhoads, ed., *Valuing Life: Public Policy Dilemmas* (Boulder, Colo.: Westview, 1980).

17 Steven Kelman, *What Price Incentives? Economists and the Environment* (Boston: Auburn House, 1981), 69–77.

18 William Ophuls, *Ecology and the Politics of Scarcity* (San Franscisco: Freeman, 1977), 173.

19 *Federal Regulation and Regulatory Reform*, 179, 510.

20 Victor J. Kimm, Arnold M. Kuzmack, and David W. Schnare, "Waterborne Carcinogens: A Regulator's View," in Crandall and Lave, eds., 243.

21 See Thomas Lenard, "Lawn Mower Safety," in Miller and Yandle, eds., 73.

22 Rhoads, *Policy Analysis in the Federal Aviation Administration*, 98.

23 Robert Socolow, "Failures of Discourse," in Laurence Tribe, ed., *When Values Conflict* (Cambridge, Mass.: Ballinger, 1976), 18. As this quotation suggests, many ecologists believe that current public and private policies will deplete our scarce resources and leave future generations with a much-reduced quality of life. They think that most economists are unduly optimistic about the future and that economists positively encourage shortsightedness by heavily "discounting" future benefits in their benefit-cost work. (Economists discount future benefits because they believe a dollar benefit received today is worth more than one received in future years: Today's dollar can be invested and thus in future years will be worth more than a dollar.)

Benefit-cost analysis considers only the preferences of today's consumers, and the practice of discounting almost completely ignores benefits received more than a few decades hence. But economists usually argue that as long as we continue to achieve positive economic growth, future generations will live better than we do. For this reason special concern for our heirs is not warranted. Economists further defend their relative optimism about the future by noting that technological improvements in the industries that extract and use raw materials continue to more than compensate for deterioration in access to raw materials so that even the costs of most raw materials themselves – whether measured in terms of labor necessary to obtain them, or in terms of price relative to other consumer goods – continue to decline as they have been doing since 1800.

Adequate treatment of the debate between ecologists and economists about the future could fill a book in itself. In any case, even the use of *discounted* future benefits may give more weight to the future than would exist in our political process if benefit-cost studies were not produced. Though economics may ignore most benefits achievable a decade or two hence, politicians may ignore most that are achievable an election or two hence. For more on these issues see Mishan, *Cost-Benefit Analysis*, chs. 25–34; Anthony Fisher, *Resource and Environmental Economics* (Cambridge: Cambridge University Press, 1981); Robert Solow, "The Economics of Resources or the Resources of Economics," *American Economic Review* 64 (1974): 1–14; Julian Simon, *The Ultimate Resource* (Princeton, N.J.: Princeton University Press, 1981), and "Global Confusion, 1980: A Hard Look at the Global 2000 Report," *Public Interest* no. 62 (Winter 1981): 3–20. Also see Simon's bitter debate with ecologist Paul Ehrlich in *Social Science Quarterly* 62 (March 1981): 44–9.

24 *Federal Regulation and Regulatory Reform*, 174.

25 Burke Zimmerman, "Risk-Benefit Analysis: The Cop-out of Government Regulation," *Trial* 14 (Feb. 1978), as quoted in Lave, *Strategy of Social Regulation*, 4.

26 Green, "Faked Case against Regulation," C-5.

27 "Comparisons of Estimated and Actual Pollution Control Cost for Selected Industries" (Prepared by Putnam, Hoyes, and Bartlett, Inc., for Office of Planning and Evaluation, Environmental Protection Agency, Feb. 1980, Mimeo).

28 Lenard, in Miller and Yandle, eds., 68.

29 Green, "Faked Case against Regulation," and Mark Green and Norman Waitzman, *Business War on the Law* (Washington, D.C.: Corporate Accountability Research Group, 1979). Also see James Miller III, "The (Nader) Green-Waitzman Report on the Benefits of Social Regulation" (Working paper no. 2 in government regulation, American Enterprise Institute, May 15, 1980).

30 Green, "Faked Case against Regulation," and the introduction to Green and Waitzman, *Business War on the Law*.

31 *Washington Post*, April 1, 1984, F-1.

32 Lawrence White, *The Regulation of Air Pollutant Emissions from Motor Vehicles* (Washington, D.C.: American Enterprise Institute, 1982), ch. 8.

33 "Environmental Protection Agency's Proposed Revisions to the National Ambient Air Quality Standard for Photochemical Oxidants" (Report of the Regulatory Analysis Review Group, submitted by the Council on Wage and Price Stability, Oct. 16, 1978); Robert Crandall, *Controlling Industrial Pollution* (Washington, D.C.: Brookings Institution, 1983), 140; Lave, *Strategy of Social Regulation*, 103–8.

34 Alan Williams, "Cost-Benefit Analysis: Bastard Science?" in Richard Zeckhauser et al., eds., *Benefit Cost and Policy Analysis, 1972* (Chicago: Aldine, 1973), 58.

35 Freeman, *Benefits of Environmental Improvement*, 161.

36 Kneese, "Measuring the Benefits of Clean Air," 36.

37 Bailey, *Reducing Risks to Life*, and W. Kip Viscusi, "Regulating Product Safety" (Working paper no. 14 in government regulation, American Enterprise Institute, Nov. 18, 1981), ch. 2, p. 14.

38 See the discussion in ch. 2.

39 *Washington Post*, March 22, 1982, A-7.

40 See, e.g., Lave, *Strategy of Social Regulation*, 27, 32, and Miller and Yandle, *Benefit-Cost Analysis*, 10.

41 Edgar Browning and Jacqueline Browning, *Public Finance and the Price System*, 2d ed. (New York: Macmillan, 1983), 431.

42 Uwe Reinhardt, "Diagnosing the Great American Bellyache," *Princeton Alumni Weekly*, Feb. 22, 1982, 23.

43 For examples of regulation-related corruption not connected to the Mandel case see *Washington Post*, Jan. 15, 1978, A-3, and May 9, 1978, A-1.

44 Though there were few complaints, there were lots of requests for the thousand free copies that were still to be made available: *Washington Post*, July 20, 1982, A-15.

45 Lave and Crandall, eds., 136.

46 See Lave, *Strategy of Social Regulation*, 80, and Rhoads, *Policy Analysis in the Federal Aviation Administration*, 95–6, for examples of how relatively simple analyses of risk levels and of program effectiveness can be illuminating.

47 Lave, *Strategy of Social Regulation*, 36.

48 Steven E. Rhoads, *Valuing Life: Public Policy Dilemmas* (Boulder, Colo.: Westview, 1980), 301–3, discusses at greater length than ch. 9 some reasons why current benefit-cost values for life should not be mechanically applied in the policy-making process.

49 Rhoads, *Valuing Life*, Introduction and 303–6. Also note how then Secretary of Health and Human Services Patricia Harris responded to the complaint of a letter writer who was outraged at suggestions that she had said that heart transplants may be "too expensive." Harris simply sent up smoke, saying cost was not the motivating concern while concluding her letter by suggesting that it certainly was; *Washington Post*, June 21, 1980, A-14.

50 For further discussion see Hapgood "Risk Benefit Analysis," and Rhoads, *Valuing Life*, 303–6.

51 For an analysis of criteria for judging political rhetoric see Harry Jaffa's discussion of Lincoln's rhetoric on slavery in *Crisis of the House Divided* (Seattle: University of Washington Press, 1973), ch. XVII.

52 Christopher Leman and Robert Nelson, "Ten Commandments for Policy Economists," *Journal of Policy Analysis and Management* 1 (Fall 1981): 107.

53 See section entitled "Who Benefits and Who Loses."

54 See ch. 2 end of section, "Should Life-Saving Programs be Exceptions?"

55 Kelman, "Cost-Benefit Analysis," 36.

56 Green, "Faked Case against Regulation," C-5.

57 For other critics of analysis who nonetheless find that it has uses see Peter Self, *Econocrats and the Policy Process* (Boulder, Colo.: Westview, 1975), esp. 66, 68, 89, 92, 124, and Baruch Fischhoff, "Cost Benefit Analysis and the Art of Motorcycle Maintenance," *Policy Sciences* 8 (1977): 177–202.

9. THE ECONOMIST'S CONSUMER AND INDIVIDUAL WELL-BEING

1 On the market production of information see George Stigler, "The Economics of Information," *Journal of Political Economy* 69 (June 1961): 213–25, and Milton Friedman and Rose Friedman, *Free to Choose* (New York: Avon Books, 1979), 213.

2 Alan Schwartz and Louis Wilde, "Intervening in Markets on the Basis of Imperfect Information: A Legal and Economic Analysis," *University of Pennsylvania Law Review* 127 (1979): 653; *Consumer Information Remedies: Policy Review Session* (A briefing book prepared by staff of the Federal Trade Commission, June 1, 1979), 83.

3 *Washington Post*, June 19, 1981, C-15; *Washington Post*, Jan. 15, 1982, A-14. There are also examples of companies withholding information from their employees about the long-term health risks of their firm's occupations. See Steven Kelman, *Regulating America, Regulating Sweden* (Cambridge, Mass.: MIT Press, 1981), 57; *Washington Post*, April 17, 1982, A-21.

4 *Information Disclosure* (A report produced by the Project on Alternative Regulatory Approaches and its support contractor SRI International of Menlo Park, Calif., 1981), 24–5.

5 *Information Disclosure*, 12.

6 *Comparative Performance Information* (A staff task force report of the Federal Trade Commission, Sept. 1981), 47. On this general problem also see W. Kip Viscusi, "Regulating Product Safety" (Working paper no. 14, American Enterprise Institute, Nov. 18, 1981), II-17–II-20.

7 *Consumer Information Remedies*, 273.

8 *Washington Post*, Oct. 24, 1981, A–1; *Charlottesville Daily Progress*, Dec. 10, 1981, C-6; *Regulation* (Jan./Feb. 1982): 15.

9 *Information Disclosure*, 42–3, and *Consumer Information Remedies*, 93–4.

10 Michael O'Hare, "Information Strategies as Regulatory Surrogates," in Eugene Bardach and Robert Kagan, eds., *Social Regulation: Strategies for Reform* (San Francisco: Institute for Contemporary Studies, 1982), 229.

11 Richard Zeckhauser says this in "Uncertainty and the Need for Collective Action," in Robert Haveman and Julius Margolis, eds., *Public Expenditures and Policy Analysis* (Chicago: Markham, 1970), 114.

12 *Consumer Information Remedies*, 96; also see *Information Disclosure*, 23–4.

13 *Regulation* (March/April 1979): 15. For additional examples of government information policy failure see *Comparative Performance Information*, 8, and George Stigler, *The Citizen and the State* (Chicago: University of Chicago Press, 1975), 184–5.

14 Claude S. Colantoni, Otto A. Davis, and Malati Swaminuthan, "Imperfect Consumers and Welfare Comparisons of Policies Concerning Information and Regulation," *Bell Journal of Economics and Management Science* 7 (Autumn 1976): 613; also see Schwartz and Wilde, "Intervening in Markets," 668; Walter Y. Oi, "The Economics of Product Safety," *Bell Journal of Economics and Management Science* 4 (Spring 1973): 3–27; Victor Goldberg's critique of Oi's paper and Oi's rejoinder in *Bell Journal of Economics and Management Science* 5 (Autumn 1974): 683–95. Despite the fancy mathematical models used, the empirical situation is so unclear that Oi ended this exchange of opinion by referring to his own preference for throwaway pop bottles even though *he* knew they were more likely to explode.

15 See, e.g., Gordon Tullock, *The Logic of the Law* (New York: Basic Books, 1971), 233–37.

16 *Information Disclosure*, 44.

17 *Consumer Information Remedies*, 84.

18 Steven Kelman, "Regulation and Paternalism," *Public Policy* 29 (1981): 229.

19 Richard Nelson, "Comments on Peltzman's Paper on Automobile Safety Regulation" (Working paper 5-13, Institution for Social and Policy Studies, Yale University): 15.

20 Roland N. McKean, "Non-Profits and Information Production" (University of Virginia, Feb. 1977, Mimeo): 30; also see Otto Davis and Morton Kamien, "Externalities, Information and Alternative Collective Action," in Haveman and Margolis, eds., esp. 78–81.

21 Nelson, "Comments," 15; also see Charles Schultze, *The Public Use of Private Interest* (Washington, D.C.: Brookings Institution, 1977), 37.

22 As previously indicated, very little has been written by economists on these sorts of contemporary issues. This shows the lack of policy relevance of much of the economics of information literature.

23 See, e.g., Arthur Okun's brief comments in Martin Feldstein, ed., *The American Economy in Transition* (Chicago: University of Chicago Press, 1980), 559. Also see the letter to the editor from Alfred Kahn in *Washington Post*, June 19, 1982, A-14.

24 See, e.g., McKean, "Non-Profits and Information Production," 32, and McKean, "Government and the Consumer," *Southern Economic Journal* 69 (1973): esp. 486–8.

25 *Washington Post*, Feb. 28, 1975.

26 Ralph Nader, "A Citizen's Guide to the American Economy," *New York Review of Books*, Sept. 2, 1971, as quoted in Ralph Winter, Jr., *The Consumer Advocate vs. the Consumer* (Washington, D.C.: American Enterprise Institute, 1972), 7.

27 Thorstein Veblen, *The Theory of the Leisure Class* (New York: Penguin Books, 1979), and see the discussion of Veblen in William Breit and R. L. Ransom, *The Academic Scribblers* (New York: Holt, Rinehart & Winston, 1971).

28 Karl Marx, *Economic and Philosophic Manuscripts of 1844*, in Robert C. Tucker, ed., *The Marx-Engels Reader* (New York: Norton, 1978), 93.

29 See Jean Jacques Rousseau, *Discourse on the Origin and Foundations of Inequality Among Men*, in Roger Masters, ed., *The First and Second Discourses* (New York: St. Martin's Press, 1964), and Jean Jacques Rousseau, *Émile*, trans. and ed. Allan Bloom (New York: Basic Books, 1979). Also see Bloom's introduction.

30 John K. Galbraith, "Economics as a System of Belief," in *Economics, Peace and Laughter* (Boston: Houghton Mifflin, 1971), 68–82. "Economics as a System of Belief" is a particularly good statement of Galbraith's differences with mainstream economists on the issues discussed here. Also see *The Affluent Society* (New York: New American Library [Mentor Books], 1958), ch. XI.

31 Assar Lindbeck, *The Political Economy of the New Left* (New York: Harper & Row, 1977), 43, and M. Bruce Johnson, ed., *The Attack on Corporate America* (New York: McGraw-Hill, 1978), 240.

32 Harold Demsetz, "Advertising in the Affluent Society," in Yale Brozen, ed., *Advertising and Society* (New York: New York University Press, 1974), 67–77.

33 Galbraith as quoted in Friedrich Hayek, "The Non-Sequitur of the 'Dependence' Effect," *Southern Economic Journal* 27 (1961): 347.

34 *Washington Post*, Nov. 7, 1982, A-14; *Washington Post*, Dec. 12, 1981, A-23. For a description of Soviet youth's passion for items like blue jeans, rock music, stereo equipment, and frisbees see Andrea Lee, *Russian Journal* (New York: Random House, 1981).

35 Lester Lave, "Conflicting Objectives in Regulating the Automobile," *Science*, May 22, 1981, 894.

36 For economists' views on advertising see Douglas Greer, *Industrial Organization and Public Policy* (New York: Macmillan, 1980), 371–95; Jules Blackman, *Advertising and Competition* (New York: New York University Press, 1967), esp. 113, 143; Lester Talser, "Some Aspects of the Economics of Advertising," *Journal of Business of the University of Chicago* 41 (1968): 166–73; Douglass North and Roger Miller, *The Economics of Public Issues* (New York: Harper & Row, 1980), ch. 13; Mark Albion and Paul Farris, *The Advertising Controversy* (Boston: Auburn House, 1981), esp. 167, 180–1.

37 E. J. Mishan, *The Costs of Economic Growth* (New York: Praeger, 1967), 130, 119.

38 Sidney Schoeffler, "Note on Modern Welfare Economics," *American Economic Review* 42 (1952): 883, 887.

39 Richard Weckstein, "Welfare Criteria and Changing Tastes," *American Economic Review* 52 (1962): 133–53.

40 Kelvin Lancaster, "A New Approach to Consumer Theory," *Journal of Political Economy* 74 (April 1966): 149–50. For an example of economists building on Lancaster's work see Colantoni, Davis, and Swaminuthan, "Imperfect Consumers and Welfare Comparisons."

41 See the very brief discussion of studies in Albion and Farris, *The Advertising Controversy*, 77–84. For another who shares my assessment see Duncan MacRae, Jr., *The Social Function of Social Science* (New Haven, Conn.: Yale University Press, 1976), 151.

42 Jerome Rothenberg, "Welfare Comparisons and Changes in Tastes," *American Economic Review* 43 (1953): 887.

43 E. J. Mishan, *Cost-Benefit Analysis* (New York: Praeger, 1976): 318.

44 For discussion on a related subject see Leo Strauss, *Natural Right and History* (Chicago: University of Chicago Press, 1953), chs. I, II.

45 Robert Solow, "A Rejoinder," *Public Interest* no. 9 (Fall 1967): 119.

46 William Baumol, *Welfare Economics and the Theory of the State* (Cambridge, Mass.: Harvard University Press, 1969), 29.

47 William Vickrey, "Goals of Economic Life: An Exchange of Questions Between Economics and Philosophy," in A. Dudley Ward, ed., *Goals of Economic Life* (New York: Harper & Brothers, 1953), 159.

48 Dean Worcester, Jr., *Welfare Gains from Advertising: The Problem of Regulation* (Washington, D.C.: American Enterprise Institute, 1978), 124. For additional mainstream reaction to the Galbraith–Mishan argument see Abba Lerner, "The Economics and Politics of Consumer Sovereignty," *American Economic Review* 62 (1972): 258, and William Breit and R. L. Ransom, *The Academic Scribblers*, 169–70, 200.

Alfred Kahn differs with many of his colleagues on many of these issues. Kahn wants the Federal Communications Commission to continue to require those awarded broadcasting licenses to air a certain amount of public-service programs. He decries the fact that there are no longer any regular weekday network shows designed for children. He expressed such views on public television's "Nightly Business Report," April 15, 1983, and July 8, 1983.

49 "Does Advertising Persuade Consumers to Buy Things They Do Not Need?" In Johnson, ed., 239.

50 Mancur Olson and Christopher Clague, "Dissent in Economics: The Convergence of Extremes," *Social Research* 38 (Winter 1971), reprinted in Ryan Amacher, Robert Tollison, and Thomas Willett, eds., *The Economic Approach to Public Policy* (Ithaca, N.Y.: Cornell University Press, 1976), 86. Also see Steven Kelman, *What Price Incentives? Economists and the Environment* (Boston: Auburn House, 1981), 19–20.

51 Gordon Tullock, "More Thought About Demand Revealing," *Public Choice* 38 (1982): 167.

52 Kenneth Arrow, *The Limits of Organization* (New York: Norton, 1974), 16. Also see Richard McKenzie and Gordon Tullock, *The New World of Economics* (Homewood, Ill.: Irwin, 1981), chs. 1, 21.

53 James Buchanan and Gordon Tullock, *The Calculus of Consent* (Ann Arbor: University of Michigan Press, 1965), 306. Hume said, "Reason is, and ought only to be the slave of the passions"; *A Treatise of Human Nature* (Oxford: Clarendon Press, 1958), book II, pt. 3, sec. iii. Also see Thomas Hobbes's formulation: "for the thoughts are to the desires as scouts and spies, to range abroad and find the way to the things desired."; *Leviathan* (Indianapolis: Library of the Liberal Arts, 1968), pt. I, ch. 8, 68.

54 In addition to the literature cited in the text, see the work on regulation done by George Stigler, Sam Peltzman, and their students. As James Kau and Paul Rubin note, this work is based on the theory of "rational, self interested voting . . . individuals as voters are concerned primarily with the impact of government decisions on their personal incomes"; *Congressmen, Constituents and Contributors* (Boston: Martinus-Nijhoff, 1982), 12. Kau and

Rubin discuss and cite the relevant literature.

There are also, of course, some economists who quarrel with their colleagues' assumptions about narrowly self-interested behavior. See Earl Brubaker, "Free Ride, Free Revelation, or Golden Rule?" *Journal of Law and Economics* 18 (1975): 147–61; Alfred Kahn, "The Place of Ethical Values in a Market System," National Economic Research Associates *Topics* (Jan. 1981); Kau and Rubin, *Congressmen, Constituents and Contributors*, esp. 49–53, 80–81, 123.

55 David O. Sears, Richard Lau, Tom Tyler, Harris Allen, Jr., "Self-Interest vs. Symbolic Politics in Policy Attitudes and Presidential Voting," *American Political Science Review* 74 (1980): 670–84; Helen Ladd and Julie Wilson, "Who Supports Tax Limitations?" *Journal of Policy Analysis and Management* 2 (1983): 274; James Q. Wilson and Edward C. Banfield, "Voting Behavior on Municipal Public Expenditures," in Julius Margolis, ed., *The Public Economy of Urban Communities* (Washington, D.C.: Resources for the Future, 1965); James Rodgers, "Explaining Income Redistribution," and Otto Davis and John Jackson, "Representative Assemblies and Demands for Redistribution," both in Harold Hochman and George Peterson, eds., *Redistribution through Public Choice* (New York: Columbia University Press, 1974).

D. Roderick Kiewiet finds that the predominant political impact of economic issues results from voters' perceptions of such issues as pressing national concerns – regardless of the voters' personal circumstances; *Macroeconomics and Micropolitics* (Chicago: University of Chicago Press, 1983). Even in a period of economic decline such as the 1970s, Donald Kinder finds that "in evaluating the president, citizens seem to pay principal attention to the nation's economic predicament, and comparatively little to their own"; "Presidents, Prosperity and Public Opinion," *Public Opinion Quarterly* 45 (Spring 1981): 17, as quoted in Seymour Martin Lipset and William Schneider, *The Confidence Gap* (New York: Free Press, 1983), 402.

56 James Buchanan, *Public Finance in Democratic Process* (Chapel Hill: University of North Carolina Press, 1967), 198.

57 Davis and Jackson, in Hochman and Peterson, eds., 286.

58 Davis and Jackson, in Hochman and Peterson, eds., 284. Also see Buchanan, *Public Finance*, 198.

59 Buchanan, *Public Finance*, 198. Also see Bruce Bolnick, "Toward a Behavioral Theory of Philanthropic Activity," in Edmund Phelps, ed., *Altruism, Morality and Economic Theory* (New York: Russell Sage, 1975), 198.

60 William Breit, "Income Redistribution and Efficiency Norms," in Hochman and Peterson, eds., esp. 11, 18.

61 Bolnick, in Phelps, ed., esp. 198–9. For discussion of other economists who have seen altruism as being "silly" or "irrational" see Gerald Marwell and Ruth Ames, "Economists Free Ride, Does Anyone Else?" *Journal of Public Economics* 15 (1981): 299.

62 An economist reader of the first draft does not agree that "too large a component of altruism in preferences strips economic theory of its predictive value." My position is, however, supported by some economists. Geoffrey Brennan and James Buchanan have said: "For the purposes of predictive science, the elements in individual utility functions must be specified in clear, recognizable and measurable terms. Application of the *homo economicus* construction for empirical or predictive purposes requires something like the assumption of net wealth maximization as a surrogate for maximization of consumption more broadly achieved"; "The Normative Purpose of Economic 'Science,' " *International Review of Law and Economics* (Winter 1981): 161–2, as quoted in Richard McKenzie, *The Limits of Economic Science* (Boston: Kluwer-Nijhoff, 1983), 9. See also McKenzie's interesting book and Ronald Coase, "Economics and Contiguous Disciplines," *Journal of Legal Studies* 7 (1978): 201–11.

63 Gordon Tullock, "Does Punishment Deter Crime?" *Public Interest* no. 36 (Summer 1974): 106; see Tullock, *Logic of the Law*, esp. 164–5, 213. Also see sociologist Serapio Zalba's comments in Simon Rottenberg, ed., *The Economics of Crime and Punishment* (Washington, D.C.: American Enterprise Institute, 1973), 62.

64 W. B. Arthur, "The Economics of Risks to Life," *American Economic Review* 71 (1981): 55, 61.

65 John Morrall III, "OSHA after Ten Years" (Working paper no. 13, American Enterprise Institute, Nov. 18, 1981), III-7, III-6, III-16. Like Arthur, Albert Nichols and Richard Zeckhauser's analysis of OSHA makes no mention of psychic external costs to the kindhearted; "OSHA after a Decade," in Leonard Weiss and Michael Klass, eds., *Case Studies in Regulation* (Boston: Little, Brown, 1981), esp. 208–9.

66 See Tibor Scitovsky, "The Place of Economic Welfare in Human Welfare," *Quarterly Review of Economics and Business* 13 (Autumn 1973): 12–13. Also see Scitovsky's *The Joyless Economy* (Oxford: Oxford University Press, 1978).

67 Richard Easterlin, "Does Money Buy Happiness?" *Public Interest* no. 30 (Winter 1973): 10. Also see Easterlin, "Does Economic Growth Improve the Human Lot?" in Paul David and Melvin Reder, eds., *Nations and Households in Economic Growth* (New York: Academic Press, 1975); the Gallup Poll of Dec. 9, 1963 (*Washington Post*, A-6) and the Harris Poll of Nov. 8, 1976 (*Washington Post*, A-8) support Easterlin on the lack of progress in subjective sense of well-being among Americans. However, a Gallup Poll of

Nov. 7, 1976 (*Washington Post*, A-4) shows the average level of felt well-being to be far higher in the wealthier Western democracies than in under-developed countries.

68 Alan Blinder, "The Level and Distribution of Economic Well-Being," in Martin Feldstein, ed., *The American Economy in Transition* (Chicago: University of Chicago Press, 1980), 471–2. In a letter Leland Yeager has reminded me that Friedrich Hayek makes an interesting defense of economic progress. Yeager paraphrases Hayek as follows: "Most people derive real satisfaction from the perception that their economic condition is improving. If people are to be able to have this satisfaction, their society must be an economically 'progressive' one. People by and large will be happier than otherwise, even though levels of happiness may not rise over time." Hayek's argument is in *The Constitution of Liberty* (Chicago: University of Chicago Press, Phoenix ed., 1978), 40–2.

69 For arguments and data that bear on one or more of these parts of life see Mishan, *Costs of Economic Growth*, esp. 160–6; Scitovsky, "Economic Welfare in Human Welfare," and *The Joyless Economy*, esp. 90–2; Kelman, *What Price Incentives?* 30–6; Robert Lane, "Markets and the Satisfaction of Human Wants," *Journal of Economic Issues* XII, no. 4 (Dec. 1978): 799–827; and Angus Campbell, Philip Converse, and Willard Rodgers, *The Quality of American Life* (New York: Russell Sage, 1976), esp. chs. 9–11. Also see the review of Campbell by Richard Merelman in *American Political Science Review* 75 (1981): 763–4, and Richard Rose and Gary Peters, *Can Government Go Bankrupt?* (New York: Basic Books, 1978), 244.

70 This is not to deny that there are minor exceptions. An advertisement for a new housing development may mention the good school system. A book store's advertisement may mention a book about religion. And churches do sometimes pay for time to promote brotherhood. These types of examples are peripheral to modern commercial life, and they do not address the benefits of strong bonds with family and friends. A quotation from Frank Knight at the end of this chapter addresses this same issue.

71 E. J. Mishan, *The Economic Growth Debate* (London: Allen & Unwin, 1977), 174. This chapter, "Love and Trust," is excellent on some of the themes discussed here.

72 Plato, *Gorgias*, intro. W. C. Helmbold (Indianapolis: Bobbs-Merrill, 1952), esp. 83. This dialogue will be of interest to readers who want to think more about the general problems raised in this chapter.

73 Ronald Sharp, "Friendship as Gift Exchange," a draft chapter from a manuscript on friendship, tentatively titled *Friendship, Form and the Spirit of Gift*.

74 Something similar happened at my university although, in this case, it was after the track coach's death.

75 Tullock, *Logic of the Law*, 254–5.

76 Aristotle, *Nichomachean Ethics*, in Richard McKeon, ed., *Introduction to Aristotle* (New York: Modern Library, 1947), book IX, ch. 4 and ch. 9, 502 and 514. See also Adam Smith, *The Theory of Moral Sentiments* (Indianapolis: Liberty Classics, 1976), pt. III, ch. 2.

77 Julius Margolis, "Public Policies for Private Profits: Urban Government," in Hochman and Peterson, eds., 301.

78 Richard F. Fenno, Jr., *Congressmen in Committees* (Boston: Little, Brown, 1973).

79 Ben Wattenberg, "A Decent Man," *Washington Post*, Sept. 4, 1983, C-7; also see Sept. 3, 1983, A-14.

80 UPI report of a study done for the Connecticut Mutual Life Insurance Co. in the *Charlottesville Daily Progress*, May 9, 1981, C-5.

81 Gerald Marwell and Ruth Ames, "Economists Free Ride, Does Anyone Else?"

82 A. Rapaport and A. M. Chammah, *Prisoner's Dilemma: A Study in Conflict and Cooperation* (Ann Arbor: University of Michigan Press, 1965), 29, as quoted in Amartya Sen, "Rational Fools," *Philosophy and Public Affairs* 6 (Summer 1977): 341. James Buchanan (as quoted in Brubaker, "Free Ride, Free Revelation, or Golden Rule?" 150) and Edgar Browning and Jacquelene Browning (*Public Finance and the Price System* [New York: Macmillian, 1983], 26–7) have also equated narrow monetary self-interest (i.e., acting as a free rider) with rational behavior. Brubaker dissents (154).

83 Plato, *Gorgias* and *The Republic.*, trans. Allan Bloom (New York: Basic Books, 1968), chs. II and IV and Bloom's interpretive essay, esp. 348, 375.

84 Robert Jastrow, *The Enchanted Loom* (New York: Simon & Schuster, 1981), 132–3.

85 *Washington Post*, July 9, 1974; also see July 2, 1980, A-11.

86 *Charlottesville Daily Progress*, May 30, 1981, B-10. Note also a recent study of psychiatrists that found that a majority of the small minority of therapists who repeatedly had sexual intercourse with patients believed that their conduct "was bad for both therapist and patient"; *Washington Post*, Sept. 1, 1983, A-3.

87 Thomas Schelling, "The Intimate Contest for Self-Command," *Public Interest* no. 60 (Summer 1980): 110.

88 "Tobacco and Liquor Taxation" (Fall 1964, Mimeo).

89 Irving Kristol, *Two Cheers for Capitalism* (New York: Mentor Books, 1978), 82.

90 First results were reported in Louis Harris poll in the *Washington Post*, Sept. 18, 1978, A-4; the second from Harris poll of May 23, 1977, A-10. Other polls have found that far more Americans think we are less happy because of increased affluence than think we are happier. Low-income respondents do not equate happiness with economic well-being any more than do high-income respondents; Jennifer Hochschild, "Why the Dog Doesn't Bark: Income, Attitudes and the Redistribution of Wealth," *Polity* (Summer 1979): 509.

91 Cited in Scitovsky, *The Joyless Economy*, 163–4.

92 For somewhat different arguments on the general subject of this and the next two paragraphs see David Braybrooke, "From Economics to Aesthetics: The Rectification of Preferences," *Nous* 8 (1974): 13–24, and Scitovsky, *The Joyless Economy*, esp. pt. II. Also see Steven Kelman, "Cost Benefit Analysis: An Ethical Critique," *Regulation* (Jan./Feb. 1981): 38.

93 Leo Strauss, "What Is Political Philosophy?" *Journal of Politics* 19 (Aug. 1957): 351.

94 Arnold Weinstein, "Individual Preference Intransitivity," *Southern Economic Journal* 34 (1968): 336; also see Arthur Maass, "Benefit-Cost Analysis: Its Relevance to Public Investment Decisions," *Quarterly Journal of Economics* 80 (May 1966): 216; Duncan MacRae, "Normative Assumptions in the Study of Public Choice," *Public Choice* 16 (Fall 1973): esp. 32–3; Amartya Sen, "Behavior and the Concept of Preference," *Economica* 40 (Aug. 1973): 241–59.

95 James Buchanan, "Individual Choice in Voting and the Market," *Journal of Political Economy* 62 (Aug. 1954): 336.

96 See also Kenneth Arrow, *Social Choice and Individual Values* (New York: Wiley, 1963), esp. 17–18. But note MacRae's discussion of Arrow in "Normative Assumptions in the Study of Public Choice," 32–3.

97 Sen, "Behavior and the Concept of Preference," 257.

98 A. Myrick Freeman III, *The Benefits of Environmental Improvement* (Baltimore: Johns Hopkins University Press, 1979), 97. For an economist who disagrees with his colleagues' frequent unwillingness to use questionnaires or self-testimony as a route to understanding see Donald McCloskey, "The Rhetoric of Economics," *Journal of Economic Literature* (June 1983): 481–517.

99 Since the federal cigarette tax has not been raised in many years (and may even be cut in 1985) and since soaring health care costs are making the external costs of smoking loom larger, the present tax may soon be justified on externality grounds alone.

100 John Stuart Mill, *Utilitarianism* (Indianapolis: Hackett, 1979), 10.

101 Martin Bronfenbrenner, "Poetry, Pushpin and Utility," *Economic Inquiry* (Jan. 1977): 98.

102 Robert Samuelson, "Let's Play Scrooge and Cut the Budget," *Washington Post*, March 11, 1980, D-7.

103 Roger Bolton, "The Economics and Public Financing of Higher Education: An Overview," in *The Economics and Financing of Higher Education in the United States*, a compendium of papers submitted to the Joint Economic Committee, U.S. Congress (Washington, D.C.: Government Printing Office, 1969), 33. For a thoughtful discussion of "groping upward" and higher values by an economist who would disagree with Bolton, Samuelson, and Bronfenbrenner see Robert Dorfman, "An Afterword: Humane Values and Environmental Decisions," in Laurence Tribe et al., *When Values Conflict: Essays on Environmental Analysis, Discourse and Decision* (Cambridge, Mass.: Ballinger, 1976), 153–73.

104 Gideon Doran, *The Smoking Paradox* (Cambridge, Mass.: Abt Books, 1979); James L. Hamilton, "The Demand for Cigarettes: Advertising, the Health Scare, and the Cigarette Advertising Ban," *Review of Economics and Statistics* (Nov. 1972): 401–9.

105 Charles Frankel, "The Moral Framework of the Idea of Welfare," in John Morgan, ed., *Welfare and Wisdom* (Toronto: University of Toronto Press, 1966), 179, 184. Also see MacRae, *Social Function of Social Science*, 217; George Will, *Statecraft as Soulcraft* (New York: Simon & Schuster, 1983), esp. 81–2, 94.

106 At the moment the public is willing to spend large amounts for purposes such as preserving air quality at national parks; Allen Kneese, "Measuring the Benefits of Clean Air" (Draft of a study done for the Environmental Protection Administration, Feb. 1982) 54–5.

107 William F. Baxter, *People or Penguins: The Case for Optimal Pollution* (New York: Columbia University Press, 1974), 5, 7, 8. Though Baxter, a former law professor who recently resigned as assistant attorney general for antitrust, is not a professional economist, he bases this book on the welfare-economic framework.

108 See Charles Frankel, "The Rights of Nature," and Tribe, *When Values Conflict*, 93–113, 61–91. Also see George Will's columns, *Washington Post*, Aug. 27, 1981, and Jan. 18, 1981.

109 Richard Lipsey and Peter Steiner, *Economics* (New York: Harper & Row, 1981), 17–19.

110 See the brief discussion of the relationship between welfare economics and logical positivism in Leonard Merewitz and Stephen Sosnick, *The Budget's New Clothes* (Chicago: Markham, 1971), 79–80. It is interesting that, unlike economics, contemporary philosophy shows no such deference to its positivist forebears.

111 Tullock, *Logic of the Law*, 3, 256. Though Roland McKean has written thoughtfully on the larger issues raised by economics, he too sees disagreement about values as evidence that there can be no ultimately correct criterion of the public interest; *Public Spending* (New York: McGraw-Hill, 1968), vii.

112 Tullock's "Comment on Rae's 'The Limits of Consensual Decision,' " *American Political Science Review* 69 (1975): 1,295.

113 Leo Strauss, *Natural Right and History* (Chicago: University of Chicago Press, 1965), p. 10.

114 Amartya Sen, *Collective Choice and Social Welfare* (San Francisco: Holden-Day, 1970), 64. Also see 56–63.

115 David Long, Charles Mallar, and Craig Thornton, "Evaluating the Benefits and Costs of the Job Corps," *Journal of Policy Analysis and Management* 1 (Fall 1981): 61.

116 Some economists have noted that an additional crime may lead to other societal costs in the form of additional expenditures to protect oneself from crimes; James Buchanan, *The Limits of Liberty* (Chicago: University of Chicago Press, 1975), 122.

117 Readers may wish to remind themselves of the effects of street crime on psychological well-being discussed in ch. 8.

118 Timothy Hannan, "The Benefits and Costs of Methadone Maintenance," *Public Policy* 24 (1976): 200–1; Gary Becker, "Crime and Punishment: An Economic Approach," *Journal of Political Economy* 76 (1968): 169–217; Richard Posner, *Economic Analysis of the Law* (Boston: Little, Brown, 1972), 357–9. My discussion here has produced contrasting criticisms. One public administration student thought it unfair to suggest that most economists would count the benefits to thieves in their cost-benefit work since he could not believe "that most economists would go this far." An economist reader could not believe that I would exclude all benefits to thieves. He reminds me that the thief could be a mother stealing from the rich to feed her children.

119 Jeffrey Sedgwick, "Welfare Economics and Criminal Justice Policy" (Ph.D. diss., University of Virginia, 1978), 156–7.

120 Richard Nelson, *The Moon and the Ghetto* (New York: Norton, 1977), 151.

121 Mishan, *Cost-Benefit Analysis*, 312–15, 385–8.

122 Leland Yeager makes a similar point in "Pareto Optimality in Policy Espousal," *Journal of Libertarian Studies* 2 (1978): 208–9.

123 John Stuart Mill, *Utilitarianism*, 13. Also see Mill's "Civilization," in

Dissertations and Discussions: Political, Philosophical and Historical, 3 vols. (Boston: Wm. V. Spencer, 1864), I, 186–231.

124 Adam Smith, *The Wealth of Nations*, 2 vols. (Chicago: University of Chicago Press, 1976), vol. 2, book V, ch. 1, 303, 308.

125 Alfred Marshall, *Principles of Economics* (London: Macmillan, 1910), ch. VI, xiii, 14, p. 720 and ch. III, vi, 6, p. 137. Adam Smith was willing to go beyond encouragement to stimulate better expenditure patterns by the rich. He advocated higher tolls on luxury carriages than on freight wagons so that "the indolence and vanity of the rich" could "contribute in a very easy manner to the relief of the poor"; *Wealth of Nations*, vol. II, book V, ch. 1, pt. III, art. 1, 246.

126 Philip Wicksteed, *The Common Sense of Political Economy* ed. Lionel Robbins (London: Routledge & Kegan Paul, 1950), book II, ch. 1, 431, 434.

127 A. C. Pigou, *The Economics of Welfare* (London: Macmillan, 1938), 13, 17. 18.

128 Frank Knight, *The Ethics of Competition* (London: Allen & Unwin, 1935), 22–3, 52n, 71.

129 Thomas Carlyle, "Pig Philosophy," a section of "Jesuitism," in *Latter Day Pamphlets* (Andover: Warren F. Draper, 1860), 400–3.

130 The words are J. J. C. Smart's in Smart and Bernard Williams, *Utilitarianism: For and Against* (Cambridge: Cambridge University Press, 1973), 24.

131 Kenneth Boulding, *Economics as a Science* (New York: McGraw-Hill, 1970), 156.

132 See last paragraph of section "Which Preferences?" McCloskey reaches a conclusion similar to mine; "The Rhetoric of Economics."

10. A SECOND LOOK AT EXTERNALTIES

1 Even if these psychic costs of crime to third parties were somehow estimated and included, I would still oppose counting gains and losses to criminals when evaluating public policy. In my judgment, when deciding how much to spend on the criminal justice system, only the costs of police, courts, and prisons on the one hand and the costs of crime to victims and third parties on the other are relevant. The gains and losses of outlaws should be irrelevant for the reasons offered in the previous chapter.

2 Kenneth Boulding comments on this general tendency in "Economics as a Moral Science," *American Economic Review* 59 (1969): 6.

3 E. J. Mishan, *Cost-Benefit Analysis* (New York: Praeger, 1976), 386.

Arthur Okun also seems to support Mishan's view. See *Equality and Efficiency* (Washington, D.C.: Brookings Institution, 1975), 78.

4 E. J. Mishan, *Welfare Economics: An Assessment* (Amsterdam: North Holland, 1969), 36–7.

5 *Cost-Benefit Analysis*, 387–8; E. J. Mishan, *Economics for Social Decisions* (New York: Praeger, 1972), 90.

6 James S. Duesenberry, *Income, Saving and the Theory of Consumer Behavior* (New York: Oxford University Press, 1967), 100–1, and Geoffrey Brennan, "Pareto Desirable Redistribution: The Case of Malice and Envy," *Journal of Public Economics* 2 (1973): 173–83. Also see William Breit and Roger Ransom's discussion of Veblen in *The Academic Scribblers* (New York: Holt, Rinehart & Winston, 1971), 42.

7 See chapter six, "Pareto Optimal Redistribution."

8 Leonard Merewitz and Stephen Sosnick, *The Budget's New Clothes* (Chicago: Markham, 1971), 78.

9 *Cost-Benefit Analysis*, 387.

10 Friedrich Hayek, *The Constitution of Liberty* (Chicago: University of Chicago Press, 1960), 145.

11 Kenneth Arrow, "Political and Economic Evaluation of Social Effects and Externalities," in Julius Margolis, ed., *The Analysis of Public Output* (New York: Columbia University Press, 1970), 16; Arrow, *Social Choice and Individual Values* (New York: Wiley, 1963), 18; Amartya Sen, *Collective Choice and Social Welfare* (San Francisco: Holden-Day, 1970), 82.

12 Leland Yeager, "Pareto Optimality in Policy Espousal," *Journal of Libertarian Studies* 2 (1978): 203–4.

13 This fact is commented on in Dennis Mueller, *Public Choice* (Cambridge: Cambridge University Press, 1979), 205, and Charles Rowley, "Market 'Failure' and Government 'Failure,' " in James Buchanan et al., *The Economics of Politics* (West Sussex, England: Institute of Economic Affairs, 1978), 36. For citations to the entire literature on the subject see Amartya Sen, "Liberty, Unanimity and Rights," *Economica* 43 (Aug. 1976): 217–45.

14 Claude Hillinger and Victoria Lapham, "The Impossibility of a Paretian Liberal: Comment by Two Who Are Unreconstructed," *Journal of Political Economy* 39 (Nov./Dec. 1971): 1,404–5.

15 Dean Worcester, Jr., *Welfare Gains from Advertising* (Washington, D.C.: American Enterprise Institute, 1978), 116.

16 Douglass North and Roger Miller, *The Economics of Public Issues* (New York: Harper & Row, 1980), chs. 3, 4.

17 Milton Spencer, *Contemporary Economics* (New York: Worth, 1974), 118.

18 Gordon Tullock, *Private Wants, Public Means* (New York: Basic Books, 1970), 150, and *The Logic of the Law* (New York: Basic Books, 1971), 248.

19 James Buchanan and Gordon Tullock, *The Calculus of Consent* (Ann Arbor: University of Michigan Press, 1971), 270.

20 Irene Diamond, "Pornography and Repression: A Reconsideration," *Signs* 5 (1980): 697

21 Michael Goldstein and Harold Kant, *Pornography and Sexual Deviance* (Berkeley: University of California Press, 1973), 73, and Diamond, "Pornography and Repression," 694.

22 Quoted in Diamond, "Pornography and Repression," 698.

23 *Washington Post*, Oct. 16, 1982, A-13.

24 Quoted in a review by Walter Berns, *Public Interest* no. 6 (Fall 1981): 149.

25 *Washington Post*, Oct. 16, 1982, A-13.

26 Neil Malamuth and Ed Donnerstein, "The Effects of Aggressive-Pornographic Mass Media Stimuli," in Leonard Berkowitz, ed., *Advances in Experimental Social Psychology*, vol. 15 (New York: Academic Press, 1982), 108–113.

27 Malamuth and Donnerstein, in Berkowitz, ed., 115.

28 Irving Kristol, *On the Democratic Idea in America* (New York: Harper & Row, 1972), 32. Also see James Q. Wilson, "Violence, Pornography, and Social Science," *Public Interest* no. 22 (Winter 1971): 57–8.

29 Harry Clor, "Obscenity and Freedom of Expression," in Clor, ed., *Censorship and Freedom of Expression* (Chicago: Rand McNally, 1971), 99–100. It is interesting that the much-publicized gang rape in a New Bedford, Mass., bar was preceded two months before by a similar "photo fantasy" in *Hustler*. In the New Bedford rape, other customers watched and cheered while the woman was repeatedly raped on a table. In *Hustler* a waitress is sexually assaulted on a pool table by four leather-clothed men. but she is portrayed as enjoying it. Ellen Goodman comments: ". . . we have the pornography hustlers, exploiting the most destructive impulses, fanning the most dehumanizing fantasies to life. I don't know whether the men in New Bedford read this seamy magazine. I don't know how great a distance it is from the reader to the voyeur to the cheering squad. But in our world, the real world, a woman cried out and four men were arrested for rape"; *Washington Post*, April 1, 1983, A-15.

30 Jackie Howell, a Los Angeles police investigator, says of the children involved in child pornography, "Very few just 'get their pictures taken.' The children experience overwhelming relief when we find them. They cry, thank us, call us, report when they are back in school''; *Washington Post.* Jan. 30, 1977, C-2.

31 This is not the place to attempt to establish standards. For a thoughtful attempt to come up with legal definitions of obscenity see Harry Clor, *Obscenity and Public Morality* (Chicago: University of Chicago Press, 1969), esp. 245. On the more general issue of pornography see Clor's book and Walter Berns, *The First Amendment and the Future of American Democracy* (New York: Basic Books, 1976), ch. 5.

32 As quoted in Kristol, *Democratic Idea in America*, 34.

33 See *Washington Post*, Jan. 10, 1982, D-3, and June 9, 1970, B-1.

34 Kristol, *Democratic Idea in America*, 46.

35 Willard Gaylin, ''Obscenity is More than Just a Four-Letter Word,'' in Clor, ed., 170.

36 Tullock, *Private Wants, Public Means*, 238.

37 Those with elephant man's disease are regularly subjected to public ridicule. A reporter spending a day with Siamese twins joined at the head found that they encountered the following comments when walking on the street. '' 'Oh, gross!' 'Why would they come out in public?' a tight-lipped woman snapped as they passed, sounding personally offended; 'It's a joke isn't it?' shrilled one woman. 'Tell me,' she persisted, almost begging, 'isn't it a joke?' '' (Quotations from *Washington Post*, Aug. 27, 1981, B-7.)

38 These are Mishan's suggestions, *Cost-Benefit Analysis*, 387.

39 I wish to thank my colleague from economics, William Johnson, for first suggesting this explanation to me.

40 Even when violence is not in pornography, harm to women may occur. The ''spreader'' pictorial magazines show naked women with their legs spread wide apart. All the indicators of human personality have been removed. The observer sees a sexual organ at his disposal; Clor, ''Obscenities and Freedom of Expression,'' 99–102. Even if they escape beatings and rapes, women are probably less likely to be treated with genuine love and concern by men who become devotees of such literature.

41 George H. Gallup, *The Gallup Poll*, 2 vols. (Wilmington, Del.: Scholarly Resources, 1977), II, 1,029, 1,031.

42 Tullock, *Logic of the Law*, 243–4.

43 One news account suggests that there might be quite a market. In 1976 a quickly forming crowd of 300 egged on a sixteen-year-old girl who was slashing her wrists and about to slash her throat on the steps of a Roman Catholic church in Hartford, Conn. ''Do your thing, sister!''

'' 'Anything that she did that looked like it was going to draw blood, they cheered,' said police detective William Fremont . . . 'The guys [police at the scene] told me they were just like animals,' Fremont said. 'It was like they were witnessing a spectacle at a football game.' '' *Washington Post*, Aug. 22, 1976, A-8.

44 *Chicago Tribune*, Sept. 1, 1974, 5.

45 Tullock, *Private Wants, Public Means*, 188.

46 Tullock, *Logic of the Law*, 244. Tullock does suggest a "suitable tax on the fighting to pay the full cost" of state care for those crippled in such fighting.

47 Finding a way to effectively end the practice of dueling was an important concern of political men of earlier eras. See, e.g., Jean Jacques Rousseau's discussion, *Politics and the Arts: Letter to D'Alembert*, ed., Allan Bloom (Ithaca, N.Y.: Cornell University Press, 1960), 67–75; Susan Jacoby, *Wild Justice* (New York: Harper & Row, 1983), 125–8.

48 Joseph Cropsey, "What is Welfare Economics?" *Ethics* 65 (Jan. 1955): 124. See also Walter Berns, "The Behavioral Sciences and the Study of Political Things: The Case of Christian Bay's *The Structure of Freedom*," *American Political Science Review* 55 (1961): 550–9.

49 Kenneth Arrow, "Social Responsibility and Economic Efficiency," *Public Policy* 21 (Summer 1973): 303–17. George Akerlof's "The Market for 'Lemons': Quality Uncertainty and the Market Mechanism" [*Quarterly Journal of Economics* 84 (Aug. 1970): 488–500] covers similar problems but looks to devices such as guarantees, brand names, and licensing rather than ethical codes as possible solutions.

50 Research suggests that greater cooperation by victims and witnesses in the community would do more than anything else to improve police performance in fighting crime; Mark Moore and George Kelling, '' 'To Serve and Protect': Learning from Police History," *Public Interest* no. 70 (Winter 1983): esp. 50.

51 Leland Yeager, "Economics and Principles," *Southern Economic Journal* 42 (1976): 569.

52 James Buchanan, *The Limits of Liberty* (Chicago: University of Chicago Press, 1975) 118-19.

53 Roland McKean, "Some Economic Aspects of Ethical-Behavioral Codes," *Political Studies* 27 (June 1979): 264. Also see McKean, 260–5 and Buchanan, *Limits of Liberty*, 76–7, 107, 117–21, 175. McKean notes that people do sometimes "compulsively sacrifice their selfish interests to support customs or rules" (265). But the quotation cited in the text clearly suggests that "increased literacy and sophistication" make one less religious and more ready to behave in a narrowly self-interested manner. Thus, again one sees an economist indicating that for the individual, the narrowly self-interested course of action is the best informed and thus in some sense the most reasonable one. As was argued in the last chapter, Aristotle's gentleman, though literate and sophisticated, would not agree. Nor would the "Meals on Wheels" volunteers discussed later in this chapter.

54 A wag might note that professional self-interest could explain economists' failure to propose public policies that might reinvigorate ethics and goodwill. Because the free-rider experiments show that entering economics graduate students are less willing than others to forget narrow self-interest so as to achieve fair outcomes for a broader public, one policy that might increase ethics and goodwill would involve discouraging people from studying economics.

55 Ed Olsen has recently brought to my attention an article by Burton Weisbrod that argues that some utility (preference) functions may be superior to others on economic-efficiency grounds because they generate fewer external costs for others; "Comparing Utility Functions in Efficiency Terms or, What Kind of Utility Functions Do We Want?" *American Economic Review* 67 (1977): 991–5. Weisbrod notes that one can thus assess educational and religious efforts to shape preferences within a conventional allocative-efficiency framework. Olsen tells me that Weisbrod's views are clearly atypical of most of the economics profession. He also says that Weisbrod had trouble getting his article published and that it has been largely ignored. I have learned in a similar third-hand manner that the superb article by Leland Yeager, "Pareto Optimality in Policy Espousal," was turned down by one of the mainline economic journals before being published in the *Journal of Libertarian Studies*.

56 Yeager, "Economics and Principles," 567; also see 569.

57 Buchanan, *Limits of Liberty*, esp. 117-18, 175, and *Public Finance in Democratic Process* (Chapel Hill: University of North Carolina Press, 1967), 229–300.

58 James Buchanan's "Appendix 1: Marginal Notes on Reading Political Philosophy," in Buchanan and Tullock, *the Calculus of Consent*, 310 (also see 267, 309, 311), and Buchanan's "Good Economics – Bad Law," *Virginia Law Review* 60 (1974): 486.

59 Charles Schultze, *The Public Use of Private Interest* (Washington, D.C.: Brookings Institution, 1977), 17–18.

60 For other examples of lower economic costs resulting from ethical behavior see McKean, "Ethical Behavioral Codes," 262.

61 Charles R. Tittle, "Punishment and Deterrence of Deviance," in Simon Rottenberg, ed., *The Economics of Crime and Punishment* (Washington, D.C.: American Enterprise Institute, 1973), 91. Tittle, a sociologist, summarizes the experimental findings reported in Richard D. Schwartz and Sonya

Orleans, "On Legal Sanctions," *University of Chicago Law Review* 34 (Winter 1967): 274–300.

62 See Franklin Zimring's work for the National Institutes of Mental Health, *Perspectives on Deterrence* (Washington, D.C., 1971), cited in Jeffrey Sedgwick, *Deterring Criminals* (Washington, D.C.: American Enterprise Institute, 1980), 44. Also see George Will, *Statecraft as Soulcraft* (New York: Simon & Schuster, 1983), 86–7.

63 McKean, "Ethical Behavioral Codes," 256.

64 Theodore Caplow, "Religion in Middletown," *Public Interest* no. 68 (Summer 1982): 80. Also note that Middletown is by no means unusually pious (85).

65 See Walter Berns, *The First Amendment and the Future of American Democracy*, chs. 1, 2.

66 George Will, "Tax Breaks with Charity," *Washington Post*, May 7, 1978, C-7. For a discussion of public-policy changes that would eliminate unnecessary barriers hindering the work of church-affiliated social welfare agencies see Peter Berger and Richard Neuhaus, *To Empower People* (Washington, D.C.: American Enterprise Institute, 1977), 26–33.

67 Will, "Tax Breaks with Charity."

68 Wilson and Kelling describe some interesting psychological experiments that have shown this mushrooming effect. "Broken Windows," *Atlantic Monthly* (March 1982): 29–38. Also see Wilson's *Thinking About Crime* (New York: Basic Books, 1975), esp. ch. 2.

69 Peter Singer, "Altruism and Commerce: A Defense of Titmuss Against Arrow," *Philosophy and Public Affairs* 2 (1973): 319. The experiment Singer describes and similar ones are discussed in D. Wright, *The Psychology of Moral Behavior* (London: 1971), 133–9. See also Peter Skerry, "The Charmed Life of Head Start," *Public Interest*, no. 73 (Fall 1983), 18–40.

70 *Charlottesvile Daily Progress*, Oct. 17, 1982, F-1, and March 14, 1982, B-1. The perverse, dependency-creating incentive effects discussed in ch. 6 are not of great concern for programs in which volunteers help the elderly. Tutoring programs, programs that help victims of violence, and a number of other volunteer activities are also relatively safe in this regard.

71 It is interesting that today's economists fail to follow one of their favorite forebears here. Though Bentham thought people always sought to maximize their personal satisfaction, he also thought they could be trained and educated to get the maximum satisfaction from helping others. See John Hospers's discussion of Bentham in *Human Conduct: Problems of Ethics* (New York: Harcourt Brace Jovanovich, 1961), 145.

72 Contrast the tax study results reported in this chapter with Tullock's matter-of-fact discussion of the wisdom of narrowly self-interested calculation when contemplating tax evasion (see ch. 9, "Subjectivism, Selfishness, Materialism").

73 See Michael Walzer, *Radical Principles* (New York: Basic Books, 1980) and Robert Heilbroner "What is Socialism?" *Dissent* (Summer 1978): esp. 342.

74 *Federalist Papers*, nos. 10, 51, 56, 44. Also see Marc Plattner, "American Democracy and the Acquisitive Spirit," in Robert Goldwin and William Schambra, eds., *How Capitalistic is the Constitution?* (Washington, D.C.: American Enterprise Institute, 1982).

75 Arthur Okun, *Equality and Efficiency*, 30–1.

76 Elzinga thinks it is and points to the added power of a diversified firm with facilities in over a hundred districts and legal counsel in Washington; Kenneth Elzinga, "The Goals of Antitrust: Other than Competition and Efficiency, What Else Counts?" *Pennsylvania Law Review* 125 (1977): 1,197. Other economists, however, note that decentralized industries such as agriculture, trucking, and the independents in the oil industry have often been the most successful politically; Harold Demsetz's rebuttal to Senator Gary Hart, "Should Government Deregulation Be Coupled with Deconcentration of Industry?" in Bernard Siegen, ed., *Government Regulation and the Economy* (Lexington, Mass.: Lexington Books, 1980), 103.

77 Joseph Schumpeter, *Capitalism, Socialism and Democracy* (New York: Harper Colophon, 1950), 140–1. Paul Samuelson has recently expressed what he describes as his new respect for Schumpeter's practice of considering the effects of economic policies on social consensus and political stability. See his very interesting remarks as part of a debate with Milton Friedman, *The Economic Responsibility of Government* (College Station: Texas A&M University, 1980), 22–3.

78 Final Report of the Select Committee on Small Business, 88th Congress, 2d sess., 1964, House Report no. 1944, ser. no. 12621-6, p. 2.

79 *Washington Post*, Nov. 23, 1982, C-14.

80 Though in one section Schumpeter says capitalism is "constitutionally unable to produce" emotional attachment to the social order (145), he elsewhere makes it clear that the small businessman is an exception (140–2).

81 "Letter to John Adams," *The Writings of Thomas Jefferson*, ed. Andrew Lipscomb, vol, XIII (Washington, D.C.: Jefferson Memorial Association, 1904), 401; *Notes on the State of Virgina* in Saul Padover, ed., *The Complete Jefferson* (New York: Duell, Sloan & Pearce, 1943), 678–9. Also note Aristotle's view that "it is the greatest good fortune" for a state when those who engage in politics "have a middling and sufficient property"; *The Pol-*

ictics of Aristotle, ed. Carnes Lord (Chicago: University of Chicago Press, 1984), Book IV, ch. 11, 135.

My colleague Matthew Holden, recently honored as the leading black political scientist in the country, believes that the fact that his family owned the land they farmed near a small Mississippi town was important in his development. Charles Willie describes a recent conversation with Holden: "Holden said there was 'a sense of uprightness and of being somebody which went with owning a little piece of land ...' Holden said, that sense of uprightness associated with ownership of property 'was extremely important.' " Charles Willie, *Five Black Scholars* (Cambridge, Mass.: Abt Books, in press).

82 *Los Angeles Times*, June 28, 1981, pt. VIII, 23. Also see Robert Samuelson, "Homeowner Tax Break: An Entrenched Hoax," *Washington Post*, Oct. 28, 1980, E-1, and Martin Feldstein and Kathleen Feldstein, "Tight Money and Tax Cuts: A Mix that Works," *Washington Post*, July 21, 1980, A-15.

83 Tullock, *Logic of the Law*, 85–90.

84 Alexis de Tocqueville, *Democracy in America* (New York: Random House, Vintage Books, 1955), 295–6. In supporting Tocqueville's praise for the civil jury I in no way mean to defend the existing jury selection process in many cities. Too often those called for jury duty wait day after day and are never assigned to a trial.

85 Tullock, *Logic of the Law*, 257, 205–6.

86 Lord, ed., *The Politics of Aristotle*, Book II, ch. 8, p. 73.

87 Jean Jacques Rousseau, *Discourse on the Origin and Foundations of Inequality Among Men*, in Roger Masters, ed., *The First and Second Discourses* (New York: St. Martin's Press, 1964), 82.

88 *Federalist Papers*, no. 49.

89 Buchanan, *Limits of Liberty*, 98–9.

90 James Buchanan, "A Defense of Organized Crime?" in Rottenberg, ed., 128.

91 Annelise Anderson, an economist, makes this point in her comment on Buchanan's paper, but the two other economist respondents do not mention it (pp. 171, 172–8).

92 Two of the most interesting treatments are Carl Kaysen, "Some General Observations on the Pricing of Higher Education," *Review of Economics and Statistics* 42, pt. 2, supp. (Aug. 1960): 55–60, and David Breneman and Susan Nelson, *Financing Community Colleges* (Washington, D.C.: Brookings Institution, 1981), esp. 45–54. One influential governmental report, however, ignored the externality questions when suggesting that effective use of resistance and thus inducing institutions to be more "responsive" to them. What students find pleasing is not necessarily what society considers effective or worthy of subsidy. [See Department of Health, Education and Welfare, *Toward a Long-Range Plan for Federal Financial Support for Higher Education: A Report to the President* (Jan. 1969), 38.] Also see the discussion of the report in Alice Rivlin and Jeffrey Weiss, "Social Goals and Federal Support of Higher Education," in U.S. Congress, Joint Economic Committee, *The Economics and Financing of Higher Education in the United States: A Compendium of Papers* (1969), esp. 550.

93 Edward Banfield, "Some Alternatives For the Public Library" in Banfield, ed., *Urban Government* (New York: Free Press, 1969), 645–54.

94 John Vaizey, *The Economics of Education* (London: Faber & Faber, 1962), 14. Also see Milton Friedman, "The Higher Schooling in America," in *Public Interest* no. 11 (Spring 1968): 111.

11. REPRESENTATIVES, DELIBERATION, AND POLITICAL LEADERSHIP

1 E. J. Mishan, *Cost–Benefit Analysis* (New York: Praeger, 1976), 318.

2 William Baumol, *Welfare Economics and the Theory of the State*, (Cambridge, Mass.: Harvard University Press, 1969), 29.

3 Thomas Schelling, "The Life You Save May Be Your Own," in Samuel Chase, ed., *Problems in Public Expenditure Analysis* (Washington, D.C.: Brookings Institution, 1968), 161. Leland Yeager dissents from many of his colleagues and makes a powerful case for deliberation in "Pareto Optimality in Policy Espousal," *Journal of Libertarian Studies* 2 (1978): 199–216.

4 James C. Miller III, "A Program for Direct and Proxy Voting in the Legislative Process," *Public Choice* VII (Fall 1969): 107–13, reprinted in Ryan Amacher, Robert Tollison, and Thomas Willett, eds., *The Economic Approach to Public Policy* (Ithaca, N.Y.: Cornell University Press, 1976), esp. 373; Kenneth Greene and Hadi Salavitabar, "Senatorial Responsiveness, The Characteristics of the Polity and the Political Cycle," *Public Choice* 38 (1982): 263-9; Ryan Amacher and William Boyes, "Cycles in Senatorial Voting: Implications for the Optimal Frequency of Elections," *Public Choice* 33 (1978): 5–13.

5 James Buchanan and Gordon Tullock, *The Calculus of Consent* (Ann Arbor: University of Michigan Press, 1965), 20.

6 See, e.g., James Buchanan, *Public Finance in Democratic Process* (Chapel Hill: University of North Carolina Press, 1967), 176. Also see Duncan MacRae's discussion, *The Social Function of Social Science* (New Haven, Conn.: Yale University Press, 1976), 197.

7 Greene and Salavitabar, "Senatorial Responsiveness," 263; Edgar Browning, "More on the Appeal of Minimum Wage Laws," *Public Choice* 33 (1978): 93; William Niskanen, "The Pathology of Politics," in Richard Selden, ed., *Capitalism and Freedom: Problems and Prospects* (Charlottesville: University of Virginia Press, 1975); Julius Margolis, "Public Policies for Private Profits: Urban Government," in Harold Hochman and George Peterson, eds., *Redistribution Through Public Choice* (New York: Columbia University Press, 1974), esp. 301; MacRae, *Social Function of Social Science*, 197.

8 Miller, "Program for Direct and Proxy Voting in the Legislative Process."

9 Gordon Tullock, *Private Wants, Public Means* (New York: Basic Books, 1970), 112–13. Martin Shubik has expressed reservations about Miller's proposal, but his suggested amendment to it (that legislation not become law unless passed in two public pollings at least six weeks apart) is a fairly minor one; "On *Homo Politicus* and the Instant Referendum," *Public Choice* 9 (Fall 1970): 79–84, reprinted in Amacher et al., eds., 376–81. William Niskanen has also discussed Miller's proposal sympathetically though he supports other forms of referenda and "direct democracy" devices; "The Pathology of Politics," in Selden, ed., and "Toward More Efficient Fiscal Institutions," *National Tax Journal*, 25 (1972): 343–7.

10 Dennis Mueller, Robert Tollison, and Thomas Willett, "Representative Democracy via Random Selection," *Public Choice* 12 (Spring, 1972): 57–68; reprinted in Amacher et al., eds.

11 Alexander Hamilton, James Madison, and John Jay, *The Federalist Papers*, ed. Clinton Rossiter (New York: New American Library, 1961), nos. 9. 10, 49, 58, 63, 71.

12 For a defense of this view see Martin Diamond, Winston Fisk, and Herbert Garfinkel, *The Democratic Republic* (Chicago: Rand McNally, 1970), ch. 4. For a discussion of contending views see Diamond's "Conservatives, Liberals, and the Constitution," in R. A. Goldwin, ed., *Left, Right and Center* (Chicago: Rand McNally, 1965), 60–86.

13 "The Perpetuation of our Political Institutions: Address before the Young Men's Lyceum of Springfield, Illinois," January 27, 1838, in Roy P. Basler, ed., *The Collected Works of Abraham Lincoln* 8 vols. (New Brunswick, N.J.: Rutgers University Press, 1953), I, 108–15; also see "Speech in the Illinois Legislature, January 11, 1837," *Collected Works*, I, 69.

14 Jefferson's letters to John Taylor, May 28, 1816; to Isaac Tiffany, Aug. 26, 1816; to John Adams, Oct. 28, 1813; and to Pierre Samuel Dupont De Nemours, April 24, 1816, in Morton Frisch and Richard Stevens, eds., *The Political Thought of American Statesmen* (Itasca, Ill.: Peacock, 1973), 26–36. Also see Harvey C. Mansfield, Jr., "Thomas Jefferson," in Frisch and

Stevens, eds., *American Political Thought* (New York: Scribner, 1971), 23–50.

15 Letter to John Adams, Oct. 28, 1813, in Frisch and Stevens, eds., *Political Thought of American Statesmen*, 28.

16 Alexis de Tocqueville, *Democracy in America*, 2 vols. [New York: Random House (Vintage Books), 1945], I, esp. 63, 70, 94–6, 265, 309–10.

17 *Washington Post*, Jan. 21, 1977, A-17.

18 *Washington Post*, April 30, 1978, B-7; April 26, 1978, A-3; Dec. 7, 1974, A-19; Nov. 10, 1977, A-23. Also see Joseph Kraft's criticism of those who think the people can be a source of policy guidance; *Washington Post*, March 8, 1977.

19 *Washington Post*, Jan. 2, 1983, B-5; Oct. 21, 1981, A-2. For more on the low level of voter information see Stanley Kelley, Jr., *Interpreting Elections* (Princeton, N.J.: Princeton University Press, 1983), esp. ch. 8; Dorothy James, *The Contemporary Presidency* (New York: Pegasus, 1969), 140–1.

20 U.S. Council on Environmental Quality, *Public Opinion on Environmental Issues*, 1980, 33–6.

21 Tocqueville, *Democracy in America*, I, 222–3, 237–9.

22 *Washington Post*, July 22, 1974, A-2.

23 *Washington Post*, July 31, 1977, A-1.

24 Tullock, *Private Wants, Public Means*, 115; also see 119.

25 *Federalist Papers*, nos. 9, 10, 57. Also see Diamond et al., *The Democratic Republic*, 99–100, and Walter Berns, "Does the Constitution 'Secure These Rights'?" in Robert Goldwin and William Schambra, eds., *How Democratic Is the Constitution?* (Washington, D.C.: American Enterprise Institute, 1980), 59–78.

26 *Federalist Papers*, no. 10.

27 Diamond et al., *The Democratic Republic*, 99–100.

28 *Federalist Papers*, no. 10; also see no. 51. On Madison's attempt to design a government in which representatives would be unlikely to act on narrow self-interest, see Robert J. Morgan, "Madison's Analysis of the Sources of Political Authority," *American Political Science Review* 75, (1981): 613–25.

29 *Federalist Papers*, nos. 63, 71.

30 Quoted in Joseph Bessette, "Deliberation in Congress" (Paper delivered at the Annual Meeting of the American Political Science Association, Sept. 1979). The paper is based on Bessette's dissertation, "Deliberation in Congress" (University of Chicago, 1978).

31 Woodrow Wilson, *Constitutional Government in the United States* (New

York: Columbia University Press, 1908; Columbia paperback ed., 1961), 104–5. The importance of deliberation to democracy was first emphasized by Aristotle, who believed that it was only when the people met together and discussed policy that their claim to rule could be taken seriously. As Ernest Barker notes, for Aristotle, "The people at large have the merit of a good collective judgment not as a static mass, but when they are dynamic – in other words when they assemble, and when the process of debate begins"; *The Politics of Aristotle* (New York: Oxford University Press, 1962), 126. Another famous statement from the founders' era was that of Edmund Burke: "Your representative owes you . . . his judgment . . . government and legislation are matters of reason and judgment, and not inclination; and what sort of reason is that in which the determination precedes the discussion, in which one set of men deliberate and another decide, and where those who form the conclusion are perhaps three hundred miles distant from those who hear the argument?" *The Works of the Right Honorable Edmund Burke*, 3 vols. (Boston: Little Brown, 1894), II, 95–6.

32 From *Congressional Government: A Study in American Politics*. Quoted in Harry Clor, "Woodrow Wilson," in Morton Frisch and Richard Stevens, eds., *American Political Thought*, 192.

33 Clor, in Frisch and Stevens, eds., 194.

34 Abraham Lincoln, "First Debate with Stephen Douglas at Ottawa, Illinois, August 21, 1858," *Collected Works*, III, 27. See also *Collected Works*, III, 29, and Benjamin P. Thomas, *Abraham Lincoln* (New York: Knopf, 1952), 133.

35 Abraham Lincoln, "Perpetuation of Our Political Institutions," *Collected Works*, I, 108–15.

36 Abraham Lincoln, "Second Inaugural Address," March 4, 1865.

37 Though today's economists are likely to be opposed to rather than indifferent about slavery, this belief comes from sources other than their economics. Welfare economics says society will have to determine property rights and distributions of income. In Lincoln's time slaves were property, not holders of rights. If the people in some states say this is just, there is nothing in welfare economics to declare them wrong. Also see Tullock's comments on South Africa, *Private Wants, Public Means*, 238.

38 In his first inaugural address Thomas Jefferson spoke of the "sacred principle, that though the will of the majority is in all cases to prevail, that will to be rightful must be reasonable."

39 Speech at Peoria, Ill., on the repeal of the Missouri Compromise, Oct. 16, 1854, in *Collected Works of Lincoln* II, 246–83.

40 Bessette, "Deliberation in Congress"; V. O. Key, Jr., *Public Opinion and American Democracy* (New York: Knopf, 1961), ch. 21; Hanna Pitkin,

The Concept of Representation (Berkeley: University of California Press, 1967), ch. 10, esp. 212; Carl Friedrich, "Deliberative Assemblies," in *Constitutional Government and Democracy* (Waltham, Mass.: Blaisdell, 1968); Duncan MacRae, Jr., "Normative Assumptions in the Study of Public Choice," *Public Choice* 16 (Fall 1973): 38–9 and *Social Function of Social Science*, 194–200; Willmore Kendall and George Carey, "The Intensity Problem and Democratic Theory," *American Political Science Review* 62 (1968): 23; Robert Axelrod, "The Medical Metaphor," *American Journal of Political Science* 21 (1977): 432; Geoffrey Vickers, "Values, Norms and Policies," *Policy Sciences* 4 (1973): 109; George Will, *Statecraft as Soulcraft* (New York: Simon & Schuster, 1983), esp. 16, 117, 120.

41 W. Arthur Lewis, "Planning Public Expenditures," in Max F. Millikan, ed., *National Economic Development* (New York: National Bureau of Economic Research, 1967), 207.

42 Key, *Public Opinion and American Democracy*, ch. 21, esp. 536, 539, 553–8.

43 John F. Kennedy, *Profiles in Courage* (New York: Cardinal, 1956), 14.

44 Herbert Storing argues that one of the great dangers of populism is that it undermines the stateman's "confidence in his own judgment, in the legitimacy of relying on his own judgment even in the face of popular disagreement"; "American Statesmanship: Old and New," in Robert Goldwin, ed., *Bureaucrats, Policy Analysts, Statesmen: Who Leads?* (Washington, D.C.: American Enterprise Institute, 1980), 103.

45 Charles Wolf's proposal cited by Vincent Taylor in "How Much is Good Health Worth?" *Policy Sciences* 1 (1970 ; reprinted in Steven E. Rhoads, ed., *Valuing Life* (Boulder, Colo.: Westview, 1980), 69.

46 Mishan, *Cost-Benefit Analysis*, 318–19.

47 See ch. 9.

48 T. C. Schelling, "The Life You Save May Be Your Own," in Samuel Chase, Jr., ed., *Problems in Public Expenditure Analysis* (Washington, D.C.: Brookings Institution, 1968), 127–76; Mishan, *Cost-Benefit Analysis*, 162; Jan Acton, "Evaluating Public Programs to Save Lives" (Rand Corp. report no. R-950-RC, Jan. 1973).

49 Tullock, *Private Wants, Public Means*, ch. 5, and Dennis Mueller, *Public Choice* (Cambridge: Cambridge University Press, 1979), 124.

50 Tullock, *Private Wants, Public Means*, 120.

51 *Los Angeles Times*, March 26, 1983, 29.

52 Herbert Baus and William Ross, *Politics Battle Plan* (New York: Macmillan, 1968), 61; quoted in Eugene Lee, "California," in David Butler and

Austin Ranney, eds., *Referendums* (Washington, D.C.: American Enterprise Institute, 1978), 101–2.

53 Raymond Wolfinger, "Discussion," in Austin Ranney, ed., *The Referendum Device* (Washington, D.C: American Enterprise Institute, 1981), 63–4. Also see David Magleby's comments in the *Washington Post*, May 29, 1982, A-11.

54 *Los Angeles Times*, March 26, 1982, 29. Field's views are significant since he and other pollsters profit from initiatives. Interest groups and newspapers need them to assess trends in public opinion prior to election day.

55 Even when voter interest and knowledge are high, initiative proposals are often passed that include poorly thought-out provisions. Raymond Wolfinger notes that "Proposition 13 included a number of secondary provisions that illustrate some interesting things about referendums. One such provision said that the assessed value of property was to be cut to what it was in 1975–1976, except that any piece of property sold after that date would be assessed at the sale price. In a building with twenty condominiums, each assessed in 1975–1976 for $50,000, if one were sold in 1979 for $125,000 then nineteen people would be paying taxes on $50,000 and the twentieth would be paying taxes on $125,000. That is an example of the kind of kicker often inserted in the language of propositions in California. The people knew what they were voting on, but few knew that the package they were voting on included things like this $125,000 versus $50,000 situation." "Discussion," in Ranney, ed., 64–5.

56 See Richard Fenno on Congress's relative strengths in this regard; *Home Style* (Boston: Little, Brown, 1978), 245. For more on the importance of consensus building as a criterion of a good governmental process see Kendall and Carey, "The Intensity Problem and Democratic Theory"; David Braybrooke, *Three Tests for Democracy* (New York: Random House, 1968), esp. 202–7. On the failure of initiatives to encourage compromise see Michael Malbin, "The False Hope of Law by Initiative," *Washington Post*, Jan. 7, 1978, 15.

57 Malcolm Jewell and Samuel Patterson, *The Legislative Process in the United States* (New York: Random House, 1977), 118. Though Niskanen ("The Pathology of Politics") suggests that terms under a lot representative system would be short, this question, like some others, is left open in Amacher et al.'s discussion ("Representative Democracy via Random Selection").

58 Amacher, et al., "Representative Democracy via Random Selection," 390n.

59 Key believes it is important that the general public feels that it shares in and participates in the political order (*Public Opinion and American Democracy*, 547–8).

60 Richard Fenno, *Home Style*, 240–5. Also see the section later in this chapter suggesting considerable public support for independent representatives. If one knows little about the issues it may be quite rational to vote for the person who seems to have good character or judgment rather than the person who shares one's current uninformed predilections. When Jones says that Smith has good judgment, he suggests that he would probably agree with Smith if he knew what Smith has learned by participating in the legislative process.

61 See "The Poverty of the Economist's Work View." Also see Greene and Salavitabar, "Senatorial Responsiveness," 263. William Mitchell says of economists who author public-finance texts, "Almost all . . . take a perverse pleasure in announcing that voters, politicians, bureaucrats, alike, are just like all the rest of us and that our continued supplies of public goods depend not on their good will but a fine appreciation of their self-interests as political actors"; "Textbook Public Choice: A Review Essay," *Public Choice* 38 (1982): 104.

62 James Kau and Paul Rubin, *Congressmen, Constituents and Contributors: Determinants of Roll Call Voting in the House of Representatives* (Boston: Martinus Nijhoff, 1982). Kau and Rubin find that both constituent ideology and the ideology of the representative are significant in explaining congressional votes. They also find that contributions from business-oriented political action committees do not influence the voting behavior of congressional recipients, but even after controlling for economic factors, public-interest lobbies do influence voting behavior (esp. 3–5, 45, 80, 93–4, 121–4). I am pleased to be able to balance my frequent criticisms of Gordon Tullock's work by noting here that he is the general editor of *Studies in Public Choice*, a series which found room for the unorthodox and interesting findings of both Kau and Rubin and of Richard McKenzie's *The Limits of Economic Science* (briefly discussed in ch. 9).

63 David Mayhew, *Congress: the Electoral Connection* (New Haven, Conn.: Yale University Press, 1974), and Morris Fiorina, *Congress: Keystone of the Washington Establishment* (New Haven, Conn.: Yale University Press, 1977).

64 Richard Fenno, *Congressmen in Committees* (Boston: Little, Brown, 1973).

65 Bessette, "Deliberation in Congress," 18–19, and Fenno, *Congressmen in Committees, 5.*

66 Mayhew, *The Electoral Connection*, 152; Richard Fenno, *The Power of the Purse* (Boston: Little, Brown, 1966). Also see Bessette, "Deliberation in Congress."

67 This is documented at length in Bessette and in Arthur Maass, *Congress and the Common Good* (New York: Basic Books, 1983).

68 Bernard Asbell, *The Senate Nobody Knows* (Baltimore: Johns Hopkins

University Press, 1978), 267, 210, 370–1, 30, 42–3. Note also that John Manley has attributed Wilbur Mills's preeminence on the House Ways and Means Committee to "influence" rather than "power." Manley says that "influence is, in essence, a means of *persuasion* that involves giving reasons or justifications for doing certain things and avoiding others, whereas power may be taken to mean the communication of decisions that activate obligations"; *The Politics of Finance* (Boston: Little, Brown, 1970), 122. Also Bessette, "Deliberation in Congress."

69 James Buchanan, *Public Finance in Democratic Process and the Limits of Liberty* (Chicago: University of Chicago Press, 1975). Also see Thomas Willett's discussion of the consumer-ignorance problem; "A New Monetary Constitution? An Evaluation of the Need and the Major Alternatives" (Paper prepared for the Conference on Constraining Federal Taxing and Spending, sponsored by the Center for the Study of Law Structures, Claremont McKenna College and Hoover Institution, Stanford University, Oct. 21–3, 1981).

If more public-choice economists studied polling data carefully, it might affect their attitudes about changing our political institutions. Chapter 5 showed that Americans have a greatly exaggerated view of businesses' profit margins. This may help explain why a majority of Americans differ from most economists in supporting the following proposition: "In industries where there is competition, the government should put a limit on the profits companies can make rather than allowing companies to make all they can." The public also supports wage and price controls and opposes the deregulation of the price of oil; Seymour M. Lipset and William Schneider, *The Confidence Gap* (New York: Free Press, 1983), 181–2, 233–4.

70 *Federalist Papers*, no. 63.

71 *The Living Thoughts of Thomas Jefferson*, presented by John Dewey (Greenwich, Conn.: Fawcett, n. d.), 58. Jefferson and other founders also emphasized that the most able and talented men would not be attracted to offices with very short terms and little power. Economists do not discuss this incentive.

72 Miller, "A Program for Direct and Proxy Voting," 373.

73 Amacher and Boyes, "Cycles in Senatorial Voting."

74 Ryan Amacher and William Boyes, "Politicians and Polity: Responsiveness in American Government," *Southern Economic Journal* 46 (1979): 558–67; Greene and Salavitabar, "Senatorial Responsiveness."

75 Letter to Monsieur D'Ivernois, Feb. 6, 1975, in Andrew Lipscomb, ed., *The Writings of Thomas Jefferson*, 20 vols. (Washington, D.C.: Thomas Jefferson Memorial Society, 1903), IX, 299–300. Also see *Federalist Papers*, no. 10.

76 Pitkin, *Concept of Representation*, ch. 7.

77 Miller, "A Program for Direct and Proxy Voting," 373.

78 Amacher and Boyes, "Cycles in Senatorial Voting," 10.

79 Schelling, in Chase, ed., 161.

80 Pitkin reports that surveys that asked questions such as "Do you believe that a Congressman should vote on any question as the majority of his constituents desire or vote according to his own judgment?" and "Should members of Congress vote according to their own best judgment or according to the way the people in their districts feel?" brought results ranging "from two-thirds in favor of constituency feelings to more than half in favor of the representative's judgment," *Concept of Representation*, 277–8.

81 Kelley, *Interpreting Elections*, esp. 57, 163–5.

12. CONCLUSION

1 Kenneth Boulding, "Economics and the Future of Man," in *Economics As a Science* (New York: McGraw-Hill, 1970), 156.

2 Joseph Schumpeter, *Capitalism, Socialism and Democracy* (New York: Harper & Row, 1975), esp. chs. 12–14. Also George Will, "One For All – Or All For One?" *Washington Post*, Aug. 24, 1980, C-7.

3 For a discussion of federal judges who have found a specially designed remedial economics course of great interest see the *Washington Post*, Jan. 20, 1980, A-1. Even when economists are wrong about ends, they may be able to help us with means. Though economists make a mistake when they ignore the political benefits of home ownership, we would be wrong to ignore their criticisms of the ways we seek to promote it.

4 Thomas Schelling, "Economic Reasoning and the Ethics of Policy," *Public Interest* no. 63 (Spring 1981): 59.

5 *Economics as a Science*, 136.

6 Robert Samuelson, "Micro-Revolution: Compete or Stand Aside," *Washington Post*, Oct. 21, 1980, D-8.

7 Rees went on to say, "Most economists are more conservative on economic issues than, say, sociologists, because they *do* understand it." William McCleery, "A Conversation with Albert Rees," *Princeton Alumni Weekly*, March 15, 1976, 15.

8 Charles Schultze, *The Public Use of Private Interest* (Washington, D.C.: Brookings Institution, 1977), 76–7.

9 Alain Enthoven, "Defense and Disarmament: Economic Analysis in the Department of Defense," *American Economic Review* 53 (1963): 422.

10 This is a theme in George Stigler, "The Politics of Political Economists," *Quarterly Journal of Economics* 73 (Nov. 1959): 522–32.

11 Seymour Martin Lipset and William Schneider chronicle a decline in confidence that Americans express in their major political and economic institutions over recent decades. They believe that "a great deal of the decline . . . can be attributed to adverse economic conditions"; *The Confidence Gap* (New York: Free Press, 1983), 65; also see 118, 155.

12 The phrase, originally Charles Hitch's, is quoted approvingly by Arthur Okun in *The Political Economy of Prosperity* (Washington, D.C.: Brookings Institution, 1970), 6.

13 Okun, *Political Economy of Prosperity*, 6, 11.

14 Others have had similar problems in their attempts to organize systematically their reflections on the limits of economics. Ezra Mishan confesses that he has "failed to discover any central theme about which these non-formal considerations might be made to cohere in some simple pattern," *The Costs of Economic Growth* (New York: Praeger, 1967), 124. Brian Barry suggests that "economic modes of analysis apply sufficiently well to be used in some situations, though not in others. The difficulty is, of course, to provide a general description of the kinds of situation in which the economic approach is suitable. Unfortunately, I am unable to find any way of specifying the area except in an unhelpful and circular form"; *Sociologists, Economists and Democracy* (London: Collier-Macmillan, 1970), 177.

15 Though not all Republican congressional staff are free-market conservatives nor Democratic staff ADA liberals, it is still interesting that Kelman found Republican committee staff to be the group most sympathetic to economic-incentive approaches to environmental policy. The most united opponents were Democratic committee staff; *What Price Incentives?* (Boston: Auburn House, 1981), 100–7.

16 Americans for Democratic Action, "A Model Platform for the Democratic Party, 1980" (Mimeo).

17 Alfred Kahn, "America's Democrats: Can Liberalism Survive Inflation?" *The Economist*, March 7, 1981, 21–5.

18 *New Columbia Encyclopedia*, ed. William Harris and Judith Levey (New York: Columbia University Press, 1975), 2,208.

19 "A Model Platform for the Democratic Party, 1980," back cover.

20 See the interview with Tsongas in the *Washington Post*, Nov. 9, 1980, D-1. Also Tsongas's book, *The Road from Here* (New York: Knopf, 1981).

21 *Washington Post*, Nov. 6, 1980, A-25. Also note liberal *New York Times* columnist Anthony Lewis's strong praise for Kahn's article, "The Task for Liberals," reprinted in the *Charlottesville Daily Progress*, March 21, 1981, A-4. Hart's views on industrial policy and on concentration in the oil industry are, however, far from those of mainstream economists. For his views on the oil industry, see ch. 5, last pages.

NAME INDEX

SUBJECT INDEX